THE FUTURE OF EMPIRICAL THEOLOGY

ESSAYS IN DIVINITY

JERALD C. BRAUER, GENERAL EDITOR

The Future of Empirical Theology

BY FRED BERTHOLD, JR., JOHN B. COBB, JR.,
LANGDON GILKEY, JOSEPH HAROUTUNIAN,
ROGER HAZELTON, PHILIP J. HEFNER,
BERNARD M. LOOMER, BERNARD E. MELAND,
SCHUBERT M. OGDEN, JOSEPH A. SITTLER,
HUSTON SMITH (WITH SAMUEL TODES),
GERHARD SPIEGLER, PAUL SPONHEIM,
DANIEL DAY WILLIAMS

Edited by BERNARD E. MELAND

THE UNIVERSITY OF CHICAGO PRESS

CHICAGO AND LONDON

THE UNIVERSITY OF CHICAGO PRESS

CHICAGO 60637

The University of Chicago Press, Ltd., London

© 1969 by The University of Chicago

All rights reserved. Published 1969

Standard Book Number: 226-51955-4

Library of Congress Catalog Card Number: 78-83980

Printed in the United States of America

General Editor's Preface

The present volume is the seventh in a series of eight books which will be published under the general title *Essays in Divinity*. At first glance, this does not appear to be a particularly auspicious moment for such a formidable enterprise. At the very moment the so-called radical theologians announce that "God is Dead," an eight-volume series investigating various dimensions of the study of religion or of theology begins publication. Is this not an ill-timed venture?

On the contrary, the discipline of theology in America was never in a more provocative and potentially creative period. There are many new and exciting factors in the present picture. The very presence of the "God is dead" movement is evidence of a new vitality among the younger theologians. In no sense does such a movement herald the end of systematic theology or the impossibility of using God-language. It is but one attempt to focus on the serious task of reconceiving and reconstructing Christian theology; and it is by no means the only attempt.

One fact alone is sufficient to mark this new age of theological inquiry as being prescient of new possibilities — the dominance of dialogue in all aspects of divinity. Basic conversation between Roman Catholicism, Protestantism, and Judaism is just beginning, and its full effect upon theological construction is only in its preliminary stages. Before the discipline of systematic theology had passed beyond even the preliminary phase of dialogue, Paul Tillich's last lecture pointed to the future of this discipline in relation to the world religions. Dialogue between the various faiths is not to be taken as the "in" movement in religion today; but it is pervasive among critically concerned theologians and other religious scholars, and is to be understood as providing a new base that will profoundly affect, not only the systematic study of doctrines and beliefs, but every dimension of religious studies.

Another mark of the vitality of religious studies today is its active interchange with other disciplines. Studies in divinity have never been carried on in complete isolation from other areas of human knowledge; but some epochs have exhibited a greater interrelationship than others. The contemporary scene is marked by the increasing tempo of creative interchange and mutual stimulation between divinity and other disciplines. Several new theological disciplines have emerged in recent years and have documented this fact. The interplay between theology and literature, between theology and the psychological sciences, and between theology and other social sciences bids fair to reshape the traditional study of religion, and this mode of inquiry is rapidly becoming central in major theological faculties.

The emergence and increasing role of the history of religions is a case in point. Until recently, the history of religions was a stepchild in the field of religious subjects. Today it is developing a methodology that will soon prove influential in all dimensions of theological study. It might not win the day, but it will have a profound influence. History of religions, in fact, appears to be the way that most state universities are taking to introduce the serious and disciplined study of religion into strictly secular curriculums.

These are but a few of the factors that demonstrate the vitality of the study of religion today. The realization that the study of religion is now entering upon a new period of candid and fruitful inquiry makes a series of books such as this one both possible and pertinent. The occasion for the publication of *Essays in Divinity* is supplied by the one hundredth anniversary of the Divinity School of the University of Chicago, and by the university's seventy-fifth anniversary. Such occasions call for special plans.

The general editor of this series proposed to celebrate the event by holding seven conferences to be attended only by graduates and present faculty of the Divinity School. It was envisaged that out of the conferences a set of eight volumes would emerge that would at once mark the progress in the various dimensions of theological study and point to the ongoing tradition of scholarship in the Divinity School. Of course, we lose something by not inviting scholars from throughout the world to contribute to the volumes. On the other hand, we gain something by inviting only those men who have been educated or are now teaching at a single theological center of America, long noted for its scholarship and its educating of theological professors.

This limitation will enable an observer to determine the extent to which a series of generations has been shaped by, and has shaped, a particular institution. It will be possible to note the variations of approach and concern that mark respective generations of that institution. Furthermore, it will help to assess the particular genius, if any, that a given institution possesses. It will demonstrate the extent to which its graduates and professors are in the midst of contemporary theological scholarship. It is to be hoped that the series will provide both a bench mark for today's scholarly discussions and research in religion and a record from which future generations can assess the contributions of an institution at the turn of its first century.

No one of the volumes in this series pretends to be definitive in its area; however, it is hoped that each of them will make a worthy contribution to its area of specialization and that the entire series will provide an over-all assessment of religious scholarship as of the present moment. The intent is to have each volume deal with a particular issue that is of special significance for scholarly research today. Thus one will not be confronted in these volumes by a disconnected series of essays, but by a group of writings, each of which deals with a general problem from the point of view of the author's own problem. No one article in the series will undertake to deal directly with the themes cited here, such as the new emphasis upon dialogue, or the deeper concern for the problems of culture within religious inquiry. Various essays, however, will reflect these interests as their authors seek to develop their particular problems.

JERALD C. BRAUER, *General Editor*

CONTENTS

CONTENTS

Introduction: The Empirical Tradition
in Theology at Chicago
BERNARD E. MELAND

The one hundredth anniversary of the Divinity School of the University of Chicago offers an occasion to review the scholarly contributions that have defined the course of its thought and its mode of inquiry. Looking back over the years, however, has not become a habit in the Divinity School. The intensity of issues and interests in each period of present history has made the immediate work at hand all-absorbing. The past, insofar as it has persisted in the work of the school, has been made manifest in the vigor and style of its present labors. In this the school emulates the spirit of the university itself, and the cultural élan that has shaped this entire region. Thus, one may say that to this school, even in its mood of celebrating its centennial, a hundred years "is as yesterday when it is past."

It is significant, I think, that when the members of the faculty in the theological field projected the conference for its alumni and faculty, commemorating our one hundred years of history, the topic they chose to discuss was "The *Future* of Empirical Theology." This, too, was the Divinity School "breeding true to itself." Papers prepared for that conference, held in the fall of 1966, along with other contributions by alumni and faculty of the theological field, form the content of this volume.

The faculty of the theological field made one concession to past history: they agreed that the editor should write an introduction interpreting the theological tradition of the school, insofar as past history conveyed such a continuing consensus. What I have set forth in these preliminary pages is more of a survey of the various periods of our Divinity

School history in which distinctive theological concerns and emphases can be detected.

What one senses in this survey is a kind of *contrast under identity*, variations within a continuing mode of thought and inquiry. If there is one word that lifts up this continuing mode of thought and inquiry in the Divinity School to give it identity amidst the contrasts and variations in its labors, that word would be *empirical*. This is not to say that all who have labored within these halls, inside and outside the theological field, have subscribed to an empirical method. Some of the Divinity School's most distinguished scholars have taken it upon themselves to counter this emphasis, or at least to supplement it, by a methodology which they deemed more adequate or appropriate to divinity studies, if only to give balance and proportion to what otherwise could become a narrow and restrictive mode of inquiry. This interplay of rival methodologies at Chicago has been to the fore at certain periods of the school's history more than at others. At its inception, divinity education at Chicago centered more dramatically in biblical criticism and the historical study of Judaism and early Christianity than in any other field. One could argue that, insofar as this discipline was itself scientifically oriented, it implied an empirical bent of mind; and, as far as some scholars of this earlier period were concerned, such a designation would have been appropriate, notably in the work of John Merle Powis Smith and Shirley Jackson Case. Yet, one wonders if linguistic scholars like William Rainey Harper, Ernest Dewitt Burton, or Edgar J. Goodspeed would have been willing to accept such a characterization of their work. Certainly they would not have been disposed to choose the empirical aspect of their study as a singular concern to emphasize or to promote. The empirical bent of mind, mingling with historical study, persisted in men like Harold Willoughby and Allen Wikgren to a degree, though one recognizes in their work something of a compromise between the more evident empirical scholarship of Shirley Jackson Case and the literary-linguistic legacy of Edgar Goodspeed. A similar observation could be made concerning

Ernest Colwell and Robert Grant, though with marked differences in each instance, stemming from their own independent temperament and mode of inquiry. In biblical scholars such as John Knox, Amos Wilder, Coert Rylaarsdam, and Norman Perrin, however, the qualifications noted earlier clearly apply, as they do in historians Wilhelm Pauck, John T. McNeill, James Nichols, and Jaroslav Pelikan. Whatever emphasis they gave to the observation of biblical or historical study has been in the context of a historical interpretation primarily; and the historical interest has a way of taking on dimensions of inquiry and a kind of interest in happenings that diverge from what is commonly understood to be in focus whenever the empirical method is applied.

The historical work of church historians like Sidney Mead, Jerald Brauer, and Martin Marty would seem to stand in a somewhat different relation to the empirical tradition than that of the men just mentioned.[1] Clearly these three men partake of the prevailing mode of inquiry common among historians; yet, in dealing with the events and personal biographies of church history, they tend to be responsive to a wider range of data and relationships within the culture at large, and to experienceable phenomena in the more immediate, empirical sense, than is commonly dealt with in more classically oriented historical studies. Whether this is a characteristic that is to be identified more with American than with European modes of historical inquiry, or with Anglo-American than with continental methods, is not a matter on which I am able to comment; but clearly a difference in procedure or range of interest is in evidence here.[2]

[1] Similarly, one might regard the historical work of William Warren Sweet as having had affinities with the empirical method. Sweet's historical studies, however, being to a great extent the assembling and cataloguing of historical data in the form of church records, letters, and formal declarations of church bodies, were more in the nature of a gathering of source material preliminary to an empirical inquiry into American church history. Interpretation and the probing of these materials toward that end were kept to a minimum.

[2] The question arises further whether historical inquiry, as differentiated from empirical inquiry, can itself be identified as one kind of response to data within all historical disciplines having to do with

These differences between empiricists and historicists present an interesting problem which perhaps has not been sufficiently explored. For one thing, they represent two different ways of countering or moderating the abstract, philosophical, or ontological concern with religious data; and they express two different types of inquiry into what is concretely observed. Empiricists have generally been philosophically oriented in their approach, even though they have countered abstract or speculative procedures that carried inquiry too far beyond the field of experience. Historicists, on the other hand, have persistently sought to avoid even a modicum of philosophical directives or restrictions on the grounds that they were concerned to let the data of events speak to the interpreter as directly as possible and without bias, given our human fallibilities. The crucial issue between the historicist

religion. Is the historian of early Christianity who employs a socio-historical method, for example, concerned with a complex of interests comparable to that of the church historian in the more classical mode, and is their form of inquiry comparable? Or again, is historical inquiry as practiced by the church historian in interpreting the Christian religion in any way comparable to that of the historian of religion concerned with non-Christian religions; or must they be differentiated? It has always struck me as being of some significance that scholarly work done in biblical and church history rarely, if ever, coheres or has contact with scholarly work done in the history of religions. And conversely, only with rare exception do historians of religion undertake to apply their mode of inquiry to the Christian religion. The two disciplines seem relatively indifferent toward one another. To a degree, to be sure, the *Religionsgeschichtliche* as well as the socio-historical method of the early Chicago school lessened the gap between the two fields, but not to the point of generating any genuine rapport or interchange between the two disciplines. The Chicago school, for example, was content to include a brief survey on the study of primitive religions and non-Christian faiths as a prolegomenon to the study of the Christian religion; but beyond that, little or no reference was made to materials or findings in the history of religions as having any bearing upon the historical study of Christianity. The recent work of Gösta Ahlström and Jay Wilcoxin would seem to offer some improvement on this situation, in being a more genuine effort to explore biblical study in the context of the wider historical field.

After all these distinctions among historians are taken into account, however, the terms historical and historicist do stand over against terms like empirical and empiricist as having irreconcilable differences, even as they disclose affinities with one another.

and the empiricist arises precisely here; for the empiricist is wont to challenge any such presentation of bare, uninterpreted data prior to observation or explication. In defense of the historicist, one might say that he has often accepted this judgment of his procedure as being a commentary upon our human fallibility but has felt nevertheless that the less one allows presuppositions to assume prominence or priority in any form of inquiry, the less likely they are to color all that is observed; and the more likely the interpreter will be to understand events on their own terms.

However one may interpret or assess this very evident note of dissidence in Divinity School history, countering and even challenging the empirical emphasis, it would be fair to say that, from the turn of the century through the nineteen-twenties at least, the years spanning the period of the early Chicago school, the empirical method, following somewhat in the tradition of pragmatism, was dominant in the Divinity School throughout all areas of study. Empiricism continued to be prevalent at Chicago after that period; but, toward the close of the nineteen-twenties, a new kind of empirical inquiry was beginning to appear. This new mode of empirical thought was being shaped by the confluence of scientific and philosophical developments which were to give rise to what was termed "organismic thinking." In the Divinity School this mode of thought was being seriously engaged as early as 1926 in seminars by Gerald Birney Smith. The most evident and concerted move in this direction, however, occurred with the coming of Henry Nelson Wieman to the faculty, and with the subsequent absorption in the new metaphysics of Alfred North Whitehead under the stimulus of Wieman's earlier influence, and later under that of Charles Hartshorne and Bernard M. Loomer. This mode of empiricism, unlike that of earlier years, tended to center chiefly in the theological field; though, as its influence developed, it shaped inquiry in other fields of study in the Divinity School as well. For a time, in fact, following the mid-nineteen-forties, the Whiteheadian mode of empiricism became formative of theological educational policy itself in the Divinity School.

Since the purpose of this volume is to present offerings of the theological field as its contribution to the centennial series, I shall confine myself in this survey to specific developments in empirical inquiry within the theological discipline, indicating the various phases and types of empirical thinking that have taken place within the theological field at Chicago. Before inquiring into that immediate history of thought, however, we should look briefly at the larger picture of empirical concern in Western thought from which some of the Chicago empiricism stems.

I

Empiricism has been so closely identified with the temper and mode of thought that developed among English thinkers of the modern period following John Locke and David Hume, and that was to receive further generalization among British evolutionists and scientists in their study of social experience, that one is inclined to view it exclusively in these terms. It is important to recall, however, that its beginnings go back to developments antedating the modern period, in the emphasis given by nominalism during the fourteenth and fifteenth centuries. As Wilhelm Windelband has observed, nominalism "was directed toward the development of natural science. . . . Duns Scotus and Occam gave chief impetus to the movement in which philosophy taking its place beside the metaphysics whose interests had hitherto been essentially religious, made itself again a secular science of concrete actual facts and placed itself with more and more definite consciousness upon the basis of empiricism."[3] This emphasis, he continues, developed along lines of psychology, especially among the Arabs, in whom philosophy addressed itself to "establishing and arranging the facts of experience."[4]

Now there is a point to be noted in relating empiricism to the facts of experience. Other modes of thought had recognized that ultimate realities impressed themselves upon the

[3] Wilhelm Windelband, *A History of Philosophy*, vol. 7 (New York: Harper & Brothers, 1958), pp. 343–44.
[4] Ibid., p. 344.

mind and psyche of man, but only as copies of the *really real.* The truth of reality detected here was thus to be studied, not as "facts of experience" in the concrete sense of empirical inquiry, but as truths that were to be mathematically and rationally discerned. The shadow of their reality reflected in experience awakened and impelled the serious thinker to attend to this reality supervening experience.

Occam was to disavow this kind of close correlation between the human mind and reality, whereby "a copy of the latter was to arise." In so doing, he opened the way for distinctions between mind and matter, body and mind, between primary and secondary qualities, and thereby introduced the epistemological issue that was to haunt philosophical and religious thought for many centuries to come.

If modern idealism is to be seen as a persisting effort to reestablish the authority of mind in its human apprehension of reality, empiricism, beginning with Francis Bacon's *De Augmentis Scientarum,* may be taken to be a relentless effort to demonstrate that the same principles employed in observing man's bodily existence as evidenced in the sciences are to be applied to "the movement of ideas and of activities of the will" with a view to discerning "their moving force." Bacon was not prepared to carry through what he proposed, but he had created a vision of the mind that was more nearly oriented to the vital and physical processes of concrete experience of man and nature than could be acknowledged by scholastics or modern idealists. It is significant that John Dewey, in his *Reconstruction in Philosophy,* devoted an entire chapter to Francis Bacon, hailing him as one who exemplified the newer spirit.

The pivotal point, however, around which discussion of modern empiricism has revolved, has been John Locke.[5] This is due principally, no doubt, to his attack upon innate ideas directed mainly against the Cambridge Platonists. Locke reinstated the role of the senses as the stimulus to reflection, and thus, in a way, brought body and mind into a working

[5] See especially *Essay concerning Human Understanding,* 1690 (Oxford: Clarendon Press, 1904), vol. 2.

correlation which required attention to the two sides of life. Experience in its sensory aspects was thus seen to be productive of ideas, though the further process of reflecting upon them was seen to be formative and fulfilling of their implications. A superficial reading of Locke's empiricism will deduce from the Lockean thesis that sense impression is basic to knowledge and thus is to be regarded as the singularly important sphere of inquiry. Positivistic forms of evolutionary thinking, presuming to be empirical, have made this deduction, and thus have set up environment and its physical determinants as the real source of man's knowledge whatever the area of inquiry. Here the balance between the sensory and the reflective process, which Locke sought to maintain, appears lost; with the result that an environmental empiricism approximating materialistic determinism follows.

The empirical bent of mind that was thought to have originated with Locke was to culminate in the skepticism of Hume, wherein causal connections, giving hint or intimation of an ultimate reality or cosmic order, were deemed wholly subjective, residing, as Hume suggested, in custom or in modes of reflection, rather than in any objective sphere of reality.[6] Kant's response to this skeptical view of empiricism issued in a strategy of thought whereby the empirical method was salvaged for scientific inquiry, but rendered unavailable for religious inquiry.[7] In appealing to the practical reason, however, as a way of affording religious and moral inquiry, Kant could be said to have made concessions to demands encountered in experience, at least in the sphere of moral and religious experience.

Empiricism is commonly defined as the method of inquiry that presumes to find knowledge and its verification by appealing to experience. Yet one needs to ask whether the appeal to experience in all its forms is really an empirical inquiry. What hinges upon the answer to this question is the relation of the appeal to religious experience, including the

[6] Cf. *An Enquiry concerning Human Understanding* (LaSalle, Ill.: Open Court Pub. Co., 1949 [from 1777 ed.]), p. 58.
[7] *The Critique of Pure Reason* (1781).

theological method in Schleiermacher's theology, to empiricism.[8] Schleiermacher, in attending to the religious consciousness as the area in which theology was to find its data and resources, was certainly moving away from the authoritarian appeal to tradition as well as from a mathematically determined a priori. One could say, as many have said, that Schleiermacher was thereby establishing theology on a new basis in which religious experience was being given its rightful place. The concern to give full import to this innovation has often resulted in psychologizing Schleiermacher's procedure, thus making it unduly subjective in method. In doing so, one dispels what Schleiermacher sought to hold together, namely, the tension felt in the juxtaposition of the reality given in the notion of God and the reality experienced in the sense of absolute dependence. For Schleiermacher no simple psychological reading of the religious consciousness could yield what was essential to the theological task. A certain distance was maintained between what could be observed and what could be inferred from this momentous juxtaposition. Schleiermacher's way of expressing this sense of distance was to say that any language employed to speak about this reality discerned in the religious consciousness could only be symbolic. On these grounds, Rudolf Otto ascribed to Schleiermacher the rediscovery of the numinous in modern theology.[9] Now this is not empiricism as it is commonly understood, though it carries with it a kind of appeal to experience. It is more akin to the phenomenological method employed by Otto in his *The Idea of the Holy*,[10] and by Paul Tillich,[11] wherein something of the earlier Platonistic notion of reality casting its shadow upon concrete experience is recovered or restated. In no sense, within this mode of thinking, should one speak of literal processes of divinity being observed. Nevertheless, one may see in this symbolic

[8] Cf. *The Christian Faith*, 1821–22, English ed. (Edinburgh: T. & T. Clark, 1928), introduction.

[9] *Religious Essays* (London: Oxford Univ. Press, 1931), pp. 68–77.

[10] 2d ed. (New York: Oxford Univ. Press, 1950).

[11] See esp. *Systematic Theology*, vol. 1 (Chicago: Univ. of Chicago Press, 1951).

method of attending to the field of experience a mode of inquiry which has affinities with the empirical concern even as its resists empiricism as such.

The appeal to experience more commonly associated with certain nineteenth-century forms of liberal theology presents another kind of problem. Here what was lifted up was more in the form of an internal judgment of values experienced, as in Ritschlianism or in personalism; or of a selective Christian sense, enabling one to discern Christ-like tendencies in thought or action, as in the theology of William Newton Clarke.[12] To speak of this mode of inquiry as being empirical would seem to ally the empirical method too readily with intuition and feeling simply on the grounds that experience is experience, whether inner or outer in form. In this connection, it is interesting to recall that Shailer Mathews was always very insistent about distinguishing between modernism and evangelical liberalism at this very point. Modernism, he would argue, is committed to an empirical method, implying observation of occurrences in the form of public inquiry which lends itself to a critical exchange of interpretation and assessment. Evangelical liberalism, he found, resorted to an appeal to experience that was more inward and personal in its source and judgment; and on those grounds, he suspected evangelical liberalism of being a subjectivized form of supernaturalism. I recall his saying in a class in historical theology on one occasion that the appeal to religious experience could probably be thought of as being continuous historically with the Reformers' notion of the immediate access to the Holy Spirit. This preoccupation with the private, subjective encounter of the psyche with transcendent realities, whether in mysticism, Reformation theology, or evangelical liberalism, he found to be a detour from the area of data with which the modern Christian theologian should concern himself. Here was the voice of empiricism speaking as

[12] Cf. his *An Outline of Christian Theology* (New York: Scribner, 1894); and *The Use of the Scriptures in Theology* (New York: Scribner, 1906). See also William Adams Brown, *Christian Theology in Outline* (New York: Scribner, 1906).

it had developed within the Chicago school. I shall speak more explicitly of this development in a moment.

A variation upon both the appeal to religious experience in the evangelical liberal sense and the empiricism of the Chicago school, and in a sense a mediation between them, is to be found in the theology of Douglas Clyde Macintosh.[13] Macintosh was a graduate of the Divinity School of the University of Chicago. When the dean of the Yale Divinity School was considering inviting Macintosh to join their faculty, he wrote Mathews asking about Macintosh as a theologian and scholar. Mathews spoke highly of Macintosh's gifts as a theological thinker, and ended by saying, "If you don't hire him, we probably will." Had Macintosh come to Chicago, he would have introduced into the Chicago scene a kind of empirical study of religion that would have added a note of dissonance to Chicago theology. For his concern at that time was not with religion as a social process, but with religious experience as it appeared in the ordinary person or church member. His hope was to create a clinical theology that could be as explicit in guiding the work of the minister among his parishioners as medical science had been able to inform and discipline the work of physicians in their communities. Theology as an empirical science, therefore, which was the title of one of his early books, was to consist in discovering and formulating the basic laws underlying the religious response, together with the principles of behavior applicable to religious experience. In this theology, intuition, observation, and reflection were to be given parallel if not equal weight and emphasis.

In the kind of psychological studies of religious behavior such as G. Stanley Hall and his associates at Clark University undertook at the turn of the century,[14] the claim of empirical inquiry can be made more convincingly. Here theological doctrines claiming to be expressive of objective, revelatory events were translated into their psychological effects as

[13] Cf. his *Theology as an Empirical Science* (New York: Macmillan Co., 1919).

[14] *Journal of Religious Psychology and Education*, esp. vol. 1.

observed in religious behavior. Once this procedure gained ascendancy in religious inquiry, however, the theological or objective reference subsided, and the study of religion became a psychology of religious experience. Edward Scribner Ames was to partake of this mode of religious empiricism,[15] giving to it, however, a distinctly social and functional emphasis consistent with the anthropological studies that were basic to his interpretation of religion.

It is fairly easy and all too common to define empiricism in so restrictive a way as to exclude much in Western thought that proceeds from motives and correctives that are consonant with the empirical tradition. I have argued elsewhere [16] that empiricism in Western thinking has to be seen in its variety rather than in terms of any single expression of it. What looms as a determinant of its meaning when looked at in this way is the scope and nature of experience that is brought into view through observation and reflection. Experience can be taken to mean a highly selective form of sensory data, or a complex of events, subtly and ambiguously envisaged. The distinction here turns, not on whether the empiricist is precise and disciplined, as against those who are vague and undisciplined in their thinking; but rather on whether the facts of experience are understood to be the kind of data that can be attended to as isolated entities and thus scrutinized with utmost clarity of observation, or data that can be envisaged only in a context; that is, within relationships, where relationships are deemed experienceable, as in the radical empiricism of William James.[17] Where relations are conceived to be experienceable, and this is what is granted in the empiricism of James, Bergson, and Whitehead, the empirical method becomes a highly complex correlation of what Locke designated sensory and reflective activities.

[15] *The Psychology of Religious Experience* (Boston: Houghton Mifflin, 1910).

[16] Robert W. Bretall, ed., *The Empirical Theology of Henry Nelson Wieman* (New York: Macmillan Co., 1963), pp. 57–65.

[17] *Essays in Radical Empiricism* (New York: Longmans, Green & Co., 1912); *A Pluralistic Universe* (New York: Longmans, Green & Co., 1909).

A basic epistemological shift underlies this newer form of empiricism. Earlier British empiricism, following Locke and Hume, against which German theologians from Schleiermacher to Tillich have aimed their strictures, presupposed a subject-object dualism which made of perception and the knowing process a direct response to sensory stimuli evoked by objects confronting the human mind. In the radical empiricism of James and Whitehead, no such dualism is envisaged. The self lives, acts, and speaks out of a context of relations which form, as it were, the field of knowing. The "perceptual flux" (James),[18] or the "composition of events" (Whitehead),[19] presents itself to each individual consciousness as a vital immediacy, which in turn is conceptualized in marginal and tentative ways. In this mode of knowing, perception is given a primacy as being the "thicker experience." Reason is made secondary as being an abstraction from this richer context, and dependent upon recourse to it for verification and renewal.

One will see, then, that the development of the empirical method of inquiry in Western thought has not been a simple one, following a straight line of descent within a specified orientation of mind. It has assumed various turns of inquiry in accordance with the conception of experience that was held and the status given to it in formulating a theory of knowledge.

II

We turn now to the story of empirical theology as it developed within the history of the Divinity School of the University of Chicago. Here, similar variations are discerned, governed by the data which are considered to be expressive of experience pertinent to religion, specifically the Christian religion; and by scientific and philosophical notions which were deemed to be helpful in interpreting such experience.

[18] *Some Problems in Philosophy* (New York: Longmans, Green & Co., 1911), p. 49.

[19] *Adventures of Ideas* (New York: Macmillan Co., 1933), chap. 13; *Modes of Thought* (New York: Macmillan Co., 1938), pp. 122–23, 128–30, 164–68.

The empirical method of theological study in the Divinity School became explicit in the rise of the early Chicago school [20] under Shailer Mathews [21] and Shirley Jackson

[20] Shortly after I had completed the writing of this introductory survey of the theological tradition in the Divinity School, the lively and fascinating account of Divinity School history by Harvey Arnold, *Near The Edge of Battle* (privately printed by Divinity School Association, Univ. of Chicago, 1966) was published. Arnold's interpretation of the emergence of the early Chicago school differs slightly from my own in that he dates its rise from the appearance of George Burman Foster's book, *The Finality of the Christian Religion* (Chicago: Univ. of Chicago Press) in 1906, and finds in Foster himself the primal source of the Chicago school. I, on the other hand, find the beginnings of the school antedating Foster's work in the preliminary studies of Shailer Mathews and Shirley Jackson Case, and tend to regard Foster as more of a dissident voice within the School, rather than its formative influence. This difference in our views can be clarified, I think, if one recognizes that Arnold, as historian, attends to the rise of the Chicago school in terms of its becoming a public event, which it did during the controversy following the publication of Foster's book, *The Finality of the Christian Religion*. I, on the other hand, have been concerned to review theological developments more internally within Divinity School history, which has projected my interpretation into earlier beginnings as these appeared in the shaping of the theological discipline within the Divinity School. In this role, Shailer Mathews and Shirley Jackson Case were clearly the major figures; and their technical theological and historical work was done independently of Foster's influence. Arnold, however, makes a persuasive case for seeing a metamorphosis of theological thinking within the faculty of the Divinity School during this period, wherein, he points out, younger members of the faculty, apparently rallying to Foster's support, moved more decisively in the direction of a critical position; while older members, such as Franklin Johnson and others, resisted this effort, preferring a more conciliatory and conservative stance. This is a point that deserves further study.

There can be no doubt that, as a dynamic and propulsive force in behalf of the critical spirit in religious studies, Foster stood out among his colleagues, giving to the critical method a candid expression beyond university circles which, in large measure, was responsible for the public image of the Divinity School during that period. Thus, insofar as there emerged in the public consciousness a distinctive Chicago school of divinity, it centered in the restive, pro-Nietzschean spirit of George Burman Foster who, as Arnold has noted, was painfully wrestling with the haunting Nietzschean declaration, "God is dead," as early as 1906 and before.

[21] Cf. esp. *The Faith of Modernism* (New York: Macmillan Co., 1924); "The Religious Life," in *Man and His World* series, vol. 11, ed. Baker Brownell (New York: Van Nostrand, 1929); *The Atonement*

Case,[22] sometimes referred to as the socio-historical school of theology. During the early stages of that epoch of theological history, however, there were mild dissenters among them. George Burman Foster[23] and Gerald Birney Smith, for example, had been troubled Ritschlians in their earlier years. And while one can find affinities between the Ritschlian method and that of empiricism, as I have noted, it would be confusing matters to subsume the former under the latter. Ritschlianism was a valuational approach to realities carrying into theology a fusion of Kantian and Lotzean idealism. While, like empiricism, it rejected speculative procedures common to metaphysical inquiry, it nevertheless retained more of the idealizing venture of faith than empiricists were inclined to acknowledge. Among the early Chicago empiricists, and in fact among pragmatists generally, a similar recourse to valuation in the idealistic mode was evident; but here it was made more implicit and, if possible, obscured, functioning mainly as a persisting habit of mind from earlier associations, rather than as an avowed manner of thinking. Both Foster and Smith, however, were to become participants in the early Chicago school and to share in its functional method.

One can make a plausible case for tracing Foster's development as a theologian from a Ritschlian with a strong personalistic bent of mind to a functionalist in the pragmatic sense as represented by the Chicago school, and then to a humanist in whom the superstructure of realities beyond man gave

---

and the Social Process (New York: Macmillan Co., 1930); *The Growth of the Idea of God* (New York: Macmillan Co., 1931); *Christianity and the Social Process* (New York: Harper & Brothers, 1934).

[22] *The Social Origins of Christianity* (Chicago: Univ. of Chicago Press, 1923); *The Evolution of Early Christianity* (Chicago: Univ. of Chicago Press, 1925); *Jesus: A New Biography* (Chicago: Univ. of Chicago Press, 1927).

[23] Foster's most important work expressive of this approach is his *Finality of the Christian Religion*, published in 1906, though the posthumous work containing his class lectures, edited by D. C. Macintosh and published in 1921, discloses its lingering influence in the form of persisting problems. See also George Burman Foster, *The Function of Religion in Man's Struggle for Existence* (Chicago: Univ. of Chicago Press, 1909).

way to his high valuation of the possibilities in man. There
are those who characterize Foster in this way. To do so, however, is to delete all the drama, complexity, and even con-
tradictoriness that persisted in his thinking, coloring and con-
founding his thought at every step. Foster was a tormented
mind and spirit who nevertheless sought discipline and or-
derliness in his thinking. He was Nietzschean in the tenacity
with which he sought truth at whatever cost; yet he could
not accept the role of iconoclast or be content with sheer
negation of what had been historically affirmed. Foster was
an obvious admirer of Nietzsche in his ruthless quest for the
reality that inhered in the immediacies of life, even to the
point of identifying with him sympathetically in his declaration, "God is dead!" [24] Yet disavowal for Foster meant not
a dismissal of the problem in pursuit of other ends, but the
creation of a more poignant and persisting one, centering in
man's own meaning and destiny.

This persistent interplay of contradictory perspectives
upon Foster's thinking held him in the throes of incessant
battle with himself as well as with others. D. C. Macintosh,
commenting upon Foster, spoke of him as being "a remarkably sympathetic interpreter of points of view other than his
own; but in his exposition of the appreciations and viewpoint
of the Christian religious man," Macintosh added, "one knew
that it was not a case of understanding through mere sympathetic imagination; he was speaking out of the depths of
his own experience." [25]

If there was a progression in his thought from a critical
and uncertain hold on the Ritschlian method of theology to
a functional method stimulating an empirical view that emphasized man's role in the creation of value, it was more in
the nature of a compounding of interests and issues, thus
deepening and intensifying their complexity, than a simple
transition from one mode of inquiry to another. He remained

[24] Cf. George Burman Foster, *Friedrich Nietzsche*, ed. Curtis W.
Reeze (New York: Macmillan Co., 1931).

[25] George Burman Foster, *Christianity in Its Modern Expression*, ed.
D. C. Macintosh (New York: Macmillan Co., 1921), p. v.

a restive, rebel intellect in whatever company of thought he participated.

Gerald Birney Smith, as dissenter and critic within the Chicago school, shared some of the restiveness and sensitive anguish of thought that spoke through Foster; only Smith was more reticent about revealing the internal struggle that issued in his measured and critically established states of faith. Nothing incensed Smith more than glib affirmations or sanguine generalizations about Christian faith; but, like Foster, he could be equally scathing in his rebuff of the uncritical iconoclast. For both men, the experience of the day-to-day encounters with people and issues was deadly serious business, expressive of the realities to which the theologian addressed himself. In this sense, they were existentialist in their feeling for the theological task; yet the constructive effort in theology, in their judgment, demanded as well a more theoretical and objective understanding of this that pressed so vividly upon them as a personal encounter with the problem of doubt and faith. For this aspect of their work, the functional method of pragmatic inquiry served their critical purposes.

Gerald Birney Smith, in fact, was to embrace empiricism wholeheartedly and to participate in the Chicago school as a major exponent of the empirical method in theology. More open and responsive to philosophical currents of thought than either Mathews or Case, and to the changing scene within the sciences, he was less committed to the rather singular, sociological procedure implied in their theologies; though, to be sure, he availed himself of this stimulus as well, as is to be seen in his *Social Idealism and the Changing Theology*, published in 1913. Smith was really a bridge or transition between this early phase of empiricism and the one that developed under Wieman. It is particularly illumining to look at this early stage of theological empiricism at Chicago with respect to the influences that shaped it. For in this context, the nature of its empiricism is made explicit. As we proceed with an analysis of the empirical tradition in the Divinity School's history, we shall see that the term empiricism forms a large canopy or umbrella under which are to be found vary-

ing presuppositions and procedures. And though the empirical concern for regarding all knowledge as being descriptive
of experience persisted through all of them as a common bent
of mind, it assumed a variety of formulations and brought
together various combinations of disciplines and sensibilities
of thought.

The empirical effort of the early Chicago school arose out
of the stimulus of the study of history influenced by new
studies in sociology and social psychology. It partook also,
if only by a process of osmosis, of the philosophy of pragmatism which, at that time, had come into prominence in the
department of philosophy at the University of Chicago under
John Dewey. This pragmatic mode of thought in turn presupposed an evolutionary view of man with its strong emphasis upon environmental influence and functional adaptation, and thus assumed a modernistic bent of mind as being
inherent in its method, if not, in fact, but another way of
naming it. Empiricism in this context was thus a study of the
functional aspect of phenomena. A thing or movement was
known in terms of the function it served. Get at the motives
behind actions, affirmations, and words, along with the purpose for which they are employed, and you may then unmask
the real nature of the event itself. Ceremonials, prayers, beliefs, or doctrines, as well as institutional forms of legislation,
were thought to be expressive of "felt needs," as Shailer
Mathews was fond of saying. And these needs, in turn, were
traceable to a particular complex of environmental and social
circumstances or forces. In this mode of explication, theological inquiry was to concern itself with human behavior in response to what was deemed ultimate and demanding of
human adjustment. For Mathews, such inquiry was to be
addressed to the action of social groups, not to individual instances of the religious life. He appeared distrustful of individual religion, whether mystical, philosophical, or pietistical.
Yet his main reason for insisting upon focusing attention on
the social group was methodological. "History," he maintained, "unlike biography, is essentially a social study. It is
concerned with social groups rather than with individual

men and women. It is by no means indifferent to individuals, but regards them as contributors to the action of the group of which they are members." And it was the social process at work in shaping a given period of religious history with which the socio-historical method was concerned.

Mathews was to see Christian history giving rise to a series of social minds, each one of which had produced its own set of analogies and patterns that shaped the vocabularies of the Christian community within these respective periods. In his chapter in *A Guide to the Study of the Christian Religion* from which I just quoted, he outlines this series of social minds in Christian history; and in his books, *The Atonement and the Social Process*, published in 1930, *The Growth of the Idea of God*, published in 1931, and in his Barrows lectures, *Christianity and the Social Process*, published in 1934, he gives a full discussion of his thesis concerning social minds, applying it to specific doctrines. Mathews was convinced that theological doctrine was a form of analogical thinking by which the familiar terms of experience rendered revelatory insights and experience intelligible to religious men and women.

From his encounter with the biological sciences, particularly as they bore on the subject of evolution, and his continual exchanges with scientists,[26] Mathews came to assume a cosmological basis or background from which he projected the religious life as an adaptive measure, responding to felt needs. The designative area, even for theological inquiry and exposition, he held, was history and the social experience of people. Yet these were the outward, visible responses to a drama that was cosmic in scope. For in his view, persons and their historical acts followed from an interplay with "personality-producing forces in the universe," the full story of which eludes man's comprehension. Man "tunes into" this vaster cosmic scene through his own felt needs and the response he makes to them. Speaking of these cosmic activities antecedent to and continuous with our human activities,

[26] Cf. his *Contributions of Science to Religion* (New York: Appleton, 1924).

Mathews wrote, "We know not whence they come or whither they go, but we cannot evade them." "Like a vast parabola" they "touch our little circle of experience. . . . We set up relations with them similar to those which we set up with persons." [27]

Part of the act of setting up relations with these cosmic activities was that of *conceiving* of them in a certain way and addressing them by the means of employing analogies and symbols that could be expressive of them within a given social situation. Mathews preferred to have his cosmic approach to theological inquiry spoken of as "conceptual theism," by which he meant a conception of God that frankly identified it with the concepts and analogical symbols available to the thought and speech of any culture at any given time in history.

From within this perspective, Mathews resisted any form of philosophical inquiry, attending or preceding theological inquiry, that sought to probe this deeper orientation of the religious life. Questions of truth in the metaphysical sense, Mathews contended, could only detour theological inquiry from the real business at hand. That business was done in the visible acts and behavior of Christians engaged as a religious community, in the convening of church councils, or in the more commonplace deliberations and occasions of preaching, and in homiletic and polemical writings of vitally concerned churchmen preceding and following such formal church gatherings. Under Mathews, empirical theology thus became church centered, focusing observation and study upon the community of believers as a practicing congregation. These deliberations and actions within the religious community constituted the practical act of "setting up relations" with "the personality-producing forces," conducted within the idiom of speech that frankly employed analogies suitable to vivifying these realities as being relevant and redemptive, and to instructing its members in their responses

[27] A fuller account of this aspect of Mathews' thought is given in Henry N. Wieman and Bernard E. Meland, *American Philosophies of Religion* (New York: Harper & Brothers, 1948), pp. 286–90.

to them to enable them to avail themselves of the resources needed for meeting their "felt needs."

In saying that Mathews' empirical theology was church centered, I do not mean to imply that he confined himself to the study of ecclesiastical activities in a restricted way. For him the church was more than a cultus, or some esoteric group set apart from its social environs. The church was a social movement among other cultural movements. It partook of the undercurrents of society and thus reflected in its aspirations, declarations, and formulations the seed ideas that had become formative of the language of the culture of a specific period of culture. This, Mathews held, was evident in the very analogies that were employed in Christian preaching and in the declarations of the councils that issued in the formulation of doctrines, or more particularly in the "social patterns" that became expressive of firmly held and fixed beliefs.

Members of the Chicago school who practiced empirical theology in this form were more concerned with describing religious thought and practices, thereby hoping to understand them, than with evaluating them. They likewise reflected little interest in establishing any doctrinal criteria of identification between present-day and traditional forms of Christianity. That there was such identification, they readily assumed. Such identification, they held, did not need to be established in doctrinal terms. In their way of understanding the history of doctrine, concern with the commonality or uniformity of beliefs was not likely to yield much continuing identification. Insofar as there was a pivotal point toward which Christians of every age gravitated, Mathews held, it was to be found in the person and teaching of the historical Jesus. But this focal point was to be understood as a "rallying point" or directive, pointing Christians toward a way of living, rather than as an ontological problem inviting speculative inquiry or reflection. Any effort to probe the nature of this person in the sense in which christological discussions had pursued the problem, he held, could only lead away from the continuing thread of historical Christianity, and in-

volve the theologian instead in the divisive and particular-
istic aspects of Christian history resulting from ontological
speculation.[28]

One may see from this cursory analysis, then, that to the
early Chicago school empirical theology consisted mainly of
the historical study of a social movement and of Christian per-
sonalities as participants in such an ongoing historical movement. The contemporary task of theology from this point of
view was not to present an interpretation of a historically
established set of Christian doctrines, within the modern
idiom; but to convey a way of understanding the directives
of Christian faith, translated into their contemporary meaning. The shorthand way of stating this objective was to ask,
"What does it mean to be loyal to Jesus in contemporary
society?"

The historical Jesus for Mathews, and with qualifications,
for Case as well, exemplified the one in the Christian movement who had mastered the role of the religious man in response to "the cosmic forces" (which in Judaism and Christianity had been cast into the imagery of God as father), in
such a way as to assure the growth of personality. Jesus'
teachings, especially within the social realm, and the basic
notions they conveyed, were thus highly pertinent as guidelines in pursuing the Christian life. Shailer Mathews, more
than any other member of the Chicago school, worked at
specifying what this pivotal core of directives was, advancing
it in the form of "generic Christianity," which functioned, he
would say, much as a protoplasm does in genetic history, and
could be counted on "to breed true to itself."

For Mathews, then, pursuing the act of becoming more personal in the quality of life and experience constituted the
meaning of the Christian life. And this, in his judgment, not
only had cosmic support, but was continuous with the driving, evolutionary motif of cosmic history. Loyalty to Jesus
was the Christian way of pursuing this more personal mode
of existence. Commitment to him was a pragmatically veri-

[28] Cf. Shirley Jackson Case, "The Lure of Christology," *Journal of
Religion*, vol. 25 (1945).

fiable entrée into the response that would best assure the achievement of that end. For salvation, he wrote in *The Faith of Modernism*, "is an advance in the total personal life made possible by a new and advanced relationship with the personal God, the way to which is seen in the experience of Jesus. It is a still further step in human evolution which has already so largely freed personality from the control of impersonal forces through the working of a fatherly God." [29]

The pragmatic test of the Christian life among people of the churches, then, as he saw it, was its effectiveness in making people more personal in their dealings with one another, and in the social life that gave wider expression and force to their individual purposes and decisions. To a degree, he assumed he could equate this kind of response, or associate it, with their loyalty to Jesus. Initially Mathews had proposed *loyalty* to Jesus as the contemporary Christian's alternative to the traditional notion of the *authority* of Jesus. Later he was to speak of the phrase "loyalty to Jesus" as a "banner phrase" by which he meant that it had been employed historically in conventional Christianity as a social movement to rally the forces of the community and to "close ranks" around its central purpose of dedication. His interpretation of Christianity as a social movement had been shaped by an early study of the French Revolution, and he continued to view Christianity in its present context as a revolutionary movement bent on extending the centrifugal power of its rallying point as expressed in its "banner phrase." Only he recognized that, for many present-day Christians, this phrase was mainly a matter of sentiment, evoking a feeling response that could be dissipated simply in ritual or in maudlin verbiage. He was concerned to infuse into it the sense of discipline and ethical purposiveness in the way Kant had employed the *ethical imperative* and Josiah Royce had advocated *a philosophy of loyalty*. Becoming more personal was the ultimate, cosmic end; exercising "loyalty to Jesus," in the sense in which he meant to convey it, was the immediate and practical mode of participating in that end.

[29] *Faith of Modernism*, p. 152.

Mathews could be quite sanguine about the possibility of bringing all Christians around to an understanding of this more personal end of their Christian loyalty to Jesus, and he never wearied of the effort to break through the conservative façade which he felt insulated Christians from the truth of the gospel. He banked heavily on his critical method of understanding doctrine to penetrate this façade, and thus to open the minds of Christians to what lay beyond their restricted understanding of the Christian life. With this understanding of doctrine, he would frequently say to young ministers and theologues, one should be able to move sympathetically and helpfully among Christians of any persuasion, liberal or conservative, and to recognize that, however differently they may word their creeds or state their beliefs, in their loyalty to Jesus as Christian people they are potentially one in pursuing the ultimate goal of a more personal existence.

The chief work of the constructive and systematic theologian, then, according to Mathews, consisted in identifying and observing, as well as promoting, the social processes at work in contemporary society that emulated or advanced the growth of the personality-producing activities by which Christian loyalty and commitment were enacted in contemporary life. This task implied also noting the key concepts or controlling sources of ideas from which analogies appropriate to this stage of the social experience were being drawn, or could be drawn, in communicating this witness of faith, and in rendering its historical affirmations and doctrines intelligible to modern man. In all of this, one can see that, for the Chicago school, the social experience of Christian people at various stages of its history provided the locus of theological inquiry.

I spoke of Gerald Birney Smith as being a participant in the early Chicago school of empiricism. This needs some qualification, for Smith was both of and beyond this era of empiricism. In fact one must say that Gerald Birney Smith played a distinctive role in the theological history of the Divinity School. While he shared the empirical concerns of

Mathews and Case, and responded heartily to the new orientation of empirical thinking that was developing in the context of organismic thought prior to and during Wieman's first years at Chicago, he could not be considered completely committed to the theological method of either of them. G. B. Smith was warmly sympathetic toward people, and exceedingly judicious in weighing a conflict in issues; yet in his criticism of thought, whether of an individual, or of a group of thinkers presuming to express a consensus, he could be devastating. With the precision of a physician's scalpel he would cut into an issue or a proposal of thought, laying bare its pretensions and ill-considered notions, or pointing up the thin line of constructive insight which gave promise to its line of inquiry. Students and faculty alike came to depend on his judgment for winnowing out the truth and error of situations in Divinity School life and thought.

In this role, Gerald Birney Smith was less given to the constructive formulation of theological doctrine or point of view in the empirical mode than Mathews or Wieman; yet through his critical interpretation of their work, he exercised a powerful influence in shaping the net effect of their contributions as empirical theologians in the Divinity School community. This was particularly true in regard to the work of the early Chicago school. He died (April 3, 1929) before the full effect of Wieman's thought became established; yet even in those early stages, Smith's initial heralding of Wieman's new empiricism in *Religious Experience and Scientific Method*, and his subsequent disappointment with *The Wrestle of Religion with Truth*, influenced the general assessment of what Wieman was contributing in this new venture in empirical theology.

In so far as G. B. Smith pursued a constructive mode of theological inquiry, it addressed itself to discovering whether the natural universe, as described by the sciences, was hospitable to a religious response and to a doctrine of theism.[30]

[30] Gerald Birney Smith's principal works, in addition to his *Social Idealism and the Changing Theology* (New York: Macmillan Co., 1912) already mentioned, were: *A Guide to the Study of the Christian*

Here his empiricism partook of the method being advanced
by Wieman, rather than the functional method of the Chicago school; yet with a difference. For Smith was aware that
the religious response was nearer to that of the arts than to
the method of science. Thus, to him, responding religiously
to the universe, or to what was ultimate and sovereign in this
complex of data described by the sciences, entailed some kind
of response that went beyond the procedures characteristic
and normative for the sciences. His final theological efforts before his death were toward refining the steps of such a procedure, taking the form of a mystical awareness of nature,
disciplined and informed by the symbols and structures of
the arts.[31]

Edward Scribner Ames was perhaps more explicit and out-
spoken in his commitment to the functional method of pragmatism than any other member of the Chicago school. As a
member of the department of philosophy under John Dewey,
in his early years, and later its chairman, he approached all
issues in religious thought from within the total matrix of that
discipline. In its pragmatic orientation, this meant seeing the
problems of man, including his religious problems, as being
psychological and cultural phenomena, expressive of basic
human needs. And the ferreting out of these formative and
motivating drives, set in their corporate context as being expressive of the religious consciousness of a community, became his chief concern in his study of religious behavior.
Ames recoiled from the word "theology" as being an outmoded approach to the problems of the religious person,
comparable, as he often remarked, to that of astrology in its

Religion, of which he was editor (Chicago: Univ. of Chicago Press,
1916); *The Principles of Christian Living* (Chicago: Univ. of Chicago
Press, 1924); *Current Christian Thinking* (Chicago: Univ. of Chicago Press, 1928); ed., with Shailer Mathews, *Dictionary of Religion
and Ethics* (New York: Macmillan Co., 1921); ed., *Religious Thought
in the Last Quarter Century* (Chicago: Univ. of Chicago Press, 1928).
[31] Cf. his "The Nature of Science and of Religion and Their Interrelation," *Religious Education* 23 (1927): 308–10. I have quoted at
length from this article in "The Genius of Protestantism," *Journal of
Religion* 27 (1947): 285.

study of the stars.[32] In this he shared the perspective of psychologists of religion dating from the work of G. Stanley Hall, William James, Edwin Starbuck, and James H. Leuba who, at the turn of the century, set themselves explicitly to the task of discerning the psychological need or concern underlying or being expressed through theological doctrines. Ames was less concerned to translate theology as such into its psychological equivalents; he preferred instead, in the manner of John Dewey, to address himself directly to the psychological reality as having religious significance. This he did most effectively and thoroughly in his major work, *The Psychology of Religious Experience*, published in 1910. This book was a pioneer work in its field and had considerable influence in relating the material of cultural anthropology to the psychological study of religious behavior.[33]

While not directly involved in the work of the theological field, A. Eustace Haydon, as historian of religions in the Divinity School, had a presence and aura that cast a spell upon much that was done in the theological field. Haydon was an avowed humanist who affirmed the cosmic support of human values. Yet, unlike his colleagues Mathews, Smith, and Ames, who saw in this cosmic support grounds for formulating a conception of God, Haydon was intent on pressing for acknowledgment that man was the universe come to consciousness. (Cf. his *The Quest of the Ages* [New York: Harper & Brothers, 1929]). As such, Haydon argued, man himself merited affirmation and celebration in ways that had generally been expended upon deities, and in the Christian tradition, upon God. The cosmic environment had been the nurturing matrix that had produced this "earth-child," man; but it was "in the enfolding social environment," Haydon argued, "that man now found his real support and guarantor." Con-

[32] Cf. his *Beyond Theology* (Chicago: Univ. of Chicago Press, 1959).
[33] See also his book, *Religion* (New York: Holt, 1929). Two articles by Ames are particularly significant as being expressive of his approach to religious problems: "The Validity of the Idea of God," *Journal of Religion* 1 (1920): 462–81; and "Religious Values and the Practical Absolute," *International Journal of Ethics* 32 (1921): 347–65.

sequently, Haydon concluded, the social environment is to be recognized as the essential phase of the cosmic structure. In this way, Haydon's mystical naturalism assumed a socio-environmental emphasis which, in its own distinctive way, carried forward the method of the early Chicago school. (Cf. *Man's Search for the Good Life* [New York: Harper & Brothers, 1937]).

Edwin E. Aubrey, who succeeded Gerald Birney Smith in the theological field following Professor Smith's death in 1929, was concerned particularly with the psychological development of the religious life in individuals and with conditions that inhibited, marred, or released its fulfilment. Coming into the theological field after having done his major work in religious education, Aubrey saw the problems of theology and their doctrinal formulation in the context of personality development. His book, *Religion and the Next Generation*, best exemplifies this mode of theological inquiry.[34] Aubrey was, however, thoroughly conversant with the socio-historical method as it had developed in the early Chicago school, particularly under Shailer Mathews; and he remained its most effective interpreter within the theological field after Dean Mathews had retired.

Although Wilhelm Pauck[35] would recoil from being gathered into the empirical tradition of theology, no account of that tradition as it developed at Chicago would be complete without reference to his role in shaping it. Pauck's participation in the theological community at Chicago extended over

[34] *Religion and the Next Generation* (New York: Harper & Brothers, 1931). Other books by Professor Aubrey are: *Present Theological Tendencies* (New York: Harper & Brothers, 1936); *Living the Christian Faith* (New York: Macmillan Co., 1939); *Man's Search for Himself* (Nashville: Cokesbury, 1940).

[35] Wilhelm Pauck's principal publications include: *Das Reich Gottes auf Erden* (Berlin and Leipzig: W. de Gruyter and Co., 1928); *Karl Barth: Prophet of a New Christianity?* (New York and London: Harper & Brothers, 1931); *The Heritage of the Reformation* (Boston: Beacon Press, 1950); *Harnack and Troeltsch* (New York: Oxford Univ. Press, 1968); Pauck has co-authored: *The Church against the World* (Chicago: Willett, Clark, 1935); *Religion and Politics*, 1946; and *The Ministry in Historical Perspectives*, 1956.

a period of nearly three decades. He came to Chicago from Germany in 1925, and in 1926 was appointed to the faculty of the Chicago Theological Seminary as professor of church history. From 1939 to 1953 he was professor of historical theology in the Divinity School of the University of Chicago, and was chairman of the theological field during the last ten years of that period. Pauck's interest in theology was chiefly historical; though, being in the tradition of Harnack and Troeltsch, he could not be indifferent to the constructive task which was then being vigorously pursued at Chicago. Pauck's role at Chicago can best be described as that of the creative antagonist. Bringing to theological study within the quadrangles his own direct assimilation of the *Religionsgeschichtliche Schule*, as he had received it under the stimulus of Troeltsch, he found modes of inquiry in the early Chicago school with which he was familiar, but much to which he was to respond critically. Pauck's audacity and candor in confronting his colleagues with questions that were being raised about their empirical method of inquiry kept Chicago theologians alert to alternative views bearing on their problems. In this way he was an effective influence against the ingrown tendency that continually plagued the Chicago school. By virtue of his live interest in the continuing conversation of the larger theological community, both in this country and abroad, and his readiness to convey its strictures to the Chicago experience, he provided the Divinity School with a perennial source of self-criticism. But his stance was more than a negative reaction. His role as historian, and his training within the historical method, gave to his approach to theological problems a concern with concrete events and decisions that readily offered judgments to challenge what had been advanced as empirical observations. Pauck exemplified, both in his criticisms of empirical findings, as well as in his occasional concurrence with them, the issue that both divides and relates historical and empirical thinking in theology.

Pauck shared the skepticism of Troeltsch and Harnack toward doctrinaire philosophical or scientific theories which were often employed to guide theological judgment. Even

29

more than they, he insisted upon a common-sense approach to historical happenings with a minimum of preconceived notions, letting each turn of events tell its own story. Pauck's lecturing was, in its way, a highly astute and amusing mode of storytelling, re-presenting or reenacting, as it were, the human scenario within historical events out of which the issues of faith and reason arose. And with the swiftness of a gesture or turn of phrase, he could illumine an episode with a touch of humor that was unforgettable.

III

With the coming of Henry Nelson Wieman to the Divinity School faculty, a new stage of empirical theology developed. Wieman was not so much the initiator of this new empiricism as a pioneer expression of it in religious thought. I have traced elsewhere [36] the radical shift in imagery of thought that occurred in the latter part of the nineteen-twenties in which a new kind of evolutionary and organismic thought emerged, following from the earlier stimulus of Henri Bergson [37] and the metaphysical writings of William James.[38] This new organismic thought was initially formulated in the writings of Lloyd Morgan,[39] S. Alexander,[40] and Jan Smuts,[41] and was to be dramatically presented as a comprehensive world view by Alfred North Whitehead in 1929, in the publication of *Process and Reality*.[42] The role of Whitehead

[36] *The Realities of Faith* (New York: Oxford Univ. Press, 1962), pp. 109–11.

[37] Particularly his *Creative Evolution* (New York: Holt, 1911).

[38] Cf. his *Pluralistic Universe*, and *Essays in Radical Empiricism*.

[39] *Emergent Evolution* (New York: Holt, 1923); *Life, Mind, and Spirit* (New York: Holt, 1925).

[40] *Space, Time, and Deity*, 2 vols. (London: Macmillan & Co., 1920).

[41] *Holism and Evolution* (New York: Macmillan Co., 1926).

[42] Prior to *Process and Reality*, Whitehead had explored various aspects of the new vision of science that had begun to take form following the turn of the century. Before 1915 he was occupied almost wholly with mathematics, and from 1910–13, with Bertrand Russell, produced the massive three-volume work, *Principia Mathematica*. In 1919, Whitehead wrote two significant books which may be considered his initial ventures in a metaphysical direction, though they were not

during this period has usually been misinterpreted. His literature is so complete in itself as a summary view of all that preceded his efforts that he is generally taken to have been the instigator, and thus the one seminal voice expressive of this new age of thought. It is truer to say that he was the systematizer, and comprehensive formulator of seminal insights furnished by a host of scientific, philosophic, and religious thinkers who preceded him and by contemporary philosopher-scientists, especially in England, who comprised what was then known as a movement in organismic philosophy. These men were bent on countering the prevalent notion of mechanism as a scientific and philosophical imagery. Whitehead himself acknowledged this fact in the opening pages of *Process and Reality*, but to those who know Whitehead, and no one else in the development of the new empiricism, this acknowledgment of other sources is taken to be an understandable assertion of humility appropriate in a scholar of sensibility. But this blurs the facts of the situation. It is true that the thoroughness with which Whitehead pursued the systematic task, analyzing and drawing out explicit implications of the various fundamental notions being affirmed, makes his work more than a mere summation of what preceded. It is rather a creative philosophical vision, exemplifying in summary form the various thrusts of organismic

---

presented in that form: *Principles of Natural Knowledge* (Cambridge: Cambridge Univ. Press, 1919), and *The Concept of Nature*, given as the Tarner Lectures in Trinity College in 1919, but published in 1920 (Cambridge: Cambridge Univ. Press). His book, *The Principle of Relativity*, in which he took issue with Einstein, was published in 1922. And then, in 1925 and 1926, two books appeared that were to have a wide hearing in religious circles as being the beginning of a new metaphysical vision of religious realities: *Science and the Modern World* (New York: Macmillan Co., 1925); and *Religion in the Making* (New York: Macmillan Co., 1926), followed by his *Symbolism: Its Meaning and Effect* (New York: Macmillan Co., 1927). *Process and Reality*, published in 1929, brought these several strands of metaphysical and religious inquiry into systematic expression and established Whitehead's thought in the minds of many as a new, modern Summa. Subsequent to *Process and Reality* he was to publish three supplementary works of importance: *The Function of Reason* (Princeton: Princeton Univ. Press, 1929); *Adventures of Ideas*; and *Modes of Thought*.

thinking that lay back of his systematic effort. But when one says, "I don't need James, or Bergson, or S. Alexander, I have Whitehead," one closes out all the subtle, yet important, issues within this new empiricism which introduce into organismic thinking a creative dissonance and a breadth of insight that can keep inquiry within this perspective open and fruitful. Restricting this newer mode of empiricism to Whitehead's formulation of it makes of his thought a form of philosophical orthodoxy or scholasticism which overlooks Whitehead's own tentativeness and responsiveness to alternative emphases.

Contrasts between Whitehead's use of organismic insights in his philosophy of organism and these earlier strands stand out in my mind rather vividly because of the initial impact he made upon me and others who sat in Gerald Birney Smith's seminars in 1926, shortly before Wieman was to join the Divinity School faculty and just after the publication of Whitehead's *Religion in the Making*. We had spent several quarters exploring this organismic thought from Bergson's *Creative Evolution* through S. Alexander's *Space, Time, and Deity*, and Lloyd Morgan's several works on emergent evolution, principally his major work by that name. Smith's temper of mind led him to address himself to subtle distinctions in emphasis and turns of thought and to follow through the implications of such deviations. He was wary of any free generalization that carried the explication or amplification beyond the observable facts. At this level of inquiry he would rather take account of a carefully annotated series of thinkers with affinities and contrasts than to lump several related views together into a movement of thought. And if anyone moved hastily into synthesizing the several facets thus noted, Professor Smith was quick to enter his demur. I found myself readily acquiring this sensibility and style of inquiry. Had Whitehead's *Process and Reality* appeared at that time, I fear we might have dismissed him summarily as one who had prematurely imposed a closure upon a fruitful line of inquiry by importing into it reconditioned and misplaced remnants of Platonic forms. Even with so tentative a synthesis as

Science and the Modern World and *Religion in the Making*
offered, our guards were up. Not until Wieman on that memorable occasion in Swift Commons had translated the esoteric terms and phrases of Whitehead's special discourse into
language that could be assimilated wholeheartedly into an
empirical understanding, shorn of Platonic overtones, were
we disposed to give Whitehead his due. It is interesting to
reflect upon the fact that Wieman himself, at first an enthusiastic exponent of Whitehead's thought, and possibly the one
most responsible for introducing it into discussions of theology and philosophy of religion at Chicago in those early
years, was to reject first "the domes and spires" of Whitehead's
metaphysics expressed in his consequent nature of God, retaining only that phase of Whitehead's system that centered
in the primordial conception of God; and then to relinquish
even that portion of Whitehead's thought as being overspecu-
lative. There, perhaps, is a mite of justice, however ironical,
in the fact that in subsequent years, Whitehead's philosophy
was to take over so completely in the Divinity School to the
exclusion of his progenitors James and Bergson. How much
my own resistance to this Whiteheadian "take-over" has
stemmed from an initial conditioning, I am unable to say.
In the interest of preserving my self-esteem, I have, of course,
defended my action on the grounds of *setting the record
straight,* and in my more zealous moments, of insisting upon
seeking more rigorously *the truth of the faith.* So be it!

But to return to the era of Mr. Wieman: Wieman's empirical theology within this organismic imagery was at first taken
to be consonant with the empirical concern of the early Chicago school. Shailer Mathews, for example, was quite convinced that he and Wieman were after the same things in
what they set forth. This judgment referred, no doubt, to
to their common stress upon cosmic activities which in
Mathews' thought took the form of "personality-producing
activities," and in Wieman's theology, a cosmic behavior or
process, upon which "human life is most dependent for its security, welfare and increasing abundance." Yet their modes
of thought and their ways of focusing inquiry differed radi-

33

cally at the time when Wieman was first undertaking his theological work. It is possible that his present emphasis upon "creative interchange," in which the resources of the social sciences loom so prominently, could be more closely compared with the earlier theology of social experience. But in the twenties, Wieman's empiricism introduced a different orientation of inquiry, and quite a different understanding of empirical method.

In addition to the difference in imagery of thought that underlay Wieman's efforts, there were other distinctions between him and the earlier Chicago school. His concern at that time was to reformulate religious issues on a philosophical basis, on the assumption that theology and the religious affirmations to which theologians had adhered were bankrupt. In his initial writings, Wieman was utterly impatient with all doctrinal or historical inquiry that simply sought to set forth a Christian consensus of belief. Every apologetic for Christian belief, or for the perpetuation of Christian thinking, was in his judgment suspect. And to persist in such inquiry was simply to ignore or to veer away from the task that had become crucial in the present day. That task was to undertake to designate in concrete and explicit terms what it is that any religious person, Christian or otherwise, believer or even Jesus Christ himself, means when he employs the word God. Empirical theology here had gone beyond all simple appeals to religious experience, as well as descriptive analyses of the social experience historically identified as a Christian movement, to ask theologically what logical positivists were asking of all modern thought. Wieman at no time, to my knowledge, identified his thinking with that of logical positivism; but I have always considered his earlier views to be a form of logical positivism applied to religious thinking.[43] Wieman's concern with the definition of meaning in religious discourse, however, went beyond that of semantics in religious thought. His prior and basic concern was security and certainty in matters of religious faith and commitment. The source of the

[43] Cf. my "Religious Awareness and Knowledge," *Review of Religion* 3 (1938).

collapse of efficacy in formal Christianity, he believed, and possibly of other forms of religious belief grounded upon sentiment or feeling and the emotive use of words, or simply upon an authoritative consensus, lay in their indulgence in illusory notions, untested as to their accuracy or efficacy. Hence, the solution of the modern religious man's problem, he concluded, lay in the direction of testing whatever conception of religious reality formed the ground and basis of religious faith and commitment. The course of Wieman's inquiry was, in effect, dictated by his definition of God, or more precisely by the context in which the theistic problem was to be explored. Wieman's initial interest as a religious thinker, dating at least from his work on his doctoral thesis at Harvard, was in the search for a philosophy of value.[44] Many strands of influence shaped his early thinking on this problem, the significant ones being those of Josiah Royce, William Ernest Hocking, Henri Bergson, and John Dewey. Through Royce and Hocking he acquired a vision of an ultimate reality, cosmic in scope, which somehow commanded adjustment and, in turn, provided resources for human growth and fulfillment. Although he turned away from the more explicit form of the idealistic argument for this vision under the later influence of Bergson and Dewey, he nevertheless retained a haunting sense of this ultimate presence as absolute idealism had formulated it. His hope was to deduce from this vision, or to translate it into, an explicit object of inquiry, concrete enough to invite and warrant direct observation and

[44] A thorough investigation of this earlier phase of Wieman's thought has been made by Charles Rich, now of Temple Buell College, Denver, Colorado, in his doctoral thesis at the University of Chicago, "Henry Nelson Wieman's Functional Theism as Transcending Event" (1962), in which he analyzes Wieman's doctoral thesis done at Harvard University in 1910, and the persisting concern with value that follows from this earlier study by Wieman. More recently, Professor Rich has come to the judgment that Wieman's "method of bipolar empirical inquiry, consisting of attention to mystic immediacy and structural analysis, has its philosophical roots in the American neo-realism of Ralph Barton Perry, E. B. Holt, and William P. Montague." The arguments he advances for this judgment are persuasive and suggestive (letter, May 24, 1968), and merit further exploration.

reason as a "science of God." [45] In this effort, he found the early philosophical writings of Whitehead, especially his *The Concept of Nature* and *Principles of Natural Knowledge*, highly suggestive. In Wieman's first book, *Religious Experience and Scientific Method*, there appears a strikingly prophetic passage to the effect that in these early philosophical writings, Whitehead had offered tantalizing suggestions for a new metaphysics. Wieman then adds the plaintive words, if only he would venture more boldly into a metaphysical construction, we would have the vision we need for the work that is before us. Wieman's prophecy was fulfilled, though in a way that far outran not only his expectations but his acceptance. The metaphysical vision that Whitehead projected in *Process and Reality* at once intrigued and repulsed Wieman's empirical bent of mind.[46] Although he retained a deep sense of indebtedness to Whitehead, he was later to part company with him on the grounds that his metaphysical route ultimately carried religious inquiry away from empirical evidence into visionary areas of metaphysical reflection and speculation in which the emotive use of words could be reinstated.

Wieman's empirical theology *was* thus rigorously functional and instrumental in intention, with as little concern with abstract or speculative ventures in thought as his own abstract vision of reality permitted. But the persistence of this veiled absolute in his thought, derived from his earlier idealism, gave to his functional, instrumental empiricism suspicious overtones which were readily detected by pragmatists like Edward Scribner Ames and John Dewey, impelling them to recognize that Wieman's thought, though having affinities with their own, was of "a different spirit."

Yet Wieman was not content with being dismissed as an unreconstructed idealist, nor was he willing to be gathered into the company of pragmatists who practiced a kind of truncated idealism. That "reality is — as it is experienced," as

[45] *Religious Experience and Scientific Method* (New York: Macmillan Co., 1926), chap. 1.

[46] "Review of Whitehead's *Process and Reality*," *Journal of Religion* 10 (1930): 137–39.

pragmatists had been wont to acclaim, could not, Wieman contended, be equated simply with man's experience. Whenever this kind of truncation occurs, he argued, there is a forfeiture of an ultimate dimension of experience. To such a forfeiture Wieman was not willing to accede. What must be undertaken, he asserted, is an effort to reconceive this that has been envisioned abstractly as the Absolute in terms that are consonant with the texture of lived experience. Here he was introducing the imagery of organismic thought, insisting as James has insisted before him, on a *More* in experience that was not reduceable to man's acts and decisions. Yet Wieman was not willing to follow James in the direction he had indicated in proposing an experimental or "piecemeal" supernaturalism.[47] Wieman believed that the *More* that was in every event of experience could become discernible as a mode of happenings in everyday occurrences which "did for man what he cannot do for himself." There were criteria, he insisted, by which such happenings could be designated. The major portion of Wieman's scholarly work was given over to formulating such criteria. More and more these became a configuration of occurrences, or a coordination of simultaneous happenings, the total impact of which constituted "that which is supremely worthful for all mankind, and which rightfully commands man's absolute commitment of faith."

It was always difficult for the empiricist schooled in the philosophy of pragmatism or positivism to recognize Wieman's thought as empiricism. Its organismic overtones, as they were presented by Wieman, always seemed to partake of a mode of rationalistic surplusage which Wieman himself had found objectionable in Whitehead. Thus, while Wieman made much of applying the scientific method to religious meaning (by which he understood observation, reason, and experimentation), what was observed, some of his critics contended, was not experience or the data provided by experience, but a pattern of happenings presumed to be implicit in these concrete occurrences, but discernible only to those who shared

[47] *Varieties of Religious Experience* (New York: Longmans, Green & Co., 1902), pp. 520–27.

his vision of reality. Whitehead would have regarded this procedure an instance of "misplaced concreteness."

We cannot settle this issue either by finding the pragmatic empiricists right and Wieman wrong, or by declaring Wieman right and the earlier empiricists wrong. Wieman was justified in pursuing the theological effort to enlarge the scope of empirical inquiry by embracing what organismic thought and its relational mode of thinking had indicated to be a more adequate conception of concrete experience. His failure to communicate this view, I venture to suggest, lay largely in the restrictiveness of the procedure which he chose to employ, separating out too sharply perhaps, or more sharply than the situation allowed, what one logical positivist has termed that which is concretely given from the *obscure occurrent*. Wieman was so fearful of falling into illusions of mystical thinking that he tended to overdo the emphasis upon precision in the use of terms, for purposes of which he insisted upon abstracting conceivable events from immediate experience. The interrelation of what is bodily experienced and that which is perceived, or that which is experienced, perceived, and then conceived, is so complex, subtle, and elusive that it defies ready distinction or analysis. Any decisive separation of them is bound to be purely arbitrary, resulting in a forced conceptualization on the one hand and a crude designation of immediate experience on the other hand, as if it stood apart from what is conceived as a separate and distinct body of data. Any such procedure can only do violence to the concrete event, and give rise to a cognitive form of play-acting that presumes to be dealing with tested facts of experience, when, as a matter of fact, it may only be projecting fallible visions of the mind. This procedure, which has been a characteristic phase of Wieman's empirical method through the years, has always impressed me as being a lapse back into the mentalism commonly practiced by rationalists and idealists, however qualified. And to this extent I think the questioning as to whether his thought is strictly empirical is justified.

However this may be, the contribution of Mr. Wieman to

the pursuit of empirical inquiry in philosophy of religion and theology has been so impressive and unrelenting through the years that he has earned the right to be known as its major exponent in America, and the one who, more than anyone else in the Divinity School's history, rallied and consolidated interest in perfecting empirical inquiry as a theological method.

Recently, in contemplating the development of Wieman's thought, I have come to the judgment that the concern motivating Wieman's thought, especially during his years at Chicago, may more accurately be discerned and understood in relation to certain aspects of William Ernest Hocking's philosophy, principally those chapters in *The Meaning of God in Human Experience* [48] in which Hocking deals with the relation between feeling and idea, and a later section in which he develops his principle of alternation. Wieman consistently spoke of Hocking as the wisest of our living philosophers and acknowledged his indebtedness to him, though he did not openly discuss the nature of that indebtedness. Wieman's philosophical development closely parallels that of Hocking. Both men were early devotees of Josiah Royce, who had come directly under the critical stimulus of pragmatism. I once heard Professor Hocking speak of his own thought as that of an idealist bent on coming to terms with the critical insights and strictures advanced by the philosophy of pragmatism. In this critical refashioning of the tenets of absolute idealism, Hocking was faithful to what he deemed central in the idealistic tradition, namely, an unrelenting confidence in an ultimate dimension of reality to which men have ascribed the name "God." Hocking's critical appropriation of the pragmatic influence, however, led him to insist that the reality of God is experienceable, and in his magnum opus he undertook to restate the ontological argument for God.[49] In a similar way, Wieman ascribes the changes in his thought extricating him

[48] (New Haven: Yale Univ. Press, 1912). One may see in the very wording of the title of this book the scope and locus of Wieman's empirical inquiry into the meaning of God as he has pursued it through the years.

[49] *The Meaning of God in Human Experience*, part 3.

from the spell of Roycean idealism to his reading of Dewey and Bergson.

For all their differences, the concerns of Hocking and Wieman, in so far as they apply to religion, move along remarkably similar lines, holding the legacies of absolute idealism and empiricism in tension with one another; and letting the dimensions and emphases of the one serve as a corrective of the other. Hocking through the years explicitly acknowledged himself to be an idealist with empirical leanings. Wieman, an avowed empiricist, has consistently brought to the empirical method overtones of concern and reflection which have impelled him to envisage the concrete datum in terms that go beyond those normally ascribed to empiricism. The effect of Wieman's empiricism, informed by this larger view of the concrete reality, and that of Hocking's idealism, responsive to empirical demands, has been much the same in resisting the form of empirical inquiry that characterizes positivism. In both instances, the sciences have been consulted as resources to inform and discipline inquiry into the religious reality given in experience; but not in a way that makes science obviously normative, or the sole source of religious knowledge.

Wieman's indifference to the more metaphysical aspect of Hocking's thought is of a piece with his resistance to Whitehead's speculative interests, which fact suggests that however much the imagery of idealism may have persisted in his empirical inquiry into the nature of God, it formed no explicit part of his methodology. What was of indifference to Wieman in Hocking's thought was to impress his colleague, Charles Hartshorne, namely, the concern with restating the ontological argument for God. It was, in turn, to influence Hartshorne in the way he responded to the thought of Alfred North Whitehead.

IV

And this brings us to the third phase of empirical theology in the Divinity School, which was marked by a direct and conscious appropriation of the Whiteheadian metaphysics in developing a process theology. An important influence in this direction has been the metaphysical efforts of Charles Hartshorne who, more than any other philosopher within this tradition, has addressed himself directly and persistently to religious problems, particularly to the problem of God.[50] Many of the present generation of theologians who are pursuing theological inquiry within the process imagery of thought received their initial philosophical stimulus in this direction while students in Hartshorne's classes at the University of Chicago, where, for more than a quarter of a century, he taught simultaneously in the department of philosophy and in the Divinity School. While clearly committed to the philosophy of Whitehead, his former teacher and associate, Hartshorne confessed indebtedness to Charles Peirce, Hocking, Fechner, and Leibniz, whose influence modified his use of Whitehead's ideas. Furthermore, his preoccupation with the logic of the ontological argument for God has perhaps obscured the fact that the resources of his thought, by which he advances many of his logical arguments, are in the main empirically based. He is a realist epistemologically, although he admits to being an idealist ontologically. But then, "ontology," he argues, "is idealistic in the panpsychic or realistic form." Hence, he prefers to synthesize realism and idealism and to be known as a "realistic idealist." [51]

This forthright merging of the organismic stream of thought, stemming from empirical and process thinkers, with the idealistic mode has accentuated his concern with rational inquiry as an accompaniment, if not a supplement, of empirical in-

[50] Cf. his *Philosophy and Psychology of Sensation* (Chicago: Univ. of Chicago Press, 1934); *Beyond Humanism* (Chicago: Willett, Clark & Co., 1937); *Man's Vision of God* (Chicago: Willett, Clark & Co., 1941); *Reality as Social Process* (Boston: Beacon Press, 1953); *The Divine Relativity* (New Haven: Yale Univ. Press, 1948); ed., with W. L. Reese, *Philosophers Speak of God* (Chicago: Univ. of Chicago Press, 1953); *The Logic of Perfection* (LaSalle, Ill.: Open Court Pub. Co., 1962); *Anselm's Discovery* (LaSalle, Ill.: Open Court Pub. Co., 1965); *A Natural Theology for Our Time* (LaSalle, Ill.: Open Court Pub. Co., 1967).

[51] Cf. *Reality as Social Process*, p. 84.

quiry in religious thought. This mode of inquiry is clearly in the style of Whitehead, though the manner in which Hartshorne proceeds and the uses to which he applies it go beyond Whitehead in extending the rational dimension of inquiry. That Hartshorne's synthesis of these modes of thought has contributed to the empirical effort in theology is attested to by the attention which theologians like Loomer, Cobb, and Ogden have given to his thought. Loomer has often insisted that the unending task to which Hartshorne has devoted himself through the years in pursuing the ontological argument is itself basic to the empirical enterprise. This contention would be affirmed more by some than by others among empirical theologians. Nevertheless, Hartshorne's impressive accomplishments in this task have served to keep the empirical effort in theology attuned to the broader and more ultimate horizon of experience as envisaged in the ontological problem.

One of the earliest efforts to employ Whitehead's philosophy in formulating a theological method was undertaken by Bernard M. Loomer in his doctoral thesis entitled, "The Theological Significance of the Method of Empirical Analysis in the Philosophy of A. N. Whitehead" (1942).[52] Even though this manuscript has not been published, it has wielded an influence comparable to that of a published work and remains one of the basic documents in process theology. Loomer has taken the Whiteheadian philosophy to be the most adequate and comprehensive metaphysical synthesis of present-day knowledge and thus the most suitable contemporary framework of meaning in which to conceive and to interpret Christian affirmations. The metaphysics of Whitehead, as Loomer sees it, replaces all antecedent metaphysical ventures, not only in the sense that it corrects them, but in the more comprehensive sense that it subsumes their important insights as well. It thus becomes a key and critical vision of the knowl-

[52] See also Loomer, "Ely on Whitehead's God," *Journal of Religion* 24 (1944); "Neo-Naturalism and Neo-Orthodoxy," *Journal of Religion* 28 (1948): 79–91; and "Christian Faith and Process Philosophy," *Journal of Religion* 29 (1949): 181–203.

edge of the world that is available to our present understanding and, in this sense, an over-all source of criteria for judging what can be meaningful to modern man, as both a historical and a present-day utterance.

The procedure by which to project the theological task, therefore, in process theology, according to Loomer, is to master the basic categories developed in Whitehead's system and to reconceive the historic Christian affirmations within this perspective.[53] At first glance this appears to be a highly arbitrary procedure of translating theological and religious statements into their philosophical counterparts. Ultimately, it may be difficult for Loomer to gainsay this claim. His justification for proceeding in this way is that all Christian theology has assumed some philosophical perspective, explicitly or implicitly. Augustinianism presupposed a Neoplatonic world view. Thomism partook of an Aristotelian structure of thought, modified by what it retained of Augustinianism. Reformation theology, while it appeared to be disavowing all philosophical association, nevertheless showed preference for presuppositions indirectly drawn from Platonism and from current criticisms of scholasticism. And theologians who have followed within the Reformation tradition, including Schleiermacher, have disclosed such a preference in formulating Christian doctrine. The argument then implied here is that the theologian never escapes some philosophical orientation; and since this is true, it seems more responsible and realistic to become self-conscious and explicit about the philosophical orientation one has embraced.

But Loomer's forthright embracing of process philosophy as a framework of Christian thinking within the contemporary idiom follows from other reasons. In his judgment, the systematic expression of Christian affirmations calls for the most rigorous and thoroughgoing restatement of the logic of Christian faith, not just a delineation of Christian themes and their apologetic. For this purpose it behooves one, he insists, to avail oneself of that philosophy that provides the most adequate

[53] Cf. "Christian Faith and Process Philosophy."

and relevant resources for such a task. For Loomer, no philosophy of the modern period is comparable in this respect to that of Whitehead. And he would be willing to add that no philosophy antecedent to it excels Whitehead's in doing justice to the subtleties and logical possibilities of the Christian understanding of man and his world.

Acknowledging that a philosophical orientation is implied in every theological formulation, however, is not to be construed as meaning that the theologian, in order to be critically informed in his task, is simply to render the statements of faith in terms consonant with an accepted philosophy. And it is not to be assumed that Loomer rests the case of theological method with the act of explicating the faith philosophically, or of casting its themes into meanings consonant with Whiteheadian philosophy. The process is more subtle than that. Philosophy, for Loomer, becomes a kind of vision of the mind within which critical reflection in all fields of endeavor can be carried on in a disciplined and responsible way. Acquiring a competent acquaintance with the Whiteheadian categories is for him prolegomenon to entering into a careful and probing reflection upon the claims and intent of the Christian witness, giving to these claims of faith the full benefit of their historical witness, yet confronting them with the counterclaims of a reasoned faith as one's philosophical vision affords and demands. This procedure, as Loomer pursues it, becomes a subtle act of interrelating the claims of faith and reason, and of achieving through this interrelationship a constructive statement of faith that is answerable to modern intelligence, even as it presumes to be coherent with what has been historically sustained within the community of faith.

That Loomer has not always conveyed this more sensitive response to the themes of the faith which characterizes his own theological reflections upon them is due, no doubt, to his concern with the pedagogical task, to which he is committed, of demonstrating not only the relevance, but the necessity, of taking one's philosophical orientation seriously in explicating and justifying one's commitment of faith.

44

For Daniel Day Williams [54] and myself,[55] Whitehead's vision of reality forms a perspective within which theological reflection may be fruitfully pursued; but it is informed and supplemented, and often criticized, by other perspectives, both within and without the organismic legacy of thought.

Williams combines a disciplined grasp of metaphysical issues with a sympathetic and knowledgeable concern for the practical work of the ministry. His philosophical study has been undertaken with the conviction that what is affirmed as an act of faith and explicated as Christian doctrine has ontological dimensions which, when known and pondered, can illumine the life of faith, and fortify as well as enlarge the scope of theological inquiry. To this end, Williams has pursued with diligence and discernment both the ontological and the doctrinal dimensions of Christian faith. But for Williams, philosophical and theological inquiry are not ends in themselves but are to be pursued as disciplines for enlarging and

[54] Williams' major works include: *The Andover Liberals* (New York: King's Crown Press, 1941); *God's Grace and Man's Hope* (New York: Harper & Brothers, 1949); *What Present-Day Theologians Are Thinking* (New York: Harper, 1952 [published in England under title, *Interpreting Theology, 1918–1952* (London, 1953]); *The Minister and the Care of Souls* (New York: Harper & Brothers, 1961); *The Spirit and the Forms of Love* (New York: Harper & Row, 1968). To these major works should be added two essays: "Deity, Monarch and Metaphysics: Whitehead's Critique of the Theological Tradition," in Ivor Leclerc, ed., *The Relevance of Whitehead* (New York: Macmillan Co., 1961); and "How Does God Act? An Essay in Whitehead's Metaphysics," in William L. Reese and Eugene Freeman, eds., *Process and Divinity* (LaSalle, Ill.: Open Court Pub. Co., 1964).

[55] My major theological works include: *Modern Man's Worship* (New York: Harper & Brothers, 1934); *Seeds of Redemption* (New York: Macmillan Co., 1947); *The Reawakening of Christian Faith* (New York: Macmillan Co., 1949); *Higher Education and the Human Spirit* (Chicago: Univ. of Chicago Press, 1953); *Faith and Culture* (New York: Oxford Univ. Press, 1953); *Realities of Faith; The Secularization of Modern Cultures* (New York: Oxford Univ. Press, 1966). To these should be added three articles: "Interpreting The Christian Faith within a Philosophical Framework," *Journal of Religion* 33 (1953); "Theology and the Historian of Religion," *Journal of Religion* 41 (1961); "The Structure of Christian Faith," *Religion in Life*, Winter 1969.

strengthening one's understanding and living of the Christian life.

In his earlier years, Williams was the most eclectic of the process group of empiricists in his selection of sources and perspectives, concerned that empirical theology be attentive to a broad canvas of alternatives within the theological tradition. His philosophical orientation through the years, however, has remained consistent with that of process metaphysics. More recently he has given full attention to Whitehead's philosophy and has become one of its most cogent and eloquent interpreters among process theologians.

In advancing his theological concern, Williams has addressed himself explicitly to the task of the churches in conveying the historic witness of faith as a contemporary word. In this role, he has been instrumental not only in mediating between the concerns of process theology and the work of the ministry, but in mediating between process thinking and other modes of theological thought that offer alternative ways of bringing contemporary force to the Christian understanding of man and the resources of faith. Williams' sharper focus upon theological doctrine as such from within the perspective of process thought has enabled him to speak directly and effectively to groups concerned with concrete issues of Christian experience. Williams aptly stated the key to his theological concern in the preface to his book, *God's Grace and Man's Hope*: "We need an interpretation of the Christian faith which can guide moral effort and sustain the exercise of social intelligence while it strengthens our hold upon the reality of God's judgment and his mercy." [56] This way of focusing the theological concern arose out of Williams' sensitivity to the life of the church, which impelled him, in turn, to address himself explicitly to the task of the churches, which embody the historic witness of faith both as word and act in contemporary form.

Williams' role as theologian is best exemplified in his patient and careful delineation of Christian themes as these bear upon immediate issues of the day. Here Williams clearly re-

[56] Williams, *God's Grace and Man's Hope*, pp. 11–12.

veals his identification with the sensibilities of thought cherished by historic liberals who made a virtue of patience and careful discrimination in meanings, looking toward understanding and reconciliation among people of diverse points of view. Yet Williams has employed this gift of mediation not only to clarify issues that have divided opposing factions, as in the recent encounter between liberals and neo-orthodox theologians, but to oppose vigorously any caricature of thought or overstatement that did injustice to the point of view being opposed. He has, in fact, carried on a continual encounter of his own, in his writings, between neo-orthodox and liberal views, countering the positions of theologians in reaction against liberalism as readily as he has sought to correct the imbalance of judgment and bias in contemporary liberals. His strictures upon Kierkegaard, as well as upon Barth, Brunner, and Reinhold Niebuhr, in his *God's Grace and Man's Hope*, are sharp and discerning yet done with a grace that is disarming. And he concludes his analysis by advancing the thesis that,

> as contemporary Protestant Christians, we are not forced to make a simple choice between liberalism and neo-orthodoxy. The conviction has been growing among many that we cannot make such a choice, partly because there is truth on both sides, but especially because both have left something out which is the very basis of all Christian experience. That is the fact of redemption.[57]

Since joining the faculty of Union Theological Seminary in New York, Williams has concentrated on exploring and expounding the resources of process thought for offering a viable interpretation of the constructive insights of the Christian faith. His inaugural address and various essays dealing with Whitehead's philosophy in books to which he has contributed further advance this focus of theological interest. His most substantial and persuasive expression of this concern appears in his recent book, *The Spirit and Forms of Love*.

My own form of empirical theology stems from an initial

[57] Ibid., p. 32.

and prolonged concern with the nature of the religious response as this problem was informed by the historical study of religion and philosophy of religion.[58] I had gone the full way of the modernist's critique of historical religions, as this mode of inquiry had developed under the stimulus of Shailer Mathews and Gerald Birney Smith and the early writings of Henry Nelson Wieman. But in pursuing the nature of the religious response as a constructive issue, I was led to confront the problem of faith in its post-liberal-modernist setting. By post-liberal setting I mean the present-day orientation of thought in which concern with dimensions of human existence that go deeper than conscious experience, as modern idealism had formulated it. Liberal theology, for all its variations, moved within a strategy of thought that had been initially conceived by Kant and modified by Hegel. Since the turn of the century within the modern era, this imagery of thought had been under attack as being unresponsive to insights into depths of occurrence within existence that are preconscious and subconscious, giving to the nature and meaning of human existence a far more complex and problematic aspect than our idealizing ventures within the liberal ethos had recognized.

The theological task, as it formulated itself in my mind, became one of reassessment and reconception. I was not to relinquish the critical stance of liberal scholarship, despite these disclosures of distressing inadequacies in its orientation of thought. Nevertheless, the tragic turn of events within Western history, reinforcing what new evidence was revealing concerning the depth and complexity of human existence, compelled a reevaluation of the liberal estimate of man and his resources. Thus my program of theological reconstruction took the form of working simultaneously upon a probing inquiry into the history of liberal theology to understand its essential character and ethos, while exploring the problematic of faith within this post-liberal setting.

Modern culture looked at from within a perspective of its so-called depth motivations and shaping presents a different

[58] Cf. *Modern Man's Worship*.

48

picture of its history and character than the one commonly set forth on the basis of explicit conscious acts, expressed in its conceptualizations. Religiously speaking, one is made aware of the role of indirect discourse and symbolism as expressed in mytho-poetic language, and its impact upon our more overtly conscious acts and conceptualizations, even when this impact is not recognized. Thus my concern has been to reconceive and, in a sense, to reenact the historic liberal's effort at bringing discipline and intelligibility into the act of faith, giving attention to this depth of motivation and shaping of the culture's life which historic liberalism neglected, and in fact essentially denied.

On the surface, this program of constructive theology appears to be the direct opposite of that to which Bultmann has addressed himself in his program of demythologization, and to which Schubert Ogden has spoken so incisively in his *Christ without Myth*.[59] Actually, however, the problem that concerns each of us is basically the same problem; though our interpretations of how it is to be met and solved within this contemporary period, and our estimates of the resources at hand for solving it, differ considerably.

How to articulate the witness of faith, expressed as an enduring mythos of the culture, to critical and secular minds of modern culture in a way that can inform and enhance our secularity with ultimate demands and resources was to become the prime objective of my effort in constructive theology. Here the influence of Whitehead's empirical metaphysics was to become a structural resource in providing fundamental notions with which to express, in part, this depth of motivation and shaping which continues to give character and direction to our cultural élan, the analyses of our radical, death-of-God theologians to the contrary notwithstanding. I have recently come to the judgment that our empirical realism, in juxtaposition with and hopefully in collaboration with

[59] Schubert Ogden, *Christ without Myth* (New York: Harper & Brothers, 1961). My response to this work appears in an article, "Analogy and Myth in Post-Liberal Theology. *Perkins School of Theology Journal* 15 (1962): 19–27.

phenomenology, may be able to probe this basic inquiry more fruitfully than either of them has done in going its separate way.

During this period of preoccupation with Whitehead, prior to the formation of the new fields of ethic and society, James Luther Adams as a member of the theological field brought a wide range of supplementary intellectual and cultural stimulus to bear upon the study of theology, extending from various historical developments within the left wing of the Reformation and modern nonconformist theories through the more systematic studies of Max Weber, Ernst Troeltsch, and Paul Tillich. He was later to become chairman of the field of ethics and society in the Divinity School, before joining the faculty of the Harvard Divinity School.

During the same period other men were to contribute to this later stage of empirical study within the theological field: George Gordh in historical theology, W. Barnett Blakemore in psychology of religion, Preston Roberts before he assumed chairmanship of religion and literature, and Perry LeFevre in theology and higher education before moving to the field of religion and personality. Later John Hayward participated in the theological field within the area of theology and culture.

Loomer, Williams, and I, along with others just mentioned, were early influenced in our thinking by Professor Wieman. Wieman's selective use of Whitehead's thought in his earlier works, centering upon his primordial conception of God, to the exclusion of the consequent nature of God, accented the empirical thrust of Whitehead. This emphasis is found to some extent in Loomer, though more particularly in Williams and in my own writings, in contrast to process theologians like John Cobb [60] and Schubert Ogden [61] who have pursued more fully the metaphysical concerns of both Whitehead and

[60] Cf. John B. Cobb, Jr., *Living Options in Protestant Theology* (Philadelphia: Westminster Press, 1962); *Varieties of Protestantism* (Philadelphia: Westminster Press, 1960); *A Christian Natural Theology* (Philadelphia: Westminster Press, 1965); *The Structure of Christian Existence* (Philadelphia: Westminster Press, 1967).

[61] Cf. Ogden, *Christ without Myth; The Reality of God and Other Essays* (New York: Harper & Row, 1966).

Hartshorne. Although Schubert Ogden and John Cobb have not been members of the Divinity School faculty,[62] their theological contributions stemming from earlier associations with the school have clearly been within its tradition and have been significant expressions of the movement of process thought that has centered in the Divinity School. Both Ogden and Cobb have the merit of having wrestled intimately and strenuously with hermeneutical issues pertinent to the theological task, particularly as these issues have been redefined by Bultmann and his critics. Thus, they bring to their discussions of theology within the process perspective problems and issues that immediately involve them in theological talk that is alive to theologians abroad who have little or no concern with their empirical interest.[63]

In this connection it is pertinent to note that Professor Jaroslav Pelikan, during his years at Chicago, had a great deal to do with influencing young theologians, even as they continued to be involved in pursuing the process method of inquiry, to take fuller account of issues being posed by other theological methods. In this respect he inherited the mantle of Wilhelm Pauck as creative antagonist to the empirical tradition, functioning both as a critic of process theology, and as an interpreter of alternative methods of reconstruction within the modern period. Under his guidance and critical challenge an impressive group of younger theologians wrote their doctoral theses; many of these men have since spoken incisively to current theological issues in recent years. The list includes, among others, such names as Schubert Ogden, Gerhard Spiegler, Philip Shen, Philip Hefner, and Paul Sponheim.

That process theologians, even among the younger repre-

[62] In the fall of 1969, Schubert Ogden will become University Professor of Theology in the Divinity School of the University of Chicago.

[63] Cf. John Cobb, Jr., ed., with James M. Robinson, *The New Frontiers in Theology* series: *The Later Heidegger and Theology* (New York: Harper & Row, 1963); *The New Hermeneutic* (New York: Harper & Row, 1964); *Theology as History* (New York: Harper & Row, 1967). Cf. also Ogden, *Christ without Myth*; Ogden, trans. and ed., *Existence and Faith: Shorter Writings of Rudolf Bultmann* (New York: Meridian Books, 1960); essays on Sartre and Heidegger and on writings of European theologians are included in his *Reality of God*.

sentatives, have not seemed to be actively engaged in pressing for the concerns of the so-called radical theologians, or the demand for "secularizing the gospel" is not to be taken as an indication of disinterest in the problems involved. Much that represents itself today as being "radical theology" appears from within the process perspective to be a delayed recognition of issues that confronted religious thinkers when the notion of relativity first began to be taken seriously in philosophical and religious thought. In its technical aspects, it expresses reaction against the theologies of reaction that emerged a generation ago under Barth and Brunner, which had, in turn, reacted against nineteenth-century theology stemming from Schleiermacher and Ritschl. The "radical theology" of the present day is a reassertion of the themes of Feuerbach and Nietzsche within a confessional context that is informed by a commitment to the christological reality as successor to the God that is dead. This christological commitment is expressive for them of what endures in our secular society as the surviving and living increment of the Christian hope and expectation.

The concreteness of their orientation allies these radical theologians with the empirical thrust of process theology and with the phenomenologists' emphasis upon "lived experience," as against doctrinaire assertions of an absolute theism. But their state of being ill at ease with the relativistic discourse of contemporary disciplines and their desperate, even uncritical, concern to come to terms with it would seem to suggest that they have yet to encounter the critical issues bearing upon modern perspectives which relativity imposes, issues with which process thinkers and many phenomenologists have concerned themselves for more than a generation. In this respect, the outlook of the radical theologians can be said to be radical only in contrast to the evangelical stance which they only recently rejected, but virtually naïve in relation to the revolution in fundamental notions of thought that has been reshaping the modern idiom within the cultural disciplines since the turn of the century — a revolution which has been basic to the form of empirical thinking that has issued

in process thought, and which has stimulated much phenomenological thinking in its concern to focus upon "lived experience."

It must be acknowledged, however, that those who have
embraced process thought or phenomenology uncritically
may not be fully aware of the revolution in thought in which
they are participating; they may see it only as a swift way of
resolving the problem of faith with which they were left upon
becoming disillusioned with an earlier biblicism, or even as a
substitute for the doctrinaire confessionalism they have had to
reject. Insofar as process thought thus serves simply to sustain or to reaffirm a sanguine confidence in theism, it reasserts
what the radical theologians are rebelling against.

V

That process theology is empirical in method is difficult for
some observers to recognize or concede. In contrast to pragmatic and instrumental empiricism, it is so obviously concerned with delineating or explicating a total structure of
thought or vision of reality that it rarely gets around to asserting its empirical claims, or to inquiring into them. Its preoccupation with basic categories and logical structure, it is said,
identifies it more readily with rationalistic procedures than
with the empirical method. In practice this criticism may not
easily be set aside by process theologians. They may deny it,
but they may have difficulty making their point when confronted with their own preoccupations and procedures. The
argument against understanding process thinking as a form
of empirical inquiry, however, overlooks the concrete character of the data with which the process thinker concerns himself. On closer scrutiny, one will discover that the concern
with categories, such as the process thinker discloses, is not
in the traditional metaphysical mode of erecting an abstract
framework of thought into which the many items of common-
sense experience are to be fitted; but in the empirical tradition
of attending to concrete, individual events to discover the
persisting and commonly shared characteristics of concrete
experience whenever and wherever they occur, and lifting

them to the level of a guiding vision of experience, tentatively embraced, and subject to subsequent verification and correction as further data of experience make themselves known, or as new understanding of known data impels a revision. Experienced events, or what empiricist and phenomenologist alike speak of as "lived experience," provide the data of reflection in process philosophy and theology. In this sense, then, the method is basically empirical, though empirical with a difference. It becomes a way of generalizing the commonly shared features of concrete experience, thus lifting what might otherwise be an ambiguous flux of occurrences into a working vision of experience as a whole. Whatever the shortcomings of this process way of thinking may be, and there are some to be noted, they do not add up to an absorption in abstractions. On the contrary, the complex interweaving of internal relations giving rise to concrete occurrences, with their light and shade, their coming into being and perishing, their waxing and waning of good and evil, hope and tragedy, are vividly brought into view. In a sense, it becomes a way of thinking existentially, only with configurative and communal dimensions of individuality, as contrasted with the drastic solitariness of the lonely transcendental ego. The difference here hinges upon the contrasting conceptions of individuality as it occurs among events and people, and upon the issue of whether relations are experienced as objective occurrences, or impressed upon reality by the subjective ego in exercising its sensibilities and demands. It is easier to see the empirical bent of mind in Bergson and James than it is in S. Alexander or Whitehead, for the reason that the former allowed the flux of experience to appear in its undifferentiated pluralism, unsorted or unstructured, and more readily afforded it priority in determining the truth value of conceptualized experience. But these empirical procedures and emphases, so readily recognizable in James and Bergson, are present in Whiteheadian philosophy as well, and form the bases from which speculative ventures take their rise to which they return for verification and further stimulus to imaginative effort.

54

VI

It will be seen, then, that the scope and character of empirical theology as it has developed within the Divinity School of the University of Chicago has undergone continual transformation, as understanding of the human problem and of the nature of experience itself has widened and deepened. In our own day, the influences of cultural disorders and the dislocation of the human spirit consequent to these occurrences have radically altered the setting in which religious issues are being posed. In the face of the traumas and demonic disclosures that have haunted our generation during these latter days, the bland, objective study of religious functions, or assured efforts at acquiring religious knowledge, hardly seem to go to the heart of the matter. A more probing and relevant form of inquiry into the deeps of human experience and behavior, and into the strange, recalcitrant forces shaping or frustrating human action, would seem to be demanded. Pertinent contributions along this line, supplementing and challenging empirical inquiry, have begun to appear with fresh power of perspective in the literature of more recent existentialists and phenomenologists, where more direct recognition of these grim incalculables of existence is in evidence.[64] Phenomenology and existentialism are not unrelated to the empirical concern; although the stance of each with regard to the issues of existence and the pursuit of knowledge differ in major respects. Modern phenomenologists have been generous in acknowledging their indebtedness to certain progenitors of the modern process form of empiricism, notably to William James and Henri Bergson, and even to Charles Peirce, as being significant sources of stimulus in their own efforts. And one finds some recognition among empiricists

[64] Cf. Jean-Paul Sartre, *Being and Nothingness* (New York: Philosophical Library, 1956); Martin Heidegger, *Existence and Being* (Chicago: Henry Regnery Co., 1949); M. Merleau-Ponty, *The Phenomenology of Perception* (London: Routledge & Kegan Paul, 1962), *The Primacy of Perception* (Evanston: Northwestern Univ. Press, 1964); Paul Ricoeur, *Fallible Man* (Chicago: Henry Regnery Co., 1965), *History and Truth* (Evanston: Northwestern Univ. Press, 1965), *Symbolism of Evil* (New York: Harper & Row, 1967).

and among phenomenologists who formerly regarded themselves as empiricists, that the phenomenological approach to "lived experience" opens up fruitful lines of inquiry into problems that concern phenomenologists and empiricists alike. Whether or not a convergence between these two modes of thought is now actually occurring, it would not be too much to suggest that each of them could benefit by a degree of rapport sufficient to enable the one to partake of the critical influence and concern of the other.[65] This may, in fact, be a next stage in the development of religious inquiry.

The coming of Paul Tillich to the Divinity School faculty [66] greatly accentuated such a rapport and interchange of thought between empiricists and phenomenologists at Chicago. The exchanges between Charles Hartshorne and Tillich were memorable; and though they could appear only occasionally in public events, the genuineness of their interest in one another's perspective gave evidence of a sustained and even personal rapport between them. Tillich's own method was that of a "critical phenomenologist," as he termed it; and his approach to Christian doctrine was by way of an existentialist concern.[67] In collaboration with Mircea Eliade he extended the appeal of this mode of religious inquiry along a wide front of studies in divinity. Tillich's presence in the Divinity School, in fact, brought the phenomenological and empirical methods sharply into juxtaposition and awakened among divinity students and faculty alike a vigorous interest

[65] Cf. John Wild, *The Challenge of Existentialism* (Bloomington: Indiana Univ. Press, 1955), and *Existence and the World of Freedom* (Englewood Cliffs, N.J.: Prentice-Hall, 1963). See also George Guthrie, "The Importance of Sartre's Phenomenology for Christian Theology," *Journal of Religion* 47 (1967): 10–25.

[66] Professor Tillich began lecturing in The Divinity School of the University of Chicago one quarter a year in 1955, and on his retirement from Harvard University in 1962, he was appointed the John Nuveen Professor of Theology in the Divinity School, a post he held until his death in 1965.

[67] Cf. esp. his *Systematic Theology*, vol. 1, where he explicitly develops his method of critical phenomenology. In his later volumes, 2 and 3, he continues to employ this method in dealing with *Christology* and issues bearing on *Life and the Spirit, History and the Kingdom of God.*

in pursuing their distinctions and correlations. This critical encounter between the two methods is being furthered by other members of the faculty, notably in the fields of history of religions, ethics and society, religion and personality, and theology and literature.

Among members of the current theological faculty of the Divinity School, this interest persists along with others. With secularist theologians, in reaction against the dialectical era of evangelical theology, reasserting the claims of the pragmatic emphasis, even lifting up the pragmatic bent of Karl Barth's theological procedure,[68] the theological conversation of our time tends to evoke an active mood of reexamination and reassessment. In the background of this most recent and publicized eruption in theological circles, giving implicit sanction to the whittling down of theological assumptions, stand the language analysts who, on their own, even before it was rumored in public print that "God is dead," provoked their own extended season of skeptical inquiry, challenging the validity of religious language and the legitimacy of the theological discipline as well as that of metaphysics. In this critical and probing effort at reappraisal, Langdon Gilkey has been especially incisive and persistent.[69] Not only has he debated extensively with theologians and philosophers on the issue of "God-language," but he has confronted process thinkers with queries concerning their form of empirical theology, arising out of current studies in language analysis. Being convinced that theology today has no option but to be both empirical and secular, Gilkey has in a sense identified himself with the stance that takes the claims of each of them seriously; yet he has been candid in expressing skepticism about the way each

[68] Cf. Harvey Cox, *The Secular City* (New York: Macmillan Co., 1965), pp. 79, 81–84.
[69] Cf. for example, his articles, "Cosmology, Ontology, and the Travail of Biblical Language," *Journal of Religion* 41 (1961): 194–205; "The Concept of Providence in Contemporary Theology," *Journal of Religion* 43 (1963): 171–192; "The God is Dead Theology and the Possibility of God-Language," *The Voice* (Jan. 1965); "Secularism's Impact on Contemporary Theology," *Christianity and Crisis* (Apr. 5, 1965), et al.

of them has undertaken to *do* theology in the present situation. His rapprochement with these two contending fronts of theological inquiry, even as he is openly critical of their procedures, lends an irenic and clarifying touch to what he advances as a stricture upon their theologizing, even when the implications are devastating.[70] Furthermore, there are intimations in his criticisms that he is struggling to cut through the impasse that has blocked him off from a clear perception of the way to go beyond process theology as well as beyond the negation of God-language so as to meet his own criticisms constructively. In this restive mood of reappraisal and reconception, Gilkey, himself attuned to a neo-phenomenological mode of restating and examining the dimension of the *religious* in our secular era, is influencing empiricists to take a fresh look at their history and present opportunity.

If, in fact, one were to characterize the prevailing temper of mind of the current theological field as a whole in the Divinity School, one would have to say that this mood of reappraisal and reconception applies also to Gilkey's colleagues Joseph Sittler and Brian Gerrish, as it did to Joseph Haroutunian before his death.

Haroutunian [71] was no stranger to the empirical tradition. His long-time interest in pragmatism, particularly as expressed in the philosophy of John Dewey, combined with a Calvinistic concern with the biblical ground of theology, enlivened his interest in issues now being posed by the secularist theologians. Their bent of mind, focusing upon the import of theological issues as they speak to the concerns of people generally within modern society, coheres with what Haroutu-

[70] Gilkey's major publications include: *Maker of Heaven and Earth* (Garden City, N.Y.: Doubleday & Co., 1959); *How the Church Can Minister to the World without Losing Itself* (New York: Harper & Row, 1964); *Naming the Whirlwind: The Renewal of God-Language* (Indianapolis: Bobbs-Merrill Co., 1969).

[71] Haroutunian's principal works are: *Piety Versus Moralism* (New York: Holt & Co., 1932); *Wisdom and Folly in Religion* (New York: Scribner's Sons, 1940); *Lust for Power* (New York: Scribner's Sons, 1949); *Calvin Commentaries* (London: SCM Press, 1958 [The Library of Christian Classics, vol. 23]); *God with Us* (Philadelphia: Westminster Press, 1965).

nian had long insisted upon in his effort to *do* theology within the context of a lay, Protestant Christianity. In recent years he attempted to give this emphasis a more explicit cultural setting by addressing himself to the religious ethos of the American experience as a distinct and authentic epoch of Christian experience, with its own characteristic understanding and application of the biblical heritage.

For all his concern with the lay aspect of the theological task, however, Haroutunian was insistent upon observing the demands of the theological discipline. "After all," he was fond of saying, "there is such a thing as systematic theology"; by which he meant to assert that the theologian brings to the "expostulations" of people within the churches and in society a mode of critical reflection, shaped by a theological tradition that has an important bearing upon the present-day protest and concern of people speaking spontaneously out of their volatile experiences. Here Haroutunian combined what has been commonly ascribed to the traditional role of theology with the empirical concern. Insofar as he offered the distillations of Christian doctrine as a resource of disciplined reflection, he avoided the onus of imposing the authority of tradition upon experience. And, in the final analysis, he was inclined to be responsive to the lay utterances of the churches and society as having an integrity to which both tradition and the erudition of the theologian must bow, at least to the degree of taking them seriously as data for theological inquiry. Thus, in his fashion, Haroutunian partook of the empirical tradition, even as he sought to be faithful to the historical witness of faith.

While Joseph Sittler [72] has made no pretence of being involved in the empirical mode of theological inquiry, his persistent concern with the *ecology* of human acts, religious and

[72] Sittler's published works include: *Doctrine of the Word in the Structure of Lutheran Theology* (Philadelphia: Muhlenberg Press, 1948); *The Structure of Christian Ethics* (Baton Rouge: Louisiana State Univ. Press, 1958); *The Ecology of Faith* (Philadelphia: Muhlenberg Press, 1961); *The Care of the Earth* (Philadelphia: Fortress Press, 1964); *The Anguish of Preaching* (Philadelphia: Fortress Press, 1966).

otherwise, suggests that, in making his theological observations, he travels a path that encompasses a terrain well in sight of those presuming to be empirical observers. And he addresses himself to problems in ways that cohere with the empiricist's concern. Furthermore, his ribaldry of language, enhancing his eloquence in describing those acts, marks him as one freed from the sacral idiosyncrasies of the theological idiom, despite the fact that the only way he knows how to do theology, as he himself has said, is to speak out of the life and language of the church with its age-old tradition. Yet, his doing of theology is always a contemporary act of articulating, and thereby preserving and nurturing, the disciplined expression of this classical Christianity in ways consonant with the needs and demands of the times.

The clearest evidence of Sittler's responsiveness to what empiricist and phenomenologist alike are attentive to appears in his insistence upon seeing the work of grace, and the denial of it, within the concrete occurrences of nature and the human community. Not only is he attentive to such occurrences as they appear in tensions provoked by our cultural pluralism and the miscalculations of human decisions, erupting into social conflict, but in the tribulation of people in sorrow, or of individuals caught up in the perplexities of personal failure. In this respect, Sittler's theologizing is an act of ministry in the most direct and empirical sense.

Sittler's distinctive effort in theology, however, whether empirical or otherwise, has been evident in his concern to close the gap between nature and history, and to break through the impasse which modernity, aided by the idealizing strategy within much of modern theology, has effected between nature and spirit, or even between nature and personality. Through a reassertion of the doctrine of creation, in explicating the work of grace, he has sought to reaffirm nature as a dimension of our humanity. And on the same basis, he has sought to overcome the dichotomy that has arisen between nature and civilization, where nature has been given the connotation of a resource untouched by human hands, as in the pastoral scene of the countryside, in contrast to the industrial and technological mode of life in the city. Nature, in Sittler's view, is to be envisaged within the technological developments of modern civilization; or, to state it more precisely, technology, insofar as it expresses our natural resources and energies harnessed and fashioned into forms suitable for the city and its modern civilization, is itself nature under a different aspect, and is to be cherished and appreciated as such. Here Sittler, whether he acknowledges it or not, is compelling the theological heritage to express itself in a secular idiom that accords simultaneously with the liberating spirit of the Reformation in its modern expression and the modernizing thrust of the empirical tradition.

Like Haroutunian, Brian Gerrish[73] too finds the Calvinistic temper of mind congenial in pursuing theological problems, both historically and constructively within the modern context. And his concern with this mode of inquiry has been reinforced by his close study of language analysis and other aspects of modern philosophy addressed to the clarification of religious meaning. Because of this orientation of his thought, Gerrish has remained unimpressed by modern forms of empirical inquiry that have sought to give metaphysical explication to experience, or to extend the import of events beyond the intimations of their concrete occurrence. Gerrish is not, however, indifferent to all forms of empirical inquiry, as is evidenced by the fact that he finds the socio-historical method of Shirley Jackson Case's historiography cogent and illuminating, and would seem to be renewing interest in that mode of historical study, along with others.

Theological study in the Divinity School, then, as this survey discloses, has produced a variety of responses to a persisting tradition of empirical inquiry. These variations upon a familiar theme suggest that within this historical tradition, itself pluralistic in procedure and concern, continuity has depended, not upon reiteration, but upon a congenial and crea-

[73] Gerrish's published works include: *Grace and Reason* (New York: Oxford Univ. Press, 1962); ed., *The Faith of Christendom: A Source Book of Creeds and Confessions* (Cleveland: World Publishing Co. [Meridian Books], 1963); ed., *Reformers in Profile* (Philadelphia: Fortress Press, 1967).

tive dissonance made possible by the recurrence of fresh exemplification of its underlying sensibility of thought. Nevertheless, it is to be acknowledged that the present period of theological inquiry in the Divinity School is clearly transitional, marking, on the one hand, an interim of reaction and reassessment, following upon a vigorous and highly productive period of systematic reinterpretation of Christian faith and doctrine; and, on the other hand, opening into an era of unprecedented ecumenical opportunity in which Protestant and Roman Catholic scholars alike are participating with zest and expectancy. And, simultaneous with this awakening of the new ecumenical vision of Christianity and the theological task and, in fact, within the ecumenical stirrings themselves, one may discern evidence of a renascent interest in process thought, particularly that stemming from the influence of Whitehead, the contribution of which to the larger Christian community of faith and inquiry appears yet to be made. Ironically enough, it would appear that this renewed interest in process thought is being currently pursued more intensively in other seminaries and universities than in the Divinity School of the University of Chicago. Nevertheless a live and serious concern with it persists in encounter with the new mode of phenomenological inquiry in religious studies that is also gathering momentum. What form this interaction of thought will take theologically is not yet clearly evident, though some intimation of it is given in several of the essays that follow.

PART 1
Methodological Inquiries

1

Present Prospects For Empirical Theology
SCHUBERT M. OGDEN

I

Whitehead once wrote, "The word 'experience' is one of the
most deceitful in philosophy." [1] A similar comment could be
made about the phrase "empirical theology." It is notorious
that this phrase may be used with a variety of meanings reflecting different senses both of "empirical" and of "theology."
Therefore, I must begin by clarifying its intended meaning
in the present discussion.

Take, first, the word "empirical." I propose that we understand the meaning of this word to be essentially the same as
that the word "experiential," defined as pertaining in some
way or other to our common human experience. I then ask
that we agree to call any kind of thinking "empirical," provided only that what it ultimately appeals to for the meaning
and truth of its assertions is that same common experience in
one or another of its different fields. This request assumes, of
course, that the scope of experience is not narrow but broad
and that there is more than one way in which the appeal to experience may be made. But while this assumption is crucial,
as the subsequent discussion will prove, it is scarcely gratuitous. The fact is obvious that "experience" as we ordinarily
understand it is a field-encompassing word. We invoke it in
speaking of a whole range of observings, encounterings, and
undergoings, from perceiving the world through our senses to
becoming aware of the beautiful and of the claim of the

[1] *Symbolism: Its Meaning and Effect* (New York: Macmillan Co.,
1927), p. 16.

good.[2] Supposing my request to be granted, then, we are agreed that to call theology "empirical" means that even a theological kind of thinking would appeal somehow to our experience simply as men in providing the final justification for its claims.

This is with the understanding, naturally, that what is meant by the word "theology" is some kind of thinking or reflection. But now, what kind? My proposal is that we take "theology" to refer to the kind of thinking which seeks an appropriate conceptual interpretation of the witness of Christian faith. This is to say that the sense of "theology" intended here is not the generic sense in which we are otherwise required to use it, but the specific sense that only the words "Christian theology" make fully explicit. In this sense, theology is the particular hermeneutical task of so understanding the Christian witness at the level of reflective thought that the resulting interpretation proves to be fitting to the essential claims of that witness. Without going into the details of just what this involves, I would note the one point which is important for the present discussion. The primary (although not the only) test of whether any interpretation is thus fitting is whether it shows itself to be appropriate to the given testimony of Holy Scripture. Whatever else theology may be, it is not theology as understood here unless it is in its own way or at its own level *ministerium verbi divini* — service to that divine word to which the Old and New Testaments bear witness.

[2] Cf. John Dewey, *Experience and Nature*, 2d ed. (LaSalle, Ill.: Open Court Pub. Co., 1929), p. 426: "It is as irritating to have experience of beauty and moral goodness reduced to groundless whims as to have that of truth. Common-sense has an inexpugnable conviction that there are immediate goods of enjoyment and conduct and that there are principles by which they may be appraised and rectified. Common-sense entertains this firm conviction because it is innocent of any rigid demarcation of knowledge on one side and belief, conduct and esthetic appreciation on the other. It is guiltless of the division between objective reality and subjective events. It takes striving, purposing, inquiring, wanting, the life of 'practice,' to be as much facts of nature as are the themes of scientific discourse; to it, indeed, the former has a more direct and urgent reality."

Therefore, the phrase "empirical theology" as intended in this essay refers to a kind of thinking which would be theological in this specific sense, and yet would also be empirical in that it would acknowledge no final basis for its claims except our common human experience. What we must now consider are the prospects for such an empirical theology, given the limits and resources of our present situation.

II

At first glance, these prospects appear to be good — at least if we judge from concerns now being widely felt and expressed by Protestant theologians. According to one observer, who is far from pleased about it, "What we see is a complete change in today's theological weather. The winds are blowing out of another quarter and the religious climate is being decisively affected." Specifically, "The prevailing wind may be identified as an anti-supernaturalistic theology of meaningfulness, a theology purporting to give the *true* meaning of traditional religious statements no longer acceptable at their face value. The eddies within the wind arise from different estimates of the 'meaning' of religious statements because of different notions held concerning the nature of the world known to modern man. . . . But, wherever the bounds are drawn, it is agreed that nothing can exist outside them." [3] The reference here is to the renewed concern with its apologetic task which is the most striking development in recent Protestant theology. Ever since the Second World War, the conviction has grown that the purely dogmatic concern of much so-called "neo-orthodoxy" fails to exhaust theology's total responsibility. Theologians have come to realize that insofar as the Christian witness advances the claim to be true, it assumes an obligation which can be fully discharged only by a reflective justification of its claim. This has seemed particularly clear in our situation today, where the traditional statements in which this witness has found expression are fundamentally

[3] Kenneth Hamilton, *Revolt against Heaven: An Enquiry into Anti-Supernaturalism* (Grand Rapids, Mich.: William B. Eerdmans Pub. Co., 1965), pp. 13, 25–26.

problematic as regards their meaning as well as their truth. Simply to repeat these statements without in any way trying to justify them is to deprive the Christian witness of a serious hearing and to reduce theology to cultural irrelevance. But this is to say, in effect, that what our situation appears to many of us to demand is a theology that would be in its own way empirical. The reason for this is the definitely empirical outlook of the contemporary Western mind, which is disposed to accept no statement as meaningful or true that cannot somehow be justified by the experience in which each of us shares.

It would be wrong to infer, however, that a new interest in meeting our apologetic responsibility is our only concern as contemporary theologians. Despite our evident dissatisfaction with a merely dogmatic repetition of traditional religious statements, we seem to be in general agreement with what is after all the main emphasis of neo-orthodoxy. We recognize that no theology can pretend to be Christian unless it is prepared to be tested as an appropriate interpretation of the witness of Holy Scripture. Thus, as the statement previously quoted acknowledges, even the new "theology of meaningfulness" purports to give the true, which is to say, *scriptural,* meaning of traditional Christian doctrines and symbols. To what extent this claim is to be credited is, naturally, a question which both can and must be raised. But the fact that the claim is so widely made, even by those whose interpretations are radically revisionist, attests to another concern which is fundamental to our present theological efforts. The object of our common quest is clearly a theology which may be called Christian as well as contemporary and which can prove its right to the name by its essential congruence with the claims of the scriptural witness.

To judge from our main concerns, then, the prospects for an empirical theology as here understood seem bright enough. Yet, on further consideration, this first impression is not easy to sustain. The nub of the difficulty is that the usual attempts to develop such a theology have hardly done justice to both of the concerns that presently account for its promise.

That this is so of the earlier of these attempts is evident from the discussion during the 1930s between Douglas Clyde Macintosh and Henry Nelson Wieman.[4] Both of these theologians were committed to the proposition that theology can and should be genuinely empirical. And yet, when either of them appraised the work of the other, he found it to be flawed by a fundamental weakness. From Macintosh's standpoint, Wieman's "doctrine of a Superhuman God without a Superhuman Soul or Mind or Conscious Intelligence and Will" was "strongly reminiscent of behaviorism in psychology." It succeeded in "adding to the assurance *that God is*" only by "subtracting so drastically and, it would seem, so permanently, from *what God means*." Hence Macintosh concluded that "if it should turn out that the idea of God as Superhuman Mind and Will cannot be reasonably believed to be literally true, even Wieman's ingenious, interesting, and valuable definitions will hardly save the day for much of what has been most dynamic and uplifting in the best religion, we have known" — by which Macintosh meant, of course, the religion of the Christian scriptures.[5] For Wieman, on the other hand, Macintosh's attempts to show the truth of the scriptural idea of God required him to sacrifice the certainty which only a strict empiricism can provide. "The reason I object to the procedure of Mr. Macintosh is that he develops a system of concepts about what God 'ought to be,' instead of applying observation and reason to the actual God he has, when he strives for the greatest good." As Wieman saw it, "The religion of infallible devotion must take the place of the religion of infallible belief." This meant that "we must have certainty [about the reality of God] at least as great as we have for the existence of wife or child or home or country or any other object of great love and devotion which can be known by observation and reason. When preservation of the content is reversely proportional to the preservation of certainty, then the content must go."[6]

[4] See Henry Nelson Wieman, Douglas Clyde Macintosh, and Max Carl Otto, *Is There A God? A Conversation* (Chicago: Willett, Clark & Co., 1932).

[5] Ibid., pp. 24, 23, 29.   [6] Ibid., pp. 118, 52, 45.

To follow the course of this discussion is to reach the conclusion that both parties made valid points. Wieman did succeed in preserving religious certainty only by drastically reducing the content of the traditional Christian witness. This was so much the case, in fact, that to this very day his revision of the conception of God has won only a small minority of adherents among Protestant theologians. On the other hand, Macintosh's concern to preserve a more traditional understanding of God did require him to break out of the limits of what, by present-day standards as well, would generally be regarded as empirical.

It is easy to show that something like the same kind of impasse has also been reached by current attempts at an empirical theology. There are, to be sure, important differences between the discussion taking place today and the earlier one which I have briefly reviewed. The most striking of these is our present tendency to approach the whole question in explicitly linguistic terms. We generally ask about the proper use of religious or theological language and are concerned to find an answer which will prove fitting to the witness of Scripture, while also fully respecting empirical criteria of meaning and truth. Yet, in spite of this and other differences, we still find ourselves confronting the same basic difficulty. Where interpretations of the scriptural witness are unimpeachably empirical, they entail such radical revisions of traditional theological claims as to seem quite inappropriate to that witness. This is especially true of interpretations which contend that the traditional assertion of the reality of God may be completely dispensed with because the scriptural use of the word "God" is a wholly "noncognitive" use. In the case of other interpretations, where this contention is denied and the reality of God is still asserted with something like its traditional meaning, there is the opposite problem of whether an empirical outlook is not thereby abandoned. Certainly for those whose empiricism is strict and who therefore incline to the first kind of interpretation, any assertion of God as transcendent personal reality is open to the same sort of objection that Wieman urged against Macintosh. It preserves the content of the Christian witness only by relinquishing the certainty that experience alone is able to provide as to the meaning and truth of any of our assertions.

And so the question remains of the prospects for a theology which would be truly Christian as well as firmly based on our common human experience. Granted that our concerns today make such a theology desirable, can we really suppose that these concerns are compatible and that "empirical theology" as here defined is more than simply a contradiction in terms?

III

There are some theologians whose answer to this question is emphatically negative. They regard the project of an empirical theology as absurd because it seeks to combine matters that are by their very nature incompatible. The whole point of the scriptural witness, in their view, is to attest to a supernatural revelation, whose claim to be meaningful and true utterly transcends the competence of human experience and reason. This revelation is in every respect *sui generis*, so that any attempt to try to justify it by exhibiting its congruence with what we are otherwise able to know already entails its abandonment. From this standpoint, an empirical theology involves an even more serious compromise of the Christian witness than the "natural theology" of the theological tradition. The competence of natural theology as usually conceived has been severely limited, since the most it has been thought able to establish is such presuppositions of revelation as the existence of God, the freedom and responsibility of man, and an objective order of law or moral obligation. Hence, even where natural theology has been affirmed, the claim of revelation has still been accepted as wholly supernatural and therefore exempted from any rational or experiential tests. In the case of empirical theology, however, this traditional exemption is withdrawn, and revelation itself is brought within the bounds of man's reason and experience. But just this, these theologians argue, explains why all the attempts to develop an empirical theology not only have failed, but also had to fail. What can be justified in terms of human experience simply cannot be appropriate to the Christian revelation; and a theology which would do justice to that revelation must resist the demand for any such justification.

I noted earlier that it is this general position against which recent Protestant theology has increasingly reacted. The reason for this reaction we saw to lie in the growing conviction that a purely dogmatic approach to theology's task renders it irrelevant to the empirical outlook of the contemporary mind. But the fact must be faced that this by itself is not a sufficient reason for rejecting such a position. If those who take the position are right, it is the very nature of the Christian witness to point beyond our human experience to a reality which utterly transcends it. Therefore, the question we must ask is whether this is correct, whether the faith attested in Holy Scripture does thus make any attempt at an empirical theology impossible.

The answer I wish to defend is that this is so far from being correct that the precise opposite must be affirmed: from the standpoint of the faith attested by Scripture, an empirical theology is necessary. In arguing for this answer, I am well aware of the inconclusiveness of all such lines of argument. No one can deny that any interpretation of the scriptural witness has to move within the hermeneutical circle by which all our efforts at understanding are circumscribed. There is always the possibility that the meaning one professes to read out of Scripture is really the meaning he first had to read into it in order even to understand it. Furthermore, the very phrase, "*the* scriptural witness," points to a nest of problems that anyone who is historically sophisticated recognizes to be extremely difficult to solve. I do not suppose, therefore, that what I shall be saying is free from objections or beyond the need of more extensive support than I am here able to provide. I offer it simply as a sufficiently plausible interpretation of the scriptural teaching to be deserving of serious consideration.

There are two main points in the argument. The first follows from the understanding of God's transcendence which is more or less adequately expressed in the scriptural texts. Granted that the language in which these texts for the most part speak of God is the language of myth, there can be little question that what they wish to say about him is very imperfectly represented in mythical terms. The God to whom they seek to bear witness is not simply one being among others, even though he be a supreme monarch whose habitat is the highest heaven spatially remote from the earth. Rather, the God of Scripture is the utterly transcendent One of whom Paul says, finally, that "from him and through him and to him are all things" (Rom. 11:36). This God is properly conceived only as "the Being of all beings," in the sense that he is the all-inclusive reality that establishes the whole difference between something and bare nothing. Whatever is, or is so much as even possible, has its beginning and end in his love for it and, but for the reality of that love, would have neither being nor value in any public or objective sense. But this understanding of God's transcendence clearly entails the assertion of his universal immanence — the claim that if anything at all can be experienced, whether as actual or as merely possible, God, too, must be experienced as its necessary ground.

The second point in the argument is explicitly made in the scriptural statements about man as radically free and responsible. Nothing is more striking in Scripture, even where the language it uses originally expressed a quite different meaning, than its understanding of man as having full responsibility for his existence. If he is to realize his authentic possibility, this can never be apart from his own free decision; and if he fails of such realization, this is always because he himself bears the guilt for the failure. The point to be noted is the reason Scripture assigns for understanding man as thus accountable. As Paul expresses it, "the wrath of God is revealed from heaven against all ungodliness and wickedness of men" because men "suppress the truth." "For what can be known about God is plain to them, because God has shown it to them. Ever since the creation of the world his invisible nature, namely, his eternal power and deity, has been clearly perceived in the things that have been made. So they are without excuse; for although they knew God they did not honor him as God or give thanks to him, but they became futile in

73

their thinking and their senseless minds were darkened"
(Rom. 1:18–21).

According to a venerable exegetical tradition, these words
provide one of the main scriptural warrants for natural theology. Indeed, they have been commonly interpreted as giving specific sanction to the cosmological argument for God's
existence whereby from a knowledge of the contingent existence of creatures an inference may be made to the necessary
existence of the Creator. Yet it seems fairly clear that this traditional interpretation reads more into Paul's words than may
be justifiably read out of them. He says nothing whatever
abut a process of inference, whether mediate or immediate,
but states simply that the nature of God has been clearly perceived in (or through) the created order. More important,
Paul does not give the slightest indication that what is thus
perceived of God is merely what falls within the competence
of human reason in abstraction from God's own initiative through revelation and grace. He affirms, rather, that
"what can be known about God," which means, presumably,
all that can be known about him, is plain to men for the
very good reason that God himself has shown it to them.
In short, Paul seems innocent of the distinction between a
"natural" and a "revealed" knowledge of God. His point is
the quite different one that every man simply as man is already
the recipient of God's self-disclosure and, therefore, may be
held strictly accountable for what he makes of his existence.

Thus, whether we begin with Scripture's understanding of
God as radically transcendent, and so also universally immanent, or with its understanding of man as radically free and
responsible, we are led to the same conclusion: an empirical
theology such as we are considering here is a necessary implication of the witness of Christian faith. If God were not
somehow experienced by us in our experience of anything
whatever, he would not be the God to whom the faith of
Scripture bears witness, and that faith could neither be true
nor have any consistent meaning. Likewise, unless every man
were in the position to verify the claims of faith in terms of his
own experience, he could not bear the responsibility for his

existence which the scriptural witness plainly affirms to be his.

The chief objection to this argument will no doubt be that it fails to take account of the scriptural testimony to the universality of man's sin. Granted that Scripture does hold that God is universally present in our experience and that we are each responsible to the gift and demand of his love, it also attests that not one of us has measured up to that responsibility. In fact, the very passage in which Paul asserts that the knowledge of God is universal, his controlling purpose is to show that "there is no distinction, since all have sinned and fall short of the glory of God" (Rom. 3:22–23). In view of this, it is almost certain to be objected that the conclusion for which I have been arguing is subject to an important qualification — that, while it may indeed be true *in principle* that the claims of faith can be justified in terms of our experience, this is hardly also true *in fact*.

The reply to this objection is that, if the universality of man's sin is a fact, the universality of God's grace is none the less so. Here again, I appeal to the understanding of God and man which, in spite of the inadequate mythical language in which it is often expressed, is evidently intended in Holy Scripture. The only God attested by the scriptural witness is "the living God, who is the Savior of all men" and "desires all men to be saved and to come to the knowledge of the truth" (I Tim. 4:10, 2:3–4). This means that the God who is the transcendent ground and end of all things never ceases to seek us out despite all our sinful attempts to evade his gift and demand. He is the One from whom literally nothing is able to separate us except our refusal of his love, which even then continues to sustain us and to claim us for itself. This is the reason why the scriptural understanding of man's sin is as radical as it is. Paul's unqualified judgment, "So they are without excuse," assumes just this universal prevenience of God's grace, whereby from the creation of the world all men are confronted with the truth that they are creatures of the Creator. Thus, on Paul's view, and I believe on the view of Scripture generally, man as sinner taken merely in himself is as much an abstraction as the purely "natural" man who is supposed to be the subject of natural theology. When he is considered in the full concreteness of his actual existence, every man is already the recipient of God's saving grace, and John Wesley's statement is correct that "no man sins because he has not grace, but because he does not use the grace which he hath."[7]

If this is so, however, it must be possible in fact as well as in principle to justify the claims of the Christian witness by appeal to our common experience simply as men. The sole aim of this witness is to re-present the true or authentic understanding of our existence by which each of us actually lives insofar as he lives as a man at all. From the standpoint of faith itself, there is no human being whatever who is not in a position to verify its claims in terms of his own experience. This does not mean, of course, that every man must have already reflected his experience at the level of full self-consciousness. We all perceive things of which we may not be reflectively aware, and this is particularly likely in the case of the field of experience to which the claims of faith refer. Because these claims have to do not with the inessential details of our experience, but with its essential structure — with the reality that makes any experience even possible — they may very well be the last thing about which some of us become fully conscious. Even so, if the witness of Christian faith is right, none of us is ever wholly unaware of this essential reality, and the different religions and ideologies give evidence that mankind generally has in fact reflected it with varying degrees of adequacy. It is in this sense, then, that, so far as faith itself is concerned, an empirical theology is not impossible, but rather necessary.

IV

The importance of this conclusion, if it can be maintained, is to exclude one possible explanation of why the various essays at empirical theology have usually failed. If the reality to

[7] Thomas Jackson, ed., *The Works of the Rev. John Wesley*, A.M. (London: Wesleyan Methodist Book Room, 1829–31) 6:512.

which Christian faith bears witness is affirmed by that witness to be present in every man's experience, it is not the nature of faith's own claims which accounts for the failure. But what could account for it, then, except the understandings of experience, of its nature and scope, by which efforts at empirical theology have generally been determined? This plainly seems to be the answer, and I now want to show why I believe it to be correct.

Generally speaking, one must say that there have been two somewhat different understandings of experience which have been taken for granted in the usual attempts to develop an empirical theology. One understanding may be more readily discerned in some of the earlier of these attempts, while the other tends to predominate in some that are more recent. This is at best a rough indication of emphasis or tendency, since it would be easy to point to exceptions in the one respect as well as the other. And there is a good reason for this: the boundary between the two understandings is in the nature of the case not fixed but fluid, and it is difficult to find any empiricist who is not to some extent determined by both, whether he explicitly acknowledges the fact or not. For the purpose of this discussion, however, it will be useful to characterize each understanding independently before considering them together, although it is important to keep in mind that we will thereby be dealing with ideal types, rather than with the actual thought of any theologian or philosopher.

The defining characteristic of the first type is that experience is understood to be primarily, if not exclusively, the perception of ourselves and the world which takes place by means of our senses. This is the understanding which has been prominent in modern philosophy ever since the seventeenth century, being variously presupposed not only by the empiricisms of Locke and Hume, but by the transcendental idealism of Kant as well. Its origins go back to the Greek philosophers, for whom the palmary instance of experience was visual sensation. But, given Descartes's insistence that the starting point of philosophy must be in "clear and distinct ideas," the primacy of sense perception inevitably became the main assumption of most modern philosophers. If the marks of the fundamental elements in our experience are clarity and distinctness, there can be little question that those elements are the impressions or data supplied by our five senses, and particularly by our sense of sight. The point of interest here, however, is the conception of knowledge or cognition which this first type of empiricism involves. Consistent with its understanding of experience as primarily sense perception, this view holds that the only solid core or our knowledge is comprised of assertions that may be directly or indirectly verified by appeal to such perception. Thus, in the case of any claim to truth, the relevant questions are always two: Can it be proved true or false by means of our senses? (in which event it is a meaningful cognitive claim) and, Does it in fact prove true when tested by this means?

The second type of empiricism is considerably less restrictive, although, as its proponents claim, correspondingly more adequate to our actual experience. It is defined by the understanding that sense perception is neither the only nor even the primary mode of experience, but is rather derived from a still more elemental awareness both of ourselves and of the world around us. Before we ever undertake the comparatively high-level discrimination of reality by means of our senses, we are already aware of ourselves and others as causally efficacious powers mutually interacting with one another. Thus our primitive sense of identification with our own bodies, which is betrayed, for example, by our certainty that we see *with* our eyes, is not the product of sense perception but its underlying presupposition. And so also with our vague awareness of a circumambient world beyond our own bodily life, or our clearer perception of ourselves as centers of experience with memories of the past and anticipations of the future.

This understanding of experience as vastly richer and deeper than mere sensation has been repeatedly represented in recent philosophy. It was more or less fully developed in the continental "philosophy of life," whether in Bergson's manner or in Dilthey's, and it was persuasively expounded in

James' "radical empiricism." So far as Protestant theology is concerned, the most influential expression of such an understanding has been provided by the existentialist philosophy of our own century. Whether through Heidegger or through others, several theologians have come to think of man as, first of all, "being-in-the-world," instead of as the perceiving subject of the older empiricism. Prior to the kind of thinking which is properly called "objective," because it rests on the objectification of reality through sense perception, man has the understanding of himself and the world which these theologians distinguish as "existential." By this they mean that the foundation of all man's experience is his awareness not only of the being of others as essentially related to his being, influencing and influenced by it, but also of his own unique existence as radically free and responsible. But this typical existentialist relativizing of the "subject-object schema" is simply one way of making explicit the broader scope of experience and cognition as understood by the second, more radical type of empiricism. On this understanding, our knowledge comprises far more than we are able to verify by appeal to our senses alone. It also includes — indeed, as its most essential elements — assertions representing the inner, nonsensuous perception of ourselves and of the world as the primal realities disclosed in our experience.

Despite this significant difference, the two types of empiricism are in complete agreement at one crucial point. They both assume that the sole realities present in our experience, and therefore the only objects of our certain knowledge, are ourselves and the other creatures that constitute the world. But if this is the assumption underlying all the usual attempts at empirical theology, their repeated failure has an obvious explanation. The whole point of the Christian witness is to attest the reality of God's love as the transcendent ground and end of all things and as the sole basis of man's authentic existence. Hence, by the very nature of this witness, there is no possibility of justifying its claims by appealing either to the perceptions of our senses or to the more basic awareness of our own existence as being-in-the-world. On either understanding of experience, the phrase "empirical theology" can only be self-contradictory, and one is faced with just that tragic choice which has been made again and again by empirical theologians. If he takes the course of insisting on an empirical verification of his assertions, he has two main possibilities: either he must refer the word "God" to some merely creaturely reality or process of interaction, or else he must deny it all reference whatever by construing its meaning as wholly noncognitive. If he pursues the other course of asserting God's reality as genuinely transcendent and personal, he must abandon all hope of an empirical justification of his assertions. The fact that he frankly admits this or even represents it as a theological virtue is of little avail. The difficulty remains that he cannot show his claims to be meaningful or true in terms of our shared experience.

V

Thus we are led to ask whether the usual types of empiricism exhaust the possibilities presently open to us. It seems evident that if the project of an empirical theology is to succeed, this can only be because of an alternative understanding of our experience as not closed but open to the divine reality attested by the Christian witness. Yet is such an understanding possible? I believe it is, and I would support this belief by appealing to several philosophies where just such an empiricism is clearly implied and, in some cases, actually made explicit.

I observed earlier that there is no absolutely fixed boundary between the two more conventional types of empiricism and that neither of their respective insights seems to have been wholly absent from the actual thinking of most empiricists. I would now make a somewhat similar observation about the second of these types and a still more comprehensive empirical outlook which certain philosophers have explicitly worked out. Both in the existentialist philosophy of the Continent and in the kind of thinking typified by James' "radical empiricism" there has been a definite tendency for the predominant understanding of experience to develop into a less restrictive understanding. One illustration of this tendency, which has been recognized by some as theologically significant, is the thinking of the later Heidegger, in which the existentialism of *Sein und Zeit* is expanded and deepened in the direction of a new philosophy of being.

But my present concern is not to canvass all the lines of thought that might appear to converge on a third type of empiricism. I wish, instead, to point to the one philosophy where I find such an empiricism most fully elaborated — namely, Whitehead's. I realize, of course, that there is nothing new in the association of Whitehead's thought with the cause of empirical theology. Both Wieman and Macintosh already appealed to it in working out their positions, and the same is true of a number of others who have continued to think along the same general lines. Even so, I seriously question whether Whitehead's achievement has been fully appropriated in most of the theological thinking on which it has been influential. The fact, for example, that Wieman and Macintosh alike regarded his doctrine of the consequent nature of God as transcending experience, and hence as speculative, indicates the limits of the usual kinds of appropriation. Therefore, I am bold to think that the following considerations may point up resources in Whitehead's thought that still wait to be exploited by Protestant theology. His contribution to theological reflection may well lie less in the conceptuality provided by his imposing metaphysical system than in the understanding of experience of which that system is but the explication.

The general features of Whitehead's empiricism may be readily summarized. Its controlling purpose is to offer a clear-cut alternative to the "sensationalist doctrine" which has been prominent in modern philosophy since Descartes. This it seeks to do by developing a theory of nonsensuous perception — or what, in Whitehead's technical terminology is called perception in the mode of "causal efficacy." According to this theory, the most basic mode of experience is not "presentational immediacy," or perception of the contemporary world as passively illustrating certain sensa, but an intuitive awareness of our own past mental and bodily states and of the wider world beyond as they compel conformation to themselves in the present. Hence our insistent conviction that we live "amid a democracy of fellow creatures" and are members of "a contemporary world throbbing with energetic values" is not a questionable inference from mere sensation, but immediately arises from our nonsensuous perception of the efficacious past.[8] And, in general, the evidence on which the interpretations of our experience are based "is entirely drawn from the vast background and foreground of nonsensuous perception with which sense-perception is fused, and without which it can never be."[9] Because this is so, Whitehead argues, the conventional doctrine of the primacy of sense perception has been completely mistaken. "Experience has been explained in a thoroughly topsy-turvy fashion, the wrong end first."[10] "The whole notion of our massive experience conceived as a reaction to clearly envisaged details is fallacious. The relationship should be inverted. The details are a reaction to the totality. They add definition. . . . They are interpretive and not originative. What is original is the vague totality."[11]

It is evident that the general features of Whitehead's understanding of experience relate it quite closely to the second main type of modern empiricism. It is also evident that there are many places in his writings where, to judge from his explicit statements, his thought remains well within the limits of this type. Consider, for example, the following sentences: "The perception of conformation to realities in the environment is the primitive element in our external experience. We conform to our bodily organs and to the vague world which lies beyond them. Our primitive perception is that of conformation vaguely, and of the yet vaguer relata 'oneself' and 'another' in the undiscriminated background."[12] It seems

[8] *Process and Reality: An Essay in Cosmology* (New York: Macmillan Co., 1929), p. 78; *Adventures of Ideas* (New York: Macmillan Co., 1933), p. 282.

[9] *Adventures of Ideas*, p. 232.

[10] *Process and Reality*, p. 246.

[11] *Modes of Thought* (New York: Macmillan Co., 1938), pp. 148–49.

[12] *Symbolism*, p. 43.

clear that Whitehead's intention here is limited to holding that the primary mode of our experience discloses a vague totality comprised of but two relata — the self and another. By "another" he presumably means simply our own bodies and their natural environment, in which case he affirms nothing more than a nonsensuous perception of ourselves and of the world. But the fact to which I would draw attention is that there are other passages where Whitehead explicitly breaks out of the limits of even this second type of empiricism. The clearest statement of what I take to be his final understanding of the matter is given in Parts I and II of *Modes of Thought*, and it is this statement that I now wish to consider somewhat more closely.

In the series of lectures which makes up the parts of this book to which I refer, Whitehead begins by distinguishing between "systematic philosophy" and what he calls "philosophical assemblage."[13] Prior to any effort at systematization, philosophy is "the entertainment of notions of large, adequate generality," or, as he also expresses it, the examination of "those general characterizations of our experience which are presupposed in the directed activities of mankind."[14] Disclaiming any intention of framing a philosophical system, he then undertakes to consider several such general ideas, insisting throughout that his final appeal is to "that self-evidence which sustains itself in civilized experience."[15] Thus he comes to the central question of the last lecture: "What is the dominating insight whereby we presuppose ourselves as actualities within a world of actualities?"[16] His answer, in general, is to restate his theory of nonsensuous perception and to argue that it is by a mode of awareness more basic than sensation that "we know ourselves as creatures in a world of creatures."[17] "At the base of our existence is the sense of 'worth.' . . . It is the sense of existence for its own sake, of existence which is its own justification, of existence with its own character."[18] Striking, however, is the way Whitehead

[13] *Modes of Thought*, pp. 1–5.
[14] Ibid., pp. 4, 1–2.
[15] Ibid., pp. 144–45.
[16] Ibid., p. 146.
[17] Ibid., p. 147.
[18] Ibid., p. 149.

proceeds to elaborate this answer. The following excerpts convey the gist of his argument:

> The primitive stage of discrimination is not primarily qualitative. It is the vague grasp of reality, dissecting it into a three-fold scheme, namely, The Whole, That Other, and This-Myself.

> This is primarily a dim division. The sense of totality obscures the analysis into self and others. . . . There is the vague sense of many which are one; and of one which includes the many. Also there are two senses of the one — namely, the sense of the one which is all, and the sense of the one among the many.

> . . . There is the feeling of the ego, the others, the totality. This is the vague, basic presentation of the differentiation of existence in its enjoyment of discard and maintenance. We are, each of us, one among others; and all of us are embraced in the unity of the whole. . . .

> Our enjoyment of actuality is a realization of worth, good or bad. It is a value-experience. Its basic expression is — Have a care, here is something that matters! Yes — that is the best phrase — the primary glimmering of consciousness reveals, Something that matters.

> This experience provokes attention, dim and, all but, subconscious. Attention yields a three-fold character in the 'Something that matters.' Totality, Externality, and Internality are the primary characterizations of 'that which matters.' They are not to be conceived as clear, analytic concepts. Experience awakes with these dim presuppositions to guide its rising clarity of detailed analysis. They are presuppositions in the sense of expressing the sort of obviousness which experience exhibits. There is the totality of actual fact; there is the externality of many facts; there is the internality of this experiencing which lies within the totality.

> These three divisions are on a level. No one in any sense precedes the other. There is the whole fact containing within itself my fact and the other facts. Also the

dim meaning of fact — or actuality — is intrinsic importance for itself, for the others, and for the whole.[19]

The import of this argument, as I see it, is twofold. First,
it makes the point that the most primitive mode of our experience is an awareness at once of being and of value; it is our
dim sense of reality, as such, as something that matters or has
worth or is of intrinsic importance. The argument then makes
the second and crucial point that this sense of reality which
underlies all our experience comprises infinitely more than
is sometimes supposed. It is the awareness not merely of ourselves, and of our fellow creatures, but also of the infinite
whole in which we are all included as somehow one. The very
nature of our experience, Whitehead argues, is such as to compel recognition of this third essential factor. Just as we are
never aware of our own existence except as related to the
being of others, so our sense that both we and they are important is our sense of the encompassing whole without
which such importance could never be. Thus Whitehead explains in an earlier lecture, "Importance is primarily monistic
in its reference to the Universe. Importance, limited to a finite
individual occasion, ceases to be important. In some sense or
other, Importance is derived from the immanence of infinitude in the finite. . . . Importance passes from the World as
one to the World as many." [20] Or again, he tells us: "Apart
from this sense of transcendent worth, the otherness of reality
would not enter into our consciousness. There must be value
beyond ourselves. Otherwise everything experienced would be
merely a barren detail in our solipsist mode of existence. . . .
Human experience explicitly relates itself to an external standard. The universe is thus understood as including a source
of ideals. . . . The sense of historic importance is the intuition
of the universe as everlasting process, unfading in its deistic
unity of ideals." [21]

The last sentence makes explicit that our primitive aware-

[19] Ibid., pp. 150–51, 159.
[20] Ibid., pp. 28–29.
[21] Ibid., pp. 140–42.

ness of reality as comprised essentially of ourselves, others, and the whole is in fact "the sense of Deity," or what Whitehead also refers to as "the intuition of holiness . . . which is at the foundation of all religion." [22] If we ask now the nature of the deity whom we thus experience, there is no doubt of the answer. He is precisely the One who is conceived in Whitehead's mature metaphysics as necessarily consequent as well as primordial. He is "that final mode of unity in virtue of which there exists stability of aim amid the multiple forms of potentiality, and in virtue of which there exists importance beyond the finite importance for the finite actuality." [23] But this means that the assertion of God as transcendent personal reality is far from a mere speculation which is empirically groundless. Given Whitehead's type of empiricism, this assertion is the only way whereby we can do full justice to what each of us actually experiences. Because at the base of whatever we say or do there is our primitive awareness of ourselves and the world as both real and important, all our experience is in its essence religious. It rests in the sense of our own existence and of being generally as embraced everlastingly in the encompassing reality of God.

Consequently, to our current question of the proper use of religious or theological language Whitehead enables us to make a straightforward reply. The function of all such language is to re-present symbolically, or at the level of full self-consciousness, this underlying sense of ourselves and others as of transcendent worth. That there should be a variety of ways in which we reflect this field of our experience is only to be

[22] Ibid., pp. 140, 164.
[23] Ibid., p. 117. Cf. the allusion to God as "that ultimate unity of direction in the Universe, upon which all order depends, and which gives its meaning to importance" (p. 68); also the statement: "The notion of a supreme being must apply to an actuality in process of composition, an actuality not confined to the data of any special epoch in the historic field. Its actuality is founded on the infinitude of its conceptual appetition, and its form of process is derived from the fusion of this appetition with the data received from the world-process. Its function in the world is to sustain the aim at vivid experience. It is the reservoir of potentiality and the co-ordination of achievement" (p. 128).

expected. Aside from obvious differences in language and in reflective capacity, we are faced with any number of conditions that can obscure our sense of worth or render our efforts to understand it problematic. There are the inescapable facts that we must suffer and die, and that our lives are ever exposed to the workings of chance. Any of these conditions can become the occasion of our reflection and thereby focus our understanding of the worth of existence in a particular way. Furthermore, there is that dark fact about our nature to which the Christian witness refers when it speaks of sin. Instead of looking to God alone as the ground of our importance, we erect some idol alongside him as being equally essential to a meaningful existence. From this, also, there naturally arise alternative understandings of our experience, and thence the different religions and ideologies which the history of culture so abundantly illustrates. Yet beneath all such differences as their underlying dynamic is the same awareness of ourselves and the world as of worth to God. It is this awareness which all religious language seeks to express, and the criterion of its truth is the one implied by Whitehead when he states, "Importance is primarily monistic in its reference to the Universe. . . . Importance passes from the World as one to the World as many."

To this reply, as to the whole understanding of experience on which it rests, there is the obvious objection that experience fails to justify so comprehensive an empiricism. I do not wish to question the legitimacy of this objection. Here, too, it seems to me, our thought unavoidably moves within a hermeneutical circle which excludes any simple resolution of fundamental differences. Whitehead himself expressly recognizes this when, in opposing his doctrine to a more conventional empiricism, he admits, "The only mode of decision can be by an appeal to the self-evidence of experience." [24] Nevertheless, I am convinced that the type of empiricism Whitehead elaborates remains sufficiently close to essential features of our experience which everyone must recognize that no one can simply dismiss it. If our experience has a narrower scope

[24] Ibid., p. 152.

than he understands it to have, there is much of what he speaks of as "the directed activities of mankind" that cannot be explained but only explained away.[25]

This expression of conviction is not intended as a conclusive argument for a third type of empiricism. The purpose of the preceding considerations, as of my earlier interpretation of the scriptural witness, is simply to suggest why I myself incline to be hopeful about the future of empirical theology. If I am right, neither the claims of Christian faith nor the resources of empirical philosophy require that attempts at such a theology must inevitably fail. But whether this is right or not, the discussion may at least have clarified the conditions on which the prospects for empirical theology definitely seem to depend.

[25] In this connection, I find it significant that the greatest of Whitehead's contemporaries among American philosophers, John Dewey, often expressed the same kind of comprehensive empiricism. In addition to *Experience and Nature*, where Dewey's view is most fully expounded, cf. the following sentences which conclude his early book, *Human Nature and Conduct: An Introduction to Social Psychology* (New York: Modern Library, 1930): "Every act may carry within itself a consoling and supporting consciousness of the whole to which it belongs and which in some sense belongs to it. With responsibility for the intelligent determination of particular acts may go a joyful emancipation from the burden for responsibility for the whole which sustains them, giving them their final outcome and quality. There is a conceit fostered by perversion of religion which assimilates the universe to our personal desires; but there is also a conceit of carrying the load of the universe from which religion liberates us. Within the flickering inconsequential acts of separate selves dwells a sense of the whole which claims and dignifies them. In its presence we put off mortality and live in the universal. The life of the community in which we live and have our being is the fit symbol of this relationship. The acts in which we express our perception of the ties which bind us to others are its only rites and ceremonies" (pp. 331–32).

2

*What Is Alive and What Is Dead in
Empirical Theology?*
JOHN B. COBB, JR.

The notion of the empirical is many faceted. I have chosen, not to offer a single definition as a basis for a critique, but to treat a wide range of themes more or less closely associated with "empirical theology." In the process I shall distinguish those senses in which I believe in empirical theology from those senses in which I feel compelled to reject it. My essay will be little more than a cataloguing of issues together with a taking up of a position on them; but only in this way can I indicate in brief compass what I see as living and what dead in empirical theology. I shall treat first those senses of "empirical" in which I find it necessary to reject empirical theology.

I. What is Dead in Empirical Theology

In all its uses "empirical" points to experience, but in many of its uses it is conceived more narrowly than experience as a whole. For example, when one speaks of empirical psychology he is likely to be consciously distinguishing his subject matter from depth psychology. The latter also deals with human experience, but the experience it describes is not directly accessible to observation.

Similarly, when one speaks of what can be empirically known about man, he may be distinguishing this from the kind of knowledge of ourselves that is derived from introspection and from the kind of understanding of others in which our introspective knowledge of ourselves plays a major role.

He is referring away from this knowledge to what can be called "behavioral" science.

In both of these instances and in many others, "empirical" points to that aspect of our knowledge that originates in sense experience of our environment and that tests itself repeatedly against further sense observations. It is the kind of knowledge that has proved its reliability and importance in the natural sciences.

In *this* sense of empirical, I do not believe an empirical theology is either desirable or possible. A rigidly empirical approach provides no possibility for speaking of oneself or of other persons as subjects, much less of God. It makes nonsense of all talk about the past. It provides no basis for value judgments or ethical thought. And, indeed, it is quite inadequate for understanding both the operations of the natural scientist and the world about which he speaks.

In this extreme sense, I assume, no one seriously advocates a purely "empirical theology." What *is* sometimes advocated is that theologians base their reflection primarily on the results of empirical inquiry into religion. Those who study religion in this way, as psychologists or sociologists, often, and understandably, complain of the neglect of their findings by theologians. Their call for an "empirical theology" is a demand that the verifiable knowledge they are prepared to offer be treated as the major data of theology. However, in common with most theologians I reject this demand, not because I suppose that in principle these data should be ignored, but because, in the midst of all the welter of ideas and facts that compete for our attention, the results of the research of strictly empirical psychologists and sociologists thus far generally appear relatively uninteresting and unimportant. It is when psychologists and sociologists have gone beyond research oriented toward sense data that their work has contributed significantly to theology.

A much more serious question arises with respect to the possibility of empirical theology when the term "empirical" is more loosely defined. Suppose we do not limit the empirical to that which is given in sense experience, but rather include also every other aspect of experience, such as the emotional, the volitional, the evaluative, and the cognitive. Can we then not gain the advantages of the more strictly empirical disciplines, their reliability and the cumulative character of their results, without omitting that which is essential for the treatment of matters of ultimate concern? This is one way of viewing Wieman's brilliant attempt.

There is, however, a difficulty in this approach upon which it is ultimately shattered. The movement toward wholeness in the treatment of experience proceeds in the opposite direction from the movement toward reliability and certainty. The natural sciences and their imitators achieve their positive results by a high degree of abstraction. First, sense experience is abstracted from the totality of experience, and second, the sense "data" are abstracted from the total event of sensation. Furthermore, only some sense data are taken as relevant, and these are abstracted from the whole flow of such data. By this process it becomes possible to achieve almost total agreement among trained observers regardless of their cultural, personal, and ideological differences. We discover that we inhabit a common world, which in crucial respects presents itself to our sensory experience in a self-identical way. By abstracting from the totality of experience toward that part which is least influenced by the rest, we achieve the possibility of widespread agreement and progressive corroboration. On the other hand, when we confront each other in our total experience we find no such ready agreement. The same sense data mean something quite different to one person and to another as they interact with different memories and needs, hopes and fears.

This does not mean that there is no way of displaying a common element in our several experiences beyond that upon which the empirical sciences capitalize. But it does mean that we cannot find these additional common elements by expanding the "empirical" to include other elements. Instead, quite new and different methods are required, such as those of Husserlian phenomenology. Therefore, insofar as empirical theology involves the attempt to take the common world found by abstracting certain sense data from concrete experience and then to expand it to include the whole of that experience, I reject it as confused and confusing.

Closely related to this attempt to expand the sphere of the empirical is the attempt to avoid speculative, confessional, and perspectival elements in theology. The empirical sciences generally repudiate speculation and see no need to confess the peculiarity of the perspectives from which they operate. They make good their claim by the extent to which agreement can indeed be reached across confessional and perspectival barriers. Sometimes empirical theology is taken to mean a theology which is similarly able to achieve assured results acceptable to all honorable and careful observers. One could then expect that such an empirical theology, based upon all those modes of inquiry in which progressive agreement is achievable, would gradually replace the manifold religious opinions which now divide mankind into conflicting parties, just as other disciplines have brought mankind toward agreement on questions in which speculation and party spirit formerly prevailed.

The argument is an attractive one, but illusory. There are many questions which objective research can settle, but there are also many which it cannot settle. Positivism and logical empiricism have helped to clarify the limits of that thinking which is subject to public and definitive confirmation; and although they can properly be charged with excessive rigidity, it is clear that these limits are much narrower then optimists have often supposed.

The attempt to limit theology to what can be objectively demonstrated is suicidal, for the beliefs that matter most cannot be found there. Therefore, we must recognize that as theologians we deal with ideas on which there exists a diversity of responsible opinion and no agreement as to how the diverse judgments are to be adjudicated. That means that we are condemned to speculation, and our task is to learn how to make that speculation as responsible as possible. Even the view that theological problems can be solved without speculation is already a speculation, and, in my opinion, a poor one. We should abandon "the quest for certainty" in theology and fully recognize that, in a vast range of questions of utmost importance for us, our task is the imaginative quest for illuminating insight tested by honest reflection and open-ended discussion. Certainly the reliable results of objective inquiry constitute an indispensable check, but by themselves they are unable to provide the insights. Hence, I reject empirical theology insofar as it is an attempt to avoid either speculation or the acknowledgment of the particularity and peculiarity of the perspective from which one thinks.

Another short step brings us to the consideration of empirical theology as opposed to ontology. One may suppose that even if some speculation is inevitable in the formulation of hypotheses and the interpretation of data and in extrapolation from data, one can avoid many of the traditionally divisive questions by avoiding the ontological problem. By the ontological problem I mean the question of what it is to *be*. Cannot theology deal with the acts and events that relate persons and things to one another without asking the ultimate question of what things are in themselves? And if so, can it not, in an important sense, remain empirical?

Once again, my judgment is negative. Theology cannot avoid the ontological question by dealing with acts and events; for any serious thought about acts and events involves a conscious or unconscious understanding of what an act or event is. And that means either that acts and events are themselves viewed as ontologically ultimate, *or* that they are seen as manifestations of another type of reality underlying them (substances? persons? material entities?). One can avoid raising these questions, but one cannot prevent the whole fabric of this thought from being permeated by his implicit ontology. When the ontology is not made explicit and thus subjected to critical reflection, it is likely to be naïve, vague, and self-contradictory. Insofar as the appeal to the empirical has encouraged indifference to the articulation and clarification of ontology, it is to be repudiated.

Finally, "empirical" in its reference to experience usually singles out human experience. Again, there is an initial plausibility to this restriction. My experience *is* human experience, and I have no direct access to any other kind. Even my indirect access to experiences other than my own is primarily through language, and this is a human phenomenon.

Nevertheless, there is a strong tendency, often encouraged by reference to the empirical, to draw too sharp a line around human experience. The problem of knowledge about human experience other than one's own is too lightly passed over, whereas the difficulty of *some* knowledge about nonhuman experience is exaggerated. Instead, we should recognize that in *all* belief there are experiences other than our own, and that all belief about such experiences involves a transcendence of the strictly empirical. We should consider the process by which we come to our fixed conviction that such experiences exist. We will then find that the nonempirical grounds for attributing experience to others do not justify so sharp a distinction between men and other entities as empiricism seems sometimes to suppose.

II. What Is Living in Empirical Theology

Thus far I have been describing what I find unacceptable and misleading in empirical theology. I reject, on the one hand, any narrowing of attention to sense data and, on the other hand, any attempt to attribute to other aspects of experience a status similar to that of sense data. I have argued also that theology must go far beyond the areas of general consensus based on commonplaces of experience and cannot hope to achieve certainty by eschewing speculation. I have insisted specifically that theology cannot avoid the controversial and divisive questions of ontology which empiricists generally attempt to skirt. And finally I have suggested that the problem of our knowledge of experiences other than our own deserves an attention rarely accorded it by empiricists, and that such attention will militate against the sharp separation of human experience from that of other entities.

I want now to turn from this negative treatment of empiricism to a positive one. Despite all of these criticisms, I identify myself as, in a broad sense, empirically oriented. And it is in this very broad sense that the Chicago tradition as a whole can be called empirical.

At Chicago, one acquired an empirical temper of mind in the sense that one attempted to form his beliefs on the basis of evidence. One learned not to settle questions by appealing to authority. I do not mean simply that one was to reject all claims to settle issues by the intrusion of a supernaturally sanctioned answer. I mean something much more subtle and much more important. A person learned that he should believe *only* what commends itself to him in its own right. He should not believe something because it is the *Christian* thing to believe. If he remains Christian it is because he finds that Christian faith, properly understood, seems *true* in the light of all that one can learn.

I wish to highlight this simple point because of my conviction that it is the most valuable legacy of the Chicago tradition, a legacy peculiarly important today. Ours is a generation of self-conscious rebellion in theology. Younger theologians outdo one another in demonstrating how very radical they are. This mood in theology is primarily to be understood as the successor to neo-orthodoxy. Neo-orthodoxy for our present purposes can be described as a theological temper which prided itself on the purity of its loyalty to the distinctively Christian, and its indifference to objective evidence of the truth of Christian beliefs. Theology was the exposition of what one believed *qua* Christian.

The problem was that there often remained a gulf between what one believed *qua* Christian and what he believed *qua* man, college educated, and immersed in the twentieth-century world. In speaking of this gulf I am not referring to the greatest of the creative expositors, but rather to the second generation to which the results of the creative period were presented as authoritative. For members of this generation really to perceive the world *qua* Christian has often required that they work themselves into a rather special frame of mind. As some of those schooled in this theology began to recognize the inauthenticity of this strained act of Christian belief, they rebelled; the spread of the rebellion is a mark of the quest for a new integrity on the part of many.

My point is that those of us who most fully absorbed the empirical temper of Chicago have been freed from the necessity to rebel. Our theological education may have been deficient in many ways, but it did not inculcate in us that inauthenticity I have tried to describe. Perhaps we believed *less* than those of our generation who were educated at schools that were tradition-bent in their orientation; but what we did believe we really believed, since it was the result of a total involvement in the questions, rather than a learning of what *qua* Christian we *should* believe. If in the years since then our views have changed, this has been the result of further reflection and maturation. To put it quite simply, we were freed at Chicago to believe what really seemed to us to be true. Having once received that freedom we can now have concerns that are positive and constructive. We do not have to be "angry young men."

The most fundamental heritage of "empirical" theology, I am saying, is a spirit of total openness before the evidence — all the evidence on whatever question is at issue. It is my conviction that the evidence, *broadly* conceived, militates against empirical theology, *narrowly* conceived. Hence I have devoted considerable attention to attacking the restrictive connotations of "empirical" which have in fact plagued its history in philosophy and theology. But I would like to testify that even when I find some of these criticisms applicable to individual proponents of the Chicago school, it has always been the broad and open appeal to evidence, rather than narrow and rigid definitions of data and method, that has characterized Chicago. It is this which I wholeheartedly affirm.

What I have said thus far does not distinguish the empirical from the rational; and indeed I would not want to juxtapose these sharply to one another. Every rationalist begins with experience, and every empiricist employs reason in his treatment of the empirical data. The issue is one of balancing these factors in a way appropriate to a particular inquiry, not of affirming one and rejecting the other. Yet on the spectrum of positions between extreme empiricism and extreme rationalism, I find myself somewhere toward the empirical end. I find myself more interested in experiential evidence than in formal proofs. My own speculations commend themselves to me especially as they seem confirmed by experiences, whether these are of the ordinary or the extraordinary variety. I am more disturbed by the appearance of experiential evidence against my views than by my inability to achieve total consistency; although I believe also that one must ever strive toward that as well. I am more excited by a perceptive account of an illuminating experience than by a formal argument based on the analysis of what is entailed in a concept. In general I regard the task of reason as explaining why we experience what we do as we do, and I am skeptical of every rational system that draws conclusions that seem in conflict with immediate experience. For example, I regard it as the task of reason to explain the freedom and subjectivity that I in fact experience myself as having, as well as my experienced certainty that I live in a shared world. If instead, in the interest of consistency or simplicity, a rational system concludes that such phenomena are illusory, or explains them in a way that seems artificially superimposed upon the experience, then I am skeptical of the rational system.

In these rambling comments I am confessing to an empirical temper in distinction from a rationalistic one; I am not affirming an empiricist doctrine over against rationalism. I believe that a strong dose of the empirical temper is healthy, but I do not believe that the criteria of the rationalist are invalid. If a rational system that seems not to do full justice to my spontaneous interpretation of experience commends itself to my reason, if I can find no fallacy in it and can provide no better explanation, then I must finally also recognize that my primary understanding of my own experience is also fallible, subject to correction by reason as well as to explanation and clarification.

My empiricism is not only a general insistence that we come to our beliefs in honest and open interaction with the evidence and that the most important evidence is of the experiential sort; my empiricism also becomes an ontological doctrine. I can state this in two propositions. Nothing is actual that is not experiential in character, and experience is always individual. These two principles can as well be called idealist as empiricist, but the idealism they describe is of a special variety — precisely that variety which is most closely associated with the empiricist tradition. These principles can be attributed to Berkeley, but not to Hegel. They are, I believe, the inevitable corollary of the empirical temper when this is extended to answering the ontological question.

There is another quite general way in which I find myself deeply informed by the empirical temper. I find myself always concerned to achieve directness and literalness of language. That does not mean that I desire to do away with all use of metaphor, analogy, and indirect discourse. But it does mean that I see the task of theology, in distinction from prayer, praise, and preaching, to be the literal and direct statement of what is intended and believed.

Part of the issue here is terminological. *If* one supposes that "literal" and "direct" language is limited to the account of those aspects of sense experience selected for attention by the empirical sciences because of their relatively objective character, then "nonliteral" and "indirect" language is required for most normal discourse and certainly for theology. But I find the identification of literal language with that of the empirical sciences contrary to common usage and all too likely, by grouping them all together, to overemphasize the similarity of these many other forms of language. If I say that I feel pain in my left wrist, or that I resent the tone of voice in which someone has addressed me, I am not speaking the language of the empirical sciences, for I am describing an aspect of my experience as it is accessible to me, and that is quite different from the way it is accessible to other observers. Yet most people would normally regard such statements as literal and direct. Similarly, Heidegger's analysis of the structures of human existence does not belong to the sphere of the empirical sciences, but it is confusing to say that his language is not literal and direct.

On the other hand, some of the language of depth psychologists is nonliteral. This is the case whenever psychic forces are described in language that has its primary and proper application to objects known in sense experience. It may be necessary at certain stages in the development of a new discipline to borrow models from other areas of thought, but it is important to recognize that this procedure has great dangers and that it is the task of the new discipline to work toward a more suitable and hence a more literal language. It may continue to be necessary to use nonliteral language to communicate with laymen, but it will be a mark of failure if the theoretician cannot explain quite literally also his reasons for using this nonliteral language and the respects in which it is appropriate and inappropriate. This is possible only if his own grasp of his subject is independent of the language he explains and subject to more literal articulation.

The question for theology is whether for it also the resort to nonliteral language is a mark of weakness it should strive to overcome, or whether the nature of its subject matter is such that the aim at literalness is false. I am here associating the empirical temper with this aim at literalness. Let us apply it first to the understanding of such literature as the Old Testament accounts of creation and fall and the parables of Jesus.

There exists a considerable literature of uneven but impressive merit that intends to explain to us the meaning of these stories. Such explanation is literal and direct. We are confronted also with theories to the effect that the full meaning of these stories, like that of a poem, exceeds every prosaic formulation. Acceptance of the latter point need not affect the decisive importance of the literal formulation of the meaning, or of such aspects of the meaning as one cognitively grasps. Presumably all poems and stories possess meanings lacking in the direct and literal explanation, but not all are equally appropriate for use in the church. The question of appropriateness of use can only be decided responsibly by discussion of the literal meaning or by literal reflection on the kinds of noncognitive meaning which the art conveys.

The critical question is that of our language about God.

Should we here also strive for literalness? Or should we accept the traditional view that only negative statements about God can be univocal? This issue requires discussion on many levels. Religiously there is the question of whether the "otherness" of God involved in his holiness and transcendence is so radical that any reality of which we speak univocally cannot be God. Philosophically there is the question of whether the grounds for affirming the reality of God are such that God must be conceived as inconceivable. Although I do not believe that negative answers can be confidently given to these questions, I am also convinced that the confident positive answers they so often receive are not warranted. What is required is the fullest exploration of what can be affirmed of God in univocal language to provide a basis for both religious and philosophical criticism. The attempt to press the limits of literal discourse as far as possible is, I believe, a further and important extension of the empirical temper.

III. The Empirical and the Historical

In conclusion I want to address myself to a quite different set of issues to which the idea of an empirical theology points. These arise when the empirical temper is juxtaposed to historical thinking. I am not speaking here of the opposition of a narrow empiricism which supposes that all truth is to be discovered *de novo* in a scientific fashion over against an authoritarianism which affirms that truth was given once for all in the past and needs only to be repeated. Such views are not to be taken seriously. I am interested rather in the fundamental understanding of the role of the theologian, and, for simplicity and clarity, I can formulate two significant, intelligent, and relevant definitions of his task. There is the view, oriented to historical thinking, that his task is that of re-presenting and interpreting for our time the Christian message historically given. And there is the view, oriented to empirical thinking, that the theologian's task is to help our generation understand its situation and find meaning within it. According to both definitions the theologian must concern himself both with the past, including particularly the Christian past, and with the present; but there remains an important, if subtle, difference. In the first view, the theologian's task centers on the reinterpretation of the normative documents of Christian faith in the light of our present situation, so as to display the already presupposed decisive relevance of the Christian message for our situation. In the second view, the Christian tradition is initially viewed as one among many factors explanatory of and relevant to our situation; and if it is held to play any peculiarly important role in the quest for meaning within our situation, this is to be shown rather than presupposed. From the point of view of the first definition of theology, those who follow the second course are not theologians at all. From the point of view of those committed to the second approach, the first betrays its origins in supernaturalistic authoritarianism even when its practitioners are extremely radical in their biblical criticism and their openness to the modern world.

I find myself peculiarly ambivalent on the issue as thus defined. On the one hand, my empirical temper inclines me strongly to the second alternative. It seems to me essential that any distinctive normative claim made for aspects of the Christian tradition be justified in relation to the present situation in terms of the criteria to be found within that situation. At the same time, it seems to me clear that in fact those who have attempted to speak as religious leaders of our time, without conscious and explicit commitment to the Christian faith in its historical distinctiveness, have generally been superficial. Indispensable for the self-understanding of our time is the intensive, critical study of the Bible, a study likely to be motivated only by a judgment of the importance of that literature exceeding that which seems warranted by empirical considerations. One task of our generation is to provide, from the side of the empirically oriented understanding of the theologian's work, an explanation of the normative importance of the Bible and the Christian tradition generally without special pleading or the appeal to arbitrary decision.

3

Empirical Propositions and Explanations in Theology
FRED BERTHOLD, JR.

To some extent the notion of "empiricism" is vague. The attempt of the so-called logical empiricists to clarify the notion has been most impressive and fruitful, yet not wholly successful. As Israel Scheffler has shown, the efforts to construct a pure or perfect empiricist language — one that would contain in addition to logical terms only a finite number of sense-observation terms — has run into difficulties.[1] If one constructs such a language, it would seem that translatability of any statement into it is a sufficient but not a necessary condition for considering that statement empirically meaningful. In short, while it may be possible to describe the "heartland" of empirical discourse, one cannot with any certainty indicate its boundaries.

The most central and crucial statements of Christian theology are located, not in the empiricist heartland, but somewhere near, or possibly beyond, the boundaries. Thus, the vagueness that besets the notion of empiricism makes difficult a simple and convincing estimate of the prospects for an empirical theology.

Such vagueness, however, should not be exaggerated. At least we know the bent and direction of empiricism. We know what the empiricist is after, what he is looking for; the problem is just how far he can attain it, and what attitude he takes towards those types of inquiry whose status as "empirical" is debatable.

The following essay will not settle the question whether

[1] I. Scheffler, "Prospects of a Modest Empiricism," *Review of Metaphysics* 10 (1957): 390–96.

Christian theology can be empirical. It will, I hope, do two things: show that the notion of an empirical Christian theology is not absurd, nor even as dubious as some recent writers have contended; and make a bit clearer what some of its major characteristics would be.

I want to stress the "verification principle" because, with its aid, I can both describe the heartland of empiricism and evaluate the disputes as to whether this or that theological statement does or does not lie beyond the boundaries of empiricism. The verification principle demands that any statement, if it is to be regarded as empirically meaningful, be related in certain ways to evidence — to experiential data which is in principle open to any human observer. And this also defines what I take to be the central concern of the theological empiricist — that at least some important theological assertions be open to evaluation in terms of public evidence.

Propositions and Explanations

I define a proposition quite simply as a factual statement, a statement about which it is relevant to ask whether it is true or false. Obviously the empiricist is much concerned with propositions. He wants to know "the facts" — and, indeed, in his strictest mood has been known to say such things as "The world is everything that is the case."[2]

Consider the statement, "Jesus died and on the third day rose again." Is that a proposition? Is it intended propositionally by the man of faith, or by the theologian? It might seem that I have chosen a poor example; for surely one could find a less controversial one. However, precisely this example has figured largely in the recent arguments which I want to examine. In any case, I would contend that one can make out a strong *prima facie* case that, for most of the classical Christian theologians, this statement was intended as a proposition.

Consider a more general statement: "God loves mankind."

[2] L. Wittgenstein, *Tractatus Logico-Philosophicus*, with an introduction by B. Russell (London: Routledge & Kegan Paul, 1922), p. 31.

Is this an empirical statement? If it is meant empirically, it might be regarded simply as an empirical generalization, or perhaps as a "law," and, if a law, then in addition it might play a role in empirical explanation. Obviously it is some sort of generalization. I shall ask if it may be considered as a law-like statement which is part of an empirical explanation.

What is an "explanation"? It is often said that explanation, in an empirical sense, consists of "subsuming" a particular event or fact under a general law; that is, showing that a particular event is an instance of an order regularly noticed among events of a certain kind. We can readily see why this is of such great importance. Suppose that there were a sort of "scientific prophet" — an incredible fellow who, upon examining any experimental setup (or, say, any extant set of climate conditions), could infallibly predict exactly what would happen "when lever x is pulled" (or, in the climate case, exactly what conditions would obtain five minutes hence). Enlarging upon the principle involved, we could imagine knowing all the facts. This, however, would still not constitute a *science*; for science is interested in particular facts not just in themselves, but insofar as they may lead to an understanding of patterns of connection. To explain something, then, is to see it as an instance of a general pattern, which, insofar as it is recognized as a familiar and dependable ordering of the discrete bits of experience, leads us to say that we understand.

> The central aims of science are . . . concerned with a search for understanding — a desire to make the course of Nature not just predictable but intelligible — and this has meant looking for rational patterns of connection in terms of which we can make sense out of the flux of events.[3]

Similarly, the theologian is not primarily interested in isolated facts (did the axe-head really float on the waters of the Jordan? did Moses really receive the ten great command-

[3] S. Toulmin, *Foresight and Understanding*, (New York: Harper Torchbooks, 1961), p. 99.

ments all at once and inscribe them on stone?) but in a certain general pattern which allegedly ties them together. The many events narrated in the Bible are all given significance by being tied together and explained by some grand pattern; for example, God in his steadfast love has made a covenant with Israel.

Among those who labor to clarify the logic of explanation there are still a number of disputed issues. Insofar as my argument depends upon special interpretations, I shall try to indicate these at the relevant points. The explications worked out by Hempel and Oppenheim seem to me to be reasonably clear and defensible, although, as I shall argue later, we must not overestimate this clarity nor underestimate the difficulties which remain in achieving a precise concept of adequate explanation.[4]

In any empirical explanation we have an *"explanans"* (that which does the explaining) and an *"explanandum"* (that which is explained). The *explanans* must contain at least one general law, by virtue of which it is possible to deduce the *explanandum*. In addition it must have empirical content: that is, the general law or laws in the *explanans* must be "well confirmed" by available empirical evidence.

Now, we may distinguish two somewhat different cases: one in which the explanation (*explanans*) does contain, in addition to the general law or laws, some statements which are not laws but which describe the conditions which obtain some particular situation (the so-called "initial and boundary conditions"); and the other case in which the explanation contains only general laws. For our purposes, it is necessary only to give examples of the two types. Insofar as the distinction is relevant to my discussion at a later point, further comments will be added at that juncture.

Hempel and Oppenheim suggest the term "causal explanation" for the case in which the *explanans* contains statements of initial and boundary conditions. A very simple example:

[4] See C. G. Hempel and P. Oppenheim, "Studies in the Logic of Explanation," *Philosophy of Science* 15 (1948): 135–75.

1. Water freezes at or below 32°F.
2. At time "t" a pail of water is sitting at point "P" and the air surrounding this point stands at 30°F.
3. Therefore, the water in the pail will freeze.

But we may also speak of explanation when there is no such reference to specific conditions, when, for example, one general law is derived from another. A simple example would be the derivation of Newton's laws from Einstein's theory of relativity.

The Verification Principle

I am assuming that it is well known how the original statement of the verification principle has been modified. In any case, when I appeal to the verification principle, it is to its later, and more valid, formulations. The principle may be stated as follows: a statement is empirically meaningful (or, is an empirical statement, or makes empirical claims, etc.) if and only if it is possible in principle to specify some state of affairs which, if it obtained, would count for or against (would tend to confirm or disconfirm) the truth of the statement. To the extent that the implications of this formulation of the principle need to be amplified or clarified for our purposes, this will be done in context as the argument develops.

Most of the discussions of the verification principle have been directed to the problem of finding a criterion for deciding whether *propositions* are empirically meaningful or not. We should note, however, that it is not difficult to extend the principle to cover *explanations* as well as propositions. A deductive relationship exists between explanation and that which is explained. If it is possible to specify the latter in terms of some observable state of affairs (or, in the case where the explanandum is itself a general law, to specify some state of affairs in turn implied by it), we can then get the confirmatory or disconfirmatory relationship. If the explanandum is *not* thus specifiable, we are not dealing with an empirical explanation.

Does Christian theology contain at least some important

empirical propositions? Does it contain empirically explanatory statements? I believe that most of the important issues
involved in trying to answer these questions will come out
in the course of a critical examination of an interesting and
influential essay by Alisdair Macintyre, entitled "The Logical
Status of Religious Belief." [5] Not only is his attack upon empiricism vigorous, but, if I am at all right, it depends upon
just those confusions and misunderstandings which have
been credited and used by most of the theological anti-empiricists in the last fifty years.

Theology and Empirical Propositions

Christian theology neither makes empirical propositions nor
offers empirical explanations, according to Macintyre. The
former can be seen in connection with the proper understanding of an assertion such as "Jesus died and left the tomb three
days later." The latter can be seen in connection with a proper
understanding of an assertion such as "God loves mankind."

Macintyre accepts, as I do, the verification principle; that
is, he agrees that we must invoke this principle if we are trying to decide whether a proposition or explanation is meant
empirically or not. In one place (p. 171) he appears to narrow the verification principle in a way that seems to me objectionable: that is, he seems to be saying that the confirming
or disconfirming state of affairs must be specifiable in terms
of "sense-experience." However, in most instances, he states
the requirement in more general terms — "that some state of
affairs is to be found to the exclusion of others." [6]

[5] A. Macintyre, "The Logical Status of Religious Belief," Part 3 of
Metaphysical Beliefs, ed. A. Macintyre and R. G. Smith (London:
SCM Press, 1957).

[6] Ibid., p. 180. This distinction is not trivial. The demand for confirmation by "sense-observation" alone is less and less common. Also,
the more general way of putting the principle is required if we are to
make use of Wisdom's distinction between "perceiving" and "notic-
ing" — or of Waismann's notion of the "open texture" of empirical
terms. See John Wisdom, "Gods," reprinted in *Logic and Language*,
ed. A. Flew (Garden City, N.Y.: Anchor Books, 1965), pp. 194–214.
In the same volume, pp. 122–51, see the article by F. Waismann,
"Verifiability."

Let us consider first his case against the notion that theology contains empirical propositions. Incidentally, he does not use the term "empirical," preferring a descriptive circumlocution, but it is clear that he is talking about empiricism: "The theologian would do well to abandon any suggestion that his assertions are in any sense connected with the way the world goes, as factual assertions are related to the evidence that is relevant to their verification or falsification."[7]

"Jesus walked out of the tomb" is, according to Macintyre, a theological assertion involved in Christian belief.[8] Now, as we all know, many Christian theologians of late have insisted that such an assertion is not meant empirically, not meant as a statement of fact. One can discern a variety of grounds for such an opinion. I think that it is the case, however, that one ground common to all who reject any empirical interpretation is precisely the one staged by Macintyre: historical investigations, attempting to recover records describing the events that allegedly happened, are irrelevant to the belief. "Everything of importance to religious faith is outside the reach of historical investigation."[9]

We need to be clear as to which of two possible points is being made. Most of the discussions of this issue have lacked the clarity which is required, and therefore it has been impossible to assess the arguments. Does Macintyre mean that everything of importance to faith is *in fact* outside the reach of historical investigation? Or is he making the more radical claim that it is *in principle* beyond such investigation? The logic of the general position he seeks to establish requires us to take his assertion in the latter, more radical form; but the specific arguments he uses to defend his assertion are relevant only to the former, less radical claim.

The problems and confusions of this position can best be seen if we begin with the assumption that Macintyre is making the more radical claim: that such an assertion as "Jesus walked out of the tomb" is in principle beyond the reach of

[7] Macintyre, "Logical Status of Belief," p. 182.
[8] Ibid., p. 207.
[9] Ibid., p. 206.

historical investigation. "We are not in fact asking a question which future historical investigation might settle." [10]

If this is Macintyre's position, there can be no doubt that it is incompatible with empiricism, for it denies that any specifiable state of affairs would be relevant as evidence counting for or against the assertion. At this point empiricists sometimes erupt: "But 'Jesus walked out of the tomb' is so *obviously* making a factual claim!" We cannot concede, however, that this is obvious. Such a statement may, indeed, be given a perfectly acceptable nonempirical interpretation without any logical impropriety. The statement might be intended, for example, as part of a myth. We understand perfectly well what is meant by "Oedipus killed his father and married his mother" even though most of us, I suspect, would think it both odd and foolish to undertake an intensive search for documents, or archaeological remains, which would constitute evidence for or against the statement. It would seem, from Macintyre's positive statements about the function of religious language, that he would want to interpret the resurrection story as myth. Summarizing his account, we may say that religious language functions as a comprehensive myth, directive of a whole way of life. Such a myth takes the form of a dramatic story. In the story we find narrations of ordinary factual events: the hero falls in love or dies, etc. We know the meaning of this language from ordinary experience. It is clear, however, that *in the myth* such narrations are bracketed (to use Macintyre's term). That is, we understand that the narration is a part of a total imaginative creation, and not ordinary history. The entire biblical myth is directive of a whole way of life, for believers, in much the same way that Bunyan's *Pilgrim's Progress* provided guidance for generations of English nonconformists. We accept or reject a role which the myth offers us.[11]

All of this, so far as it goes, makes perfectly good sense. It represents one way of understanding theology which is thoroughly nonempirical.

[10] Ibid.
[11] Ibid., pp. 190–93.

While I do not doubt that this position *can* be made logically consistent, I am not sure that Macintyre has done so. What puzzles me in his distinction between two possible meanings of the term "historical event." He says that sometimes it means "an event to be investigated by historians" and sometimes simply a "past event." This distinction can certainly be defended insofar as the term "past event" is intended to cover stories and myths about things that happened long ago, or once upon a time. But then Macintyre goes on to say, "The essence of the New Testament claim, as we have seen, is that certain past events can be part of a religious belief, that is that they can be believed in on authority." [12] I find this most puzzling. Why do we need to rely on authority at all, if these "past events" are *not* the sort that are alleged to have "really happened in the ordinary world outside the story" and thus are not the sort which the historian might investigate — and, on the other hand, if they *are* the sort of "past event" that we find in novels and myths?

I certainly need no authority in order to accept the statement, as part of the story, that "Christian fell into the slough of despond." All I need to do is to read the story and *see* that, indeed, that assertion is made. And I do not see how Macintyre is entitled to raise such a question as: did such a "past event" really happen, not only as an event narrated in the story, but in "real life" — "outside" the story? For then he has removed his "brackets" — and with them any logical warrant for claiming that these events, unlike some others, are in principle beyond the investigation of the historian.

That Macintyre has in fact slipped into an inconsistency is also strongly suggested by the following two consecutive sentences:

> To believe that a past event happened is usually only reasonable if historical inquiry warrants the belief. But the essence of the New Testament, as we have seen, is that certain past events can be a part of a religious belief, that is that they can be believed in on authority.[13]

[12] Ibid., p. 207.
[13] Ibid.

From this it seems quite clear that Macintyre is *not* consistent in following out the lead suggested by the concept of myth. In the passages presently under consideration he seems, on the contrary, not to be suggesting that the "past events" of the Bible have a different sort of meaning and logic than those which interest the historian; but rather that they have the same sorts of meaning but different sorts of evidential backing. To stick consistently with his mythological lead, Macintyre *should* have said, the essence of the New Testament claim is found in a story that relates certain "past events," and *not* that we can *believe in* certain past events on the basis of a certain authority. The latter locution, especially with its "believe in," very strongly smacks of the language of the historical, the non-mythological, way of speaking. To return to the example from Bunyan, it would be most odd for someone, having read and understood the story, to say "By George, I *do* believe that Christian fell into that slough of despond — just as the man said!" Of course he did — just as the man said! For the man's saying it constituted his doing it.

We may just raise the question, without trying to answer it, whether in fact the biblical writers and classical theologians did intend their assertions about the resurrection to be understood mythically — even if they might have done so without logical fault.

Perhaps the most important point for our purposes is to note the utter confusion and the invalid arguments which accompany Macintyre's rejection of the empirical understanding of such apparently historical assertions as "Jesus walked out of the tomb." His case rests in no small part upon his attempt to show that an empirical interpretation is logically indefensible.

He asks us to "consider how any evidence that might be discovered would be assessed." [14] If historians were to turn up a document from the right period, allegedly attested by Caiaphas, asserting that he had seen Jesus walk from the tomb, what would we be entitled to conclude? Either that Caiaphas had seen Jesus walk from the tomb, or that the

[14] Ibid., p. 206.

document is a forgery, or that Caiaphas had been a convert and deliberately produced the document for propagandistic purposes. On the other hand, suppose historians were to turn up a document, certified by all the Apostles, asserting that Jesus did not walk out of the tomb but that they had spread a false rumor to this effect. We might logically conclude that this document is but an anti-Christian forgery, or that the Apostles were mistaken, or that in fact Jesus did not walk out of the tomb. The evidence neither verifies nor falsifies; therefore, Macintyre concludes, the assertion is not an empirical one.[15]

This line of argument fails because an absolutely essential distinction is ignored. It is, I think, universally recognized by proponents of the verification principle that we must distinguish between propositions which can in fact be verified (or have in fact been verified) and those which we are not at present in a position to verify. The latter would include many historical assertions, for which evidence might be flimsy or even totally absent, as well as all predictions about the future. In order for a statement to pass the verification test, and thus be accounted empirically meaningful, it is not necessary that we be able in fact to produce the verifying or falsifying evidence; it is required only that we be able to specify what evidence (evidence obtainable *in principle*) would, if available, tend to verify or falsify the statement.[16]

Furthermore, Macintyre's argument leads to the absurd conclusion that any historical statement about an alleged event, with regard to which people have strong feelings and little documentary evidence, is intended as a nonempirical statement (e.g. "Leif Erikson discovered America").

If belief in the resurrection includes a belief that Jesus walked out of the tomb, it is a straightforward empirical, historical belief, even though, as Macintyre contends, we will

[15] Ibid., pp. 206–7.
[16] See C. G. Hempel, "Problems and Changes in the Empiricist Criterion of Meaning," *Revue internationale de philosophie* 4 (1950): 41–62; and by the same author, "The Concept of Cognitive Significance," *Proceedings of the American Academy of Arts and Sciences* 80 (1951–54): 61–77.

probably never have much or very good evidence by which to judge it. Further, we should note that not only many pious Christians, but also a distinguished theologian like Aquinas has in fact treated "the testimony of the Apostles" just the way in which one treats ordinary testimony regarding matters of fact.[17]

Macintyre offers a second argument in support of his contention that the historical assertions of Christian theology (again his example is the resurrection) are not empirical. "Since a belief in an historical event is always a factual belief, it is always provisional in the sense that new evidence as to the facts could always turn up. But religious faith, as we have already argued, is never provisional."[18] In the entire essay this contention looms large: that religious faith is never provisional or tentative. I shall return to this point later, for it is important in connection with another portion of Macintyre's thesis — one which I want to examine in some detail. Suffice it to say, for the moment, that we have here an instance of confusion between the grounds for belief and the characteristics of belief.

With regard to belief in the resurrection, Macintyre makes one important and valid point. He notes that Christians believe not merely that something happened, but that it was *an act of God*. I readily admit that this raises a more complicated issue: are Christian assertions about God in any sense empirical? However, if Christian historical statements are in other respects like empirical statements, does asserting them to be acts of God render them nonempirical?

If the other reasons for regarding them as nonempirical fall to the ground, it would seem to me most plausible to say something like the following: belief that "x" has occurred, in the ordinary historical sense of "occurred," is a necessary but not sufficient ground for regarding "x" as an act of God.

[17] See St. Thomas Aquinas, *The Summa Theologica*, translated by the fathers of the English Dominican Province (London: Washbourne, 1914), part III, no. 2, question 55, articles 5 and 6, especially pp. 411, 413–14.

[18] Macintyre, "Logical Status of Belief," p. 207.

Theology and Empirical Explanation

If we look at such a typical and crucial example of Christian language as "God loves mankind," we can see, says Macintyre, that Christians do not intend this empirically. It is not, for example, offered as an explanatory hypothesis to account for the sorts of things that happen to people.

A number of objections suggest themselves at once: (1) Christians do talk as if God's love for mankind explains some things that happen (John 3:16, Psalm 106, etc.); (2) at least a good many Christians have seemed to be concerned to refute evidences from experience which some have thought incompatible with the assertion; and (3) some people have apparently lost their Christian faith because they have thought it incompatible with the sorts of things that happen to people. In the face of such considerations, why does Macintyre wish to deny that "God loves mankind" is meant to be explanatory and thus connected "with the way the world goes"?

He rightly observes that, if such language is meant to be explanatory, it is to be tested in terms of the verification principle. That is, one must be able to specify some state of affairs which would tend to confirm or disconfirm the statement. However, according to Macintyre, Christians neither do, nor should, relate the statement "God loves mankind" to evidence in the way required for empirical statements.

If "God loves mankind" is meant empirically, it is a hypothetical statement. It is related to evidence in an "if . . . then" way. If the alleged explanation is true, then we should *not* expect situations or events of a given sort, and we *should* expect others. However, we can never know with certainty that a hypothetical explanation is true or untrue; for at no point in human experience is all the evidence available or counted. Therefore, if "God loves mankind" is meant empirically, it must be held tentatively; it must in principle be revisable in the light of possible further evidence. This consideration alone is sufficient to show that such an assertion is not meant empirically, for "such adherence (provisional and tentative) is completely uncharacteristic of religious belief." [19] "Part of the content of Christian belief is that a decisive adherence has to be given to God. So that to hold Christian belief as a hypothesis would be to render it no longer Christian belief." [20]

But let us suppose that the assertion in question is meant as a hypothesis, only that it could be so highly confirmed that, for all practical purposes, we should be entitled to regard it as demonstrated. This will not do either, says Macintyre, for it would "produce the kind of certitude that leaves no room for free decision." "If the existence of God were demonstrable, we should be . . . bereft of the possibility of making a free decision to love God." [21]

However, entirely apart from such considerations, we can see that such assertions are not meant empirically, because the believer will not permit any conceivable evidence to count against them. In other words, the believer rejects the application of the verification principle. No amount of evil and suffering leads, or should lead, him to say: "Well, I guess I was wrong in thinking that God loves us."

We all recognize, of course, that believers frequently resist or reject the "weighing of evidence" regarding God's goodness and love. What are we to conclude from this? Says Macintyre, we are to conclude that the believer in principle regards evidence as irrelevant. This interpretation is rendered more plausible if one holds, as Macintyre does, that, if evidence is to be admitted as relevant, it *obviously* counts *against* belief in a loving God. The problem raised by the verification principle

> for theistic assertions is not that they are unfalsifiable but that they are either unfalsifiable or false. Either the believer allows that the facts of evil count against his assertion, or he does not concede this. If he takes the latter course, his assertions are no longer in a meaningful sense assertions. If he takes the former course . . .

[19] Ibid., p. 181.
[20] Ibid.
[21] Ibid., p. 197.

what we have seen already (even if all of the evidence is not yet in) is enough to make theism either false or fantastic, if its evidences are of this kind.[22]

"Thus, if religious beliefs are explanatory hypotheses, there can be no justification whatever for continuing to hold them."[23]

By way of rebuttal I would note, first, that the hypothetical nature of explanatory schemes is quite compatible with the decisiveness of faith. We must insist, with Luther, Barth, and Tillich, that Christian faith is not to be confused with "assent of the intellect." The faith of the believer is not directed to the theoretical adequacy of his theological formulations, but to the "promises of God." Now, it might seem that, by making this distinction, we are playing Macintyre's game. "Aha! (we might imagine him saying) Then you do agree after all that the assertions of faith are not intellectual propositions but something else." Not at all. I am suggesting that we distinguish the life of faith, which we believe to be somehow a gift of God's grace, from what the theologian is trying to do when he makes statements about it. In short, we must not confuse the experience of faith with theology. If we decide to do theology (as distinct from worshipping), if we decide to make some statements *about* God, on the basis of what we believe to be our experience *of* God, then one kind of statement that would seem to be possible (and, indeed, abundantly actual in the history of theology) is an ordinary propositional affirmation regarding patterns of events which we believe to be implied in what we have experienced. What if we venture such a proposition, and it fares badly when confronted by evidence? This, I think, is the prospect that troubles our timid anti-empiricists. I shall discuss precisely this question a bit later. At this point I want simply to say that, should we formulate such a proposition and then be confronted by a considerable amount of adverse evidence, the next move, even for an impeccably pure empiricist, is not

[22] Ibid., p. 182.
[23] Ibid., p. 196.

117

necessarily obvious (e.g. reject the explanatory proposition as false). What is, of course, quite clear from an empiricist point of view is that some "next move" is called for — that we cannot just rest content with a discordancy between explanatory statement and experiential evidence.

Further, I should like to point out that holding a proposition tentatively is quite compatible with a decisive and continuing orientation of one's life in ways implied by the proposition. I can conceive of the falsification of "God loves mankind" but that does not mean that in fact I believe it to be false, nor that I may not reasonably act decisively on the presumption of its truth. I can conceive of the falsification of the proposition, "My wife is loving and faithful," but from that it does not follow that in fact I am doubtful of its truth. Here again we do well to note that all that is required by the verification principle is that we be able to *conceive* of some state of affairs that would tend to confirm or disconfirm the statement — not that we think that such a state of affairs is likely to turn up. The papa of modern empiricism, David Hume, taught that any given state of affairs *might conceivably*, for all we could demonstrate, be followed by any other, however contrary the two might seem to our thought. Some have held that, logically speaking, Hume should have been much more timid about sitting down in chairs than he actually was. Such wise men have misunderstood Hume in the same way that Macintyre misunderstands the implications of empiricism for theology: they have confused the logic of evidence with that of feeling, belief, and decision. Especially if it be true that Christian belief is not merely theoretical, but inevitably expressed in one's style of life, then belief and decision have an all-or-none character. On the other hand, evidence is very much a matter of degree.

Empiricists have been attacked because, it is sometimes said, they think of faith too much in terms of propositions — they are inclined to "reduce" the God-man relationship to something that can be described in factual statements. Ironically, however, such allegations usually depend, as they do in Macintyre's essay, upon making the very assumption of which the empiricists are accused — and, as it happens, falsely accused. For Macintyre's logic runs thus: if Christian assertions are propositions, and therefore tentative, then faith is tentative. Macintyre also offers an example of the obverse: if Christian assertions are propositional, and have been "demonstrated" to be true, then faith is necessary or coerced. Either or both of these arguments depend upon a confusion of faith with the propositions which a person may employ to express his faith.

But no such confusion is necessary to empiricism. In fact, to cite one prominent example, such an empiricist as H. N. Wieman never tired of distinguishing between faith, as a decisive act of commitment involving the total self, and the beliefs which may be associated with faith. Faith is an all-or-none business, in the sense that either one does or does not live in a certain relationship. Beliefs are our attempts to articulate what we think to be the situation, by virtue of which such an act is warranted. There is no logical contradiction at all between a decisive commitment — and an intellectual inability to back such a commitment with an incontestable warrant.

Conversely, even if we could demonstrate that God exists and that he loves us, this would not *necessitate* our loving him in return. As the Christian doctrine of sin might well suggest, it is not inconceivable that we might fear or dislike such a God, that we, like the devils mentioned in James 2:19, might "believe and tremble."

If I am right, tentativeness of belief is not inconsistent with a firm decision or practical faith. There must be some additional reason why Macintyre is opposed to the notion that religious statements such as "God loves mankind" are propositional and therefore hypothetical. It is not far to seek; for he holds that, if such a statement is offered as an empirical statement, it is *so obviously false* that we cannot understand how so many apparently intelligent people have maintained it. They must not intend it as an empirical statement, as an explanation of the way the world goes. We have already noted that Macintyre is driven to the same conclusion by the (alleged) fact that believers do not permit anything that happens to count against their belief that God loves mankind.

It would appear that Macintyre has a plausible position. But I believe he overshoots the mark, because he is thinking in terms of the way an empirical generalization is related to the evidence which tends to confirm or disconfirm it. If we construe "God loves mankind," however, as one component of a complex explanation scheme, his objections may perhaps be met. And, as I hope to show, such an explanation scheme involves an empirical sense of the statement under consideration.

It is of utmost importance to note something which Macintyre himself mentions but does not, I think, sufficiently bear in mind in the present context: namely, "We cannot say what, e.g. 'God loves us' means in isolation.[24] To understand what a religious man means by an utterance we must see it in the typical contexts in which he, the believer, uses it.

But we, and Macintyre, have been talking about the way in which Christian believers speak. Surely there is something odd in arguing that the facts of innocent suffering refute "God loves mankind" as that utterance is intended by one who firmly believes that the greatest revelation of the love in question is to be seen in the death of an innocent man on the Cross. It is gratuitous to assume that the believer, when he says "God loves mankind," has simply forgotten for the moment about such a monstrous event.

To be sure, the juxtaposition of the assertion with the evil event presents a problem — but Macintyre's solution is neither the only one, nor is it really a very convincing one. For his solution amounts to denying that the assertion "God loves mankind" is meant to explain the way things happen in the world. Rather, it is part of a comprehensive myth, which functions to shape one's total attitude toward life. It is hard for me to escape the judgment that this constitutes an irresponsible or irrelevant sort of wishful thinking, as if to say: we all know unfortunately that this is a cruel and evil world, that the way things actually happen in the real world is incom-

[24] Ibid., p. 174n.

patible with any notion that it is governed by a beneficent will, but, in spite of this, let us be guided in our basic attitudes and policies by the happy thought that "God loves mankind."

Macintyre's solution simply erases the problem. But there are other ways to attack it. I certainly cannot here even mention all the types of solution which have been suggested. My main point, however, is simply that the attempts at a "theodicy" makes sense if and only if the assertion of God's love is taken to imply certain states of affairs and not others. In other words, the so-called facts of evil constitute an intellectual problem only for the theist.

The nontheist, of course, faces "evil" as a practical problem; but only someone like the Christian finds here a theoretical problem; and he does so precisely because his assertion of God's love *does* imply something about the way the world goes — something which seems to be thrown into question by the facts of evil.

This whole discussion, however, should make us sensitive to the possibility that various assertions may be empirical in various ways. I talked earlier about straightforward, historical statements. Empiricism is concerned to examine the status of the evidence for believing in alleged facts. In connection with our discussion of "God loves mankind" we have seen that this cannot be construed as a simple description of a few facts. Rather it purports to indicate a pattern or structure, a relationship among many facts. It functions as a general explanatory hypothesis. Before turning to some final comments on the nature of empirical explanation, however, it may be well for me to state simply and positively the sense in which I would want to take "God loves mankind" as an empirical assertion to which factual evidence is relevant.

First, when the Christian makes such an assertion he has in mind certain positive experiences. These can be referred to summarily as experiences of "grace" — that is, some good is received which, one feels, is not merely the result of one's own effort or proportional to one's merit. He experiences, in connection with Christ, a new courage, a clearer sense of duty, an acceptance in spite of shortcomings, and the like. When seen in the total context of Christian doctrine, "God loves mankind" functions (in part) as a statement which accounts for, explains, the experiences one has had.

Further, I think we can see from the way in which theodicies (or individual apologetic arguments) develop that the facts of evil *are* seen as counting against one's faith. That is precisely why the effort has to be made to show that, when rightly and fully understood in the context of all the facts, they are compatible with faith.

Also, I see no reason why, in the case of "God loves mankind," we cannot satisfy the verification principle — that is, specify a state of affairs which, if it came about, would tend to falsify the statement. If the world were a place where the majority of people not only suffered cruel and undeserved evils but also never met these with courage or dignity or creative effort, if we never saw an instance of a man strengthened by adversity, if we never felt that "the risen Christ" referred to a renewing and redeeming power in our lives, and so on — then I for one feel that I *should* conclude that the evidence counts against the truth of the Christian faith. If, as a matter of fact, I continued, in spite of all, to cling to my faith, I should (whether or not I would) regard this as a fact of greater interest to the psychologist than to the philosopher or theologian.

I suggest, therefore, that some theological assertions — for example "God loves mankind" — are intended to serve an explanatory function. The logic of empirical explanation is often described in terms that seem simple and clear. When this is done, one seems to possess a fairly straightforward criterion by which to decide whether an apparently explanatory statement is in fact explanatory. I suspect that Macintyre is working with some such clear and simple concept of explanation in mind. The test is: whether it is possible to deduce from the (lawlike) statement some particular state of affairs which would occur, if the statement is true, and if the "initial and boundary conditions" are thus and so. As we have seen, Macintyre rejects the notion that "God loves mankind" is explanatory *because* one can deduce nothing specific from it — it "is compatible with the occurrence of any and every catastrophe to the human race."[25] To put it another way, a statement is explanatory only if it is possible to specify some state of affairs that would falsify it.

The difficulty is, however, that the criterion suggested in the above sounds a good deal more precise and rigorous than it actually is. It sounds as though an explanation is related to descriptions of deduced states of affairs in a very simple way: thus,

    1. Lawlike statement: Water freezes at or below 32°F
    2. Initial and boundary conditions: here at point "P" we have a beaker of water, and the atmosphere surrounding the beaker is 30°F.

    3. Deduction: therefore the water in the beaker at point "P" will freeze.

By analogy, we presumably get something like this:

    1. God loves mankind.
    2. John Jones is a human being, who is critically ill with bone cancer.

    3. Therefore, God will cure John Jones' bone cancer.

No one, so far as I know, would deny that the first example stands as a kind of paradigm of empirical explanation. The scientist would like to have things always just as straightforward as this. Problems and complexities begin to arise, however, when the scientist seeks for explanations in areas of experience where the patterns of connection are not well known in common-sense experience. To be useful, the concept of explanation must be capable of extension to alleged patterns of relationship which may or may not exist, to cases which are not decidable in such obvious fashion. In short, for a statement to be put forward or intended as explanatory, and therefore to be subject to the logical canons governing

[25] Ibid., p. 180.

explanation, by no means implies that we know in advance that it is explanatory.

In his well-known essay, "Verifiability,"[26] Friedrich Waismann discusses the relations which are often said to hold between a law and the statements of observation which supposedly *follow* from the law. He notes first that, since an unlimited number of consequences can be derived from a law (under endlessly various conditions), the ideal of complete verification is unattainable. One can at most say that, if a predicted consequence is observed, that tends to some degree to confirm the law. However, it has often been said that a single contrary observation serves to overthrow a law; that is, that while a law cannot be completely verified, it can in principle be completely falsified. From the law, together with a statement of the conditions, one predicts "x." But if "not-x" occurs (something logically incompatible with "x"), the law is presumably overthrown. But, as a matter of fact, this is "unrealistic." It does not correspond to the way in which scientists actually work with laws and observations.

Suppose that, according to Kepler's laws, an astonomer predicts that planet "P" will appear at point "Y" at time "t." At time "t" he points his telescope in the direction of point "Y" and observes, much to his disgust, that planet "P" does not appear right there but some considerable distance away. Does such an observation falsify Kepler's laws? Before reaching such a conclusion, one would have to consider a whole host of other possibilities and qualifications. One of the lenses in the telescope was perhaps not ground perfectly. Perhaps the stopwatch was inaccurate, or the astronomer did not push its button at precisely the right moment. On the other hand, perhaps some hitherto unnoticed heavenly body (or concentration of gases, or something unknown) has obtruded into the field.

Before deciding about the law (explanatory hypothesis) in question, one would have to reconsider many things; but, to put the matter simply, one would have to weigh against each other two main sorts of "evidence": (1) observational evi-

[26] Waismann, "Verifiability."

dence, including those things that turn up when you deliberately look for other factors that may not have been noticed at first; and (2) the entire system of scientific laws and theories into which Kepler's laws were thought to "fit." In short, the business of relating law to observations is "system dependent."

> Even then [when all known observational and theoretical possibilities have been canvassed] the refutation would not be valid finally and once for all: it may still turn out that some circumstance had escaped our notice which, when taken into account, would cast a different light upon the whole.[27]

> The mere fact that a single counter observation *s* can always be reconciled with a general law *L* by some accessory assumption shows that the true relation between a law and the experiential evidence for it is much more complicated and only superficially in accord with the customary account.[28]

In short, "the observational statement *s* does not follow from *L* alone, but from *L* plus a number of further premises which are often not expressly stated.[29] It would seem then that the situation is somewhat as follows: If we have an alleged law (or explanatory hypothesis) and from it, together with a statement of the conditions, we deduce "x"; and if we then observe "not-x"; we may conclude *either* that the law does not hold, *or* that some ancillary (and perhaps unstated) premise is unwarranted. (Or, we may note a further possibility, commented on by S. Toulmin: namely, that the law is valid only within a narrower range of conditions than we had hitherto suspected.[30])

This sort of qualification is, I think, essentially correct, but it is important to note a further complication. We are not

[27] Ibid., p. 132.
[28] Ibid., p. 133.
[29] Ibid.
[30] S. Toulmin, *The Philosophy of Science* (New York: Harper Torchbooks, 1960), p. 79.

able, even in the case of simple experiments, to state all of the premises operative in the statement of the law, or in the selection of the relevant features of the situation which we choose to note in our observation statements.

What is stated is only a *part* of the conditions, viz., those which, e.g., can be isolated in experimental technique and subjected to our will, or which can be readily surveyed, etc. The others merge into one indistinct mass: the vague supposition that "a normal situation subsists," that "no disturbing factors are present" . . . What is, in fact, conveyed by these words is only that, in case of a conflict between theory and observation, we shall *search* for disturbing factors whilst considering ourselves free to adhere to the theory.[31]

Very frequently explanatory statements or laws are system-dependent in another sense, in a sense which can be recognized when we consider not "causal explanation" but the more general sort in which a law is deduced from a still more general law. In such cases what counts *for* or *against* an explanatory law is not a finite set of observations but, as it were, the mutual support, or fit (or lack thereof) between several theoretical systems, considered along with observational evidence which may be rather indirectly related to the laws in question.

It is now possible to state how all of this bears upon alleged theological explanations, such as "God loves mankind." First, we must note that this is a very general statement, of a high level of abstraction. Just as there is no reason to suppose that from Einstein's theory alone one can deduce particular states of affairs, one should not expect to be able to go in one easy logical step from "God loves mankind" to a conclusion about what to expect in the case of John Jones' bone cancer. The connection with particular states of affairs is more remote and cannot be specified, apart from the specification of a great many other related things. In the case of the theological statements for example: the meaning and implications of "God loves mankind" would be system-dependent upon statements regarding the nature and (possible) limits of God's

[31] Waismann, "Verifiability," pp. 133–34.

126

power, some doctrine concerning His purposes, some specification of the nature and meaning of the term "love" when viewed christologically — to mention only a few of the central considerations.

Let me put my point as simply as possible. The Christian statement that "God loves mankind" has its meaning and use in a complex, total system. There is no simple way of verifying or falsifying that statement in isolation from the total system; nor is it possible to specify precisely at what point we can be sure that we have taken into account all of the relevant observational (experiential) data. Perhaps "God loves mankind," when compared with other doctrines of the total system, might seem to be the "weakest link" (weakest in terms of relative difficulty in squaring it with the data of experience); but at the same time, it might find considerable support from another direction — that is, it might be a logical corollary of certain other doctrines of the total system for which we have, or deem that we have, strong warrant.

Death by a Thousand Qualifications?

In the so-called "university discussion" of theology and falsification, Antony Flew characterized the peculiar danger of theological utterance. The theologian offers a statement which seems to be an empirical hypothesis. When confronted by problems, or by bits of evidence which seem to be contrary to the hypothesis, he qualifies it; and this process continues until the original force of the statement is dissipated. "A fine brash hypothesis may thus be killed by inches, the death by a thousand qualifications." [32]

Have I not, in my discussion of the nature of theological explanation, illustrated the truth of Flew's contention? It depends upon where you lay the stress. I for one would not deny that he has, indeed, pointed out one of the chief dangers for any theology which claims to be empirical. At the same time, I would want to recall the sorts of qualifications

[32] A. Flew, "Theology and Falsification," reprinted in *New Essays in Philosophical Theology*, ed. A. Flew and A. Macintyre (London: SCM Press, 1955), p. 97.

found necessary by F. Waismann in characterizing the relations between alleged laws of science and the data relevant to their confirmation or disconfirmation. Perhaps the danger which Flew points out is not peculiar to theology alone.

We must admit, however, that Flew's comment constitutes a challenge for empirical theology. Much work must be done to fill in the enormous gap between hypothesis (or purported explanation) and the data relevant to the evaluation of its truth or falsity. If empirical theology has a future, it will require the labors of a generation more sensitive than those of the past to the various theoretical levels of empirical discourse. It will no longer do to try to jump directly from concrete data to such high-level theoretical statements as "God loves mankind." Nor will it do to ignore the logical complexities which lie behind such a deceptively simple-sounding notion as "checking the hypothesis against the data." In particular, we need to distinguish the varying degrees of complexity attending the principle of verification when applied to simple factual statements, to empirical generalizations, and to hypotheses or explanatory schemes of varying scope.

In my opinion those who have begun to think of theological systems in terms of the "logic of models" are at least aware of the magnitude of the task, and of many of the issues which need careful analysis before we will be in a position to make a very significant judgment on the prospects for empirical theology.

4

Empiricism: Scientific and Religious

HUSTON SMITH (WITH SAMUEL TODES)

In the seventeenth century a missionary-monk named Ramon Lull built a primitive computer, a

> logic machine, in which the subjects and predicates of theological propositions were arranged in circles, squares, triangles, and other geometrical figures, so that by moving a lever, turning a crank, or causing a wheel to revolve, the propositions would arrange themselves in affirmation or negation, and thus prove themselves to be true.[1]

Father Lull was convinced that the Trinity and the Incarnation could be established by logic so clean cut that even a machine could manage it.

We smile at the distance that divides his age from ours. No one today presumes that logic can prove Christianity's decisive tenets. The question is whether, in matters religious, reason can prove anything. Some theologians would settle for a gentlemen's agreement to the effect that in matters religious reason not seek to *dis*prove.

What has happened to make the three hundred years that separate us from Father Lull seem like eons? The answer, of course, is modern science and the canons of knowledge it enthroned. These canons did not take shape instantaneously, but by the eighteenth century they were sufficiently formed to merit a title: scientific empiricism. Glossing over details, we can characterize it as a weave for four components: [2]

[1] *Catholic Encyclopaedia* 12:670. Quoted in E. L. Allen, *Christianity among the Religions* (Boston: Beacon Press, 1960), p. 15.
[2] This formulation and a number of points following have been in-

129

1. Self-validating observations: sense-data reports, expressions of feeling and of how things appear to the observer.
2. Analytic truths: nonfactual, true by virtue of their meanings alone, purely deductive relations; the truths of pure mathematics.
3. Inductions from observations, using logic, to statements about public, testable objects and states of affairs.
4. Statements about theoretical entities (such as electrons or photons) which are not observable. The status of these is arguable, but they are most safely regarded as names or summaries of, or shorthand or ideal postulates for, the real entities located by 1–3.

Hume and Kant were quick to perceive the consequences of this epistemic model for theology. With a clarity none has surpassed and few have equalled, they saw that it allows no compelling inferences from man or nature to God. No event, however strange or marvelous, requires reference to a divine cause to account for it. The term "God" and references to God's action — in creation, for example, or through providence — are vacuous as explanations of anything that happens in this world. Our concepts are restricted to our space-time world and must beat their wings in the void when they try to transcend it. For purposes of hard and reliable cognition, intuition, analogy, and unmediated experience carry little weight.

This view of epistemological finitude, especially Hume's formulation of it, expresses the scientific sense of belonging to this world with built-in limits to what we may validly believe. It meshed beautifully with the Reformation's distrust of natural theology, its resort to revelation and man's response in faith. Convinced by it, Schleiermacher sought to establish theology on an independent basis in the feeling of absolute dependence, Ritschl in judgments-of-value, Otto in the experience of the Holy, Tillich in Ultimate Concern. It drove

fluenced by an unpublished paper by Harmon R. Holcomb titled "Natural Theology: New Explorations in an Old Tomb."

Kierkegaard to stress the radical paradoxes of faith, and Barth to hew to a christocentric "word" with a determination scarcely precedented in theological history.

Still, something there is that doesn't love a wall, so there have been other religious voices less willing to settle for the reason/faith dichotomy. First among these were the latter-day natural theologians — men like Paley and Bishop Butler who, too early to be fully schooled in Hume and Kant, continued the medieval confidence that patterns in nature and history do evidence a godly creator. The second group, and here we move temporally into the twentieth century and spatially to the University of Chicago, has been led by Henry Nelson Wieman. Wieman does not use empiricism, working on the world as a whole, to prove it is God-created. Instead he uses empiricism to identify what within the world deserves to be regarded as God because it merits man's ultimate commitment. Where he has failed to carry the religious mind with him, we fear, is in his move from "X is the most worthy event in the natural world" to "X can, on a wide scale, evoke religious fervor." Wieman's position carries force for thinkers (a) who accept rational empiricism as the royal road to knowledge, and (b) who, having been nurtured in a religious tradition, feel their lives should be committed to *something*. The first sentence of one of Mr. Wieman's recently published items evidences his assumption that something within the empirical world merits religious commitment. In his contribution to the Hocking Festschrift, Wieman writes: "The religious philosophy of William Ernest Hocking is empirical in the sense that he finds in human experience *the* reality which calls for worship and religious commitment."[3] The revealing word in this sentence is the second article which Wieman enters as definite rather than indefinite — "*the* reality" rather than "a reality." How few are the persons who meet the conditions stated in both (a) and (b) above is evidenced by the smallness of the inroads of Wieman's theology into Christian

[3] "Empiricism in Religious Philosophy," in Leroy Rouner, ed., *Philosophy, Religion, and the Coming World Civilization,* p. 184. Italics added.

churches. The moral is: even if something is the best there is, this is not necessarily enough to evoke religious fervor.

This chronicle of religious empiricism is sketchy to the point of caricature, but we are concerned here only with its conclusion: Religious empiricism today is not very vigorous. We can respond to this fact in one of two ways. So much for religious empiricism, we may say, and close our books on the whole undertaking. The alternative is to see if there is not something enduringly valid in the enterprise which was aborted in the modern period through certain mismoves.

We choose the second alternative. Religious empiricism, we shall argue, has a future, but it needs to separate itself more clearly than it thus far has from scientific empiricism.

The basic mistake of religious empiricism in the modern period lay in its failure to perceive the degree to which the epistemic model "scientific empiricism" was shaped by scientific purposes. Failing to see this, religious empiricism accepted scientific empiricism as paradigmatic of knowledge generally, including religious knowledge. But since science is not religion, the model of knowledge tailored to science turned out to fit religion poorly.

Science is the attempt to gain rigorous knowledge of the objective world; which is to say, the world insofar as it elicits consensus. Since consensus — insofar as it pertains to the world and is not simply a report of how symbols can be manipulated in logic and mathematics — is most readily obtainable regarding the world's physical aspects (this being the part of the world that impresses all human observers in much the same way because their sensing apparatus is similar), scientific knowledge tends to be about man's physical, at some point visually perceivable, environment. Technology is the attempt to turn such knowledge to purposes of human control.

Science and technology are not life's whole; even if their aims were realized completely, vital human needs would remain unmet. So science and technology cannot save us. (They can in instances save scientists and engineers, a point which discloses the ambiguity between science as an endeavor and science as the yield of this endeavor, between science as process and science as product. This is an interesting point which, if pursued, would reinforce our thesis, but only by way of a detour too long for the present essay.) Science cannot save us because its objective data and theories can never shape into a *lebenswelt,* a lived world, which by its very nature must be shot through with purposes, hopes, and valuations that skew the objective findings of science in ways analogous to the way visual perspective skews the relationships in scientific space. Behind the lament "We know so little," there is often the assumption that if we had enough objective knowledge we would be well off. Not necessarily — better off, perhaps, but not necessarily well off. For objective knowledge is like a straight line which though extended indefinitely cannot curve to provide the encircling orientation our lives require and will in some way achieve, however malformed the circle.

Technology, for its part, cannot save us either, and here there are two reasons. (1) Happiness cannot be received; it must be achieved, won. This means: no matter how many benefits technology showers us with, these benefits cannot add up to happiness. Technology can relieve distress, providing food when we are hungry, antibiotics when we are ill. It cannot bestow happiness. (2) The second reason technology cannot save us is that man's power to control (which technology enlarges) calls for a balancing capacity to surrender (which the spirit of technology tends to cauterize). The more resolved we are to have things our own way, the less open we become to possible virtues in alternative ways. (Pages of illustrations, several from current American foreign policy.) Shorn of our capacity to surrender — to another in love, to obligations in acknowledging their claims on us, to life in general in basic trust — we let cynicism and nihilism take over. The basic reason Sartre concludes that "man is a useless passion"[4] is that he is free floating. Ungrounded, unattached, there is nothing beyond himself to which he can appropriately give himself. The most profound philosophical

[4] Jean-Paul Sartre, *Being and Nothingness* (New York: Philosophical Library, 1956), p. 615.

voice arguing the contrary today is that of the later Heidegger. We refer to his notions of "openness to Being," "waiting on Being," "releasement toward things," and "meditative as distinct from calculative thinking," as these appear (in one instance) in *Discourse on Thinking.*[5]

Since science and technology cannot save us, the endeavor to extract life's saving truths by means of an epistemic model forged to abet science's purposes is doomed, in advance, to fail.

A more direct way to put this point is to say that religion, to be alive, must *define* reality, not take its cues from a view arising out of some alternative human concern. For example, religion could remain wholeheartedly alive for Augustine because he built his notion of reality (and correlatively of objectivity) on a religious base: the objective is what harmonizes the soul, fulfills, and in this sense saves. By contrast, religion ends up for Hume dead because he takes his view of objectivity (reality) from the natural sciences. For him objectivity is the discovered and projected order of experience, and against the standards of "event," "truth," "actuality," and "reality" this view stipulates, the arguments of natural religion (miracles, first cause, design) fail. Hume then concludes that the only defensible religion is a form of faith utterly disjoined from reason, because (we add) unsupported by Hume's interpretation of reason. Hume was correct in his judgment of what natural religion could demonstrate within his view of reality; he was mistaken in believing a religion of irrational faith is the only religious alternative. Religions, like people, leave corpses when they die. The corpse of dead re-

[5] Martin Heidegger, *Discourse on Thinking* (New York: Harper & Row, 1966). We add in passing that philosophers seem not to realize fully the way the most unchallenged requirements of contemporary philosophy — the requirement of clarity — serves technology's ideal of control. The sharper the questions we put to life (nature, existence, what have you), the more we force its hand, the more we say in effect, "Don't tell us anything except what bears on what we choose to ask you. All else is irrelevant." We do not, it is true, control the answers that are returned to us, but we do control (and with every sharpening of our questions control more precisely) the kinds of answers we will accept as relevant.

ligion is a body of specific beliefs, practices, feelings, objects, and institutions which are considered to be in fact *true* (required, profound, inviolate, and authoritative) but are not considered definitive of *truth* (requirement, profoundity, inviolability, and authority). Such specific religious beliefs, attitudes, and so on, held and expressed in the context of some secular sense of reality, are spasmodic twitches of religious corpses. The real battle for the religious mind, the religious sense of reality, has been lost. The old religious expressions, couched in the new sense of reality, continue the old religion as little as the waving of Confederate flags for Goldwater in the 1964 election continued the Civil War.

The moral thus far is: religious empiricism will not work if it builds on an epistemic model devised to serve other than religious purposes. If knowledge is to be equated with scientific knowledge, it must withdraw from other areas of experience. What does this leave for art and religion? Emotion, perhaps? "Art," Hans Reichenbach tells us, "is emotive expression,"[6] and mysticism, per Bertrand Russell, "little more than a certain intensity and depth of feeling in regard to what is believed about the universe."[7] "Like hell!" we can expect artists and mystics to respond.[8] "Could anyone for a moment doubt that the artist, in his acts of apprehension, is making a statement with cognitive content?" asks Herbert Read.[9] Self-respecting mystics and prophets would ask the same.

Positivism restricted meaning to statements of scientific genre. Wittgenstein showed us that that is absurd; moral, aesthetic, and religious utterances can be meaningful even if not verifiable in any scientific sense. The question now concerns truth. *Meaning* having been shifted from verification to use, can *truth* be comparably liberated?

Here is the point in the discussion where one is tempted to

[6] *The Rise of Scientific Philosophy* (Berkeley: Univ. of California Press, 1956), p. 313.

[7] *Mysticism and Logic* (New York: W. W. Norton, 1929), p. 3.

[8] See, for example, Herbert Read, "The Limitations of a Scientific Philosophy," in *The Forms of Things Unknown* (Cleveland: Meridian Books, 1963), pp. 15–32.

[9] Ibid., p. 17.

give up and simply await another Wittgenstein. The achievements of modern science are so magnificent that they render the epistemic model that has produced them nearly sacrosanct. With heroic effort we might be able to imagine alternatives to the scientific route to truth, but to make a case for their deserving confidence — this seems too much to ask. Nevertheless . . .

Our plan from here on out has three parts. Beginning with a *via negativa*, we shall try to loosen the hold of scientific empiricism by showing that it does not deserve unquestioned epistemic allegiance. Thereafter we shall proceed to the more difficult task of suggesting the lines along which an alternative epistemology might proceed. Finally we shall indicate the places in this alternative epistemology where empiricism can be useful.

I

Scientific empiricism does not deserve to serve as knowing's paradigm.

A. Philosophers of science have been unable to give a satisfactory account of what it is. So great, indeed, are the difficulties they have encountered in their attempts to do so that if scientific empiricism is not falling apart, it is at least creaking at the joints. Quine has questioned its sharp distinction between analytic and synthetic truth, the distinction which formed the prongs of the fork on which Hume delivered theological texts to the flames. Even more suspect is the presumption that sense data present themselves innocently — simply as "given," and therefore self-certified and not open to question. With the collapse of this "dogma of the Given," the presumption that there exist clear criteria for specifying observables or staking out an "empirical language" has fallen as well; the props have been knocked from under it. Finally, the program has found itself incapable of giving a satisfactory account of theoretical terms designating nonobservables like "electron" or "neutron."

B. While philosophers of science have been trying to say

what scientific empiricism is (or should be), historians of science have been busy showing how little it has been the method by which science actually proceeds.[10] What an age takes to be the norms of knowledge — its sense of what shall count as "fact" or "true" or "explanatory" or "reliable inference" or "evidence" — is a function of many factors, not all directly derived from science. And when one epistemic model displaces another, some of the reasons are (again) extrascientific. For no noetic paradigm is simply an induction from "the facts." All tell the directions to look and what kinds of things shall be called "facts." To admit this is simply to be realistic about the way finite man manages his beliefs and stabilizes his tentative and fallible relation to his environment.

Michael Polanyi's *Personal Knowledge*[11] and T. S. Kuhn's *The Structure of Scientific Revolutions*[12] provide the most interesting documentations of this point. According to Kuhn, science is understood better as a historical enterprise than as a logic, and scientists better as a human community than as computers.[13] A universally recognized scientific achievement that provides model solutions (and problems) for a community of practitioners Kuhn calls a paradigm. Such a paradigm serves as "normative science" until seriously challenged. Paradigms are sturdy webs of commitments, some conceptual, others methodological, still others theoretical. Invariably included are quasi-metaphysical commitments which guide selection and evaluation. No such network of commitments is directly implied by the facts; all have their source in current metaphysics, other sciences, and accidents, both historical and personal. Thus a paradigm is not just a set of rules and

[10] Note, for example, a typical recent comment like the following: "The impulse to make psychology 'operational' by restricting theory construction to the formulation of generalizations about behavior has waned in proportion to the abandonment of operationalism in philosophical accounts of the older sciences" (J. A. Fodor, "Could There Be a Theory of Perception?" *Journal of Philosophy* 63 [1966]: 369).

[11] (Chicago: Univ. of Chicago Press, 1958).

[12] (Chicago: Univ. of Chicago Press, 1962).

[13] Harold Schilling, too, makes this point impressively in *Science and Religion: An Interpretation of Two Communities* (New York: Scribner's Sons, 1962).

theories. It is that from which rules and theories are abstracted.

There are, according to Kuhn, no neutral scientific languages; tests of important theories must proceed from within one or another paradigm. Disputes between paradigms cannot be settled by proofs. Decision resembles a conversion experience that vectors the whole fact-theory network.

C. Empiricism tries to hew to the facts. But facts have turned out to be so implicated with theories that it is difficult (if not impossible) to isolate them to the point where they can stand judgment on theories. This point has been touched on in both preceding ones, but it deserves separate and more extended statement.

Instead of flowing in one-way traffic from observations toward theory, meaning flows both ways. The theory-fact dichotomy is not sharp-edged. Developed sciences contain no clear criteria by which the meaning of observations can be wholly separated from the meaning of theories embodying nonobservables. That facts are theory laden is no new discovery, but we are coming to see with ever greater clarity (a) the ways in which powerful conceptual systems alter in the natural sciences problems of meaning, truth, and justification, and (b) how crude — destructive even — would be the results if we tried to apply general canons of induction and deduction untailored to the contours of the system in question.

Enough of what we want to say hangs on this point to warrant rolling up a couple of big guns to support it. Rudolf Carnap argues that it is possible to talk sense about the world only from the vantage point of a framework: no sentence is true of the world apart from its framework's matrix. It follows that one must distinguish questions that arise within a framework from those that arise about a framework. Considerations relevant to the latter are noncognitive. Whether we find one framework more suitable to our purposes is a pragmatic question. The "true" framework is a fiction.

Willard Quine makes much the same point by way of language. "Studies of the semantics of reference . . . make sense only when directed upon . . . our language, from within. . . . Unless pretty firmly and directly conditioned to sensory stimulation, a sentence S is meaningless except relative to its own theory; meaningless inter-theoretically."[14] Sentences thus "firmly and directly" tied to sensory irritations, ones that can be converted without loss into statements about nerve-hits, overt behavior, ostensive definition, and the like, "are sparse and . . . woefully under-determine the . . . hypotheses in which the translation of all further sentences depends" (p. 72). As a consequence, conceptual schemes differ in ways that can seldom be empirically adjudicated and force choices of surprising latitude. All this holds for scientific theories as well as for others; "true" can be applied sensibly only "to a sentence couched in the terms of a given theory and seen from within the theory complete with its posited reality" (p. 24). Even in the ideal long run "countless alternative theories would be tied for first place" (p. 23), giving different accounts of the world each within the terms of its ontic theory. Still, "to call a posit a posit is not to patronize it, [for] everything to which we concede existence is a posit from the standpoint of the theory-building process, and simultaneously real from the standpoint of the theory that is being built" (p. 22).

We are not interested here in Carnap and Quine as individual philosophers; we cite them as representative contemporary philosophers of science and language. Turning from them as individuals to contemporary epistemology generally, we summarize its prevailing themes that bear upon our problem as the following:

1. Human beings are historically conditioned creatures in a staggeringly complex and fast-changing world.

2. To cope with such change and complexity, quite clearly articulated conceptual frameworks are required.

3. These conceptual frameworks sit with considerable looseness on what-there-is.

[14] *Word and Object* (Cambridge: M.I.T. Press, 1960), pp. ix, 24. All page references in this paragraph are to this book.

4. There is no criterion for detecting which types of expressions are authentically referring ones and which are not.

5. Statements can be said to be "true of . . ." only within the context of a given theory or system.

6. There is no general criterion of reality, truth, or meaningfulness by which some kinds of language can be considered meaningful while others are denied this status.

7. In knowing, something must always be posited. It is never possible to prove everything that theories need.

8. The number of legitimate frameworks is multiple; they cannot be reduced to one.[15]

Up to this point we have sought to effect a disengagement. Since facts are controlled by theories and theories by their purposes, we have argued that religious empiricism can come to little as long as it tries to build with materials and methods devised primarily for other purposes, notably those of science. Should anyone wonder whether such disengagement is needed, we appeal to two quotations. On the question of whether science-oriented empiricism is utilized in religious philosophy, John Passmore writes:

> "Positivism is dead," so they say. Rightly, too, [save] where it touches religion.[16]

The second quotation summarizes the consequences for religion of this presence:

> The empiricist's model is . . . not the neutral model . . . which it pretends to be. It is atheistic in the sturdy, old-fashioned, belligerent sense of the word, for it prohibits *any* cognitive employment of theological language. In effect, it rules that "God" must name either a finite, manipulatable entity or be an empty term.[17]

In the interests of disengagement we have argued that religious empiricism need feel no responsibility toward scientific

[15] We acknowledge again the influence of Harmon Holcomb's paper, "Natural Theology," on the section of our statement just completed.

[16] "Review Article: Christianity and Positivism," *Australasian Journal of Philosophy* 35 (1957): 125.

[17] Harmon Holcomb, "Natural Theology."

empiricism, the moral at this point being capsuled in the old rabbinic saying: "If you can't believe in God, the next best thing is at least not to believe in idols."

Released from scientific empiricism, religious empiricism must proceed to develop its own logic with attendant canons of reality, which logic must fit its distinctive purposes.

What are these purposes? We have no alternative but to go right back to the beginning, to cut back to the ground. This requires that what follows be general and in some sense simple because (we hope) fundamental. It seeks to indicate in broad strokes the direction for a religious epistemology within which religious empiricism can be effective.

II

Knowing arises from doing; knowledge is a consequence of action. The world does not form for us as a result of our gazing at it passively. It takes shape in the course of actions we undertake within it. Chickens hobbled from birth do not see space as including the dimension of depth. They must move into space — stumble and fall — before depth comes into existence for them. We see because first we look; we hear because first we listen. Our entire sensory equipment, on which all our knowledge has been founded, has been produced by our particular kinds of interaction with our environment.

Knowing, then, results from doing. And doing, in turn, is propelled by needs. Latent, amorphous, and partially indeterminate, these needs come as close to defining a human being as anything in his original makeup.

The problem facing everyman is the problem of casting his life in a form which will satisfy his needs. Traditionally Christianity assumed that such satisfaction would result when a life discovered God's purpose for it, which purpose man could find by searching. With the "death of God" (read eclipse of God) this assumption has faded. The alternative proposed by the existentialists is that insofar as life acquires meaning this meaning must be created from scratch, *de novo* and *ex nihilo*. This view overestimates man's freedom. If a man assumes that all logically possible life-styles are equally available to him in the sense that any one he chooses stands an equal chance of fulfilling him, he will be brought up short. Individuals are not that protean.

Between the possibilities of finding life's meaning, on the one hand, and creating it, on the other, stands the possibility of founding it in a way analogous to the way our founding fathers founded our nation. They did not find the United States, nor did they create it. By bringing latent and partially indeterminate materials to viable resolution, they founded it. Something analogous is required of every life.

Much of life's problem arises from the fact that we do not know at the outset what our needs are. This may not be entirely a matter of ignorance; in their early stages needs may be amorphous and our inability to discern them clearly due to the fact that at this stage they have little form to be discerned. They do, however, give off clues to their nature in the form of wants. We have a better idea of what we want than of what we need. When we get what we want and that getting satisfies us, we see that what we wanted was also what we needed. In reverse cases we thought that what we wanted was what we needed but see in retrospect that we were mistaken.

The import of this relation of wants to needs for life's founding is that it requires venturing; it requires ploys. One casts one's life into a form suggested by one's wants. If the consequences satisfy, one's form of life is consonant with one's needs, otherwise not. In such proof of the pudding through its eating we discover retrospectively what our needs were by experiencing how they do or do not work their way to satisfying resolution through the form our lives have assumed.

Though it is impossible to know in advance what an individual's precise profile of needs is, we know (from the fact that he is a human being) that they are of two kinds, practical and passional. He must eat, and he will feel. He needs to eat reasonably well and to feel reasonably well.

Among man's passional needs are his need for (a) a sense of home (not just a house), (b) a sense of vocation (not just a job), and (c) intimations of a "more" (not just quantitative but qualitative) beyond what he currently apprehends. Both secular and religious men agree in acknowledging these needs; they differ in the extent to which they think they can be satisfied. Religious man thinks it possible (a) to bring life to the point where it can be at home in the world at large, not just in some intimate enclave within it, (b) to live in a way wherein one's entire life, not just one's job, is sensed as vocation, and (c) to experience life *sub specie aeternitatis*, irradiated by intimations of a nonobvious dimension of existence that intersects each moment with power to transfigure it. Secular man at his most profound says to religious man: I resonate to your hopes, but I don't think you will make it. It is in this spirit that we should read Wittgenstein's last public statement: "This running against the walls of our cage is perfectly, absolutely hopeless. . . . But it is . . . a tendency in the human mind which I personally cannot help respecting deeply and I would not for my life ridicule it." [18]

Being human, man has a mind, which mind can help fulfill both his practical and his passional needs. On the practical side thought enables man to build better bear traps. On the passional side it enables him to devise imaginal forms — symbols, images: bear songs, bear dances, totemism — that deepen and resolve how he feels about bears. The mind working to assist man with his practical needs is technology. Assisting him with his passional needs it is philosophy, art, and religion.

The average man is no more capable of forming his imagination in ways that resolve his feelings nobly than he is capable of being his own scientist. Both tasks require genius. Geniuses in the art of shaping man's imaginings are artists, philosophers, prophets, and seers. Over time their creations coalesce and distill into cultures. As the religious forms of traditional Judaism and Christianity are losing their power to inform the contemporary mind, the West desperately needs religious geniuses who can create new imaginal forms, convincing to the contemporary mind, which consummate man's needs for home, vocation, and transcendence.

[18] "A Lecture of Ethics," *Philosophical Review* 74 (1965): 12.

III

Against this sketch of the human condition and the place of knowing and religion within it, we are prepared to ask: what is the appropriate function of religious empiricism?[19]

A. It can be alert to evidence bearing on whether the sketch of human condition, just given, is true. In particular, it can ask whether man has the religious needs we indicated.

The fact that archaeologists and anthropologists have discovered no societies without religion suggests that he does. Or should we say did, inasmuch as sociologists are divided on whether religion is importantly present in contemporary megalopoli? This is an important question. Before we conclude that the advance of secularization shows man's religious impulse to have been transitional we should remember that Japan's position as the most literate and technologically developed nation in Asia has not obviated the need for over five hundred new religions since World War II. Science and secularization are doing puzzling things to man's religiousness in our time, especially that of the young, but we are not convinced that they are dispelling it. On the one hand college students are making a left end-run around the prophetic (this-worldly) wing of the church to tackle directly such issues as Vietnam, racial injustice, and the problems of poverty. More recently they have been making a right end-run around the priestly (other-worldly) wing of the church to link up with Zen, Tibet, parapsychology, Sokagakai chanting sects, Maharishi meditation societies, and pharmacological mysticism via the psychedelics. Theological supernaturalism is being replaced by psychological supernaturalism defined as belief in the existence of saving truths accessible only through trans-normal states of consciousness. Empirical inquiry can help us

[19] As conceived in this essay, religious empiricism differs from empirical theology. Empirical theology works with facts as these are shaped by its theory. Paralleling the fact-theory correlation manifest in the developed sciences, empirical theology moves primarily within a given theological circle. Religious empiricism works with facts on a looser, more common-sense level. It asks what there is in man's common understanding that can bear on religious understanding and belief.

to see whether man is by nature or only transitionally *homo religiosus.*

B. Beyond this, empirical inquiry can help us to ascertain whether there are certain forms which man's imaginings must exemplify if they are to resolve satisfactorily his religious reachings. In this, its second opportunity, religious empiricism becomes religious phenomenology. The founder of modern phenomenology, Edmund Husserl, derived from Frege the distinction between ideas (which are momentary, unrecurring, and privately apprehended psychological events) and meanings (which are enduring, publicly apprehensible, nontemporal entities, and — the point he stressed — active in organizing man's experience). An infant's visual field may be dominated by a house; it remains nondescript until the meaning "house," along with others like "lawn" and "trees" and "sky," enter to structure it and make it meaningful. Husserl shared with gestalt psychologists a fascination with the way meanings work to order human experience and make it intelligible. Religious phenomenology asks whether there are religious meanings (in the Husserlian sense) that order and give form to man's religious experience.

A finding from the new science of linguistics can help to indicate the religious phenomenologist's objective. Linguists have discovered a striking fact about language. All natural human languages share a common depth grammar, which grammar is arbitrary in the sense that alternative depth grammars, no more complicated, are possible. The surprising point is that the human mind appears to be incapable of learning languages constructed on depth grammars other than the single one which human languages exemplify, this despite the fact (just noted) that these alternative grammars are logically no more complicated. This finding has led Noam Chomsky and others to conclude that in the course of its evolutionary development man's mind has been "programmed" to learn a single depth grammar. Has it been comparably programmed to organize its religious intuitions in definite patterns that recur in all religions, all cultures? This is the chief question for religious phenomenology, equally designatable as religious empiricism in one of its plausible undertakings.

C. A third opportunity for religious empiricism is to furnish materials the religious imagination can shape into religious hypotheses.

If we expect facts to tell us what to do or what to believe, we are naïve. Even in science, as Norwood Hanson points out, no inductive move can carry one from discrete data to explanatory hypotheses. Hypothesis recognition is like pattern recognition: data neither require nor control it. Similarly, no amount of objective data gleaned from science and common sense shapes itself into religious hypotheses, religious visions. But objective data can be so shaped. An example is Teilhard de Chardin's *The Phenomenon of Man.* When the distinguished British biologist P. B. Medawar challenged Teilhard's claim that he had written a scientific book, Medawar was right. It is not a scientific book, it is a theological (and philosophical) one. But the fact that it is built of scientific materials is not incidental to the fact that a reader as intelligent as Lillian Smith found it the most important book in her later life. Empiricism can discover suggestive facts for the religious imagination to work with. It may even be the case that in this scientific age the religious hypotheses that stand the best chance of mustering the convictions of contemporary men will be ones that make striking use of scientific findings.

Religious empiricism can be useful, but after it has done its most it must wait upon insights and disclosures that are revelatory. It can be a noble partner but not sole master. For as in science observations are idle without theories that infuse them with meaning, so in theology observations indicate nothing by themselves. They must be shaped by the religious imagination in ways that cannot, in full, be empirically delivered.

PART 2
Some Theological Problems
Empirically Considered

5

Empirical Theology within Process Thought
BERNARD M. LOOMER

Empirical theology has emerged in Western thought as a response to forces that have created the modern world and the modern mind. It could not have arisen at an earlier period. Science in both its theoretical and its applied senses has been the dominant factor in the development of the modern Western mind and its world. Its methods, its attitudes, its understandings, and its technological results have revolutionized the world and re-created the mind of man. Its influence is ubiquitous. There is no place to which we can flee in order to escape its theoretical and applied consequences. Science may not be the final determiner of truth, but most if not all modern philosophy has been shaped directly or indirectly, and to a greater or lesser degree, by science.

The major intellectual discoveries of recent centuries, represented by such men as Copernicus, Darwin, Marx, Freud, and Einstein, have had double-edged repercussions. On the one hand, they have reduced the importance and status of man in his own eyes. They have brought in their wake a startling and humiliating self-knowledge to man. His limitations have been revealed and his pretensions exposed. This knowledge has been perceived as a threat, for even the religiosity of Western man has been transformed. On the other hand, the forced reconception of the universe and his place in it, along with his painfully acquired self-knowledge, has had significant consequences for man's understanding of his relations to his fellows. These intellectual discoveries have broken down the justifications for the barriers and distances, such as classes and castes, that man has erected between himself and his fellow human beings.

In short, these seminal ideas have disclosed both sobering realities and creative possibilities beyond the imagination of premodern man. Greater heights and depths, more awesome wonders and deeper mysteries lie before contemporary man. He is simultaneously impressed with his control over nature and the final unmanageability of both nature and history. The self-knowledge by which he is threatened is also the means for his freer access to his fellows and theirs to him. The secularizing of his world and of himself is one of the grounds for his finer and more concrete humanization.

I

The modern mind has been in the making for several centuries, dating back to the beginning of modern science. The modern mind, which differs from all other historical and animal forms of mind, may be superseded in succeeding centuries by other forms of mind. We cannot conceive of these future minds, of course, since we are bound by the structures of our language and the limitations of our historical epoch. But we can imagine that they may differ from our own by at least that emergent gap of discontinuity by which we differ from our historical forefathers. The various forms of mind achieved in natural and human history may involve a type of progress or qualitative advancement. The higher may be grounded on the lower, and the higher may always carry within itself something of the lower, however transformed the lower may be. But there is loss in every gain. Since every form of mind is itself a selective functioning, relative to its contextual world, every historical form of mind illustrates a loss of emphasis and sensitivity exemplified by earlier forms.

The conclusion of this may be that there is no normative form of mind. Certainly the modern mind, however it is described, is normative only to itself. Obviously this applies to all previous types of understanding. The several forms and dimensions of meaning (which is a relationship) and understanding are natural and historical achievements. The hermeneutical problem arises in religion and theology most obviously because the great religions originated and developed in the context of the ancient mind and world.

The following brief characterization of the modern mind is probably parochial (in terms of the Western mind). It is obviously restrictive, since I do not deal with the industrial, economic, political, aesthetic, and cultural facets of the modern world and the modern mind. It is certainly somewhat selective in its emphasis. It is too intellectualistic for more general analytic purposes.

1. The whole movement of modern thought and experience has been in the direction of the fundamental thesis that this world is the locus of meaning and value. The world of the transcendental has been relinquished. It has lost its explanatory power and salvatory appeal, even if it remains as a somewhat residual or even vestigial point of reference for our emotional and spiritual needs as these are classically understood. This is surely one of the dimensions of the secularization of life. We are not pilgrims simply passing through a vale of tears and testing en route to our eternal destination. The earth and all that dwells therein is our home. We aspire to the stars; and yet even in our aspirations, we are creatures of the earth. As recent "clock" experiments have indicated, we are earth-bound or earth-oriented to an incredible degree. The most elemental and fundamental orientations of all organisms are dependent on the relative motions of the relevant masses of our universe.

All this has been perceived as a tremendous reduction of dimensions and resources, at least at first. But further reflection discloses that all the heights and depths, the originating causes and final ends, the realities symbolized by the principalities and powers (including the demons and angels) that were formerly thought to inhabit the lower and upper worlds, are now found within the many mansions of this world. This is so for some, at least, even when the inevitable implication is drawn that God must be identified, in whole or in part, with this world.

2. This shift of focus to the transcendent qualities of the immanental relationships of this world has been accompanied

by a strongly empirical bent of mind. Reason is the servant of concrete facts. Whether we speak as scientists, or Marxists, or existentialists, or psychoanalysts, or pragmatists, or radical empiricists, or as devotees of process forms of thought, or as linguistic analyst, there is a common methodological refrain running through the thematic variations. This refrain is the general empirical principle that the world of meaning and value, and the world of the knowable, are the world of the experienceable, however this latter term may be defined. If the term is used with sufficiently personalistic denotations even philosophic idealism, at least in part, could be gathered under the umbrella of this empirical axiom. Usually "experience" is much more restricted extensionally. In any event, most of us perceive ourselves as living in the warp and woof of natural, historical, and personal causality. These are distinguishable but not isolable or autonomous forms of causality. Each type contains efficient and deterministic aspects. Each type exemplifies elements of indeterminacy with respect to prediction, and each may illustrate qualities of spontaneity or even originative qualities of emergent novelty.

3. Perhaps the single most fertile concept in modern intellectual history is the notion of relativity. In its scientific meaning it implies that the objective determination of an object is dependent upon the standpoint of an observer. That is, objectivity as a nonrelational concept must be relinquished. The ideal of simple objectivity illustrates Whitehead's "fallacy of simple location." This predicament has given rise to the epistemological theory of "objective relativism" which is a relativistic form of realism. The repercussions of this principle were carried over into the discipline of value theory, as I have observed, in Wieman's axiological studies.

The philosophical generalization of this principle involves the negation of substantive theories of reality, including the nature of the self. Conceptions of independent, self-existing, underlying identities or substances, whether these be bodies, atoms, minds, souls, or selves, are replaced by the understanding of units of reality as interdependent. "It belongs to the nature of a 'being' that it is a potential for every 'becoming.'

This is the 'principle of relativity'" (Whitehead). The further extension of this principle suggests that the reference to what a thing is in itself is a way of indicating an object's process of subjectivity. But a thing's subjectivity is not a state which it possesses apart from its constitutive relations. It is not an instance of transcendental solitude. What a thing is in itself is what it is for itself. To put the point in terms of existentialist language, the being of a thing for others is a reflection or a perspective of its being for itself, just as its being for itself is an emergent from its causative or constituent relations derived from others.

We have seen in our day the rise and development of another extension of the physical principle of relativity, namely the concept of historical relativity. This notion catches up into its complex meaning insights derived from a great variety of social sciences, including the sociology and psychology of knowledge, and anthropological studies pertaining to the development of mind and the origination of the self. It has drawn heavily from the historical disciplines, especially from the methodological principle or approach which we may call historical understanding. This is a comparatively novel form of understanding to which historic theological liberalism made such a decisive contribution through its biblical and historical studies. It was a discovery the full implications of which we have only slowly perceived and appropriated.

In terms of this mode of understanding we realize, in H. R. Niebuhr's neo-Kantian language, that not only are we in time and space, but time and space are within us. Our theories and judgments about external realities may tell us more about ourselves than about the objects into which we inquire. Not only our knowledge but our very being is contextual in character. But not only *our* being. The being and nature of all past historical (and natural) realities were contextual in form. Their justification for being what they were was contextual. But contexts change and develop, and specific justifications become outmoded. All ideas, principles, forms of mind, types of understanding, institutions, and activities have historical origins, and they are in principle datable. We are creatures but not

captives of our past. I regard this as a fundamental hermeneutical principle of theological inquiry.

When this approach is conjoined with a generalized evolutionary outlook (as it was, historically; in fact, historical relativity and evolutionary thought may be understood as being
two manifestations of the same basic impulse), we conclude
that everything that can be said to be in any concrete sense
has evolved. Relativity and evolution are to be understood as
universal principles. The degree to which one is unable or unwilling to acknowledge exceptions to the universality of these
principles is a measure of the extent of his departure from
the classical tradition.

In keeping with this understanding of evolved and relative
contexts, in which not only truth but also reality are perceived
as perspectival, many or most if not all the classical absolutes
are given up. The idea of an absolute beyond all relativities is
itself a historically originated notion. Like the notion of perfection, it is a relative meaning. It need not necessarily be an
expression of a primordial rationality or logos, nor need it be
necessarily a demand correlative to an original restiveness of
the human spirit. All forms of the human spirit and of human
spirituality have evolved. The logics of rationality, of motivation, and of religious aspiration are historical achievements.
These forms and these logics may exemplify the contextual
limitations of their origins and historical evolvements.

The modern mood is not a preoccupation with a nonrelative best. It is a concern for a relative best. Or, rather, it is an
involvement with the better in contrast with the worse. It is a
meliorism rather than a perfectionism. I suggest that the classical devotion to nonrelative absolutes has been replaced, in-
tellectually and operationally, with a modern involvement in
mutual religious, political, and cultural relativities. The rise
of new centers of military strength and political power has
been accompanied by some redistribution of intellectual
strength and a pluralistic denial of religious imperialism. And
through it all are the hungry millions whose degree of self-
transcendence takes the form of a desire for a "better" that lies
beyond their impoverishing state. I suggest that for us the

search for the content of meaning of a hypothetical or valid nonrelative absolute should take the form of living and thinking in terms of a religious relativity that attempts to take into itself all other significant and creative relativities. At the level of history, we have no transformation equations by which the world as seen from one perspective can be transposed into views of the world as seen from other perspectives.

4. Along with the theory of relativity, the principle of the ultimacy of becoming defines and distinguishes the modern mind from previous types of mentality. The idea that events or patterned forms of energy are the basic realities of our world, that creativity is the category of categories, is not simply an illustration of how a philosophic principle may be derived by a generalization from scientific theories, although it is that also. It is a symbol of the conviction that becomingness adds an incremental gain to the content of reality, in contrast to the classical assumption that the realm of becoming is a derogation from some preeminent reality. The perspective that suggests that being is a becoming, that rest is a dimension of motion, and that the unchanging is an abstraction from change, points to the seriousness of existential decision and to man's creative urge to transcend previous limitations. It is an exemplification of modern man's awareness that he faces problems no age has encountered before, that he has no reference handbooks, and that his approach must be experimental. It is an acknowledgment of the surmise that not only life, but reality itself, may be an adventure.

The stress upon the primacy and ultimacy of becoming is not confined to advocates of process modes of thought. The heavy emphasis on temporality and history in existentialist perspectives is a parallel line of development. With some qualifications, we could conceive of process philosophy and existentialism as two variations on the common theme of temporal process. Process philosophy has been shaped in close relation to the natural and social sciences, and existentialism has been more fully identified with the humanities.

The historical disciplines, with their concern with time, change, development, and context constitute another manifestation of the same impulse. The modern replacement or even the rejection of metaphysics by history has been occasioned for some people because of their understanding of metaphysics as being basically preoccupied with the static or unchanging dimension. In this respect, process philosophy might be considered to be an historical metaphysics or a metaphysics of history.

5. The development of the social or relational view of the self is due to the convergence of insights from many sources and disciplines. It does not simply reflect the ascendancy of the Democratic party, although the Republican party does still operate with what is essentially a substantialist view of the self. Perhaps even Dickens' Scrooge was one kind of concretization of Adam Smith's theory of economic life.

The theory of the social nature of the self means more than the idea that the individual is fulfilled through his participation in the lives of others (Tillich). It means that the self is constituted by others, that the self is an emergent from its relations, whether this is understood in the manner of Mead or Whitehead.

The unity of the self is an achievement, not a presupposition. It is an emergent quantum arising out of the synthesizing of a given plurality. The difference between unity as a creative achievement and unity as a given separates the contemporary from the premodern mind. In modern thought concrete unity has a present-future rather than a past sense of direction. The logic is that of decision rather than assumption. In some types of empirical thought the concrete unity of the world, of reality itself, is a quality to be achieved, not a quality that is given. For some thinkers even the notion of the conceptual unity of the world, the abstract unity of order, should be entertained with misgivings.

6. For the modern mind the conjoining of the principles of relativity, becoming, and sociality leads with some inevitableness to the disturbing idea of the episodal or momentary or discontinuous character of the concrete self. What endure are complex personal societies with similarities of defining characteristics. Subjectivity is a fluctuating or pulsating affair, and

the objective preservation of values is the accumulated pre-
hensions of successive occasions of achievement. Once the notion of enduring substantial individuals is given up, who is to
participate in and to enjoy an eschatological kingdom?

7. Reinhold Neibuhr may be correct in speaking of the optimism of modern Western man. Modern man, says Niebuhr,
disbelieves in original sin, is persuaded of his own goodness,
and holds to the conviction that evil can be progressively
overcome in history. For these reasons modern man is curiously unteachable; his theories are always being confounded
by his experience. Man's greatest problem is himself.

I suggest, however, that there is another side to this coin.
Roughly speaking there have been two dominant theories concerning the fact of evil, related but distinguishable. The first
is theological. It states that evil is to be understood somehow
as a manifestation of the wisdom and power of a sovereign
God. Evil is preordained. The second derives from a philosophical idealism. It contends that what appears to be evil
to our limited vision may yet have its proper place in the larger
scheme of things. This larger vision is beyond our grasp, just
as the inscrutable purposes of almighty God constitute an
abiding mystery to mortal man. We can only bow our hearts
and minds in the face of God's unknowable intentions. The
Lord giveth, and the Lord taketh away. Blessed be the name
of the Lord.

Now all this may be the final truth about things. But modern man is not metaphysically or theologically oriented (in
the classic sense). He is more empirical, pragmatic, and historical in mood. He is less concerned with what may be ontologically given and more interested in what can be transformed. He may be somewhat blind to the destructive aspects
of his devotion to the idea that knowledge is power. He may
not be as realistic and mature as he ought to be with reference
to that ancient wisdom which urges us to distinguish between
those conditions which can and those which cannot be
changed. He is probably guilty of all this and more.

But modern man increasingly is not "buying" these two
traditional accounts of evil. At least he does not seem to live in

the spirit of their meaning. He is more impressed with the historical rootage and man-made quality of evil. Impoverishing conditions that once were thought to be unalterable have in fact yielded to creative labors. At least part of the justification for the rise of existentialism lies in the conviction that man by means of his decisions and actions can create himself and his world; hence the "philosophy of the act," which is a kind of behavioristic and socialized form of existentialism. For some, life is finally meaningless because this is an absurd world. And it is ultimately absurd because these people believe there is no God that answers to man's self-transcending outreach. But not all the misery, brokenness, emptiness, and despair of men derive from a metaphysical absurdity. Some of it is practical in origin. Some is traceable to chance and fortune. Besides, for all that modern man knows, God may be the great experimenter, as Hume coyly suggested.

Because of his sinfulness man may suffer an ironic defeat, as Niebuhr contends. And every advance in goodness brings with it the possibilities of greater evil, as Niebuhr has also profoundly observed. Yet modern man would rather run the risk of total destruction and perhaps achieve a common humanity than acquiesce to privileges, injustices, castes, classes, orders, and degradations that were prematurely declared to be ordained.

8. As Pauck and Tillich, among others, have taught us, ever since Luther the modern man of faith has been forced to live with the fact that doubt is an essential ingredient in his stance of faithful trust. He is aware that most if not all the classical intellectual certainties have been shaken. He knows that history cannot be rationalized. He has come to see that there is no transcendent court of appeals in which the claims of various religious alternatives can be adjudicated. He sees Jews with their Law living in ways that supposedly are possible only to Christians with their experience of grace through Jesus Christ. He knows of the theoretical distinctions between God and our ideas of God, and between God's purposes and our cultural values. But we live by meanings and ideas, and there is no religion without culture. These distinctions are dif-

ficult to exemplify in concrete life. He hears of one God, but he perceives that monotheistic trust and commitment is a rare achievement or grace, behaviorally speaking. He senses the contradictions in society and in his own life, the ambiguity of motives and goodness, his own sinfulness. He is attentive to the wisdom that God may speak a profound "no" to his hopes, aspirations, and ideals. He is sceptical about the deliverability of the promise of resources contained within the Beatitudes. He wrestles with the abiding tension between the unshakableness which is of the essence of faith and the uncertainty of doubt, the tentativeness of belief, and the defeats of personal and communal pilgrimage. Yet this tension is the character of his concrete humanity.

II

By "empirical theology" I have reference to a theological effort to interpret Christian faith with the aid of resources to be found within the philosophic outlook variously described as process thought, rational empiricism, radical empiricism, or pragmatism. These labels are indicative of various kinds of emphases, but in general this characterization refers to the Anglo-American empirical tradition. The definition is broad gauged, but it is not meant to include the labors of theologians associated with the tradition of philosophic personal idealism. This group has its own version of "empirical."

This modern effort to interpret and to communicate the meaning of Christian faith is merely the latest in a long series extending throughout Christian history. In the pursuit of this task we need not be overly concerned with the objection that we are importing foreign categories into the autonomous intellectual discipline of the Christian church. Apart from any evaluation of that particular characterization of theology, the reply must be that Christian theology has always done so, as the Bible itself testifies. The history of the church is the story of the missionary expansion of a faith that developed in one complex culture and spread to other alien lands with their cultures, including their categories of thought. The categories of all the cultures in which Christianity has appeared have found their way into the theology of the church. How could it be otherwise? To this degree at least there is nothing normative about the culture and categories of biblical literature. What is a "foreign" category?

It is important to maintain the biblical distinction between the fullness of the reality of God, including his transcending and creative purposes, and any categories, or forms of understanding, or cultural values.

In the sense in which I am defining it, empirical theology operates with a methodology which accepts the general empirical axiom that all ideas are reflections of concrete experience, either actual or possible. All propositional or conceptual knowledge originates from and is confirmable by physical experience. The limits of knowledge are defined by the limits of the experienceable, by the limits of relationship. Reason functions in the service of concrete fact and experience.

The meaning of "experience" is grounded upon a Whiteheadian or Jamesian epistemology which stresses the givenness of relations and the primacy of bodily feelings or causal efficacy from which sense experience is an abstraction. It also involves the notion of experience as a synthetic concrescence of the many into some unity, based upon the discontinuous becoming of ultimate drops of experience or quanta of events.

The metaphysics of this approach is naturalistic. It regards the world as self-sufficient. It knows nothing of transcendental causes or disembodied principles. Explanations are forms of description, and description is the analysis of coordination. Consequently in one form or another, and in keeping with its basic empirical axiom, this viewpoint holds to the ontological principle, which asserts that if there is no actual event, there is no reason. What does not communicate with immediate matter of fact "is unknowable, and the unknowable is unknown" (Whitehead). Perhaps Whitehead also furnishes us with one of the more succinct definitions of the naturalistic quality of this outlook, even though this quotation has a rationalistic coloring. "This doctrine of necessity in universality means that there is an essence to the universe which forbids relationships beyond itself, as a violation of its rationality.

Speculative philosophy seeks that essence" (*Process and Reality*, p. 6).

In this approach to theology, the doctrine of God is foundational, of course. Yet the doctrine of Christology is central. Since a revelational event is a wholly naturalistic occurrence in the metaphysical sense, revelational theology in the traditional sense is not a live option from this point of view. Revelational theology collapses into philosophical theology as the only viable alternative.[1] Yet the christological figure or event is central. It functions, methodologically, as the basis for a descriptive generalization with respect to the character of God.

III

Without setting forth an analysis of the present state of empirical theology I want to suggest a few topics which I think are relevant for the future of this kind of theology. They are elements of a possible systematic theology, if we bear in mind that every system of thought is a perspective. And a perspective is a limited style of thought and being. Even for one cultural epoch there is no "the" Christian theology. There is only the systematic development of contrasting strains or dimensions or emphases. These emphases are all part of a complex gospel as our Bible so vividly testifies.

I suggest first the doctrine of Christology. I believe that a naturalistic version of Christology is needed. On other occasions I have made a beginning on this topic. I want to indicate now some principles that might be helpful in the formulation of a naturalistic Christology.

1. A christological figure involves in some decisive manner the co-presence or even the inseparability of God and man. A christological figure is revelatory of both God and man, but revelatory of each in relation to and in the context of the other. Likewise, a christological figure is soteriological in function, but redemption is an activity of both God and man in relation to and in the context of the other.

[1] The other side of the same point consists of the notion that all philosophies or metaphysics are revelational in their grounding.

2. The fact of a christological figure as encompassing the co-presence of God and man implies that the characters of these two distinguishable realities are compatible. Christology means that the deepest and truest nature of man is at root continuous with God's nature. And conversely, a christological figure is not only logically but ontologically impossible if man and God are essentially discontinuous in nature, if God is wholly other. We must choose between the notion of God as wholly other and a doctrine of Christology. We cannot have both. The differences or discontinuities cannot be so conceived that a fundamental continuity is destroyed.

3. The attribute of being christological should not be ascribed to a man, in this case Jesus, in, of, and by himself as though he possessed his being wholly within himself, or as though his being were a function solely of the relation between himself and God. Christian theology has usually interpreted the figure of Christ in this way. The New Testament tends to picture Jesus as one who derived little if anything from his disciples and the people he encountered, except perhaps his crucifixion. Even a reference to the Holy Spirit does not help at this point. This impression is in keeping with his reported self-image: I came, not to be ministered unto, but to minister. This is of a piece with the interpretation of love as *agape*, where God's, and consequently Christ's, concern is wholly with his giving and not with his receiving.

But we perceive an individual in terms of his relational as well as his unique character. We understand a person only as a communalized self. We literally create one another. So if Christ as a man is to be understood in terms of categories descriptive of all men as men, then Christ owed, in part, not only his crucifixion but also his character as a christological figure, his messiahship, and his resurrection, to those people whom he came to serve. He was ministered unto, more than he knew or at least more than is recorded.

4. This point can be expanded. The event of a christological figure means that man, whose true nature is believed by Christians to have been disclosed, is not man in isolation. It is man in context, where context includes nature, history, society,

and the ontological dimension of reality. It is man in context because there is no man without context. Therefore the true nature of man revealed in a christological figure involves a disclosure of the fundamental character of the contextual reality. A christological occurrence means that reality as a whole, or the structure of that portion of reality sufficiently relevant to function as the context for that event, is at least permissive and perhaps supportive of the revelatory event. The christological event, as revelatory, has a fundamental character which is taken as the basic clue to the nature of ultimate reality. A Christian can be said to derive the logos character of reality by generalizing the most basic structure of the complex event we call Jesus Christ. This procedure can be characterized as a variation of Whitehead's methodological principle of descriptive generalization.

5. Christ's relations to his fellows and theirs to him were constitutive of his very being. As revealer of man's true nature Christ disclosed that the servanthood of suffering love is the truest and deepest form of the relational life which is constitutive of His being.

6. If we combine this proposition concerning man's relational life with the proposition that Christ is the revealer of the natures of both God and man in relation to each other, we arrive at the notion that as individuals we are constituted in large part not only by our relations to our fellows but by our relation to God. Not only man's true nature, but his very being as man, whether saint or sinner, involves his relation to God as a necessary dimension of his concrete being. God is a part of man's necessary context. Man's true nature, as well as his existential being as natural and historical man, is neither disclosed, present, or possible apart from God's presence. Man has his very being within the constitutive context of grace.

7. So God is part of the context on which man depends. But in terms of the figure of Christ the converse is also true. Man and the other creatures are the necessary context for God. The point can be put in the form of a syllogism: If man's true nature as the suffering servant is grounded in the relational character of his being, and if man's true nature is con-

tinuous with God's, then God's nature as love is grounded in the relational character of his being.

God as disclosed in Christ was revealed as essentially related. God was not disclosed as one who is essentially unrelated but who chose to become related. In naturalistic theology there is no basis for a kenotic theory of God's action in Christ. In the figure of Christ we are not referring to God's emptying himself of his divinity in order to redeem man. We refer rather to God's fulfillment of himself through the redemption of his creatures. For suffering love, relations are neither optional nor incidental nor external. Their internality is of the essence of love as suffering.

8. Since a christological figure is the disclosure of man's true nature, the being of this revelatory figure is not of a different order than the being of any man. And the nature of man disclosed is not foreign or alien to man as such. In some fundamental sense what is disclosed is continuous with, even if transformative of, what man as such already knows and is. As Schubert Ogden has contended, what Jesus revealed is a way of life for man as such (always in relation to God). I would only add that this was so in the sense of an abstract possibility. It is now a more concrete or real possibility for us because of the historical achievement in Christ. His life was a historical achievement not only on our behalf. It was a historical breakthrough which is empowering; it makes our exemplification a nearer possibility.

9. The principle of historical relativity applies not only to our relation to Jesus Christ as a revelatory event (as H. R. Niebuhr has taught us). The principle of relativity must be applied to the revelatory event itself. Jesus Christ is the answer to a particular question that emerged in the life of a particular people with a particular history. The question can be phrased in various ways. One way is this: How can the strength of our egocentricity be transmitted so that we can live for others? The answer, the unsurpassable answer to that question is the cross. This is the answer for every man if, in fact, all men ask this question.

IV

I suggest that the doctrine of God constitutes part of the unfinished business of empirical theology. At this point I can but touch upon some of the issues.

A residual question concerns the use of the term "God." For the empirical naturalist, of course, God must be identified with the world, or part of it, in some respect or other. This is a departure from the tradition. If the term "God" can be used only to refer to a divine reality of a transcendental sort with a fundamental dissociation from the world, in no basic way dependent upon or conditioned by the world, or who stands in an ultimately external relation to the world (external to God, although internal to the world) much as a creator stands apart from his creation, or who transcends the world in such a way that the being of the world is not his being, then for modern man this God is indeed dead. And he has been dead for a longer period of time than Altizer and his death-of-God colleagues indicate.

But I know of no adequate theological reason why the term "God" can be used only in reference to a reality with a preeminent metaphysical status. Apart from any bias arising from an empirical stance, the principles involved in historical understanding should free us from this tyranny. It is of the essence of both historical understanding and historical existence that tradition should embody the principle of self-transcendence. History can be overcome only by history and not by dogma (Cf. Harnack and Troeltsch).

There may be a persistent consensus that the term "God" should refer to that which is both worthy of man's worship and influential with respect to his salvation. But, beyond this, historical understanding implies that there is no primordial or normative conception of the Godhead, especially with respect to its metaphysical status and attributes. The same principle may apply to the religious and secular functions of God since these cannot be conceived of in total independence of all ontological frameworks. All theological understandings and presuppositions are historical achievements.

The point at issue involves, to be sure, the whole hermeneutical question. But in terms of both historical understanding and Christian commitment, we are not bound to the idols of created meanings, even biblical idols. We are bound to truth, to the living God as encountered, as experienced and experienceable. We know no other living God. This God is the concern of empirical theology.

In reading the God-is-dead theologians many of us, I am sure, have wondered what all the fuss was about, since the game without the name has been played for some time. Altizer may be said to prefer to use the Germanic dialectical method in order to arrive at the position that the English-American style gets to more easily. My anxiety about this somewhat ponderous proclamation of God's death is that it may become an obstacle to an appreciation of the God who is living, under somewhat different metaphysical auspices, to be sure. Much of the point of Altizer's basic thesis rests in part on the assumption of the univocal use of the term "God."

The problem concerning the concept of God is at least two-fold. Reinhold Niebuhr's basic criticism of any naturalistic theology is that there are no unambiguous processes in either nature or history. In other words, if God is to be defined as a reality with integrity, then there can be no naturalistic God, no God in and of this experienceable world. I think the logic of Niebuhr's criticism necessarily implies that there is no experienceable work of God in the world either, even when God is conceived under the best traditional Christian auspices. There may be an unambiguous work of God but on Niebuhr's terms it would not be experienceable. Consequently, it would be unknowable and thus unknown.

Wieman's conception of the fourfold character of creative good could constitute a reply to Niebuhr. In the *Library of Living Theology* book in honor of Wieman, I have tried to pay my inadequate tribute to him for this concept. I do not think it has received the attention it deserves. My contention is that the behavior of this process is unambiguous, although it operates through ambiguous materials and contexts. Nonetheless the whole point merits further attention, especially when the tortuousness of historical forces is taken into account. I would also contend that Whitehead's concept of the primordial nature of God deals with the same problem.

The related issue involves the concrete or consequent nature of God, the sense in which God is a concrete unity, and ultimately the problem of the sense in which the universe may be said to be a concrete unity. The organic unity of Wieman's creative event seems to some to be an episodic affair, a here-and-there and now-and-then type of thing. I grant that Wieman's actual description is not adequate to his conception. But if the temporal extensiveness of the four processes ingredient within the creative event were to be seen in its full and complex scope, I think we would experience a greater sense of organic unity.

Whitehead's ontological principle, in one form or another, is basic to all empirical thought. Everything has to be somewhere, and "somewhere" means in one or more concrete actualities. So in Whitehead's thought God's conceptual nature, his envisagement of the whole realm of eternal objects, has to be someplace concrete, and this is God's consequent nature. (*In Science and the Modern World* God's concreteness was denied.) Whitehead is not too clear about this consequent nature, as is well known. But it seems to involve the idea of the universe as one organic unity in some sense. But this is precisely the problem. Empirical methodology requires the ontological principle, a concrete experienceable God. God's consequent nature fulfills this demand. But the concept of the consequent nature of God in Whitehead's philosophy may not be an empirical concept. It is perhaps a speculative concept where "speculation" means that it is not empirically confirmable in principle. Wieman's objection to this concept is that there is evidence against it, namely that some values are lost.

My impression is that Whitehead's concept of the consequent nature of God can be established only by rationalistic methods. Hartshorne's ontological argument is an attempt to prove by rational means that Whitehead's concrete God necessarily exists, that the universe is one organic unity and that it necessarily exists (although the actual state of affairs is not necessary). But this option is not available to an empirical theology.

One alternative is to define the concrete nature of God up to the limit of a rational empirical approach. This would imply that God's concrete unity is a growing or developing unity, an emergent. Concretely, God would be one process among several, and the idea of the universe as one organic unity might constitute an ideal to be achieved. Again, unity would not be a given, but a future emergent.

If this alternative were to be followed, the conceptual aspect of God, the abstract nature, should be reconceived. It might involve, for example, the notion that even the basic order of the world would be an instance of emergence on the grand scale. This line of inquiry is closer to Wieman and Mead than to Whitehead. It would mean that there is no exception to the principle of evaluation.[2]

The implications of this whole issue are too numerous even to mention. But it was considerations such as these that forced Wieman to define God in terms of value rather than of power. The traditional notion of God as the unity of power and goodness, in the sovereign sense, was rejected on empirical grounds.

It is the task of empirical theology to describe as best it can the God formed within our experienceable world. As Charles Hartshorne has reminded us, empirical theology does not and cannot deal with a "necessary" God. That kind of God can be known, in its necessary mode of existence, only by an a priori methodology. An empirical method deals with a God who, from a rationalistic point of view, exists contingently, a God who is perhaps finite, imperfect, and surpassable in all respects. Possibly this kind of God is not intrinsically worthy of man's worship. From the perspective of an a priori methodology perhaps an empirical theology is a contradiction in terms. The empiricist in theology is probably closer to Me-

---

[2] It should be remarked, incidentally, that we need a fresh look at the Christian doctrine of the goodness of creation.

land's "margin of intelligibility" than he is to Hartshorne's on-tological argument.

It may be the case that an empiricist in theology conceptu-alizes in terms of God's contingency while he worships, acts, and lives as though his God were a being who exists necessar-ily. Not all empiricists seem to illustrate this dichotomy. But this possible truncation and incoherence needs to be inquired into.

V

I think that we need a full statement on the nature of man in empirical theology. The foundation for this has been well laid. We have before us the detailed conception of the social na-ture of the self in Whitehead and Mead. But we have not de-veloped this approach sufficiently to take account of the di-mensions of man to which Reinhold Niebuhr, for example, is so sensitive. At least, we have not done so in any systematic fashion. I believe we ought to accept his challenge that all naturalistic or empirical analyses of the self are too flat and one-dimensional. Niebuhr claims that most modern accounts of the self, whether in psychology, sociology, or political and economic theory, lack an adequate understanding of man in his self-transcendence, his freedom, or man as spirit. I be-lieve this to be true. But I also think that Niebuhr, like most theologians, lacks a basically social conception of the self. A synthesis of these two strains is needed. This synthesis should also include, I believe, the fascinating findings of re-cent ethnological studies by such men as Ardrey and Lorenz.

In the course of this fuller statement on man, I think that reasonable justice can be done to the existential dimensions of man's development. The processive character of reality and the self is a natural base upon which to elaborate the fuller picture of the self as decision.

Furthermore, the relational and dynamic character of the self in process thought offers a resolution to the perennial prob-lem of the relation between God's action and man's action, be-tween grace and freedom. In this view the self, and especially the momentary self as in Whitehead's thought, begins its existence from a movement outside itself, where "outside it-self" may include the notion of one's previous self. The endur-ing self begins each moment of its existence as a gift from be-yond itself. It lives out its existence in the ever-present reality of grace, and grace is mediated through the action of one's fellow creatures. The self comes into being as a response to what is given for it and to it. The first movement is an initiating act of others. The self's initiative is a response to this enabling act. The grace of others and the free response of the self con-stitute the self. Each requires the other. The action of others is an enabling cause giving rise to the freedom of the self. And yet the self's free act is really its own act.

It should be clear that in defining man as made in the image of God, empirical theology need not define this image primarily in terms of man's freedom or creativity, as much tra-ditional or even recent theology has done. Man as free and creative or man as spirit involves a fundamental considera-tion. But the image should also stress man's capacity to re-ceive and extend love. This point is simply an extension of the more general theory of the social character of the self and of God. If, for example, love is the ultimate law of life (Nie-buhr), then this love is of the very fiber of man's being as such. The covenantal relationship between God and man, which includes relations between the creatures, is written on man's heart. It is an ontological given as well as a historical achievement.

In the development of a Christian anthropology in natural-istic terms, might there not be included a critique of a concep-tion that still operates in our worship and that preserves a pe-culiar understanding of grace? I refer to the notion that as sinners men are not worthy of God's grace, that they do not merit his forgiveness. This understanding derives, at least in part, from a conception of the covenantal relation as a con-tract. A contract between two or more parties involves an agreement that each party will uphold his end and fulfill his obligations. If one partner reneges on his responsibilities he has no further claims on the other, and the contract is ended. He does not merit further consideration. If the offended partner chooses to continue the relationship, this act is an act of grace which the offender has not earned.

Applied to the covenantal relationship between God and man, this means that man by his sin has broken the contract and deserves only adverse judgment. He is unworthy. He may be worthy in God's eyes because God chooses to so regard and treat him. But as a sinner he is unworthy in his own eyes and should so regard himself. If he does not think of himself as unworthy, he is prideful and perverse. He does not acknowledge his sinfulness.

But love is not a contract of this sort. To use an analogy: the child does not deserve his parents' love only when he is good, when he does what they want him to do. It is not a question of his meriting love at all. From the parents' point of view it is only a question of their relating to the child in terms of what is good for the child, whether the child is good or naughty. In either case the child is to receive love simply because they are parents of that child and he is their child. From the child's point of view, he needs to think of himself as worthy to receive love, whatever love may involve at any particular moment. As naughty he is worthy to receive love as judgment and forgiveness. If you will, he "merits" love just because he is naughty. He is worthy, in his own eyes, to be granted love from his parents because he is their child, and they are his parents. To be sure, his self-image, his value in his own eyes, is related to the appraisal of worth he receives from others. If he is unworthy in his own eyes, he thereby denies that he is of worth in the eyes of others.

After all, parents cannot be parents without children. The depths of parenthood are realized precisely when the child is a problem. The child, by his very need of forgiveness, may enable the parents to love. The parents create the child. He is the means, in part the enabling power, whereby the parents fulfill themselves. He helps to create the parents.

This is not love as condescension or option. This is love as mutual fulfillment.

Finally, in this picture of the self there might also be a statement concerning the nature of Christian personality. This topic would include a consideration of power, competition, dependence, neurotic dependence, and independence. At present we vacillate between conceptions of stoic invulnerability, republican self-sufficiency, Christian meekness, and selfless love. We might give greater weight to Hartshorne's suggestion that the one who is to exert the greatest influence is one who is himself most influenced by others.

VI

There are other issues that should be part of the future labors of empirical theologians, such as the status and role of parapsychological data, the character of a truly American theology of freedom (as Barth suggested), the formulation of hermeneutical principles from the vantage points of both a deeper grasp of historical understanding and process modes of thought, and a recasting of ethical principles. I conclude my discussion with a brief reference to an issue that is relevant to any empirical theology, the problem of falsifiability.

The problem of what would or could count against a belief in God is a tantalizing one. The question of evidence is obviously relevant, especially from an empiricist's standpoint. In science one moves from error to another hypothesis when the expectations or predictions are not fulfilled. The conditions of confirmation and falsifiability are relatively manageable, at least in principle. But in matters religious and theological the factor of evidence must be held in tension with one of the essential qualities of faith. For faith involves a clinging, a holding steadfast, even when the evidence seems to negate one's faith and one's belief in the object of one's faith.

This principle does not mean that faith is indifferent or blind to evidence. It does not mean that one's ideas and beliefs should not change. It does mean that our understanding and our faith can be transformed only if we remain faithful to the active God who is not identified with the shattered understanding and knowledge that we have used to define the meaning of our experience and our world.

Faiths are destroyed and gods do die. But one cannot abandon the object of his faith too readily or quickly. One does not lightly experience spiritual defeat or casually change his faith. There is no resurrection without the cross of defeat, despair, and meaninglessness. But the cross does not eventuate necessarily in the resurrection. The rebirth occurs only if there is a faithfulness and trust in the God whose character is somewhat other than the God who was symbolized by the inadequate understanding that constitutes the broken evidence of our despair.

In a deeply organic sense one must pour the ashes of defeat and meaninglessness over his entire being. He must live in a sackcloth and ashes, in faith and repentance, in order that the new word and the new being may be born in him.

6

Suffering and Being in Empirical Theology
DANIEL DAY WILLIAMS

The justification of empirical method in theology can only be through the demonstration that it handles theological problems more fruitfully than other methods. I have chosen to approach the question through an empirical approach to one issue, the nature of suffering and the meaning of the suffering of God. It is a question on which empirical theologians have had much to say. Their critique of traditional doctrines of God has moved toward a doctrine of God's being which involves the divine suffering. It is a test of empirical method if the doctrine of the suffering God can remove long-standing theological difficulties and lead to some new insight into the way of God with man.

In the present stage of the discussion about the meaning of theological language, the empiricist thesis about meaning and verification is of critical significance. The period of arbitrary assertion of the rights of theological language to exemption from the general canons of intelligibility and verification has passed. Empiricism has proposed a method of verification; and I shall explore this method in relation to the problem of suffering. I choose this issue not only because of the importance it has had in empirical theology, but also because it involves critical questions for every Christian theology. The significance of empirical method for Christian thought may find here a test case in relation to other methods.

Empirical theologians have replaced the impassible God of the tradition with God as the "fellow sufferer who understands."[1] Among the theologians and philosophers who have

[1] Alfred North Whitehead, *Process and Reality: An Essay in Cosmology* (New York: Macmillan Co., 1929), p. 532.

175

done this are Alfred North Whitehead, Edgar Brightman, Henry Nelson Wieman, Charles Hartshorne, Bernard Meland, and W. Norman Pittenger. One may ask whether it is empiricists alone who hold this position. Bonhoeffer's statement, "only a suffering God can help," points in this direction, but in those last letters he is seeking theological substance without exploring the technicalities of method.[2] Berdyaev affirms the suffering God within the idealist, mystical, and existentialist modes of thought; so it is not only empiricists who have made this break with tradition.[3] And one can find a few theologians with empirical methods who do not accept the doctrine of the suffering God. Generally, however, this has been a characteristic position of the empiricists, especially within the process school. They have rejected the classical doctrine of omnipotence and have asserted that God suffers in his involvement in the world's life. I hope to show that the empirical method has a way of exploring the meaning of suffering, and that it can give an intelligible interpretation of the relation of God's suffering to human experience. This is a large claim and no brief discussion is sufficient to defend it; but I want to show how empirical theology can go about this task, and I shall try to recognize its characteristic problems.

What Is Empirical Method in Theology?

On certain broad foundations of empirical method perhaps we can agree; at least I do not propose to argue them here. First, by experience I mean the felt, bodily, psycho-social, organic action of human beings in history. Experience includes the sense data, but it is not limited to them. Second, God is experienced as a power and process immanent in the world, creating and patterning communities of value in ways which are describable in rational categories abstracted from concrete experience. The dimension of transcendence is not excluded by this statement; but empirical theology asserts that God is experienced as immanent process. Third, knowledge

[2] Dietrich Bonhoeffer, *Letters and Papers from Prison* (New York: Macmillan Co., 1962), p. 220.

[3] Cf. Charles Hartshorne, "Whitehead and Berdyaev: Is There Tragedy in God?" *Journal of Religion* 37 (1957).

of the character of things is derivable from a disciplined critical analysis of the structures in experience and the testing in historical action of theological propositions about God and man. Fourth, the formal structure of our knowledge always has the status of tentative and correctable assertions, subject to criticism, and never exhaustive of the concreteness of reality.

Three special aspects of empirical method become evident in the interpretation of the suffering of God.

The first has to do with the nature of metaphysics. Whatever being is, it includes concrete process. But does empirical method give us access to anything beyond the immanent working of God as creative process? Can an empirical metaphysics penetrate to the structures in all experience to justify a doctrine of God's being in its primordial aspect as the condition of all being? The metaphysical doctrine of God requires an elaboration of the categories, time and eternity, cause and effect, perfection and finitude, personality and mystery as they are exemplified in his being. If we assert that God suffers, is this only a description of the working of the creative process as observed, or is it a statement about the metaphysical order and its exemplification in God's being? Here all the classical problems of the analogy of being, transcendence, and immanence loom up. There is involved here the question of the community of man with God and the nature of religious experience itself. What does it mean to say that God's being is disclosed to us?

Empiricists have disagreed about whether theology requires a minimal or a maximal development of metaphysical reflection on the being of God. Dr. Wieman became increasingly negative about such an extension of empirical method, but the Whiteheadians, and especially Charles Hartshorne, have elaborated the doctrine of the divine perfection as a rational extension of empirical-rational method through a search for the structures in all experience. Whichever way we take will affect our mode of interpreting the suffering of God. I agree with the metaphysicians. A doctrine of the being of God is required because the human search for meaning involves questions about the metaphysical order manifested in all things. Man lives at the boundaries of time and eternity, personality and mystery. It is his participation in being which drives him to interpret his experience in categories through which he seeks to understand the integrity of the world in the midst of its diversity. The task is difficult, but faith for human living cannot do without it.

Second, there is the question of how we get at the structures of experience. This question must receive the continuing attention of empiricists, and we can never regard our answers to it as finished. In the beginning of the empirical movement there was a tendency to hold that scientific method furnished the adequate model for religious knowledge. Douglas Clyde Macintosh and Henry Nelson Wieman could speak of theology as an empirical science, although Wieman developed the scientific model in a different way from Macintosh. But we are still faced with questions about this scientific model. Much depends upon how broadly we state the method of observation, reason, and experience when we call it "scientific." Whitehead remarked toward the close of his life that philosophy is not a science.[4] We require a method which can uncover the structures of experience as they are disclosed to a human reflection so as to describe the concreteness, complexity, and dimension of ultimacy in man's existence. The attempt to penetrate to the structures of being involves an inquiry which requires elements of total valuation and discrimination. Such reflection is not anti-scientific or irrational, but whether we should call it science seems to me doubtful.

If there is a way of getting knowledge beyond science, what is it? Here empiricists must consider the phenomenologists, who have claimed to develop methods for clarifying the nature of human experience. This claim has often been put in extravagant ways, as if the analysis of the structures of consciousness could establish the limits of all meaning (Husserl). Phenomenologists sometimes have proceeded as if man's

[4] Alfred North Whitehead, "Mathematics and the Good," in P. A. Schilpp, ed., *The Philosophy of Alfred North Whitehead* (Chicago: Northwestern University Press, 1941), p. 681.

existence as a natural organism in a developmental process was irrelevant to understanding man and his world. Merleau-Ponty can be seen laboriously working his way out of such restrictions in the phenomenological method.[5]

I hold that an adequate empiricism must incorporate the phenomenological method in getting at the distinctive structures in human experience. Man is an animal, but a strange animal, and empiricists should not forget this. We must discriminate the forms of the human way of being. Whitehead began his metaphysical construction by abstracting from human experience those features which he believed could be useful in framing the general scheme of categories, but this abstraction left much of the uniqueness of human experience unexplored. In *Adventures of Ideas*, Whitehead did give a phenomenological analysis of Truth, Beauty, Adventure, and Peace as motifs of human experience. It is such an analysis which I believe is required in a theological interpretation of human and divine suffering.

In making such an analysis I restrict my attention here to the constructive aspects of suffering. The existentialists using a phenomenological method have carried philosophy and theology forward; but on the whole, they have described suffering as a sign of man's estrangement from God, and from his own authentic being, and not its power to contribute to the fulfillment of life. Kierkegaard's analysis of the structures of the estranged consciousness in *Sickness unto Death* is a classic of phenomenological analysis; but he is concentrating on the pathology of the spirit, not its healing. We should not forget his analysis of suffering as the essential expression of "Religiousness A" in the *Postscript*; but here again, for him suffering marks only the distance between the human condition and the will to the absolute good.[6] Can we see in human suffering a key to being and to how God brings sanity to our derangement? I have hopes for a phenomenological empiricism which will unite the two types of critical method.

[5] Maurice Merleau-Ponty, *The Structure of Behavior* (Boston: Beacon Press, 1963).

[6] S. Kierkegaard, *Concluding Unscientific Postscript* (Princeton: Princeton University Press, 1941), pt. 2,A, sec. 2.

The third special aspect of empirical method is its confessional component. Empiricists have characteristically sought to get beyond the confessional position to explore the realities which are open to human inquiry, and have denied claims to knowledge which have only a private or parochial status. I fully share this concern, but I do not believe in the existence of a purely nonconfessional interpretation of human experience and the meaning of God. We live in historical communities of valuation and faith. We see from perspectives informed by primordial and historically embodied value judgments. Empirical theology will use the religious traditions in which we live as sources of data and hypotheses; but every empirical theology stands within a historical perspective. The fact that we are always within a structure of thought and evaluation does not mean that we are bound to the place from which we start. We are free to criticize and reconsider every claim. It is the empiricists who have insisted on this openness in any confessional position, and I accept it while continuing to hold that every theology is shaped within some community of faith.

I turn now to a specific inquiry into the meaning of suffering as a theological problem.

Suffering

Suffering is a vast subject. There is so much of it. We all know something about it, and each man knows something no one else can ever know, that is, just how it is with him. I propose to concentrate on a single question. What are the ways in which the experience of suffering enters into the growth of communities of personal value? I begin with phenomenological analysis. I am not trying to prove a thesis about all suffering, and certainly not denying its destructive aspects, but I ask, "Can we discriminate the forms of human existence in which suffering becomes a constructive part of selves and communities?" In a lecture in a Divinity School course many years ago, Professor Wieman gave an analysis of the growth of community in which he undertook to state certain requirements for creativity. One was that suffering must be incorporated into the system. For thirty years I have meditated on that sentence, and this paper is but an attempt to take a slight step forward within the perspective Dr. Wieman opened up.

Analysis requires an exploratory definition. What do we mean by suffering? We encounter at once an aspect of the problem which is important for a theology of a suffering God. Suffering in its widest sense means being acted upon. It is conformation to requirements imposed by something which reshapes the self. It means to bear. One use in classical Latin for *patior* is "to undertake many labors." Thus suffering is not to be equated with evil, and it does not always involve physical or mental pain. We recognize suffering wherever living things or persons are shaped by something which moves them from their present state. Within this broad meaning of suffering, however, we have the experience of being acted upon in such a way that we know pain of body or mind. We ordinarily mean by suffering an anguish which we experience, not only as a pressure to change, but as a threat to our composure, our integrity, and the fulfillment of our intentions. All acute suffering has this character of threatening our self-direction, and therefore, implicitly, our being. It challenges our capacity to maintain ourselves and retain the poise of self-direction. In the diseased body, suffering threatens the organism's unity and its capacity to continue. The suffering attendant upon athletic or artistic discipline always contains an implicit threat to our adequacy and our will to continue. In Heideggerian language, all acute suffering has the aspect of the threat of non-being.

Our question is, then, are there conditions in which this element of threat in suffering becomes a creative function in personal life? The existentialists have emphasized the threat of non-being. I believe a more adequate phenomenology will prove that this is only part of the truth. Consider three aspects of suffering: as identification, as communication, and as healing. I stress that we are not here seeking a generic description of all suffering or its functions. To adapt a saying of Whitehead's, we must never forget the "multifariousness of the world" and its suffering.

Suffering as Identification

It is in part through suffering that we begin to answer the question, "Who am I?" We all know the heightened self-consciousness which goes with suffering. Even a minor pain can elicit a self-awareness which is otherwise diffused in activity or preoccupation. Samuel Beckett's plays and novels give vivid examples. Hamm knows his father is living because he is crying. The Unnameable finds his existence confirmed through bodily pain. As a commentator remarks, "He is pained, therefore he is." [7] Notice that this "is," the self-awareness of being, is an ingredient in the experience of pain. We not only know that we are but that we are in a world, and that we are beings who must cry out and can cry out. In *The Words* Jean-Paul Sartre gives this account of an accident which befell the sculptor Giacometti:

> One evening, more than twenty years ago, Giacometti was hit by a car while crossing the Place d'Italie. Though his leg was twisted, his first feeling, in the state of lucid swoon into which he had fallen, was a kind of joy: "Something has happened to me at last!" I know his radicalism; he expected the worst. The life which he so loved and which he would not have changed for any other was knocked out of joint, perhaps shattered, by the stupid violence of chance: "So," he thought to himself, "I wasn't meant for anything." What thrilled him was the menacing order of causes that was suddenly unmasked and the act of staring with the petrifying gaze of a cataclysm at the lights of the city, at human beings, at his own body lying flat in the mud; for a sculptor, the mineral world is never far away. I admire that will to welcome everything. If one likes surprises, one must like them to that degree, one must like even the rare flashes which reveal to devotees that the earth is not meant for them.[8]

[7] Josephine Jacobsen and William R. Mueller, *The Testament of Samuel Beckett* (New York: Hill & Wang, 1964), p. 106.

[8] Jean-Paul Sartre, *The Words* (New York: George Braziller, 1964), pp. 145–46 of the Fawcett Crest edition.

Sartre's mastery of phenomenological description is evident. The hurt man comes to self-knowledge in the destruction of his hope of vocation; and, by confronting the void of meaninglessness into which he gazes, he discovers who he is. It is not merely perverse for Sartre to say that self-knowledge arises in the discovery of what we cannot do and the threat of negation of our being. "The earth is not made for us."

But that is a half truth. We may recall this passage in Sartre as we look at Giacometti's poignantly moving sculpture, for he did live to become a great artist. His human figures are wordless communications of the human condition. These gaunt, stretched bodies are put upon by the world, and the souls they express know suffering. But they are not cowed; they bear a human dignity which draws power from the suffering itself.

In a theology of community the importance of identification lies not only in self-knowledge but in self-knowledge as a requisite of love. To know myself and to know another it is required that I allow suffering to have its part in defining who we are. To reject suffering, either my own or another's, as "Not-I" marks the beginning of the loss of selfhood. Dr. Wieman's analysis, in *Man's Ultimate Commitment*, of the function of the dark realities is relevant here.[9] He lays down the requirement that creativity depends upon the self's courage to face fully the *id*, the source of the dark realities. When fully faced, the suffering entailed can be incorporated into the creativity of the self. Identification, therefore, is not merely a naming function, but an indispensable factor in self-discovery, self-affirmation, and it can be the entry into a significant community of selves. That suffering in self-awareness will lead to self-definition is of course not guaranteed. It depends upon our finding an interpretation of suffering which can be affirmed in the courage to be — for we know that our being is at stake in suffering. This metaphysical dimension recognized by Sartre is confirmed in experience. Psychiatrists are astonished at the amount of suffering people will bear unnec-

[9] Henry Nelson Wieman, *Man's Ultimate Commitment* (Carbondale: Southern Illinois University Press, 1958), chap. 3.

essarily. We cling to our sufferings as guaranteeing our identity. Our sufferings are ourselves. The self wants to hold on to anything which makes self-recognition possible rather than move toward an unknown experience. I suggest this is a pathological aspect of a positive function. Suffering is both identification of present being and the offer of a possibility of becoming. This prospective reference in suffering will occupy our attention further on.

Suffering as Communication

Shared suffering has peculiar potencies. It can, under some conditions, create communities of understanding and mutuality. We recognize this power of suffering in the common life. We anticipate it in the marriage vow, "for better for worse, for richer for poorer, in sickness and in health." We recognize it in oaths of office — "to preserve, protect, and defend." Initiation rites, liturgies, myths, and symbols in the common experience include the shared memory of past suffering, and sometimes impose suffering, real or symbolic, as a condition of membership.

Empirical theology seeks the conditions of this community-creating power. Let us follow the clue that suffering becomes a means of communication. It is a way in which persons reach out to one another in need, in love, and also, we do not forget, in destructive hatred. The cry for help, the silent anguish, the bearing of the burden, are potential elements in the syntax of personal languages in which the struggle with one another and toward communion goes on.

Certainly suffering born or inflicted on another may destroy communication. Lillian Smith's description of the suffering inflicted out of racial arrogance and hatred traces the meaning of the cruelty to the impotence and rate of the feeling of inferiority overcoming itself as it feeds on the gratification of power over others.[10] It is possible, of course, that even in the sheer clash of force with force there may be an occasion for learning something about the other which opens the way

[10] Lillian Smith, *Killers of the Dream* (New York: W. W. Norton, 1949), pp. 174–91.

to communication. But suffering may close that door. What then are the conditions under which a way to a new relationship may be opened through suffering?

First, there must be an ongoing community of interpretation which gives form to remembered experience and transmits this memory in the historical life of a people. How much human suffering is objectified and preserved in the histories! Consider Alan Clark's *Barbarossa*, the history of the Nazi campaign on the Eastern front in World War II.[11] No pages of print can of course do more than hint at the reality of the suffering, not only in the military action itself, but the meaningless human cruelties, waste, and desolation of spirit which was involved. If such suffering is to have any part in the creation of a new community in history, there must be a people, or peoples, whose language embodies this memory, objectively documents the truth, and in some way transmits the memory as a constituent element in a new consciousness. Meanings live in historical communities of interpretation. This is the insight of Josiah Royce's *The Problem of Christianity*, which, in spite of its idealistic elements, remains one of the great works of empirical theology.[12]

A second condition is that the memory of suffering in the past must be accepted and lived with in the present. There must be the will to hear, to recall, to tell about and not hide the unpalatable, even the unbearable reality. Yet, and here I venture a paradox about the creative function of suffering, there must be a kind of forgetting also. We all know that the immediacy of suffering has a way of being lost from memory. There is something operative here about which we have much more to learn, and it has to do with the prospective reference in all suffering. It looks towards its own removal. We say sometimes that we can "laugh about it afterwards." In any case we know that to remain either individually or collectively fixated on past suffering is pathological. Past suffering is not to be remembered for itself, but to take its place in an

[11] Alan Clark, *Barbarossa* (London: Hutchinson, 1965).

[12] Josiah Royce, *The Problem of Christianity* (New York: Macmillan Co., 1914).

ongoing community in which the past does not finally determine the form or the hope of the present.

Third, for suffering to be remembered constructively it must be reconceived. Its meaning is not simply a deposit in the memory but material for a new interpretation. The word "reconception" is used by Dr. Hocking in a somewhat different connection, but it is useful here in a phenomenological description of the career of suffering in the self and the community.[13] We reconceive past anguish by seeing it in context, probing its causes, and relating it to new understanding. This is a large part of what happens in psychological therapy. I do not say reconception is always creative of wider community. We can interpret past suffering so that we harden our motives of revenge or self-destruction. Reconception is no sure route to communion. But the point is that reconception may take place in the sharing of experience so that the past contributes to the sensitivity and cohesive power of a new community of persons.

When we think of the burden of suffering in the human story, to which our century has added in such incredible fashion, and we remember how in the present state of communications so much of what happens is presently and vividly available for recall, it is a critical human question how this burden of guilt, cruelty, and anguish is to be borne in the search for a tolerable and decent human life. I am pointing to the possibility that our shared knowledge of the past can enter into a redefinition of our humanity so that a more humane, just, and responsible life together may be possible. It is not *catharsis* alone we need, in spite of Aristotle, but *reconciliation* through an objectification of the past in the present and its reinterpretation in new occasions of human experience. The argument of this paper may or may not be convincing, but of this I am sure: what is at stake in the understanding of suffering is crucial for the possibility of a humane existence in which we learn who we are and live in responsibility and love with one another.

[13] William Ernest Hocking, *Living Religions and a World Faith* (New York: Macmillan Co., 1940), pp. 190–208.

Suffering and Being in Empirical Theology

In the fourth condition for the communicative function of suffering, empiricists and existentialist come together in asserting the significance of decision. The revision of the meaning of the past through its interpretation in the community does not take place without the human resolve to do it. We can refuse and turn away. T. S. Eliot remarks that man can stand just so much reality.[14] We are always missing the real glory of life because of our fear of suffering. There must be a resolve to face and transform it. We cannot by decision make suffering mean what we will. Of this more shortly as we turn to the doctrine of God; but one element in the transformation of suffering is the resolve to transform it.

Suffering as Healing

Suffering objectified can become a healing power. The process here is one of the mysteries of life. It is largely the psychologists who have given us empirical descriptions of it inasmuch as they have been concerned with interpersonal communication in the healing process.[15] They have shown that the relationship in which the feelings of one are taken into the consciousness of another without rejection, without fear, and in love, is a condition of the transformation of the self. Suffering is not only a symptom of disease, it becomes a healing potency. In his book on the atonement, F. W. Dillistone comments on a sixteenth-century mode of treatment:

> It has been suggested . . . that when those suffering from the plague and other bodily diseases arrived at the famous hospice of Isenheim and were taken (as was in fact the case) to see the great altar piece of Grunewald *first* before any kind of physical treatment was administered, it was in the hope that the view of such suffering as was displayed in the terrible picture of Christ in His agony would bring a sense of reconciliation to the pa-

[14] T. S. Eliot, *Murder in the Cathedral*, a line spoken by Thomas Becket.

[15] Cf. Karl Menninger, *Theory of Psycho-analytic Technique* (New York: Science Editions, 1961); Bernard Steinzor, *The Healing Partnership* (New York: Harper & Row, 1967).

tient's heart and set him forward on the way to receiving whatever physical relief the hospice could provide.[16]

Both phenomenologists and empiricists should find this rich with suggestion. Empiricists (some at least) would want to know the emotional profile of the sufferers before they were shown the altar and after, and a documentation of the incidence of improvement or deterioration. Phenomenologists might concentrate on the significance of the presentation of the Christ-figure, its symbolic power, and the mode of interpretation given to it by the beholder. There is so much we do not know about man and his religious experience. Why is it, for example, that the representation of the suffering Christ is uncommon in the early Middle Ages, and only later becomes a pervasive stylistic idiom?[17]

We do, however, have some means of understanding the intuition which led to the Isenheim practice. The discovery of the other who bears the consequences of my suffering and shares my condition is a powerful mode of personal communication and healing. There are at least three elements involved. First, there is the objectification of the suffering in its representation in another. Sanity depends upon objectivity about the self. This is one reason why the current vogue for rejecting all "objectivising" in theology is so misguided. What I cannot objectify I probably fear. Part of the power of healing lies in discovering another who can hear my story, experience my feeling, and not be destroyed by it. This last condition is crucial. Suffering becomes constructive only when it participates in structures which have elements of strength. The pooling of agony by itself rarely leads to creativity. It is the strength which allows the suffering to be faced that makes its transformation possible.

The second element is the offer of community in spite of suffering. There is much which I cannot develop here, but we know that suffering willingly accepted in communion with the

[16] F. W. Dillistone, *The Christian Understanding of Atonement* (Welwyn, Eng.: James Nisbet & Co., 1968), p. 235.

[17] Émile Mâle, *L'Art religieux de la fin du Moyen Age en France* (Paris: Armand Colin, 1922), chap. 3.

other becomes a language of the self which can reach the other. It is the word beyond words.

Third, there is the transformation which takes place in the meaning of suffering through love. The hard fact, beyond all sentimentality, is that either we share suffering in love or outside of love, and it is not the same in one case as in the other. Suffering with the other in love becomes a sacrament of the possibility of love in all being and is the deepest source of the transmutation of suffering. Again I am speaking descriptively of the forms of possible experience. There is no guarantee in suffering that it will take on this meaning, or be so understood. We can suffer for lack of love, or from its misunderstandings and pathologies. Love seeks no guarantees. But where the reality of self-giving, self-accepting search for communion with the other is present, suffering can enter into the power of being as it is released between persons.

Suffering has, I am saying, causal efficacy at the human level in a diversity of modes, for causality is one of the categories of being. Suffering is caused, and it also causes, and the context determines its effects. In suffering we enter in special ways into the process of becoming in personal histories. Our feelings are objectified for one another. Sartre's picture of each man as wholly *causa sui*, confined within himself, is a caricature of the metaphysical evidence.[18] It leaves no basis for that communication of meaning which he himself so skillfully achieves.

Suffering and God

We have so far remained within the human sphere. Theology needs the method of abstraction no less than other inquiries, a point which nonempirical theologies often overlook. But our ultimate concern is with suffering and being, and that means man's existence in its full concreteness of relationship to God.

There are two ways in which empirical method develops the analysis of experience in the doctrine of God. The first way may be called the pointing function of empiricism. I can

[18] Jean-Paul Sartre, *Being and Nothingness* (New York: Philosophical Library, 1956).

state it briefly, although its importance for empirical theology cannot be exaggerated. Empirical theology points to the fact that what works in human existence, so as to bring suffering into creative communities of value, is not primarily human will, action, or design, but the action of God. We experience the weaving together into one community of being of many strands of action, feeling, pain, language, memory, and expectation. Man is in the weaving, but he is not the weaver. Dr. Wieman's way of pointing to the presence of God as the creative event in experience is the foundation of empirical theology. My only footnote here to what he has said is that one way of approaching the empirical argument for God is through an analysis of the work of suffering in the creative event. In our time this may have some especial pertinence when the existentialist analysis of the human condition has described so profoundly the dimensions of anxiety, suffering, and the threat of non-being. Empirical theology will not reject this analysis, but use it to point to the divine activity within existence which existentialists have usually failed to see.

There are empirical theologians who wish to leave the matter there, with the creative event in existence. God, they affirm, is indeed much more than this, but about the more we can only speculate.

The other view of the relation of the ontological question to religious commitment, a view which I share, is that we must develop the metaphysical doctrine of God's being in relation to all the categories. The reason lies in man himself. The community of being in which we participate is not the human community alone, but the community of man with nature and with God. To use Dr. Hartshorne's phrase, the society of being has God as its supreme member.[19] The nature of this society and the relations of its members must be interpreted as far as possible if we are to have a rational faith.

Because our communion with one another and with God is within the ontological community, what we know about suffer-

[19] Charles Hartshorne, *Reality as Social Process* (Boston: Beacon Press, 1953), p. 40.

ing as identification, communication, and healing can become fruitful for our doctrine of the being of God. The way is opened to an empirical interpretation of the confessional tradition of God's creative and redemptive action. "God has shown his love for us in this that while we were yet sinners Christ died for us" (Romans 5:8). No phenomenological analysis will exhaust the depth here revealed; but within that description there can be a mode of understanding the sufferings of the man who represents every man as God's act of self-identification for us, his way of communication to us, and his healing power working among us.

The metaphysical doctrine of God's being involves the way of analogy. Its presupposition is that there is a community of participation among the real things which make up the world. I prefer the concept "community of analogous structures" to the traditional *analogia entis* doctrine, partly to emphasize that the community of real things is a field of dynamic processes, an ongoing activity. Structure, process, and valuation are the ultimate metaphysical elements. The ground of the commonality of structures is God's metaphysical function as the form-giving and power-sustaining factor in all things. He is the indispensable metaphysical participant in every world. To be is to participate in the society of being which has God as its primordial, everlasting, and ever-present source of the forms of valuation. A community of beings with analogous structures is the formal mode of participation of God in the creatures and the creatures in God.

God is not one creature among many. He is both creator and creature within the ongoing life of being. Hence all analogies require a certain reservation in the language about God. He has his being in a way which differs from the way of finite being. Creatures are not eternal. They do not possess the free and unbounded vision of the range of possibility. No creature has the power of being without which nothing else can be.

We turn then to the doctrine of suffering in God. In this empirical theology I affirm that God does suffer as he participates in the ongoing life of the society of being. His sharing in the world's suffering is the supreme instance of knowing, accepting, and transforming in love the suffering which arises in the world. I am affirming the doctrine of the divine sensitivity. Without it I can make no sense of the being of God. Sensitive participation in this world means suffering, or else our human experience is completely irrelevant to anything we can say about God.

What is often overlooked in affirmations of the divine suffering is, I hope, brought out by this analysis. That is, what suffering is, how it functions, what it may achieve depends upon the context in which it appears. *God's* suffering is the way *he* takes the world into his being, and that is the way of a perfectly adequate love. That is all we can say ontologically about it. Whitehead's great phrase, "the Fellow Sufferer who Understands," gives us the key when we give full weight to the word *understanding*. God's understanding is that of a perfectly adequate love, and knowledge in love transforms suffering. Suffering in the being of God is not just any suffering; it is the supreme instance of the transmutation of suffering. We must be clear about this if we are to have a theology of the divine suffering. I reject the traditional denial of suffering to God; but God's resources are his, not ours, and ours participate in his only within the community of experience which he makes possible. As the ground of possibility of that community he is not threatened or changed. He is.

This analysis of the metaphysical status of suffering in God leads us to a critical issue for empirical theology. It is the question of the nature of the hope which faith in God sustains. The doctrine of the suffering God, combined with the restriction on the divine omnipotence which empirical theology asserts, can lead to a consequence which is plausible, but which I believe threatens any theological meaning. If to participate in the society of being is to suffer, and if God suffers, then we might seem to be saying that the ongoing life of creative process can only exhibit a repetition of suffering, an increase of its quantity, so that the more being the more suffering. We must explore this point.

There is an "effect" in the analysis of suffering which has

been much exploited in contemporary literature, particularly among the atheistic existentialists, though not only among them. I shall call it, for short, the "Beckett effect" after Samuel Beckett, one of its most engaging and powerful dramatizers. It is the view that to be is simply to beat against the cage of suffering in a human nature bound to be put upon, hurt, and in agony forever. We see it in the painful step which Clove tries to take as the curtain descends in *Endgame* — one step toward freedom in the world, but he cannot take it. His foot is forever poised in the impotence of indecision. We hear the same theme in Pozzo's speech to Estragon in *Waiting for Godot*: "The tears of the world are a constant quantity. For each one who begins to weep somewhere else another stops. The same is true of the laugh." Everything balances out, Murphy at the judas window of the Magdalen Mental Mercy Seat flicks a switch, "flooding the cell with a light of such ferocity that the eyes of the sleeping and waking opened and closed respectively." Regardless of heart, lungs, action, toil, the place and position will be "where we were, as we were."[20]

It is of course debatable whether Beckett himself wholly sustains this doctrine of endless suffering with a constant quantum of agony. Pozzo is perhaps not the one to whom we are expected to listen most seriously. In *Waiting for Godot* the tree does sprout leaves, and, miracle of miracles, Estragon finds shoes which *fit*. But the overpowering effect in Beckett is the constancy of the human condition from which there is no escape. One interpreter even calls the fit of Estragon's shoes "one of the hellish devices of hope" by which Estragon and Vladimir are pinned to their place.[21]

The empirical doctrine of God's suffering is not caught in this impasse. I have tried to show where the issue can be drawn with Beckett, Sartre, Camus, Heidegger, and many others. Suffering does not remain a constant in the metaphysical situation. It points forward. It can be transmuted through being brought into a community of interpretation with a

[20] Quotations will be found in Jacobsen and Mueller, *Testament of Beckett*, pp. 135–36.

[21] Ibid., p. 137.

prospective dimension, that is with a hope for creativity beyond the present. Suffering can mean this, and can be incorporated within it. In an empirical theology of the divine
suffering, neither God nor man is bound to a wheel of endlessly repeated suffering; rather we are released into a new
dimension of hope through what God continually does.

The classical doctrine of God affirmed the victory of the
divine life. The glorification of rest which usually attended
this in the tradition is rejected by empirical theologians. Quiet
is not the supreme value. There is hope for a life which in-
corporates past and present suffering in a new meaning, and
that is what empirical theology asserts. We have a kinship
with the Becketts of our time and their "sadness after song."
But we have a hope, grounded in experience, a hope which
to be sure must be continually renewed in a response of faith
which is possible not through our power alone but through
the working of God.

7

Christian Coherence and Human Wholeness

PAUL SPONHEIM

I

If a reader of traditional theological discourse were to seek to isolate some basic terminological structure in the material history placed in his hand, he might very probably set upon the terms "God" and "man" and their linguistic interrelationships. He could observe that by a bare appeal to the presence of these terms it does not seem possible to discriminate between theologies he encounters and yet that these terms seem very near the logical center of gravity of those same theologies. And he would, in fact, probably have been told by such advertised antagonists as Luther and Aquinas alike, by both mystic Jacob Boehme and deistic John Toland, that not only these terms but, more ambitiously, their referents in reality were altogether central to their work. These terms qualify well both intensionally and extensionally, as the structure sought.

Of course, our reader would rightly be reluctant to make too much of the universality of "God" and "man" in theological language and intention. Linguistic universality, supported by psychological seriousness, clearly does not yet settle the problem of the logical unity or identity of usage; and surely not that concerning the ontological status of the referent(s). One lacks some kind of connection between the highly inward consensus and the wholly outward one. Perhaps even these strands of consensus would be worth pondering with respect to these problems. But these are not the problems to which this paper is directed. I have mentioned the apparent agreement concerning "God" and "man" only to make a point about theological endeavor in our time. If conventional theological discourse seems always to speak of "God" and "man," if — advancing the analysis a bit — that discourse so positions "God" and "man" that speech about either always involves the other, strong forces in our time seem to be tending toward or trying for something really new. Superficially, we seem to have chosen the way of specialization, splitting apart "God" and "man." Upon closer critical examination, much of recent and current theological literature seems hard pressed to speak coherently and persuasively about either of the two. To take a leaf from Tillich, if "God" and "man" are "poles" structuring traditional theological literature, we witness currently a "polarization." If polarity is an apt image at this point, it might seem that to turn to one "pole" alone is to lose both.

I can further indicate this pattern of polarization by observing the near commonplace that the contemporary purveyor of theological discourse can no longer assume any widespread explicit sense of some linkage between any "God" and any "man" of whom he would speak. The causes of this condition may be differently diagnosed. Perhaps the trouble which questions the reality of the relationship is rooted in its terms. The pole of "God" has often, of course, been associated with some notion of ontological superiority or priority. That such notions have had hard going in our time is an understatement. No empirical realities appear to make easily credible the concept of the unchanging. And the pain linked with that loss becomes bearable when it becomes exhilaratingly clear that it is man (or at least no superior order of being) who shall control the career of the process of change. In pop theological terminology, the "God-of-the-Given" and the "God-of-the-gaps" are gone. And where they have vanished, "God-the-Ground" seems destined soon to be found. The efforts of Bishop Robinson and his more sophisticated counterparts at this point will very probably appear to many as proposing a geographical solution to an ontological problem. They nevertheless seem to require a double order of causality.

Given this situation, little wonder should be experienced over the fact that men have come to feel that to be pure of heart theologically is to will one thing: one or the other. Shall we will man? Who can do other — even apart from the contemporary embarrassment over transcendence? And who can any longer find persuasive the claim of the godly to a special datum, a holy history, a discourse with its own rules and a community with its own cult? What do we have, after all, to add in practical terms to the profound portrayal of health in human relationships offered by someone like Erich Fromm? Perhaps we can add a lingering touch of transcendence and provide an ideological rite of passage at the same time in a dramatic construct concerning God's place in the past and his absence in the present. To do so, of course, is not to let the theological circle become an ellipse again — unless one can manage a speculative commitment to a grand historical dialectic and so gain its guarantees.

On the other hand, life at the other pole has its attractions too. "They" cannot touch you after all, for Christianity is not a religion, and all historical, psychological, or other modes of attack on religion really do free man for faith in the God who dwells beyond this brutish tinkering with the toys of belief.

It is perhaps understandable that theologians like the firm ground the poles provide. Some seem to like it well enough to try to stand at both poles at once, without yet trying to bring them intelligibly together. One may say, for example, that God is the subject of the sentence that man is the subject of faith.[1] If someone objects that such a saying simply forfeits meaningfulness, he merely reveals that single-minded human reliance on the principle of contradiction must give way to the *duality* of the God-man relationship.

Clearly this broad sketch of influential contemporary theologies lacks detail. Yet I would argue that all kinds of fascinating detail can be located by reference to the tendency of polarization, in what may be said to be either its "horizontal" diastatic development or its "vertical" dialectical development. That locating is a large order and not one which I shall

---

[1] This specific formulation is from Barth (*Church Dogmatics* [Edinburgh: T. & T. Clark, 1936——] vol. 1, part 1, pp. 280–81), but it fits a wide range of dialectical theologians. For an examination of this theme in Bultmann's ethics, for example, see Thomas C. Oden, *Radical Obedience* (Philadelphia: Westminster Press, 1964).

try to fill, except insofar as the third part of the paper draws upon such detail in its constructive concern. It is in fact the constructive interest upon which I want to concentrate, and for that purpose the broad sketch before us is sufficient.

The theological posture informing this paper yields a critical response to the diastatic and dialectical tendencies. Negation comes too cheaply to a theologian, and I shall give a larger portion of these pages to the costly work of affirmation. But the orientation which I have sought to provide thus far requires a transition which becomes a word of criticism.

On the one hand, the human role must win conscious commitment from the theologian. Despite all talk of theology as doxology, it must be insisted that man's praise of God speaks to men. More than a few theological witnesses from the centuries and nearly all those voices heard within the Chicago theological tradition have thought this requirement not unrealistic because the praise of God speaks *of* that which man knows. The appeal to experience in our history is not a masked argument from authority. The dialectical theologian who would speak of both God and man in a kind of incoherent coincidence of opposites of his own seems to fare no better before this requirement. Two words are uttered simultaneously — and the effect seems to be that of a nonsense syllable. It is only superficially less cryptic to say that "Yes" and "No" meet to become "But," since by itself — however often repeated — that word becomes meaningless sound. In like fashion it is hard to be happy with the denial of speaking literally, univocally of God, or with theories of theological symbolism which make every term, and so none significantly, speak of the divine.[2]

But what is to be done when men seem no longer to know, or to acknowledge at least, the dimension of the transcendent? Why should they? Why not celebrate the birth of man? The

[2] Tillich's widely quoted interpretation of religious language does not make clear how it can avoid this result. Given the ontological access to God for all beings, the possibility of significant discrimination seems closed unless one is willing to opt for a schema connoting degrees-of-being. That option is entertained in Tillich, but not clearly affirmed.

tutelage of our past put a searching question to the celebrants. The ascent of man appears to correlate directly with the demise of God. But how reliable is the instrument of measurement? In view of the polar character of the God-man structure, it is hard to see how a generation of theologians can check the deity at the door of their studies (or bury him there) and still in fact expect to find man. We may outdo the mythical scientist in our devotion to the stuff of life, but that does not constitute a difference of kind which could support the researcher's identity as theologian. That special identity might, of course, still be rescued without recourse to "God," by an appeal to a particular state of self-consciousness which marks the theological student of "man." It might be possible to maintain the meaningfulness of such a distinction in subjectivity, though that would have to be shown. But one might wonder whether winning that battle would not leave the victor with a distinction of such diminished significance that a burial by "nine hundred and ninety-nine qualifications" would in fact have taken place. Moreover, it may be suggested (and I shall try to do so briefly in part three) that conditions in reality outside the theologian, more than any internal instinct for self-preservation, speak for the desirability of retaining the rhythm of polarity in his work.

But this line of argument may fail to convince. We do live in a time when Occam's razor cuts away at our own identity. Can we any longer convince even ourselves with our invocations of the depth dimension in experience? Perhaps another consideration pointing to the polar procedure should be stated. We might recall that we are not done describing the structure of our faith when we have spoken of God and of man. We witness to *Christian* faith, or even to Christian atheism, to cast the net as widely as I can. It is possible to see such reference to the Christ as a kind of intellectual exercise; but that is surely not how Christians have understood themselves in making their witness. The Christ is not an abstraction, a slightly dull construct flowing from a mind making a counteroffensive against polarization. Rather he is said to be actuality, the one in whom the authentic reality of God and man is definitely realized. Faith's concern with the Christ has distinct theological identity, as surely as its speech about one called Jesus is not proposed as a colorful symbol to warm the stark logic of the principle of identity.

In explicating such speech and stating such a concern one must speak of both God and man, but of their coinherence or coherence rather than of their identity or polarization. Clearly here theologians have seemed more skilled at negation than affirmation. But something solid comes through all the adverbial exclusions. One is speaking here of a duality in which a distinction is secured in such a way that a sharing of reality repulses the rhythm of separation. That sharing involves such matters as a common world, a common concern, and a common selfhood. While all manner of sins have been committed in the name of creedal "intention," it is possible to speak of the tendency or logic of such Christological statements without returning to the immensely subtle debates of the past.

Nor do I seek to take up directly here, even in a preliminary way, the urgent task of constructive work in Christology. Precisely because the witness to Christ treats of historical reality, we may take it truly seriously when we let the intentionality disclosed in that witness direct us in our concerns to speak of God to men in a period which seems beset with new predicaments, and when moral vision fails to focus, giving way to an astigmatism of spirit. Thus will the primal act of contemporary confession come to bear flesh in those more derivative provinces roughly designated by such terms as "apologetics" or "ethics." Such speech, attendant to the meaning of the Christ, will find its cadences fashioned by the principle of coherence. Informed by the insistent actuality of the Christ, the theologian will seek to see life in terms of the primacy of relationships which that principle presupposes. That will involve a pointed correction of the ontological atomism implicit in the logic of polarization. But more specifically, the theologian so tutored will try to be open to strands of sensibility which speak of that particular relationship in which God and man share. And out of that process he will try to win a strategy for Christian witness in this time. In Part III I seek to take a first step toward showing how the fundamentally formal rhythm of coherence can bear on the situation in which we stand today.

This proposal certainly sounds officious and perhaps even pompous..For that reason, before going further, it may be helpful for me to offer a more modest interlude of historical description which shows that this sketch of the rhythms of spirit does fit at least one figure bearing flesh — Sören Kierkegaard. Here the call to Christian coherence can be seen to win effects in areas more clearly linked to faith's confessional concerns. With that instruction in hand, we may be better able to glimpse how the principle of coherence can have methodological efficacy in the more diffused areas I approach in Part III.

II

Kierkegaard's reflection reveals the same tendency toward polarization which seems to lie beneath the contrasts evident in the contemporary theological scene. That the claim to stand in his line of descent is voiced from very disparate quarters is intelligible, given the heritage of his literature and the executors of his estate. But it is unfortunate that this picture of Kierkegaard as a classic self-contradiction continues to pass nearly unchallenged, because he can show us not only the pull of polarization, but also a theological process of critical reassessment. He would move back toward coherence, though neither his life at its close nor the course of his influence up to the present really makes that apparent.

Kierkegaard's thought reflects the centrifugal character of protest. The conditions calling forth the protest carry certain similarities to some of the characteristics of our century's theological distress. An anecdote may set the stage for us. In 1838 Hans Lassen Martensen's doctoral dissertation, "On the Autonomy of the Human Consciousness," was translated into Danish. While Kierkegaard will never let us forget that it was Martensen who would go "beyond Hegel," that attempted advance was not evident or irritating, at least, to the Hegelian true believers. One such, J. A. Bornemann, published an enthusiastic review of the dissertation in which he proclaimed by way of Martensen, but in dependence on Hegel, that the principle of contradiction had been overcome. More specifically, the battles between rationalism and supernaturalism are happily past. After all, Hegel's philosophy shows us that the infinite is not a "bad" infinite, separated from the finite. Seeing now the true infinite, rationalism (which had strayed to an isolated finitude) and supernaturalism (which had sought a separated infinitude) can join hands.

Kierkegaard reacted, privately in his papers, insisting that the principle of contradiction applies in life and in thought,[3] and then publicly in offering Either/Or (1843), whose hectic eloquence courses around the cry: "Tautology is and remains still the supreme principle, the highest law of thought."[4] Moreover, a major thrust of his authorship bears forward the contention that Hegel is un-systematic in the sense that all identities dissolve within the massive mechanism of the dialectic of mediation. Caught up in this rhythm of protest, Kierkegaard recruits categories which amount to committing theological suicide. The striking thing is not that he does so (history offers examples enough), but that he sees what is happening and lets the center of his concern call him back from the brink. He might help us to see and to do likewise.

The categories carrying the protest are metaphysical. God cannot well be blurred in a vague identity with man because "God is pure subjectivity, perfect, pure subjectivity. He has no objective being whatever in him; for everything that has such objective being comes thereby into the realm of relativities."[5] Even motifs apparently affirming relatedness reveal the pull of polarization: man is created in the image of God; but that image is the image of opposites.

While the inner thrust of this distinction between God and man seems to depend on metaphysical opposition, the lan-

[3] See Sören Kierkegaard's Papirer, ed. P. A. Heiberg and Victor Kuhr, 11 vols. (Copenhagen: Gyldendals, 1909–48) V A 68–69.
[4] Kierkegaard, Either/Or, trans. Walter Lowrie, David F. Swenson, and Lillian M. Swenson, 2 vols. (Princeton: Princeton Univ. Press, 1944) 1:30.
[5] Kierkegaard's Papirer XI 2 A 54.

guage of faith can be appropriated. Thus it is in the meta-physical principle of individuation which (it would surely seem) "makes it possible that in the particular instance one can be guilty or not guilty" that Kierkegaard finds the clue to the religious reality of "total guilt." He writes:

> He who totally or essentially is guiltless cannot be guilty in the particular instance; but he who is totally guilty can very well be innocent in the particular instance. So then, not only by being guilty in a particular instance does a man denounce himself as essentially guilty (*totum est partibus suis prius*), but also by being innocent in the particular instance (*totum est partibus suis prius*).[6]

Kierkegaard saw that this line of thought is approaching a point at which "God becomes so endlessly exalted that there is absolutely no real relationship at all between God and the individual man."[7] There is material in his literary production which suggests not only Kierkegaard's approach to that point, but his arrival as well. Life at that destination does remind us of the polarizing tendencies leading into our period. We can hear in Kierkegaard a Barth insisting that "the subject of reve-lation (sc. God) is the Subject that remains indissolubly Subject. We cannot get behind this Subject. It cannot become an object."[8] Out beyond that insistence lies the oddity of writing a row of volumes about a Subject whom one can-not know and who cannot care. On the other hand, Barth's stated wariness over a lingering anthropocentrism in Kierke-gaard does see something; for the man who asked for nothing more than honesty may not be far removed from those men who now claim that nothing more *could* be asked. Subjectivity is the truth, he did say; and does it really help then to say that the true passion of faith can correspond to only one ob-ject, if you will not or cannot specify that object intelligibly?

[6] Kierkegaard, *Concluding Unscientific Postscript to the Philosophi-cal Fragments*, trans. David F. Swenson and Walter Lowrie (Prince-ton: Princeton University Press, 1944), p. 471. (Italics his.)

[7] *Kierkegaard's Papirer* X 1 A 59.

[8] Karl Barth, *The Doctrine of the Word of God*, trans. G. T. Thom-son (Edinburgh: T. & T. Clark, 1936), p. 438.

What will keep one from concluding that the dumb pagan bowing with real passion before his idol, in Kierkegaard's famous illustration, or the triumphant technician of our age with his undoubted ardor, really does have all the truth worth talking about?[9]

Kierkegaard was kept from that conclusion; and a persuasive case can be made for finding the corrective principle in his Christology. Of course, the polarizing strain can offer its own Christology. The Christ comes "to do away with the absolute unlikeness in absolute likeness."[10] We may be expected to know something of that rhythm, though Kierkegaard had such a clear vision of the distance between the poles that he permitted himself no facile preoccupation with only one in an untroubled theology of secularity. Rather does he see that it is hard enough to muster more than sheer coexistence of the two natures for the work of this Christ. And the acceptance of even that work must find its way past metaphysical meaninglessness and psychological suicide. To affirm the Christ is to act against all rational order (which is rooted in the principle of contradiction) and without any personal reason (since the certainty of suffering forbids classification as the fulfillment of subjectivity).

That price might still not be too high if by paying it one would gain admission to a faith that commends itself at other strategic points of theological interest. After all, the fee fixed for this highly disjunctive faith is not arbitrary. Given the polarizing statement of the relationship between God and man, the alternatives for christological formulation are not ample. In his literature Kierkegaard goes down the list, entertaining

[9] Thus Gerd-Gunther Grau (*Die Selbstauflösung des christlichen Glaubens* [Frankfurt: G. Schulte-Bulmke, 1963]) sees Kierkegaard's thought as suicidal. He points to two such moments: (1) a circular one in which the sheer discontinuity affirmed of "Religion B" returns that religion to an aesthetic moment by virtue of the absence of any continuity, and (2) a linear one by which a development within a temporal progression advances to the point where all hope for the temporal is lost.

[10] Kierkegaard, *Philosophical Fragments or a Fragment of Philosophy*, trans. D. F. Swenson (Princeton: Princeton Univ. Press, 1936), p. 37.

such themes as the blessed fall motif and Christ as the second stage of a single eternal creative decree. These options do not significantly alter the issue and do not really alleviate what is asked of the believer. In fact such a survey serves to show that what is really at issue is the possibility that anything that man or a God-man might do could matter to God. At the peak of polarization the only access to a sense of responsibility becomes a psychological argument concerning the self's orderly development. A while ago I suggested that the *theologian* of secularity seems able to find no more than subjective status for the distinctiveness of his vocation. Now Kierkegaard shows us how an apostleship grounded in the qualitative abyss only answers the question of ethical motivation by warning against the psychological shock associated with the sudden change sure to strike those who suppose they will resist the sovereign One.

Kierkegaard pulls away from attempting such an answer. It would be "foolish speech," for God is not mocked. And there are existential actuality and theological primitivity to the Christ witness that force Kierkegaard to look again at the auspices under which his protest has been conducted. The Christ must be acknowledged. Even at the height of the polarizing tendency, while perched on the paradox of coexistence, Kierkegaard never did accept the resolution of fictionalism. That solution is not so much finally rejected as never fully considered, precisely because Christology can never be reduced to the *derivative* status in which it can be assessed as one alternative for "resolving" tensions flowing from more fundamental theological forces.

> Offence has essentially to do with the composite term God and man, or with the God-Man. Speculation naturally had the notion that it "comprehended" God-Man — this one can easily comprehend, for speculation in speculating about the God-Man leaves out temporal existence, contemporaneousness, and reality. It is altogether a pitiful and dreadful thing that this (which one does not characterize too strongly by saying that it is a mere prank

and a way of making a fool of folks) has been feted as profundity. No, the *situation* is inseparable from the God-Man, the situation that an individual man who stands beside you is God-Man. The God-Man is not the unity of God and mankind. Such terminology exhibits the profundity of optical illusion. The God-Man is the unity of God and an individual man.[11]

The Christ witness, then, cannot be assimilated within the pattern of polarization. It becomes ascendent in a work of reconstruction. Let it be openly said: "The birth of Christ is not only an event on earth, but also in heaven."[12] Kierkegaard's employment of the kenosis motif also moves to make the point that God is fully involved in human time:

> God's servant-form is . . . not a mere disguise, but is actual; it is not a parastatic body, but an actual body; and from the hour that in the omnipotent purpose of his omnipotent love God became a servant, he has so to speak imprisoned himself in his resolve, and is now bound to go on (to speak foolishly) whether it pleases him or no. He cannot then betray himself. There exists for him no such possibility as that which is open to the noble king, suddenly to show that he is after all the king — which is no perfection in the king (that he has this possibility), but merely discloses his impotence, and the impotence of his resolve, that he cannot really become what he desires to be.[13]

Here we have not come all the way round to identity surely. There is still place enough for the tension of faith. But Kierkegaard insists that the Christian advance over the "Socratic position" "contains no self contradiction. . . . Thought is free to occupy itself therewith as with the strangest proposal possible."[14] One cannot, of course, simply deliver such a verdict

---

[11] Kierkegaard, *Training in Christianity*, trans. Walter Lowrie (Princeton: Princeton Univ. Press, 1941), pp. 83–84 (Italics his).

[12] *Kierkegaard's Papirer* II A 594.

[13] Kierkegaard, *Philosophical Fragments*, p. 44.

[14] Ibid., p. 85.

of consistency. And Kierkegaard sets about to make his payments. That process involves a turning from metaphysical opposition to religious rebellion as a way of focusing the relationship between God and man: "If the difference is infinite between God, who is in heaven, and you, who are on earth: the difference is infinitely greater between the Holy One and the sinner." [15] One cannot claim that none of the strain of polarization lingers, but the direction of the formulation is clear: "God creates out of *nothing*, wonderful, you say; yes, to be sure, but he does what is still more wonderful: he makes saints (the communion of saints) out of sinners." [16]

It is probably incorrect to try to find in Kierkegaard a full development of this turn toward coherence. Certainly a systematic statement of it is not available. Never in his short life did he welcome the professor's pen. There are, however, some delicious suggestions which could be explored in a more leisurely setting. The clearest of these lie directly in the domain of the basic theological polarity. Kierkegaard accepts the thrust of transcendence but bends it toward temporal purposes:

> Oh, marvellous omnipotence of love! A man cannot bear that his "creations" should be something directly in apposition to himself, and so he speaks of them in a tone of disparagement as his "creations". But God who creates out of nothing, who almightily takes from nothing and says, "Be", lovingly adjoins, "Be something even in apposition to me." Marvellous love, even His omnipotence is under the sway of love!
>
> Hence the reciprocal relationship. If God were only the Almighty, there would be no reciprocal relationship, inasmuch as for the Almighty the creation is nothing. But for love it is something. Incomprehensible omnipotence of love! For in comparison with this omnipotence it seems as though one could comprehend better the omnipotence

[15] Sören Kierkegaard, "The High Priest," a discourse published with *Christian Discourses*, trans. Walter Lowrie (London: Oxford Univ. Press, 1939), p. 368.

[16] *Kierkegaard's Papirer* II A 758 (italics his).

which creates out of nothing (which nevertheless one cannot comprehend); but this omnipotence, more marvellous than the genesis of all creation, which constrains itself and lovingly makes of the creature something in apposition to itself — oh, marvellous omnipotence of love! . . . So then, love, which made a man to be something (for omnipotence let him come into existence, but love let him come into existence *for* God) lovingly requires something of him. Here we have the reciprocal relationship.[17]

These adjustments, animated by the concern for coherence, establish the basis for serious work in apologetics and ethics. One who would work there can find aid in Kierkegaard. The clamor of the attack on the church and the crowd should not be permitted to conceal the essentially constructive tone of Kierkegaard's concern even in his last years. Furthermore, the turn which Kierkegaard's thought takes toward coherence could endorse an attempt to regard the pieces conventionally placed in the earliest of the stages on life's way as being much more than a sort of psychological propadeutic to Christian existence. It was after all in the *Postscript*, which surely does not fail to speak of paradox, that Kierkegaard said, "There are three stages, an aesthetic, an ethical, a religious. . . . But in spite of this triple division, the book is nevertheless an Either-Or. The ethical and religious stages have, in fact, an essential relationship to one another." [18] And in that ethico-religious *Or* he had said of the aesthetical — understanding by that term that in a man "by which he is immediately what he is": "By the absolute choice the ethical is always posited; but from this it does not follow by any means that the aesthetical is excluded." [19]

Nonetheless it is difficult to develop this type of argument without feeling that one has left the terrain of analysis and may even be skating on thin ice as far as application is concerned. The shape of the Danish situation seemed to push

[17] Kierkegaard, *Christian Discourses*, pp. 132–33 (italics his).
[18] Kierkegaard, *Concluding Unscientific Postscript*, p. 261.
[19] Kierkegaard, *Either/Or* 2:150.

Kierkegaard toward protest. And even when the pendulum of his protest does not itself swing distortedly, it reaches specific engagement with the human community most often at the opposite end of its course, out from his sensing of the domestication of transcendence in his time. It seems better, therefore, to put independently the question how a theology tutored by a similar sensitivity to the Christ witness, and so taking a similar turn toward coherence, might fit itself to the issues of our age.

III

Within the space remaining for this essay, I shall seek to add some substance to the skeletal sketch of a posture of Christian coherence by saying something about (1) the opportunity presented by the quest for wholeness in the human community; (2) a requirement imposed on any candidates seeking to fulfill that quest; (3) certain contributions being made toward such fulfillment within the human community; (4) a theological perspective anchored in the principle of coherence which can accept that opportunity and that requirement, and maximize those contributions; (5) the urgently needed process of measuring from that perspective the major material thrust of our time, technology; and (6) a specific suggestion of strategy for moving ahead with the human community toward wholeness in time.

(1) The human quest for wholeness stirs beneath the surface of our contemporary pluralism which often seems to constitute actual fragmentation. That that quest is not satisfied by the ministry of mass culture is made clear by the continuing popularity of existentialist themes. Sameness is not centeredness and deserves to be diagnosed as evasion. But the existentialist protest itself seems parasitic at this point, or at least sterile. It is difficult to manage the conversion by which anguish becomes faith, and despair the fulfillment of destiny. Perhaps both the American ethic of productivity and the existentialist protest to it represent essentially a single self-assertive thrust of the human being for self-affirmation. But man seems to be bent on finding more than either a greater gross

national product and homogenized group glories on the one hand, or more authentic absurdities on the other. Even the existentialist denials suggest this, as when Sartre seems very sure indeed what a God would look like were one to be found.

Man's achievements have brought him a novel predicament. The means for altering his destiny are in his hands, but which ends will ennoble the species? Fierce debates rage concerning the artificial production and prolongation of life. But these disputes pale before the larger question: "What do we wish 'life' to mean, knowing that we can wed wish and fact in so many instances?" That question cries for a perspective of the whole. And perhaps the matter of achievement does not really put the full point about wholeness. We achieve very well, and can do better still, and will; but we want desperately to be accepted apart from our achievements, and despite our failures. By itself the very effort to achieve seems suspiciously hollow — not empty surely, for its grandeur is most imposing — but hollow. This hollowness is what many contemporary playwrights and novelists have exposed, in a literature which can hardly be described as a statement of confidence.

More positively, we live in a time when an author in accepting a National Book Award can denounce the narrow snobbishness of the literary caste as blindness compounded by the formal posture of liberation, independence, and creativity.[20] Joined to that denunciation, a plea sounds for a return to the common world and to the use of intelligence therein. It is a time when scientists speak of questing after the ultimately simple structure of things. It would be excessive to claim that this is the stuff of which the dominant temper of the age is made. Indeed, one also witnesses tendencies to extend even further the fragmentation and specialization already at hand. But there does seem to be an increasing concern for relatedness, for relevance, within and between disciplines.

To be sure, such concern conducts its business chiefly on the level of description. It does not, consciously, or at least openly, propose material solutions. But it puts the question of

[20] Saul Bellow for *Herzog*.

wholeness, and one wonders on what grounds the theologian may decline to attempt an answer. To dismiss such data from the human community is, of course, possible. One can hold that the integrity of the divine answer requires a repudiation of this or of every human question. But such a response could only sustain itself if rooted in a "no-saying" to man at the most fundamental theological level. The principle of coherence is not so rooted, but pleads instead for a recognition of this human material as legitimately calling for an answering theology.

(2) Any answer which openly or subtly requires man to repudiate temporality will surely fail to find acceptance. It is not merely that we have buried so many absolutes in our time; it is that we know of no point of contact within us for some unchanging order of reality which would resist any compromise with temporality. That we have such notorious difficulty making distinctions of quality about things around us likely reflects the fact that the efforts to speak of multidimensional selfhood seem to tack on something artificial to the self's authentic temporal reality. In the only world we have been given, psychologists have taught us that the self's identity is derivable from its environment; [21] philosophers that a person's corporeal character is adequate to the expression of consciousness; [22] and biologists that the gap between man and machine is rapidly closing. [23] In the face of all this and more of the same we are hard put to appeal to a distinctive origin, not the least so when it appears that God, man, and machine alike can create *imago sui*. Nor does it seem probable that we can make convincing any claim to a special end. Trouble enough there is in creating interest in even a moderately long-range temporal good. We easily underestimate this reign of the sense of temporality. To ask, for example, "Why is there anything at all

[21] See the review of the contemporary discussion by Martin J. Buss, "Self-Theory and Theology," *Journal of Religion* 45 (1965).

[22] See, for example, P. F. Strawson, *Individuals* (London: Methuen, 1959) and his article "Persons," *Minnesota Studies in the Philosophy of Science* (Minneapolis: Univ. of Minnesota Press, 1958) 2:330–53.

[23] The writings of Norbert Wiener make this point in a nontechnical way. See, for example, *God and Golem, Inc.* (Cambridge: M.I.T. Press, 1964).

given?" simply strikes men today as raising an unnatural, if not wholly meaningless, question. We live with givenness, growth, decay, and death all the time.

Faced with this barrier to other-worldliness in any form, the theologian can, of course, appeal to logical gaps or psychological insecurities and bank these deficits in a *tu quoque* argument upon which he hopes to base his faith.[24] It can still be argued that neither the scientist nor his more ardent advance man, the technician, has really shown that scientific methodology does more than work well with certain limited questions in which the issue of wholeness is not yet in sight. Such an argument from silence seems in poor taste, however, and, more important, a serious error in strategy. What I am speaking of as the requirement of temporality seems to reach us from more quarters than some coterie of specialists. Moreover, we ought not to assume at the outset that the sway of temporality is bad business. Perhaps the world is doing us a favor in making it clear to us that an entity which is in no sense temporal is as good as dead, and well gone at that.

(3) Time's reign may be unchallenged from without; but its capacity completely to tyrannize man's quest for wholeness is hindered by its intrinsic tentativity. Events have their reality in a large sense in their eventuality. Thus the tendency to see the momentariness and change linked with time to be an insuperable barrier to wholeness stands in need of review. The experienceable awareness of continuity in change should occasion interest in a linear conception of wholeness which might appropriately replace the punctiliar one which dominates so much discussion of this topic.

There are forces at work in the contemporary situation which seem to move man toward such a linear wholeness. One of the better known examples is the process of psychotherapy. Men here quite openly speak of self as process and health as continuum. Carl Rogers' characterization of the direction of healing well accords with an acceptance of temporality as that with which we must work. As one moves toward (or in)

[24] See, for example, William W. Bartley III, *Retreat to Commitment* (New York: Knopf, 1962).

health the person (a) recognizes and expresses himself more freely, (b) has a sense of the immediacy of experience, (c) loosens the "cognitive map" of his experience, (d) moves away from remoteness from self and other, from rigidity. Emphasis is also placed on the fact that the instruments which move man in this direction are not essentially other than the goal intended, that the psychotherapeutic relationship, for example, is simply a particular form of responsiveness to the dynamics operating in interpersonal relationships generally.[25]

(4) These efforts to reach wholeness within time can be welcomed by a theology of coherence. In fact the pattern of the illustration has special attractiveness. "Sin" may well be said to be "shut-in-ness"; and healing to be marked by and mediated by revelation. That it is the creator God who redeems is here suggested by the fact that the reciprocal revelation of selves constitutes a specification of the inevitable relatedness of selves given with existence. The community of faith has no need to be surprised by the presence of energies working for healing among men and only mistakenly supposes its mission to be the abolition of those resources. In fact, the Christian has reason for optimism, for he does not need to speak of the "miracle" of dialogue.[26] He can appeal to his faith in a creator God and so affirm that change need not defeat the quest for wholeness any more than creativity conflicts with divine completeness.

Again here, as in Part I, a more pointed incentive to such affirmations comes from the area of Christology. God is the present source of the world's reality; and the Christian not only knows this more truly because of the Christ (though he does that), but also believes it to be more true than before. For the Christ is neither a mere logical construct combining the notions "God" and "man," nor a metaphysical miracle constituting the coherence of two unrelated realities. In the actuality of the Christ the coherence of God and man comes to

[25] See Carl Rogers, *On Becoming a Person* (Boston: Houghton Mifflin, 1961).

[26] To take the title of Reuel Howe's recent book published by Seabury, 1963.

expression, but also makes an advance meaningful for both God and man as living entities. It is thus now doubly possible that the Christian quest for wholeness can take the form of the world upon itself, and that requires immersion in temporality. It would seem natural to expect that temporality will place its mark not only on the means, but every bit as much on the "end" of wholeness. Thus one will not speak of wholeness as reunion but as genuine growth, as advance into novelty.[27]

But to accept the energies of healing at hand in the human community does not mean to accept unrealistic ideologies or expectations linked with them. If it is unrealistic to try to flee the terrestial, it is equally so to ground one's hopes on a simplistic analysis of the texture of temporality. The danger may be the greater for being the more subtle. The temporal is the tentative. The meaning of that for faith is not merely that ultimately fixed destinies are subject to temporal distribution. Those "ultimate" destinies are constituted temporally; they consist of temporality so that no certainty of supernatural telos can exercise a tyranny over the course of time. The issue or outcome has its reality in time and finds its formative causality within time. Now neither historical consensus nor present experience portrays utter uniformity or even a diversity drawn together in perfect harmony. The principle of coherence and the basic theological polarity it presupposes provide a perspective from which the discordant diversity of temporality can be viewed.

In this perspective it becomes clear that time has a tentativeness with respect to ethical status as well as successiveness of influence. Or, putting the point otherwise, unbelief is not self-deception; it is in fact a faith of its own.[28] Thus, we surely have no reason to stand with those who make all activity out to be achievement, and all achievement to be an advance. Again one must warn against letting the life of the polarity

[27] Cf. Gordon Allport's distinction between "growth religion" and "safety religion" in *The Individual and His Religion* (New York: Macmillan Co., 1950).

[28] On this point see Terrence Penelhum's critique of "Pascal's Wager" in *Journal of Religion* 44 (1964).

level out in a style bearing the simplicity of death. In coherence God and man come together not to coincide, but to share. In Part I, I spoke of sharing a world and so a self, but also a concern. The man of faith surely errs if he turns from temporality to seek an ideal which cannot be real; but the error he risks is just as great if he accepts the aims of his time without further ado. He need not do so, for he knows not only the universal relatedness of men but the specific rootage of his own community of faith as well. If revelation requires of its participants truly honest identification, the Christian who disavows his heritage has disqualified himself. Rather does he rightly let his actuality come to expression, though he does so in order that community with any contemporary can be attained. Since he would take time as ally he is open to novelty in the emerging community. And in retaining his critical capacities, he does not escape to the eternal but accepts temporality in attempting to articulate a principle of discrimination for its abundance. Attentiveness to temporality does not dictate an annihilation of judgment any more than personal wholeness means the bald togetherness of all trivia in any moment of time.

(5) An application of such critical "coherent" judgment in *this* time will require an assessment of the thrust toward technology. That point hardly seems debatable, but beyond it alternatives do become available. On the one hand, of course, we hear of the glories of technology, not only from the secular sphere with their operation on genetic bootstrap,[29] but also from the sacred where the logic of desacralization is said to permit one to see that technology is the new missionary movement which breaks down ontocratic structures.[30] On the other hand, there are the many particular problems which seem to resist glossing over. They make one pause to listen seriously to the prophets of despair who see the technological society as an irrational force incapable of self-criticism, inevitably trans-

[29] See the piece by the geneticist H. J. Muller, "Perspectives for the Life Sciences," *Bulletin of the Atomic Scientists* 20 (1964).

[30] Of the many such appeals, see Arend Th. van Leeuwen, *Christianity in World History: The Meeting of the Faiths of East and West*, trans. H. H. Hoskins (London: Edinburg, 1964).

forming quality into quantity, means into ends.[31] After listening a while, one can be attracted to the view that Christian existence is the perpetuation of Christian tradition which should not be tied to the tendencies of any one time — or at least not to this one.

A theology informed by the intentionality of coherence simply cannot settle for either of these solutions. The ethical status of the expanding technology would seem to be a matter of tentativeness. Still, it may be far too simple to say that technology is simply ethically neutral. Technology may give such a strong and specific turn to temporality that to say its ethical status is tentativity would be an understatement. Does the fact that machines are "literally minded," that consequences of machine operations reach us with frightening speed and often without review,[32] or that it seems difficult to hold the drive of technology back from not only replacing personal roles but actually inhabiting people — do such facts suggest that technology weighs against the qualities of critical reflection and free responsiveness which seem essential to human wholeness? On the other hand, we are told that technology is creating a society of abundance in which we can no longer profit at our neighbor's expense, but only at his profit; that the rhythm in the tide of our time is driving us away from producing things and towards serving people.[33] Does that development not ap-

[31] This is the formulation of one of the more extreme pessimists, Jacques Ellul, *The Technological Society* (New York: Alfred A. Knopf, 1965).

[32] This point is made with considerable force by Norbert Wiener in *God and Golem, Inc.* As a rather dramatic datum for this view, one could consult Dr. Ralph E. Lapp's article, "Do Developers Regret A-Bomb?" for World Book Encyclopedia Science Service, Inc. Lapp cites Dr. Cyril S. Smith's contribution to a list of reasons for the making of the atomic bomb by the group of scientists of which Smith was a member: "Then once we got started, the desire to do the job well took over, and carried us along to the conclusion." Lapp expands on the theme: "In general, technology is remorseless. If a bomb could be made, it would be. If made, it would be used. Technology manufactures its own momentum."

[33] See the "conversation" by Ralph Helstein, Gerard Piel and Robert Theobald, "Jobs, Machines, and People" available from the Center for the Study of Democratic Institutions, Santa Barbara, Calif., 1964.

pear to be driving us toward the kind of interpersonal involvement which facilitates wholeness according to the argument of this paper? I ask these questions not in order to try to answer them, but because they well ask that other question: "Has temporality taken such a turn that the formula of the real as neutral over against the ideal simply no longer applies?"

In any case the role of man is surely changing. What shall he now do? Serve?[34] Contemplate?[35] Play?[36] My discussion here suggests that — whatever else he may do, he shall reveal himself; and a diagnosis of the problems of our time turns up insularity as an insistent theme. We can perhaps seek to accept the apparent anonymity of technological instruments' entering into human affairs and still build in the flexibility which seems requisite for responsibly revelatory personal relationships.[37] But it seems probable that the pattern of the future will place severe strain on the structures of revelation with which we are now familiar. And so I want to give the last paragraphs of this essay to the possibility of finding new media for man's sharing of his selfhood.

(6) The urgency of the need for new inquiry into the matter and means of communication coincides happily with a contemporary willingness to lift the rigid limitations of recent views of language and expression. Scientists speak of the role of heuristic vision,[38] philosophers of varying language games,[39]

[34] See another of the Center's studies, "Toward a Moral Economy," by W. H. Ferry, and *New Careers for the Poor*, by Arthur Pearl and Frank Riessman (New York: Free Press, 1965). This is of course the view which Harvey Cox has popularized in his *The Secular City* (New York: Macmillan Co., 1965).

[35] See Josef Pieper, *Leisure, the Basis of Culture* (New York: New American Library, 1963); Sebastian de Grazia, *Of Time, Work and Leisure* (New York: Doubleday & Co., 1964); and Hannah Arendt, *The Human Condition* (Garden City, N.Y.: Doubleday & Co., 1959).

[36] See Herbert Marcuse, *Eros and Civilization: A Philosophical Inquiry into Freud* (Boston: Beacon Press, 1955).

[37] On this point, see Rogers, *On Becoming a Person*.

[38] Michael Polanyi has argued this point in several works. See particularly, *Personal Knowledge* (Chicago: Univ. of Chicago Press, 1958).

[39] For Wittgenstein's own statement on this view, see *Philosophical*

and literary analysts stress anew the role of metaphor and myth. It is becoming possible to regard language with a new excitement, to use it with greater sensitivity, and yet to reach beyond it or beneath it for other avenues of expression.

Words no longer need be regarded as a pale report on reality. They are increasingly seen as actuality, as creative, as acts of discovery. At the same time words may be only one aspect of the active intercommunication of selves. Linguistic studies show a willingness to acknowledge this, not referring to some ontological dualism demeaning to language, but to a reality "between the words," to a living field filled with tensions created by the interplay of relations which throw up meanings.[40] This recognition urges that far more serious attention be given to the relevance of imagination, metaphor, and myth,[41] as ways of creating apertures in the insularity of selves. Such a strategy is not dictated by the distance of the reality of which we would speak, but by the concern to keep our words as close to the encountered immediacy as possible.

Along with this renewed interest in language we witness an emphasis on communication of another kind. We are told to shift from favoring auditory harmonies to concern with visual syntheses.[42] Such a strategy, accepting temporality, and so its own mission as a co-creator of change, can affirm a "tactile" age without embarrassment. Some of us are going to have some relearning to do. But the personal word which reveals and makes whole may well bear flesh too. That would seem

---

Investigations, trans. G. E. M. Anscombe (New York: Macmillan Co., 1953), p. 12e. See also Strawson, *Individuals.*

[40] See, for example, the unpublished paper "Metaphor and Anti-Metaphor" by Beda Allemann prepared for the Third Consultation on Hermeneutics, Metaphor, Symbol, Image, and Meaning, at Drew University, 1966.

[41] As a sampling, see Ian Ramsey, *Models and Mystery* (London: Oxford Univ. Press, 1964), Owen Barfield, *Language, Meaning and History* (Middleton, Conn.: Wesleyan Univ. Press, 1967), and Iris Murdoch, "Vision and Choice in Morality," *Christian Ethics and Contemporary Philosophy,* ed. Ian Ramsey (New York: Macmillan Co., 1966), pp. 195–218.

[42] See Marshall McLuhan, *The Gutenberg Galaxy* (Toronto: Univ. of Toronto Press, 1962), and *Understanding Media: The Extensions of Man* (New York: McGraw-Hill, 1964).

particularly suitable if it is the case that our language is most impoverished when dealing with relationships rather than with abstracted entities or supposed substances.

The ancient peril of the pendulum is alive in these changes of course. We could without much difficulty ride the crest of these new developments into that fatal paradise where the theologian has it both ways in a reverse rationalism to which only the confused can gain admission.[43] If we speak of coherence with the world of men we must speak of order, though that be an organic order and not a mechanical one. It will be a new order — one, for example, in which things can be seen as signs of words as well as the opposite, but still an order in which both words and things reflect patterns or cycles of meaning.[44] And one who no longer holds that selves are separate substances may be permitted to hope that the very experience of transcendence may be communal in character.

[43] See the words of caution voiced by James Barr, *The Semantics of Biblical Language* (London: Oxford Univ. Press, 1961), and *Biblical Words for Time* (Naperville, Ill.: Alec R. Allenson, 1962). For a pointed illustration, see H. D. Lewis' sharp criticism of J. Baillie's *Sense of the Presence of God* in *Journal of Theological Studies*, 25 (1964), 1. Lewis writes: "Professor Baillie leans heavily on G. E. Moore's distinction between the meaning of an affirmation and the analysis of it and on Russell's idea of 'knowledge by acquaintance,' but he pays no heed to well known discussions of the former principle or to the severe limitations which Russell himself would have placed on 'knowledge by acquaintance.' We can certainly not pass without further argument, from notions like these to insistence on acquaintance with religious realities of which Moore and Russell themselves would have denied all awareness." It should be observed that Mr. Lewis finds Baillie to be not only too bold, but too "timid" as well, "because he wants to discover in the complexities of the moral life as such the sort of distinctively religious and transcendent reality which must be expressly recognized on its own account." The full statement of Lewis' reaction may be found in his "The Voice of Conscience and the Voice of God," pp. 172–80 in Ramsey, ed., *Christian Ethics and Contemporary Philosophy*.

[44] Among American anthropological linguists Kenneth Burke has been a leader in paying attention to the variety and vitality of the modes of use of language. See his *A Grammar of Motives* (New York: Prentice-Hall, 1941, in paperback, Meridian Books, with his *A Rhetoric of Motives*, 1962), and "What are the Signs of What? A Theory of 'Entitlement,'" *Anthropological Linguistics*, 4 (1962).

That community will itself not be a tensionless unity. As it changes, it may come to resemble what we now know as the church hardly at all. Yet, in all this change, we may realistically expect only commonality and not universality of insight. An eschatology of the omega point after all seems to suppress the dynamics of temporality as surely as, if more subtly than, conventional kingdoms do.

What we really need to say, I suppose, is that we simply do not and cannot know what specific forms and strategies an intentionality of coherence may require of us. The lineaments in which the present clothes the future are not that luminous. But that lack of knowledge should be no occasion for despair, but rather an opportunity and incentive to take seriously the attitude and activity of openness which the center of our faith's identity itself invites.

8

Is an Empirical Christology Possible?
ROGER HAZELTON

I

In the bewildering welter and cross fire of present-day theology there is one common feature which ought not to be neglected. I refer to a very widely shared and striking preoccupation with matters of Christology. Whatever may be one's dominant theological interest, whether in hermeneutics, ethics, secularity, or the "death-of-God" motif, this christological emphasis is noteworthy. I speak of it as christological because it evidences a general concern with the meaning of Jesus Christ for faith and unfaith in our time. I do not intend to suggest that it is engrossed with traditional problems or styled in classical doctrinal mannerisms, for this is clearly not the case. Yet surely no one can fail to see that there is a decidedly christological cast to contemporary ways of doing theology, and that this is especially prominent in the movements that like to think of themselves as being "new" or "radical" in their perspective and aim.

If I were asked to characterize the major stress in these contemporary efforts to relate thinking about Christ to present-day concerns and issues, I would have to use the word "empirical." That is, I believe, the only term that fairly describes what is actually the motive and method of this sort of inquiry. Negatively, it means that thinking about Christ is being done as much as possible without explicit reference to the transcendent, to what has traditionally been called his divine nature, even in some cases without reference to God. Positively, it means that what is sought is a christic understanding

221

of human experience and existence itself, Christ being taken as in some sense normatively, because also normally, human.

Let me specify a bit more carefully this empirical bent in contemporary Christology, or at least my own view of it for the purposes of this essay. Here we are dealing with a mode of thought that looks for the meaning of Christ within man's present experience, not beyond it; that therefore sees the theological task as providing a description and elucidation, a phenomenology, if you will, of faith's own self-understanding. Regarded as out of bounds in such an inquiry are deductive premises and conclusions having to do with the supposed divinity or deity of Christ. Matters of faith are treated, with a kind of calculated naïveté, as matters of fact. This remains true even when the events and meanings so described are not susceptible of being publicly verified by scientifically controlled observation and measurement.

This way of doing Christology is obviously at variance with the classical traditions and professes to be in basic conflict with them. Hence a careful examination may prove useful to both devotees and critics. What is commendable and what is questionable in this effort to empiricize Christ and to christify experience? Is it as radical or novel as its proponents seem to assert? More generally, is such an attempt possible and credible as Christian theology? Such queries serve to indicate the character of my concern.

II

To take the last of these questions first: Can such a reducing of the christological mystery and problem to empirical dimensions be justified theologically? The assertion that all statements about God are actually statements about man is becoming commonplace, and if accepted, would appear to give support to the current empiricist trend in Christology. However, the proposition that all theology is really anthropology is very far from being self-evident, no matter how axiomatic it may seem to some. There is, of course, a sense in which the proposition cannot be doubted: what men say about God tells much about themselves as well; faith-statements therefore constitute an invaluable source of human self-understanding. "Men show by what they worship what they are," in Emerson's familiar words; and thus religious actions and beliefs which refer ostensibly to the divine may quite properly be utilized to give significant information about what is empirically human.

We may go even further, agreeing, for example, that psychological interpretation of theological statements has shown how possible and plausible it is to account for religious phenomena "in terms of factors immanent within man's mental life without positing any supernatural or even transhuman factor at work." [1] No one in his right mind would deny that this applies also to Christology, which affords some particularly revealing glimpses of human motivation, frustration, and satisfaction.

All this is clear enough, but is not something more often implied, if not intended, in the proposition that theology is in fact anthropology? Does this mean that theology is a mode of discourse which says something about man when God is its ostensible subject, or does it mean instead that whatever is said about God must be regarded as only human self-revelation and nothing more? And if this second meaning is the one intended or implied, where does it leave us theologically? To agree with it would be to commit theological suicide, for it would involve granting that theology has nothing of its own to think about and that its work could be taken over and done better by other disciplines. Theology might still continue as a branch of the psychological and social sciences, but only at the price of abandoning its historic purpose and perspective. In that event its very name would be a misnomer, to be discarded as soon as its work could be absorbed into other fields of study.

This is naturally an appalling prospect to professional theologians, and the effort to avoid it might easily arouse suspicions of frightened self-interest on our part. Yet the issue is considerably more far-reaching and wide-ranging than that. What is at stake is nothing less than the worth and truth of

[1] John Macquarrie, *Principles of Christian Theology* (New York: Scribner's Sons, 1966), p. 25.

man's self-understanding itself. Karl Barth was quick to see this when, as William Hamilton remarks, he "loved to dangle the threatening figure of Feuerbach before the faces of anyone interested in the self, modern man, or despair." [2] For it was Feuerbach who first showed in his book *The Essence of Christianity* how Christian theology could be viewed as disguised and misguided anthropology. Using his well-known "psychogenetic method" to support the conclusion that doctrines which refer to God's acting or speaking are in truth but projections of human need or desire, Feuerbach prepared the way for Freud's later contention that religion, and a fortiori theology, constitute a last-ditch stand of the pleasure-principle which generates the wishful illusion of God's presumed reality. Pointing to Feuerbach, Barth indicated that it is always easy for a Christian thinker to slip from using experience as a theological category into an empiricism which is the dogmatic annihilation of all theology. In view of the turn taken by not a few contemporary thinkers, this warning is still timely and valid.

Surely it is not by denying the force of much in Feuerbach's analysis and argument that theologians ought to justify their intellectual vocation and its survival. Nothing can be gained by a gambit which at bottom only further illustrates the cogency of Feuerbach's position. Yet there are questions to be asked regarding this quite nonempirical assertion. Is it the case or not that man's thought of himself in terms of God is an infantile error to be removed by a more healthy and mature self-knowledge? Can theological inquiry be assimilated without loss or remainder into nontheological pursuits? Must we accept the proffered dilemma that theology in claiming to speak of God speaks in fact only of human experience or says nothing?

I have dwelt upon this general point because it has considerable bearing upon the issues posed by current work in Christology. To put it in the bluntest possible form, the at-tempt is being made to render Christ intelligible with no rel-

[2] In "The Death of God Theologies Today," *Christian Scholar*, Spring (1965), p. 36.

erence, or only the remotest reference, to God. As "the man for others," Christ is said to be "contagious" in his "freedom." Or it is said that the coming of Christ is a "secular" event which does not need to be viewed in any but empirical, non-transcendent terms. It is not what such characterizations affirm so much as what they deny that prompts our theological uneasiness. Can Chalcedon be gotten around so neatly? In other words, whatever ring of truth these characterizations have, do they succeed in giving an adequate interpretation of the very kinds of experience of Christ on behalf of which they profess to speak?

An adequate account of any experience, such as that of "being grasped" by Christ or "feeling loyalty" to him, must of course be accurate and honest. It should not claim more for the experience than the experience claims for itself. But neither should it begin by claiming less. When Paul van Buren writes that "the meaning of the Gospel is its use on the lips of those who proclaim it," [3] he gives no theological offense until he explains that what *he* means is that we must consider the use or function of the Gospel as separate and altogether different from the proclamation that is made. He claims, in short, to understand the meaning of faith better than faith can understand itself, by ruling out the very reference to a transcendent ground which alone can account for the behavior and speech of faith.

That a particular reference may be misguided or misplaced when Christians speak of Christ is always a possibility, to be sure. Then it becomes a proper matter for theological criticism and restatement. But any assertion that such reference is not or should not be made at all is one which can only be termed presumptuous and untrue. Speak of Christ without God, and you no longer have a Christ to speak about.

Dietrich Bonhoeffer is frequently appealed to in support of this secularized, functional empiricism in Christology. It is interesting therefore to observe how different his approach was from that of some of his latter-day disciples. "The chris-

[3] In *The Secular Meaning of the Gospel* (New York: Macmillan Co., 1963), p. 155.

tological question," he declared, "alone has put the question of transcendence in the form of the question of existence." [4] This means, I take it, that even the right question cannot be asked about Christ unless the meaning of transcendence is at stake. In Bonhoeffer's own terminology Christ is the one in whom *Akt* and *Sein*, act and being, come together. Although he believed that traditional discussions of the two natures of Christ, of what he called "the alchemy of the incarnation," were outdated and sterile, he nonetheless insisted upon preserving the dimension of transcendence. In changing ground from the impertinent question "How?" to the momentous question "Who?" Bonhoeffer did not transpose or invert the substance of Christology. Rather, he emphasized that in any experience of Christ we have to do with the act and being of God, or else there is no such experience.

One may also pose the question of existence in the form of the question of transcendence. Bonhoeffer did not forbid this, but he preferred the reverse order theologically. In his view it is Christ who interprets us to ourselves so that we discover our humanity in him. The central problem of Christology, he says, is the relationship of "the already given God-man," "present and contemporaneous," to "the likeness of man." [5] But, of course, this problem only arises because Christ is encountered in our experience as God's act and being *pro me*. "It is not only useless to meditate on a Christ in himself, but even godless," Bonhoeffer remarks. [6]

Bonhoeffer's Christology, it seems to me, shows how a truly empirical theology can be carried on without landing in the vacuum of a mere theological empiricism. Contemporary theologians would do well to study Bonhoeffer and take heart from his example for their work.

III

The project of an empirical Christology also raises another sort of question. Is it such a new departure as it is sometimes claimed to be? Does it represent a deliberate breaking away

[4] In *Christ the Center* (New York: Harper & Row, 1966), p. 33.
[5] Ibid., p. 46.
[6] Ibid., p. 58.

from the traditional guidelines and issues? What is its probable place in the history of Christian thought?

From one point of view, the project we are considering may be called a reassertion of the full and whole humanity of Jesus Christ. The present moment in Christology represents among other things a swing away from recent efforts to build up the meaning of Christ for faith upon the basis of a radical historical scepticism about the man Jesus, as in Bultmann. "The new quest for the historical Jesus" initiated by biblical scholars has here been given its theological appropriation and assessment. In contrast to the patristic, medieval, and Reformation periods contemporary work in Christology freely admits the elements of human limitation in the person and office of Christ. This, then, is reaffirmation of the *vere homo*, but with a significant difference. In his healings and teachings, as in his own developing life as a moral and religious man, it is generally admitted that Christ was in no way exempt from human conditionedness and finitude. Older assertions of Christ's omniscience, sinlessness, or ubiquity have no place in this present-day perspective; or they are so thoroughly reinterpreted that their new meanings are notably discontinuous with the old.

The current stress on Christ's humanity within the "new" or "radical" movements goes further than any previous theology in admitting that he is a man like each and all of us, that nothing human is alien to him. However implicit this admission may have been in the classical Christologies, it has now become entirely explicit. Especially in the thought of those identified with the "death of God" motif, the humanity of Christ is equated with his humiliation. The preference of these writers is clearly for a flawed and stricken Christ, vulnerable in all respects to the ills that mortal flesh is heir to, and bearing in his own person the burdens of our tragic finitude. In this respect contemporary Christology finds immediate rapport with the Christ-figure that has been taking shape in the arts of our time, modeled upon the image of man as a weak, broken, even absurd being.

It is as if, in order to avoid repeating the Docetic heresy,

one had simply to invert it, making human existence as we
know it in ourselves the true "nature" of Christ and then regarding his supposed divine character as a mere appearance
to be seen through theologically. Perhaps I am pressing this
point unduly, but what else can be involved in the simple
equation of humanity with humiliation? Must not both humiliation and exaltation belong to the humanity of Christ? If
not, the whole point of the Gospel, and therefore also of
Christology, is lost. "Only that which is taken up can be
healed," in the still pregnant words of Irenaeus; but that suffering and sinful humanity *is* thus healed is precisely the good
news which theology must comprehend and communicate.
But this, of course, requires that reference to transcendence
which a christological humanism wishes to avoid.

The most extreme example of this inverted Docetism is to
be found in the writings of Thomas Altizer. According to him,
the incarnation and the *kenosis* of Christ are identical. Hence
"God has negated himself in fully and finally becoming
flesh. . . . If Spirit truly empties itself in entering the world,
then its own essential or original Being must be left behind
in an empty and lifeless form; . . . the new man who is born
in Jesus is liberated by the death of God from the oppressive
power of every alien reality standing over against and beyond
humanity."[7] If the word God is still to have a Christian use,
it must be as the name of Jesus in whom transcendent and
primordial Being died for men, once for all.

Despite the fact that Altizer correctly sees his viewpoint
as a total breaking away from the orthodox Christian tradition, he nevertheless chooses to regard it as the true meaning
of the proclamation that God is love. That God truly died in
Jesus, and that this is the significance of Jesus for Christian
faith, therefore means that we should "give ourselves totally
to the world, to affirm the fullness and the immediacy of the
present moment as the life and energy of Christ."[8]

It would be fairly easy to make an external criticism of

[7] Thomas J. J. Altizer, *The Gospel of Christian Atheism* (Philadelphia: Westminster Press, 1966), pp. 67, 69, 72.
[8] Ibid., p. 157.

Altizer's position, pointing out, for instance, that in it worship is dissolved into morality, or that Hegel's doctrine of self-negating Spirit has dubious value in attempting to delineate the love of God for man. The question I would like to raise, however, is a more internal one: Does this position accomplish what it sets out to do? That is, does Altizer's vision of "Christ actually present in our flesh"[9] provide either the motivation or the interpretative force he thinks it does? Granted that what he wants to do is important, does it get done?

Take but one matter, that of "presence." For Altizer, "presence" has the same meaning as "absolute immanence"; it is not a manifesting or showing forth of Christ but a simple identity of Christ with whatever is experienced, "in faith." The idea that only what is transcendent can possibly be immanent as well has evidently not occurred to him. Christ is simply the word "radical Christians" use to designate whatever happens or confronts them. To speak of "presence" in this connection, I submit, is to use language loosely and arbitrarily. The word might as well denote absence, as Altizer admits when he says that we must be liberated "from even the memory of transcendence,"[10] which can only keep us in bondage to the past. If Christ is everywhere present, then what can presence signify? Is Christ merely a Christian's way of reading any and all experience, what Vaihinger would have called a convenient or useful fiction? It would seem so, if presence has the simple meaning of "being there" for the radical Christian who has placed his bet on Christ, being predisposed to see him everywhere he happens to look. Does this not emasculate the very notion of presence, leaving it without a referent?

But presence is not merely a "being there"; it is rather a "being with," as Gabriel Marcel has carefully shown, which is compatible with and may indeed require physical absence. If then Christ is present, he is so not only *in*, but also *to* experience, and we need signs of his presence which can help us to distinguish it from sheer illusion. In his recent volume on Christology, Wolfhart Pannenberg has dealt succinctly with

[9] Ibid., p. 156.
[10] Ibid., p. 154.

this problem of experiencing the presence of Christ. In opposition to Paul Althaus who declared that in faith we have to do primarily with what Jesus is, Pannenberg emphasizes that it is first from what Jesus was that we learn what he is for us today and how contemporary proclamation of him is possible.[11]

I do not see how this truth can be gainsaid or bypassed, for it only reiterates that ours is and must be a historical faith. Altizer of course admits this in choosing the name Christ to characterize our present experience, but the whole tendency and temper of his thought is antihistorical. A backward look in time is forbidden, he thinks, by the very nature of faith in a forward-moving incarnation, as also by the present deadness of the God whom such a look would reveal as once having lived.

Curiously enough, this interest of the new theological empiricism in the matter of presence evokes older, much older, discussions of transubstantiation in the Eucharist. In particular it suggests the odd and difficult teaching of Christ's ubiquity in Luther, in which God is said to bestow upon the humanity of Christ his attribute of omnipresence. Luther's doctrine has been criticized by Karl Rahner as involving "the divinization of Christ's finite human nature" in a way which goes against the Chalcedonian conception of the hypostatic union.[12] And Bonhoeffer called Luther's teaching an attempt to answer the question "How?" which leads to a conceptual impasse and is theologically impossible.[13]

Doctrines of the presence of Christ, whether old or new, run inevitably into many problems. They are theologically valid insofar as they interpret the mystery of presence without trying to dissipate it. The theme of the incognito Christ, which recurs in Bonhoeffer and to a lesser extent in Barth, is theologically to be preferred over such attempts as Altizer's or Teilhard's, because the former theme does justice to the hiddenness of Christ as the self-manifestation of transcendent

[11] In *Grundzüge der Christologie* (Gütersloh: Gerd Mohn, 1964), p. 22.
[12] Karl Rahner and Herbert Vorgrimler, *Theological Dictionary* (New York: Herder and Herder, 1965), p. 475.
[13] Bonhoeffer, *Christ the Center*, pp. 57–58.

Being under the conditions of our existential estrangement (Tillich), while at the same time Christ incognito is "beside us as creature, in our midst, brother with brother" (Bonhoeffer). An *empirical* Christology dare not neglect the fact that Christ is present and contemporaneous in the *scandalon* of his humiliation and exaltation. In short, it cannot do without the dialectical experience of the transcendent, paradoxical though its interpretation of that experience may appear to be.

IV

Now to the third question: How may the effort to do Christology empirically be evaluated, and with what results? It has already become plain that it is not to be rejected out of hand on the basis of some dogmatic prejudice or from behind the protecting wall of what we may please to call Tradition. Sooner or later, as Bonhoeffer wrote in his *Ethics*, every Christology must undertake to show how "Christ gains shape (*Gestalt*) among us now and here," that is, as an aspect of present Christian experience. If that task is not accepted, Christology lapses into antiquarianism or exoticism.

In order to judge correctly the achievements and deficiencies of any christological interpretation in the empirical mode, it is required that such an enterprise be seen as theologically necessary and in principle legitimate. Since Christians do read their experience in terms of Christ, their reference to him must be a datum for theological explication. Whether one conceives and practices theology as elucidating faith in its personal and interpersonal aspects, or as identifying and ordering what faith believes in, the requirement is the same. Any comprehensive and comprehensible theology will actually move on both these levels, or else it will be neither comprehensible nor comprehensive.

Yet when this rather obvious point is granted, something more remains to be said. In order to be truly empirical, Christology does not have to become a radical empiricism, humanism, or positivism. For this entails the closing of experience against the transcendent, despite the fact that it reports itself

as being experience of the transcendent. Much in christological empiricism and humanism is plausible because it confuses
a polemic against the very meaning of transcendence with at-
tacks upon particular renditions of transcendence which are
patently in error, out of date, or infantile. Undoubtedly there
is a considerable work of ground-clearing to be done, such as
theologians must do in every generation, and some cherished
notions will need to be permanently retired. But this is a far
cry from claiming that modern secular man must be the measure of all things, or that the latest rendering of Christian experience is necessarily the best.

Some of us today are having second thoughts about Schleiermacher, which may simply be a way of expressing our post-
Barthian orientation. I suspect however that it is much more:
the recognition that experience is not to be discarded but
affirmed as the locus of whatever revelation there may be,
and that its character as *Dependenzgefühl* is to be taken with
full theological seriousness. Over against the sterile, forced
antithesis so often posed today between experience and transcendence, and in opposition to any effort to reduce one to
the other, Schleiermacher at least insisted upon the fact of
man's ultimate dependence on the transcendent as disclosed
in his experience, which he called God-consciousness. In this
respect, I believe, his thought can still stimulate and fertilize
our own, which is by no means the same as saying that we
must return to his Christology in all respects.

Whether it is willing to learn anything from Schleiermacher
or not, empirical theology in our day will have to recognize
and reinterpret man's experience of the transcendent. This is
particularly and inescapably so with respect to Christology.
One cannot avoid it by concentrating upon the humanity of
Christ to the exclusion of his divinity, since it is precisely his
humanity that poses the question of transcendent Being. Nor
can one avoid it by neglecting the person of Christ in favor of
his work, for what is done and who does it are finally inseparable.

Our ways of picturing what is transcendent in relation to
Christ are bound to change, of course. Some models will be

superseded and replaced by others. The insistent claims of newer forms of Christian experience will continue to take their toll of older formulations. Yet there is no good reason for supposing that this must be solely a process of attrition in which transcendence will be seen to mean less and less as experience comes to mean more and more. Each will need to be defined in terms of relevance for the other, and neither can be reasonably isolated from the other, whether linguistically or conceptually. The illuminating statement of Nicolas Berdyaev that "God is the meaning of human existence" will remain pertinent and suggestive as we speak and think of Christ afresh.

However, this should not be taken as a call to return to any *status quo ante* in Christology. Karl Rahner has rightly said that "the clearest formulations, the most sanctified formulas, the classic condensations . . . all these derive their life from the fact that they are not end but beginning, not goals but means, truths which open the way to the ever greater Truth." [14] The consensus reached at Chalcedon, for example, may be said to have this initiating, open function. Doubtless it is definitive, as it brings to formal ecumenical expression the symbol fashioned at Nicaea and further clarified at Constantinople, thus setting the christological stage for more than a millennium. Yet the decree of Chalcedon can scarcely be regarded as conclusive; it explicates the problem for Christology in terms belonging to ancient metaphysics quite as much as to biblically grounded revelation. Merely to repeat the classic formula today is necessarily to place it in a greatly altered context, bringing to it and expecting from it structures of meaning which could not have been in the minds of its framers originally. Every "return to Chalcedon" is *ipso facto* a reinterpretation and reassessment, to be undertaken in both fidelity and. freedom.

Assuredly it is a theologian's right as well as his duty to state the meaning of Christ in the language and perspective of his own time and place. So far as possible, his belief must be articulated in terms of what he knows about his world or

[14] In *Theological Investigations* (Baltimore: Helicon Press, 1961) Vol. I, 149.

himself. In this broad sense, an empirical Christology is a permanent possibility, and something of a necessity too.

What is commendable in contemporary efforts in this direction is that they refuse to be straitjacketed or turned away by any prior consensus, but insist on thinking of Christ as one "remembered and known still" (John Knox) in the community of faith. Such efforts are more defensible biblically, and more impressive philosophically, than many of the orthodox restatements they are designed to supplant. They do, however, raise the question whether or not Christology is theology. That is, can the meaning of Christ as presently experienced be stated either properly or truly except in relation to transcendent Being?.

We have already seen that questions such as these must be answered in the negative. Christology has always had to deal with the temptation to degrade the mystery of Christ into a problem capable of being resolved on the purely intellectual level. The present empiricist trend is no exception to this rule. My contention in this essay has been only that this degradation, if and when it occurs, is a misinterpretation of Christian experience itself.

9

Towards a New Doctrine of Man: The Relationship
of Man and Nature

PHILIP J. HEFNER

I

The centennial theme of this volume impels us to focus our
thinking upon the prospects for *empirical* theology. Just what
this "empirical" theology might be is open to question and
difference of opinion. One of the leading proponents of such
a theology has said that "empirical" theology in the Chicago
tradition means simply that what one believes must be au-
thenticated by his experience, and that what one experiences
is in this sense a norm of theology whose integrity cannot be
violated. According to this understanding, the present essay
stands clearly in the Chicago tradition of empirical theology.
There are others, however, who would insist that the adjec-
tive "empirical" refers to a specific stream of Anglo-American
philosophy (in which Alexander, James, Whitehead, and
Hartshorne figure most prominently), from which empirical
theology takes its roots. Although I have no particular interest in repudiating this stream of philosophical thinking, and
in fact find it instructive, I would consider it artificial to claim
that this stream has a monopoly on experientially honest theology, and I have not consciously tried to derive my insights
from this school of thought. What follows is empirical in the
sense that it has tried to listen to the voices of the empirical
world in which the theologian lives, and it has tried to listen
to the richness and vivacity of those voices in a very concrete
manner. I would emphasize the "vivacity" of the voices from

the empirical world, because at the root of that word is "life." The importance of doing empirical theology lies in the fact that life resides in the empirical, and the task of theology is to speak from and to that world of life. It is in this sense that the theologizing represented in this essay intends to be empirical.

It is a truism to say that every generation of Christians grapples with God and his revelation in terms of the symbols and categories of knowledge that its age furnishes. These symbols and categories of the age form the lineaments according to which our knowledge of God and his revelation are cast. Our knowledge of God and his revelation are, therefore, inseparable from the forms of the age. It is improper to imagine that the symbols and categories of our age are somehow inauthentic impositions upon a timeless and authentic revelation of God. Rather, it is in, with, and under the symbols of our time that we know God. We do not deny that our ways of understanding and appropriating God's truth are continuous also with the ways of previous generations, but our integrity demands that we be faithful to our own age's categories and to the contours that they provide for our understanding.

It should be perfectly obvious that the confidence that I have just asserted in the capability of contemporary categories and symbols to be the stuff in, with, and under which God's revelation is borne presupposes a metaphysical structure which allows me to conceive of a certain and close relationship between God and the world. A number of men from the Chicago school of theology have devoted considerable effort to the refining of just such a metaphysical structure. At present, there are also other exciting attempts to forge such a metaphysical instrumentality going on in Germany, represented by the thought of Wolfhart Pannenberg and Jürgen Moltmann.[1] Whatever else an "empirical" approach to theol-

[1] Of the "Chicago" school, I have in mind the well-known writings of Bernard Meland, Daniel Day Williams, John Cobb, and Schubert Ogden. The chief work of Moltmann's is *Theologie der Hoffnung* (Munich: Chr. Kaiser, 1964); see also his "Das 'Prinzip Hoffnung' und die christliche Zuversicht," *Evangelische Theologie* 23 (1963): 537–57 and "*Die Kategorie Novum* in der christliche Theologie," in *Ernst*

ogy might mean, however, it surely implies that in some circumstances the theologian will eschew the metaphysical efforts, or at least hold them in abeyance for a time, and devote his attention solely to the empirical categories and symbols which our age provides for its own self-understanding. In such times, the theologian's confidence that God's revelation is in, with, and under the contours of our age's self-understanding liberates him to devote his efforts single-mindedly to comprehending and probing the empirical categories of his own epoch. His confidence is liberating even if it is not undergirded by an explicit metaphysical structure, although such a structure could serve as a foundation for his efforts.

The task here is to indicate what it means for me to take seriously the empirically given categories of our age in regard to one aspect of the doctrine of man, to determine what contours such categories and symbols give to this phase of our faith. I intend to do this by working through the materials which certain natural and social sciences provide us. It is safe to say that biology, anthropology, social psychology, sociology, and psychology have given our generation some of its most significant symbols and categories for understanding ourselves as men. It is unthinkable that our generation could come to know God apart from the influence of these disciplines of thought, no matter how indirect their influence may have been. Even the unlearned and inexperienced have been touched by their powerful symbol-engendering presence. In this essay, one important contour of contemporary thought will be before us, the category of man's relationship to na-

---

Bloch zu Ehren, Siegfried Unseld, ed. (Frankfurt: Suhrkamp, 1965). For Pannenberg's thought, see his *Theology and the Kingdom of God* (Philadelphia: Westminster, 1969), and *Grund Fragen systematischer Theologie* (Göttingen: Vandenhoeck and Ruprecht, 1967); *Grundzüge der Christologie* (Gütersloh: Gerd Mohn, 1964), pp. 79–85. Also pertinent are Harvey Cox, "Afterword," in *The Secular City Debate*, ed. Daniel Callahan (New York: Macmillan Co., 1966); Carl E. Braaten, "Toward a Theology of Hope," *New Theology, no. 5,* eds. Martin Marty and Dean Peerman (New York: Macmillan, 1968); and Philip Hefner, "Questions for Moltmann and Pannenberg," *Una Sancta,* 25 (1968): 3.

ture, as the life sciences have forced us to consider it as an unavoidable factor for any contemporary statement of the doctrine of man.

As I work through the materials from the life sciences that pertain to my theme, I shall be doing an exercise in empirical theology. I shall also be attempting to come to terms with the concrete, empirical challenge of the so-called "secular world." And in my conviction that these empirical secular sources demand a restatement of the traditional Christian doctrine of man, I shall be indicating how the secular impinges upon the theological task. The fact that my enterprise does not approach the secular under popular ideological phrases, such as "holy worldliness," "religionless Christianity," or "death of God," should not take away from the earnestness with which I do seek to establish what it means to be Christian in our age.

II

I intend first to focus attention on five aspects of what the life sciences tell us about man's relationship with nature and then to turn to some observations concerning their implications for a new doctrine of man.

1. The first important testimony from the evolutionary theorists concerning man's relationship to nature describes a basic equation within which man enters this world and in terms of which his later development is spelled out. This equation is composed of two members: the genetic endowment which man receives as his heritage from his ancestors, and the environment within which and over against which that genetic endowment unfolds. The genetic potential of an individual is termed his genotype, and it encompasses all of the theoretical possibilities for his development. It is the wide door of capabilities that are his; it is a wide door, but it is the only door through which he can pass as he lives out his days. The specific path which the individual will actually take through that door is determined by the particular demands his environmental transactions place upon his genotype. The particular path he takes corresponds to what the biologist

calls his phenotype, the specific configuration of development that an individual has arrived at in any given moment. The genotype is potentiality; the phenotype is the actuality of the individual's development at any given time.[2]

For my purposes in this study, it is important to note that both members of the equation within which man lives out his career are formed by *the stuff of nature*. In this sense, "nature" refers to the physical stuff out of which man and his world are made. Nature is inside man in what we call his genetic endowment. Indeed this nature is so intimately *inside* man that words can scarcely describe that intimacy. This nature inside man forms him and *informs* him. In this respect it would be better to say nature exists as man, at least insofar as his genetic endowment is concerned, but the direction and shape which that informing takes is determined by the nature *outside* man, his environment. There are only two points of input into the human organism, namely, through his genetic endowment or through his environing world; and both of these inputs are comprised of nature in the most material, earthy sense of that word "nature." This is the hard fact that faces a man at the very outset of his career in the world. Weston La Barre, the anthropologist, has put this point almost epigrammatically in his book, *The Human Animal*:

> The biologist, then, has two concepts: matter and life (which is a special phase or state of matter). He studies both living organism and material environment, environment being particular aspects of total material reality, but both, organism and environment, being wholly material entities. . . . An organism's "knowledge" is its environment. An organism, so to speak, only knows what it needs to know, or perhaps more correctly needs what it knows to need — needs being purposes. In this sense, *evolution is life learning about matter* (or what amounts to the same thing, *matter learning purposes*).[3]

[2] See Theodosius Dobzhansky. *Mankind Evolving* (New Haven: Yale Univ. Press, 1962), chap. 4.

[3] Weston La Barre, *The Human Animal* (Chicago: Univ. of Chicago Press, 1954), pp. 3–4 (italics added).

Evolution is life learning about matter, and this life is itself material in the genetic endowment which gives it its potentialities.

That which we call life, including human life, is a phase of matter. We may say, as Father Teilhard de Chardin does, that this matter in man has been spiritualized or hominized; [4] and if we use those terms "spiritualization" or "hominization" very carefully, they are quite proper and useful. But none of our terminology should divert us from the basic fact that spiritualized or hominized matter is matter, nature, under some particular condition or phase of its evolution. And in this light, if one were inclined to distinguish between man and matter or nature; or between matter and some "spirit," he could do so only with the utmost caution and careful definition of terms.

2. The first insight I can draw from the life sciences is that the equation within which man spills out his life is composed, in both members, of nature defined in material terms. The second aspect of my study has to do with a further specification of the world or nature within which man has developed and is developing.

Within the equation I described above, the career of life is spelled out in the attempts of the organism to survive — survival in this sense means maintaining the organism's life long enough for it to reproduce itself effectively. The fittest, in contemporary interpretation of "survival of the fittest," refers to the ability to produce the longest line of descendants.

In prehuman evolution, the information for survival was largely derived from the genotypic heritage which structured the organism and its instinctual behavior. Human evolution, however, increasingly involves a new source of information or instruction for generating adaptive behavior and survival in the environment.

Increasingly supplementing his genetically inherited organs and instinctual behavior, man responds to his environment by means of socially transmitted tools and patterns of behavior,

[4] Pierre Teilhard de Chardin, *Man's Place in Nature* (New York: Harper & Row, 1966), pp. 23ff.

which we call cultural inheritance.[5] Culture stands as the unique feature in man's evolution, and it is tied, biologically, to the process of fetalization. Fetalization refers to man's unusually long period of maturation, during which he is subject to the nurture of his family and society. This nurture, including education, imparts to man his own peculiar substitute for instincts, namely, culture, which in turn is the impressive new apparatus through which man evolves, responds to his environment, insures his fitness to survive, and fulfills his destiny as an organism.

The pivotal position that culture and nurture hold in man's evolution emphasizes very strongly that man is a social animal, whose development is fundamentally dependent upon society, whether society resides in the family or the educational system or somewhere else. La Barre and others point to man's sociality as the unique feature about man. La Barre writes that "the very essence of human nature, then, is its promiscuous and fantastic inter-individuality. This is initially rooted in the biological nature of the human family." [6] In his 1964 Silliman lectures at Yale, René Dubos summarized this whole matter of man's sociality and its decisive importance for man:

> If instinct is defined as a specific adaptation to environment that does not have to be learned, then the human infant is singularly ill-equipped at birth and furthermore remains deficient in this respect for several years. Because his instincts are so inadequate, personal relationships are of paramount importance during his long period of development. Man, in fact, continues to require the support and encouragement of other men throughout his life. . . . But biological innovations occur also whenever several members of one species associate to form a population, and this is particularly true of man. The individual organisms within a group interact in a variety

[5] Dobzhansky, *Mankind Evolving*, chap. 3, especially pp. 58f.
[6] La Barre, *Human Animal*, p. 237. Note also La Barre's social theory of psychosis, chap. 13, which in effect underscores the role of sociality.

of ways, and this interplay brings about the unfolding of potentialities that would remain unexpressed in the isolated state. For better or for worse, the *interplay between individual members of the human species always changes the expression of their morphological and physiological endowments, and of course their behavior.*[7]

Society and its heritage, culture, are integrally and even uniquely a part of man's evolution. More specifically, society and culture are aspects of his adaptation and response to his environment, adaptations which insure his survival as a "fit" creature. Culture has proven to be a much more effective adaptive agent for man, moreover, than biological evolution, spoken of in purely physical terms, ever would have been.[8] However, culture embraces a number of other factors that we might not ordinarily associate with evolution. It embraces, perhaps most importantly, man's use of symbols, his morality, and his purposiveness. Man's use of symbols plays an important role here, because man does not simply respond to his environment, but rather he responds to his own symbolization of his environment and its stimuli.[9] This symbolization of the environmental stimuli is what makes it possible for man to transcend what Dubos calls "simple biological urges," and actually to respond to himself in the form of the symbolic activities of his mind which interpret the world about him.[10] Man's morality enters into the evolutionary discussion, because his moral structures become extremely significant as means by which a symbol-making, socialized animal maintains himself as a social being, by which he lives with other men and thus enables the evolutionary process to continue. Finally, culture embraces man's ability to define purposes and to decide in accordance with those purposes what his action as an individual in society will be, relative to survival. Man sets himself apart from other forms of life in this very ability

[7] René Dubos, *Man Adapting* (New Haven: Yale Univ. Press, 1965), p. 8 (italics added).
[8] See Dobzhansky, *Mankind Evolving*, pp. 18–22.
[9] See the insightful discussion in Dubos, *Man Adapting*, pp. 5–7.
[10] Ibid.

to make decisions thoughtfully and to carry them out; and this is one reason why his evolution differs from that of other forms of life.[11] These are only three of the important aspects of culture which enter into man's unique evolutionary development. When put together, they suggest that man's culture is what it is because of his unique position among animals and his unique process of evolution. La Barre puts it this way: "Culture is man's adaptation to his humanity."[12] Furthermore, they suggest that even man's psychic and cultural dimensions have an important biological significance. I shall return to this point later.

These considerations lead me to conclude that as man develops beyond his origins, *the nature to which he is so inseparably related is social and cultural.* If we are to take cognizance of this testimony from the life sciences, we must acknowledge that for man, nature is not so much the mountains and climate and floods (even though these are to be considered), but rather nature is *people* and the products of people, society and its culture.[13]

But even if the concept of nature is thus reshaped when we consider man's evolution, that nature still resides in a matrix of physical, earthy matter. This social and cultural "nature" may pertain to what we call the psyche, *Geist*, or spirit; nevertheless, it has still emerged from a very earthy creature, whose existence spells itself out in terms of an earthy equation of genes and environment, and whose goals are still related to the physical enterprise of survival, however "spiritually" that survival is defined. How do we deal with this sudden appearance in man of a "spiritual or psychic" dimension of the material realm? Teilhard, who was a paleontologist, speaks of this dimension as a socialized or hominized phase of matter, which is so complex that it represents a new dimension of life, the noosphere, contrasted with and built upon the bio-

[11] See ibid., pp. xviif., and La Barre, *Human Animal,* chap. 12.
[12] La Barre, *Human Animal,* p. 213.
[13] See Joseph Haroutunian's essay on this theme, "Toward a Piety of Faith," in Philip Hefner, ed., *The Scope of Grace* (Philadelphia: Fortress Press, 1964), pp. 165–82.

sphere; that is, a complexifying tendency within the sphere of physical life, which transmutes that physical life into the psychic sphere that encompasses man's cultural phenomena (morality, politics, philosophy, the arts, etc.). Teilhard writes:

> We must enlarge our approach to encompass the formation taking place before our eyes and arising out of this factor of hominization, to a particular biological entity such as has never before existed on earth — the growth, outside and above the biosphere, of an added planetary layer, an envelope of thinking substance, to which, for the sake of convenience and symmetry, I have given the name of the Noosphere.[14]

In other words, as bewildering as the appearance of this psychic dimension of life may be, when compared with the material aspects of prehuman evolution, it does not seem adequate to separate the psychic from the material, or to form a dichotomy between them. Rather, it may be more adequate to recognize that matter under certain circumstances has reached a phase of its development that we call cultural, social, or psychic.

These reflections upon the relation between matter and psyche turn our attention further to the relation between biology and the social sciences, particularly sociology and social psychology. Just as man's evolutionary career binds together within itself matter and psyche, so it binds the natural and social sciences. Dubos writes:

> Thus, man has evolved a novel, parabiological method for adapting to his environment. He no longer relies exclusively on the forces of natural selection but instead increasingly uses sociocultural means. In final analysis, human evolution is now the resultant of the interaction between biological and sociocultural forces, and it involves a constant feedback between them.[15]

[14] Teilhard de Chardin, *The Future of Man* (New York: Harper & Row, 1964), p. 157.

[15] Dubos, *Man Adapting*, p. 13. See also La Barre, *Human Animal*, pp. 216ff.

This statement provides the basis and the necessity for the interrelationship of biology and sociology and social psychology. Sociocultural "nature" is within and without man as he pursues his evolutionary career — within as the nurturing process has fit him for life, without as the social environment to which he must respond. Sociocultural tools furnish man's arsenal, so to speak, from which he gathers strength to mold his environment. Furthermore, man's future will be determined even more by the success he attains in shaping socio-culturally the world in which he lives.

3. The third aspect of man's relationship to nature, to which I turn now, is simply a footnote to what I have just discussed, namely, that no matter how highly refined the sociocultural dimension of man's evolution becomes, he cannot hope to escape the physical, material impact of evolution in the form of natural selection. Both Dobzhansky and Dubos approach this factor through the study of disease — Dobzhansky as a geneticist, and Dubos as a microbiologist. Several factors enter in here, only a few of which need to be mentioned as examples.

Man's diseases, we are now quite sure, are intimately related to his patterns of living. Dubos goes so far as to say, "The prevalence and severity of microbial diseases are conditioned more by the ways of life of the persons afflicted than by the virulence and other properties of the etiological agents." [16] Or, again, disease is an expression of man's "responses to environmental insults and stimuli." [17] Dubos himself uses these observations as the basis for calling for an ecological approach to the practice of medicine.[18] We can refer to Dubos's insights here as biological counterparts to the work that Aarne Siirala has done in psychotherapy in his book *The Voice of Illness*.[19] Both Siirala and the biologists remind us that since psyche and matter are within the same continuum, psychic phenomena

[16] Dubos, *Man Adapting*, p. xxi. Dobzhansky, *Mankind Evolving*, pp. 303–12.

[17] Dubos, *Man Adapting*, p. 233.

[18] *Ibid.*, pp. xix–xx.

[19] Aarne Siirala, *The Voice of Illness* (Philadelphia: Fortress Press, 1964).

have biological consequences, one of the most obvious consequences being that as man's sociocultural evolution proceeds, his new ways of adjusting bring with them correlative diseases which throw light on the peculiar nature and problems of man's responses to his world. These diseases become another testimony to the manner in which man is related to nature. They indicate that the fully material and natural processes of natural selection are still crucially operative in determining man's present and future.

Another factor which applies here is the growing awareness that our advances in medicine, which have reshaped man's evolutionary development by modifying the world in which he must, for all practical purposes, live, have added greatly to the number of deleterious genes existing in our society's over-all gene pool, by preserving the lives of genetically defective persons who otherwise would have perished. That these deleterious genes may one day return to visit destruction upon us [20] is another example of the ineradicable relationship in which man stands to material, earthy nature.

4. The phenomenon of change brings before us a fourth aspect of man's relationship to nature which figures prominently in what the life sciences have to tell us about man. In his discussion of the history of Darwin's researches and writing, John Greene elaborates upon the conflict which ensued between Darwin and those of his contemporaries who believed, in harmony with Newtonian physics and conventional theology, that God had created man initially and, from the time of origins to the present day, conserved the "stability of the fundamental structures of nature." [21] These contemporaries, whose convictions have been labeled as "creationism," were unwilling to allow that change was a constitutive factor in nature, specifically in man's nature. Charles Darwin, on the other hand, was deeply impressed by the diversity of

[20] Dobzhansky, *Mankind Evolving*, chap. 11. See also Lucy Eisenberg, "Genetics and the Survival of the Unfit," *Harper's* (1966), pp. 53–58.
[21] John Greene, *The Death of Adam* (New York: New American Library, 1959), p. 15.

life.[22] He was impressed by the diversity he found within the same species. For example, in the months preceding the completion of his *On the Origin of Species,* Darwin was at work examining many specimens of a certain species of crab. Even though Darwin was an old hand at working in the field, as a naturalist, he noted in a letter to a friend that he never ceased being amazed at the individual differences within the same species.[23] Similarly, in his journeys on the *Beagle,* he found many occasions to wonder at the diversity, not within species, but between geographical areas, noting for example, that it is geographical nearness, and not topographical similarity, that is correlated with likeness between species.[24] Faced with the enormous diversity in life that his practical field studies brought before him, Darwin simply could not accept the arguments of the creationists. Indeed, his theory of evolution and natural selection may be looked upon from one angle as an attempt to resolve the problem of diversity or change.[25] The theory of evolution by natural selection provides such a resolution. Each individual's genetic endowment or genotype provides a particular pattern of adaptation to the environment. In a population, the genotype of each individual is different from that of the others in the gene pool of the population. In the processes of life in any particular environment, certain genotypes provide adaptations that fail to leave any descendants. No descendants means that this genotype was selected out, or eliminated from the gene pool. Other genotypes provide responses to this particular environment such that there are many descendants. These are adapted, and the fact that there are descendants means they have been selected. Since there are always many different environments, and since the environment in any particular place is always undergoing some kind of change, the various genotypes are always being selected by different standards in different times

[22] Ibid., p. 283.
[23] Ibid., pp. 249ff.
[24] Ibid., pp. 250ff., 283.
[25] Ibid., pp. 257ff. See also Loren Eiseley, *Darwin's Century* (New York: Doubleday Anchor, 1961). Also Andrew G. van Melsen, *Evolution and Philosophy* (Pittsburgh: Duquesne Univ. Press, 1965), p. 11.

and places. Thus the combination of varied genotypes and varied selecting environments yields diversity and change in varied patterns of life.

Greene mentions two phases of diversity that impressed Darwin: diversity within species, and diversity between geographical areas. Diversity is also built into the biologist's categories of genotype and phenotype, as I discussed them above. These terms represent diversity within the career of the single individual. To speak of a static, final man is impossible. The genotype, which theoretically contains all of man's developmental possibilities, cannot even be laid hold of or described. This genotype expresses itself only in the concrete responses to concrete environmental stimuli, that is, in the phenotype; and the phenotype changes every moment. The phenotype of the infant is not that of adolescent, and neither of these is that of the young adult or the mature man. Yet all four are spun from the same genotype, and all four are the same man. Here we hit upon a very significant example of change and diversity.

The most adequate way to deal with this diversity may be to entertain a notion of man as an *event*, that is, as a confluence of *happenings*, whose identity is comprised of a *composite*, which emerges out of the happenings of the evolutionary process, subject to the laws of natural selection. To speak of man as an event and of his identity in a composite of appearances is to accept diversity. The whole realm of physical sciences has made us familiar with the notion of defining things as events. We are accustomed to working with the composite in the metaphysics of S. Alexander and Alfred North Whitehead in their concepts of process, and in the role-playing school of sociology, represented by Erving Goffman and Peter Berger, as they suggest that the self is a composite of roles in which the person finds himself. So, too, I am suggesting that the life sciences point us towards a view of man who is defined as event — an event that emerges from genes, environment, culture, and who locates his identity, whether as a species or as an individual, in the composite of appearances that express themselves in his phenotype throughout his career. That is to say, man's being is located in the very stuff of the changing nature in which his life manifests itself. Man so coinheres in his nature that his identity is dependent upon it.

5. Finally, at least for the purposes of this discussion, I must call attention to the imperative that the life sciences seem to place before man to assume ever more intelligent and responsible control over the nature that I have discussed in the preceding four sections, as well as over his own evolutionary process within it. The preceding four sections leave us with two clear testimonies in this matter. First, the evidence cited there indicates that man is already controlling nature — the nature within and without, the physical nature and the social-cultural nature; but the question is whether he is controlling it well, that is, whether he is controlling it in a manner commensurate with his further survival. Man is controlling his own cultural nurture, for example, but is he controlling it in such a way that produces healthy individuals who can carry on the human enterprise, or not?[26] Every organism inevitably specializes in its development, in order to adapt to the stimuli emerging from its own environment. Overspecialization leads to extinction, because it cannot adapt to change. Is our culture developing so specialized a configuration that it is in danger of fossilizing? Man can influence the chemical condition within his own body through drugs and medicines; but is he doing it responsibly? Similarly, man can control his environment, produce a city, for example. But can he do so in a way that is conducive to survival? These are the kinds of questions the life sciences raise for us today in regard to our control of nature.

Second, the life sciences, particularly as I observed under section two, are opening our eyes to the fact that psychic or spiritual phenomena have biological, evolutionary significance. That is to say, what we do socioculturally, in politics, government, education, the arts, morality, or religion, has sig-

[26] See La Barre's discussion of nonadaptive cultural trends, and the possibilities of producing a psychotic culture, *Human Animal*, pp. 240–45, and chap. 13. Paul Goodman's *Growing Up Absurd* (New York: Vintage Books, 1960) is also pertinent here.

nificance for our attempts to control nature for our own advantage. These psychic or spiritual dimensions of our existence have emerged out of the biological matter of life; they have emerged out of the struggle to survive, and they serve an adaptive function.[27] Therefore, it is clear that we do not fully understand these psychic phenomena unless we understand that, besides their other meanings, they have great *biological* significance.

III

At the present, we are not in a position to erect a new doctrine of man in the light of the considerations I have sketched here. We have not progressed far enough in our thinking to produce the kind of synthesis that is necessary for such a doctrinal formulation. Despite the primitive stage of our thinking, however, we can uncover some of the basic issues that face us as we contemplate a new doctrine of man, basic issues that theologians, preachers, and, in fact, all Christians must consider as they go about their work of synthesizing. Here I want to discuss three of these issues, as they grow out of my preceding remarks and point towards a new doctrine of man.

1. *A new doctrine of man must reassess the spirit/nature dualism.* If evolutionary theory is correct, and for my purposes I am making that assumption, spirit and material nature must be considered within a single continuum, rather than as two separate realms of being. My references to Teilhard de Chardin indicate that spirit ought to be construed as a certain phase of matter, namely, the phase of its extreme complexity.[28] Paul Tillich has been one of the most instructive thinkers among us on this problem. Although he did not go into the problem in enough detail, he asserted very forcefully that man's spirit (here used as a synonym for the German *Geist*) is not a level of his being, nor a compartment of his self. Rather, Tillich insisted, spirit is a *dimension* of man's total self, which includes his body.[29] Tillich was countering, quite

[27] See Dubos, *Man Adapting*, p. 249.
[28] See footnote 3.
[29] Paul Tillich, *Systematic Theology*, vol. 3 (Chicago: Univ. of Chicago Press, 1963).

explicitly, a tradition of preaching which separated spirit and matter as a correlate of the separation between good and evil. This tradition has exhorted the individual to remain unspotted by the world of material nature, and it has given that exhortation both moral and ontological justification. Morally, the separation from matter meant refraining from actions that were too earthy or too "worldly"; ontologically, it implied that man's body was the source of his problems, his propensity and vulnerability to evil, whereas his "mind" or "soul" was pure, the seat of faith and goodness, which therefore had to be protected and liberated from evil matter.

The Reformation theological tradition has had a stake in this spirit/nature separation. For example, in his *Loci*, John Gerhard, who was one of the greatest sixteenth and seventeenth-century Lutheran theologians, quoted Augustine with approval as follows:

> The fact that man is said to have been made in the image of God must be understood not according to the body, but according to the mind, or intellect. However, it can be said that even in the body man has a unique property which somehow reflects the image of God. Such a property is the physical constitution of man, whose body stands upright. By this he is warned that he should not seek after earthly things, as the other animals do, whose whole pleasure is out of the earth, and hence they are bent and prostrated towards their belly.[30]

[30] In Herman Preus and Edmund Smits, eds., *The Doctrine of Man in Classical Lutheran Theology* (Minneapolis: Augsburg, 1962), p. 49. See also the classical Lutheran theologians Baier and Hollaz, quoted in Heinrich Schmid, *The Doctrinal Theology of the Evangelical Lutheran Church* (Minneapolis: Augsburg, n.d.), pp. 626, 628. There is some indication that the mainline Reformation understanding of faith and works also participates in this unfortunate dualism, although one might argue that the dualism is not essential to the *sola fide*. The sixteenth-century discussions tended towards this dualism when they argued (1) that when justification is under discussion, works are extraneous; (2) without faith, works are hostile to God, whereas with faith they are part of his will; (3) faith precedes good works *temporally*. For pertinent sources, see Theodore Tappert, ed., *The Book of Con-*

This spirit/matter dualism has its roots in the New Testament, including the writings of St. Paul and the spirit/flesh opposition which he represents. St. Paul's concern is to designate the seat of sin's power over man, and he did so by calling that seat of power "flesh." For Paul, flesh is not synonymous with matter, but it is not difficult to understand why it was often interpreted as if it were. So, for example, it requires a sophisticated and subtle exegesis to avoid drawing justification for a spirit/nature or spirit/body dualism from Romans 8:5–8:

> For those who live according to the flesh set their minds on the things of the flesh, but those who live according to the Spirit set their minds on the things of the Spirit. To set the mind on the flesh is death, but to set the mind on the Spirit is life and peace. For the mind that is set on the flesh is hostile to God; it does not submit to God's law, indeed it cannot; and those who are in the flesh cannot please God.

Although it is commonplace today to assert that flesh does not equal matter or nature in this passage,[31] there are several ways to account for our persisting temptation to misinterpret Paul. R. G. Collingwood roots the propensity in the rise of modern science in the seventeenth century, in which nature had to be considered lifeless, as dead matter that could be worked upon by man for his own ends.[32] Of course, life and spirit were to be seen everywhere, in contrast to lifeless nature, and their very presence made the spirit/nature dualism a serious problem that could not be ignored by the philosophers and theologians. It may well be that our own American traditions were particularly congenial to this Renaissance

cord (Philadelphia: Fortress Press, 1959), Formula of Concord, art. III, par. 29, 36; art. II, par. 20; Art. III, par. 27, 32, 40f., passim. Contemporary restatements of Reformation faith tend to maintain this dichotomy.

[31] See Werner Kümmel, Man in the New Testament (Philadelphia: Westminster Press, 1963) pp. 61ff.

[32] R. G. Collingwood, The Idea of Nature (New York: Oxford Univ. Press, Galaxy Books, 1960), pp. 111–12.

mode of thinking, since those traditions were wielded by men whose first task was to subdue a nature so as to make it malleable for nation-building; a nature that is lifeless, inert, devoid of spirit is more easily twisted and subdued than a living, dynamic nature. Reinhold Niebuhr roots this propensity not so much in the secular spirit as in heretical Christianity itself, pointing his finger at the Pelagian influence which sought to exonerate man's will from sin, and therefore placed responsibility for evil upon nature itself.[33]

Whatever the precise historical provenance of the modern theological holdovers that still subscribe to the spirit/nature dualism, contemporary Protestant theology's commitment to existentialism and the Kantianism which underlies existentialism has tended to reinforce this spirit/nature dualism. Existentialism, like its Kantian precursors, is essentially a type of phenomenology of the human consciousness; it describes the contents of the human self-consciousness as the self encounters the reality that lies outside itself. Therefore, existentialist philosophy is predisposed to view everything in terms of the distinction between the self-consciousness and that which it encounters. Nature, however defined, whether as matter, body, or whatever, must always be separated from the self-consciousness in this existentialist framework. As a consequence, the world of nature, including the human body, tends to be opposed to the self-consciousness in existentialist philosophy and theology, and this opposition becomes a matter of some significance when one considers that everything important for the existentialist happens in the self-consciousness.[34]

[33] Reinhold Niebuhr, *The Nature and Destiny of Man* (New York: Scribner's Sons, 1949), pp. 245–46.

[34] Even so sensitive a treatment as that of Karl Heim's discussion of *Leiblichkeit* carries with it unmistakably the presupposition that spirit and self-identity are dualistically opposed to nature and body. See his *Glaube und Denken*, 1st ed. (Berlin: Furche-Verlag, 1931). The current school of the "New Hermeneutic" proceeds under this same assumption, as it insists that some primordial being (*Geist?*) is unveiled in language. This dichotomy is clearly seen, for example, in the interpretive essay by James Robinson in James M. Robinson and

My earlier observations indicate that, from the point of view of the life sciences, a radical distinction between spirit and nature or matter must appear very dubious, whether that distinction is theological or philosophical. The distinctive vision of the life sciences lays bare the unity and continuity between spirit and matter, between man and his world. What we are faced with — as we stand between existentialism and the life sciences — is a kind of strange double vision on this issue of man's relationship with his world.[35] An adequate doctrine of man must synthesize both factors, so as to resolve this double vision into a unity of vision in respect to man. Christian doctrine has no overriding investment in the spirit/nature dualism. Nor does it seem to me that existentialist philosophy has such an investment. Rather, Christian theology has used this dualism in order to talk about the self-conscious and creative dimension of human being which is so crucial for man's humanity, and which seems to differentiate him from other forms of life. The spirit/nature dualism has also been employed to talk about the forces which cause man to do evil, in direct contradiction to man's inner sense that he should be doing good. Now both of these concerns are legitimate and real, the concern for the creative dimension of man's life and the distinction between the sensibility for good and the propensity for evil. These concerns cannot be obliterated, but we can no longer speak of them by postulating a dichotomy between spirit and material nature. At the very least, the life sciences call for a revolution of theological discourse at this point. This is the first important lesson that philosophy and theology must learn from the life sciences.

What I have said about the spirit and nature dualism has been set within a definition of nature as physical and material. But my conclusions are equally pertinent when nature is conceived of in sociocultural terms. The tendency in Chris-

John B. Cobb, Jr., eds., *The New Hermeneutic* (New York: Harper & Row, 1964), pp. 1–77.

[35] This "double-vision" is worthy of much more attention. Hans Jonas throws some light on it in his concepts of "physical-outward" and "vitalistic-inward" approaches to man, in *The Phenomenon of Life* (New York: Harper & Row, 1966), pp. 17f.

tian theology has often been to speak of man in individualistic terms which set him in sharp contradistinction to his socio-cultural world. It is not only the hyperindividualism of frontier American Christianity that I object to here; nor is it simply the individual orientation of existentialist theologies, focusing as they do on the contents of the individual self-consciousness. (It is true that the Buberian I-Thou existentialist approach does emphasize the dialogical character of human existence.) Rather, what seems most inadequate is the view, common to many theologies today whether existentialist oriented or not, that selfhood is an individual matter; namely, that which resides in the interior of its possessor. H. Richard Niebuhr's *The Responsible Self* is a notable exception. Coupled with this view, we often come upon a conviction that society is the enemy of the self, the "herd" or the "crowd" (to recall Sören Kierkegaard's term) which must inevitably compromise the self. Both the individualism and the polemic against society are strategies for separating man and nature, denying man's basic relatedness to and dependence upon nature, as nature is socioculturally defined.

The life sciences certainly call into question any simplistic interiorization of the self and any stereotypical rejection of society which causes a dichotomy between man and nature, socially defined. Whether one thinks of the evolutionary understanding of society as the nurturing agent that prepares man to undertake the struggle for survival; whether one thinks of the anthropologist's understanding of society as the meaning-giving agency in human existence; or whether one thinks of the social-psychological understanding of selfhood as comprised of roles that society prescribes, we must question any simplistic interiorization of selfhood and any rejection of society. Erving Goffman, the sociologist, puts this issue squarely, in a way that the evolutionary theorist and the anthropologist could also accept:

> In our society the character one performs and one's self are somewhat equated, and this self-as-character is usually seen as something housed within the body of its possessor, especially the upper parts thereof, being a

nodule, somehow, in the psychobiology of personality. I suggest that this view is . . . a bad analysis of the presentation. . . . While this image is entertained *concerning* the individual, so that a self is imputed to him, *this self itself does not derive from its possessor, but from the whole scene of his action.*[36]

In other words, the self does not reside solely in the possessor, but it is *bestowed upon* the possessor in his social interrelatedness.

If these testimonies from the life sciences have any validity at all, they call into question any simplistic dichotomy between man and sociocultural "nature." This sociocultural "nature" is so intimately related to man that it is in him; we might even say that man and his sociocultural "nature" coinhere. Once again, if we choose to speak of man's selfhood or his spirit, we must do so in a manner that includes his dependence upon society and culture as the matrix in which his distinctively human existence takes form and from which it emerges. This is the second lesson a doctrine of man must learn from the life sciences.

2. *A new doctrine of man must take change and diversity seriously.* Theological anthropology at the present time is very largely premised on a picture of man's not having altered basically since his creation by God. At least, he has not changed within his holy of holies, his self-consciousness. Even the methodologies like Martin Buber's, which build into their theologies the factor of constant dialogue with the Thou, through whom the self unfolds, do not encompass change within their purview — at least not significant change.

The life sciences have suggested to us that change and diversity are of the very fabric of life. This change is of two kinds, and we can get at these two kinds of change by borrowing the categories of Andrew G. van Melsen;[37] we can speak of change in respect to man regarded as an object and in respect to man regarded as a subject.

[36] Erving Goffman, *The Presentation of Self in Everyday Life* (New York: Doubleday Anchor, 1959), p. 252. Italics added.
[37] Van Melsen, *Evolution*, chap. 1.

When the life sciences look at man as an object, it seems clear that he is one part of a chain of life that has changed from one species to another in a long history of development, and that seems open to change in the form of future developments of life. This change was described by Ernst Haeckel in 1896: "The gist of Darwin's theory is this simple idea: that the Struggle for Existence in Nature evolves new Species *without* design just as the Will of Man produces new Varieties in Cultivation *with* design." [38] We have difficulty imagining this kind of change in life, particularly in man. It is difficult for us to take seriously any significant change in future men. Continuity in man's nature seems to be an indestructible building block in our thought. Father Teilhard is one of the few Christian thinkers who has really allowed for a change in man in the future. In his more dramatic phases of thought, Teilhard spoke of this change in terms of a point omega towards which man's ever increasing complexification is tending.[39] The intense mystical dimension of this concept of omega makes it difficult to work with. But in another aspect of his thought, Teilhard is concerned to speak, not about eschatology, but about evolution's ability to make fresh starts when a maximum amount of complexification has lessened possibilities for further development in any particular phase. He uses the image of the space vehicle which achieves one orbit, only to launch a second vehicle into a still higher orbit. Man's evolution has now reached such a preliminary height, he believes, since it has populated the entire globe, formed a world society, and entered upon the explosion of intelligence which cybernation has rendered possible. In this context, he writes:

> Still deceived by the slowness of movements that embrace the whole cosmos, we all to some degree find extreme difficulty in thinking of man as still moving along his evolutionary trajectory. We still attribute to ourselves the fixity that we now recognize as an illusion when attributed to stars, to mountains and to life's long past. . . .

[38] Quoted in Eiseley, *Darwin's Century*, p. 334.
[39] Teilhard de Chardin, *Future of Man*, pp. 120–23.

257

We must distinctly and once and for all finish with the legend that continually crops up again of an earth that has, in man and with the man we now see, reached the limit of its biological potentialities.[40]

If this change is difficult to conceive theoretically, it is all too evident in the practical developments of biological technology. Genetic engineering, electronic control of the brain and human emotions, asexual reproduction, advanced medical procedures, and more sophisticated drugs are making it clear that our conceptions of what it means to be man and of what life and death are must be changed, if they are to be meaningful.

The second aspect of change, with respect to man regarded as a subject, overlaps the first kind of change, but differs in that it is change that transpires within an individual within his lifetime, and it has to do with changes in his own selfhood. If man is the highly flexible creature I have described, whose phenotype is always changing within an equally fast-changing world to which he is intimately related, and if this world includes the sociocultural "world," then we should expect great diversity within each individual human career. This is not only the diversity that accompanies the physical changes of growth, maturing, and change in environments, but also, as the social psychologists would want to point out, the diversity of the psychological and spiritual changes that attend those physical alterations. Peter Berger, in his book, *Invitation to Sociology*, discusses the implications of the fact that man owes his self to the social context in which he lives. This view of personality, he writes,

is far more radical in its challenge to the way we commonly think of ourselves than most psychological theories. It challenges radically one of the fondest pre-

[40] Teilhard de Chardin, *Man's Place in Nature*, pp. 107–8. Leslie Dewart, in his *The Future of Belief* (New York: Herder and Herder, 1966), chap. 3, makes an interesting effort to deal with change, but omits almost entirely any consideration of what Van Melsen calls the objective aspects of change. Dewart confines his attention to the interior, subjective self, as it changes.

suppositions about the self — its continuity. Looked at sociologically, the self is no longer a solid, given entity that moves from one situation to another. It is rather a process, continuously created and re-created.[41]

I would suggest that most theological discussions of man employ a view of the self as a "solid, given entity."

Andrew G. van Melsen has given us another insight into man's interior propensity towards change by asking what the sciences, as such, reveal to us about man as subject. His conclusion is that the sciences reveal to us, first of all, that through the experimental method man is fully involved in a nature that is fully open to change; and, second, man's own cognition of that nature is always open to change.[42] The conclusion must be drawn that man's understanding of himself is always open to change, since he is caught up in fully open-ended involvements, both physically and cognitionally.

> The progressive character of human knowledge disclosed itself first in physical science, but since then man has become convinced that progressiveness is valid for the whole of human existence. It could hardly have been different. For the self-experience man has acquired in the development of physical science essentially touches his relationship with nature, and a modification of his view of nature automatically has consequences for man's view of himself.[43]

It seems clear, then, that change is a fundamental category which we must implement in our thinking about matter and nature; indeed, some years ago, Collingwood could already conclude that change was a basic category in modern man's intellectual armory.[44] Change and diversity have already made their mark on our contemporary thinking about God.

[41] Peter Berger, *Invitation to Sociology: A Humanistic Perspective* (New York: Doubleday Anchor, 1963), p. 106.
[42] Van Melsen, *Evolution*, pp. 18–23, 51–53. See Dewart, *Future of Belief*, chap. 3.
[43] Van Melsen, *Evolution*, p. 22.
[44] Collingwood, *Idea of Nature*, pp. 9–13.

On the American scene, the efforts of men like Daniel Day Williams, John Cobb, and Schubert Ogden do not need to be detailed here. On the European scene, Wolfhart Pannenberg and Jürgen Moltmann are simultaneously dealing with change and diversity under the rubric of hope and futurity. In a recent article, Moltmann put the issue well by saying that Christian theology must pay "attention to the future as a divine mode of being."[45] Pannenberg is doing precisely this as he seeks to develop an ontology of futurity which makes the future in God preeminent over past and present, and which makes God's future the prime determinant for all moments of the present. The work of Pannenberg and Moltmann, simply because it does emphasize futurity, bids fair to join forces with what seems to be a growing need and desire for a "theology of revolution" which can proceed more carefully than the rather careless, popular attempts that are rife today.

It is not at all clear, however, that we are proceeding with as much clarity and courage to implement the concepts of change and diversity in our theological thinking about man as we have in our thinking about matter, nature, and God. When we do proceed clearly and courageously in this area, our conceptions of sin, grace, and ethics will have to undergo decisive changes, since so much of the theological and philosophical tradition presupposes a static view of man.[46] Perhaps most importantly, relativity will figure even more prominently in our thinking concerning ethics and in our construction of norms for determining just what constitutes Christian life, both in the present and in continuity with the past.

I have already suggested that if theology is to form an adequate doctrine of man in the light of what we know about change and diversity, then perhaps we must say that man is himself most adequately conceived as an *event*. That is, man is himself a concatenation or juncture of biological and social forces; man is himself a bundle of energy, organized in a cer-

[45] Jürgen Moltmann, "Hope without Faith: an Eschatological Humanism without God," in *Is God Dead?* (Concilium 16; New York: Paulist Press, 1966), p. 39. See the materials listed in footnote 1, above.

[46] Van Melsen, *Evolution*, pp. 17ff.

tain manner, proceeding in a certain direction. In these terms, we could understand that man is a process, continuously created and recreated. The self, in this reconstruction, must be considered, not only as a changing entity; but, in its essential nature, it must be understood to be composite, relative, and unfinished. The self is a composite of the entire process that constitutes it. Such a view of man as event and composite would call for a corollary restatement of our doctrines of justification, sin, the image of God in man, and others. In each of these doctrines, the restatement should probably emphasize the category of *linearity* rather than substance. Here I can only sketch cursorily what "linearity" might mean for our doctrine of man. It means, for one thing, that we must define man in terms of the *structure* or shape of the components that comprise him, in terms of the structure or shape of his actions and functions. Here I would simply be following the lead of Whitehead, Alexander, Teilhard, and most scientists.[47] Linearity would also imply that we consider man from the perspective of the direction in which he is tending, rather than the substance or essence he has attained. So, for example, man's intelligence is to be described, not so much in terms of the brainpower and learning that man has attained, as in terms of the network of cybernated centers of intelligence and learning that man is building and projecting, with the concomitant changes such a network will effect. Linearity would combine changeability and instability with order and direction in defining man and his life.[48] This linearity would consist in a thrust forward in full psychosomatic unity, towards the future.

3. *A doctrine of man must come to terms with the biological significance of psychic, or spiritual and cultural phenomena.* I have indicated in the first part of this paper that the realm of biological considerations is of a piece with man's so-

---

[47] See Collingwood, *Idea of Nature*, pp. 158–74. Also the basic thesis of Karl Menninger in *The Vital Balance* (New York: Viking Press, 1963).

[48] Pannenberg offers insights along this line in his emphasis upon man's "openness" to the world and God. See his *Christologie*, pp. 196ff. and his *Was ist der Mensch?* (Göttingen: Vandenhoeck and Ruprecht, 1964).

ciocultural achievements, including his morality, politics, and so forth. Christian theology has often abhorred such intimations. Even a touch of Emile Durkheim or W. Lloyd Warner in such instances has brought howls from theologians,[49] who have insisted that the psychic phenomena with which the church has to do are God's *revelation*; and such revelation has not ordinarily been thought to possess biological significance.

This distinction between the psychic events that are revelation and the physical events of biological evolution may have been viable in a day when biology and the social sciences seemed to be unalterably discontinuous. Today, however, when biological and sociocultural considerations appear to reside in one single continuum, we must reassess theology's traditional abhorrence of the suggestion that even Christian psychic phenomena have a biological significance in the same sense that all of man's actions do. Of course, this statement needs some elaboration. A previous generation objected to Durkheim and Warner, as well as to Huxley, because their work seemed to imply that religion was simply another mechanism of adaptation to the environment. This functional approach to religion was simply too crass for theologians, and rightly so.

Today, however, we can put different constructions upon the statement that religious phenomena have biological significance. We can point, first of all, to the judgment that the term "adaptation" is not an exhaustive designation of man's activities. Man also "expresses" himself, sometimes in ways that seem to have little adaptive value at all.[50] For this reason, Dubos prefers to say that man "responds" to his environment, which includes expressiveness, rather than that man "reacts," as if he were victimized by his environing world.[51] Psychic phenomena, including religion, may very well fall under this expressive functioning of man.

[49] Emile Durkheim, *The Elementary Forms of Religious Life* (New York: Collier Books, 1958); and W. Lloyd Warner, *The American Life: Dream and Reality* (Chicago: Univ. of Chicago Press, 1962), chap. 2.

[50] See Dubos, *Mankind Adapting*, p. xviii.

[51] Ibid.

More importantly, however, we can follow the lead of Teilhard de Chardin to see that the biological significance of psychic phenomena lies in the assertion that the psychical phenomena point to the more complex phases of biological reality into which it appears to be the destiny of matter to evolve.[52] This perspective has the merit of viewing spiritual phenomena within the total continuum of nature, while at the same time showing that the purpose of those phenomena is in relationship to material nature. The realm of *Geist* or psyche is not a disembodied, and therefore scientifically suspect, realm that hovers furtively and illegitimately alongside empirical reality. Rather, the *geistige* dimensions of human life, including religion and faith, are in some sense a phase of empirical, material reality. Therefore, as both Teilhard and La Barre point out, man's morality is not simply a spiritual entity dropped into man's existence from above. Rather, it is a spiritual dimension which is appropriate to the increasing complexity of life, in its human phase, which makes it possible for that life to sustain itself. Now such an assertion may be termed a "biologizing" of morality; on the contrary, it is more to the point to see morality as a phase, that is, having to do with the destiny, of biological realities. It is in this framework that Teilhard discerns a point omega, towards which life is evolving, which will be a final step in the destiny of life, and which he believes is encompassed by Jesus Christ.[53] Whether Teilhard is to be followed in all his details is not really the question; the point is that Teilhard understands that the psychic dimensions of man, including the psychic realities that we are accustomed to terming "faith" and "revelation," are to be viewed *within* the evolutionary career of nature, and that their significance obtains within that career. Here again, it is possible to hold Teilhard's eschatology in abeyance, in order to focus on his contention that civilization is a specific phase of the life process which is marked by the socialization of the human organism, in which psychic influences predominate over oth-

[52] See Teilhard de Chardin, *Future of Man*, chaps. 10, 13.
[53] Teilhard de Chardin, *Future of Man*, chaps. 1, 6, 22, 23.

ers.[54] The work of Pannenberg and Moltmann, particularly to the extent that it has been forged out of a dialogue with Marxism, is cognizant that the movement towards the future is an *embodied*, material movement. Its idealistic root, however, must be carefully restrained so as not to lose this material dimension. This built-in concern for concreteness and materiality is an important contribution which Teilhard and American empiricism can make to the current German modes of thought that are concentrating upon the future orientation of God and the world and man.

If we do take the biological significance of psychic phenomena seriously, the results will be explosive for our anthropology. On the one hand, we will have to consider earnestly that material or natural phenomena are incomplete apart from a larger destiny which includes spiritual dimensions of the life process. By this use of the term "destiny," I am not suggesting an illicit concept of teleology. Rather, I am calling attention to the fact that if matter at a certain level of his complexity is *life*, and thus inclusive of a psychic dimension, then we cannot fully understand matter at any level unless we understand its relationship to the structure of matter we call psychic and vital. On the other hand, we cannot understand spirit or life unless we can comprehend its place and significance for the whole spectrum of matter and its process of development.

These suggestions imply at least two important implications for our doctrine of man. First, our doctrine must be sophisticated enough to take its place in a cosmic context. What we say about Christ as Lord of men must be susceptible of elaboration under the rubric of his cosmic lordship. What we say about man's sin must be continuous with what we know about the existence of the entire cosmos, from subatomic matter to God himself; sin must have relevance not only for man's neuroses, but also for the groaning and travail of the creation. What we say about grace must be capable of illuminating the redemption of nature, both physical and sociocultural. What we say under the rubric of ecclesiology must be inclusive of the sociological, psychological, political, and historical dimen-

[54] Teilhard de Chardin, *Man's Place in Nature*, pp. 85–88.

sions of church life. In other words, we must break out of a parochialism which isolates man as if he were a phase of life in separation from all others, as if his destiny and origins were separable from the rest of the cosmic spectrum.

Second, and here I draw together implications from my discussion of the spirit/matter unity and change, we must consider more carefully the sense in which the spirit *is* matter in man. In an important sense, the self *is* what it does in the material world, and this means that man's spirit can only with difficulty be distinguished from what he does. Man does know himself to be something "more" than his deeds, "more" than the empirical analyses of himself; but this "more" is itself fully embedded in materiality. It has been suggested that man's life today is well described by the term "Operator," indicating that man's very being today is spelled out in his actions of managing and directing the apparatuses he has built, whether those apparatuses be social, political, technological, or psychological.[55] As we look at man today, we can see very clearly that his selfhood, his spirit, *is* his managing and operating, since it is within that managing and operating that he understands himself, tests his possibilities, lays out his goals, performs his ministrations of mercy, works out this destiny. If this is so, we must reassess rather drastically some of our traditional notions about faith being sharply separated (soteriologically, at least) from works, about man's true self being identified with what he *is* rather than with what he *does*.[56]

Third, we must recognize that in this respect the nontheological empirical disciplines can legitimately exercise a truth judgment upon our doctrine. If morality is a characteristic of the phase of life called socialization of the human species, then theologians can hardly formulate doctrines concerning morality that are disruptive of or nonsensical in relation to that socialization. Or, to restate an argument that Joseph Haroutunian has made very eloquently, if the peculiar biological and psychical task of mankind, under God's providence, to-

[55] I first heard this term from Joseph Sittler, although I am not sure that he would want to put it to the use I have here.
[56] See footnote 30 above.

day is to achieve a mode of existence which is hyperorgan-
ized and yet inclusive of ultrapersonal freedom, then a doctrine of man that does not speak very importantly about man's
relations in community and the possibilities of divine freedom
in those relations is a doctrine that might just as well not be
written, because it will be useless and profoundly unnatural
in a time when unnatural theology is nonsense. I recognize
that such comments are dangerous in that they are easily misunderstood. I do not mean to biologize theology; I do not
mean that theologians should let social engineers write their
moral theology for them. But I do mean that if man is a natural
organism, set inseparably within a network of physical-social-
cultural relations, then our confidence in God's providence
and faithfulness demands that our theology be of such a kind
that it will move man within these relations to his fruition and
fulfillment. In other words, the cosmic goals of life, as that
life happens to be structured in a hominized form, must be
the context and even the goals of our theology as well, particularly our doctrine of man. Once again, a parochial form of anthropology cannot relate easily and adequately to these larger
goals of the process of life.

Finally, the material I have attended to here holds implications for the shape and style of theological statements. Since
the problems that are raised by the life sciences, as well as the
constructive patterns of thought that they provide, must be
taken into consideration by theology and addressed explicitly,
I cannot avoid the conclusion that theological reflection upon
man will appear more and more to be a kind of empirical
analysis. Such theological reflection certainly is beholden to
its own tradition, for both its conceptualities and its problematic. Nevertheless, the conceptualities and problematic of the
nontheological disciplines that pertain to man will increasingly pressure theology out of any intellectual ghettoism. The
revelation which the theologian seeks to bring to bear upon reflection about man will have to manifest its usefulness within
the problematic which most reflective men have found pertinent, just as it will have to relate its constructive insights to
the structures of analysis those men have found helpful.

PART 3
Related Areas To Be Explored

10

Overcoming History with History: Some Unfinished Old Business at the New Frontiers of Theology

GERHARD SPIEGLER

For better or for worse the way from the present into the future leads through the past. This holds as much for intellectual movements as for individual and social life processes, for man with his creative spirit is a child of the past though he belongs to the future. Contemporary theology as a movement of the human spirit is not exempt from this rule. It too must own its past to possess a future.

But fundamentally "owning the past" is not a matter of choice but of necessity. The issue is not whether, but how to be related to the past; and the alternative is not between denying and accepting history but between owning one's past and being owned by it. The immortality of completed actuality is a stubborn present fact for the now of the contemporary scene, and that which is dead rises as a positive or negative ingredient in the life of the present. In this sense, contemporary theology has no future apart from its past, and constructive theology has no substance apart from historical theology. This conclusion suggests itself to a theologian working in the tradition of theological empiricism.

I

The theological liberalism represented by Adolf von Harnack and Ernest Troeltsch is part of the complex rich heritage of contemporary theology. Indeed, contemporary theology is deeply immersed in the problems, if not solutions, of the critical historical tradition of theology. This cannot be obscured by the fact that attack on theological liberalism has been a dominant trend in Protestant theological circles. On the contrary, this attack, rather than witnessing to the escape from theological liberalism, is indicative of a continued, even if reluctant, involvement of contemporary theology in the liberal tradition.

Recognizing this state of affairs, some contemporary theologians have urged a renewed concern for the liberal theological tradition. Professor Rudolf Bultmann did so when writing the introduction to the new edition of Harnack's *Das Wesen des Christentums,* as did Professor Wilhelm Pauck when delivering his inaugural address at Union Theological Seminary. Bultmann writes:

> It should . . . be stressed that this understanding of Christianity, although one may label it "liberal," is in no wise a lifeless residue of a vanished era which no longer needs to be taken seriously. On the contrary this "liberal" understanding, at the very least, contains active impulses which though now obscured nonetheless preserve their legitimacy and will recover their validity.[1]

But lest he be misunderstood, Bultmann concludes his article with a warning which should be heeded by all who appeal to the past. He says,

> True loyalty is never an "archaizing repetition," but only a critical appropriation which makes the legitimate impulses of tradition its very own and endows these emphases with validity in a new form.[2]

It is not clear what Bultmann regards as the "legitimate impulses" of the liberal tradition, but it is clear that he does not advocate a simple "sliding back" into the past; and neither does Pauck, though he predicts:

> Harnack and Troeltsch will be rediscovered and their leadership will again be recognized as promising a true

[1] Adolf von Harnack, *What Is Christianity?* (New York: Harper & Brothers, 1957), p. viii.
[2] Ibid., p. xvii.

and truthful understanding and interpretation of the
Christian gospel in the modern world.[3]

What do these men have in mind when they point contemporary theologians toward their liberal heritage? What are
these valid motives which must be reexamined and repos-
sessed in a new form? What in theological liberalism promises a "true and truthful understanding and interpretation of
the Christian gospel in the modern world"? What is it that can
serve as a bulwark against a vulgar orthodoxy and a dogmatic
confessionalism which, instead of possessing the past, is possessed by it?

Pauck gives us more hints than does Bultmann concerning
the direction of the new examination of liberal theological
thought. Nevertheless it is clearer what the appeal to the liberal heritage does not mean than what it does mean. Pauck indicates the possible direction which a reexamination must
take:

> It is his [Harnack's] approach to Christianity as a living
> faith which needs to be freshly understood and re-evalu-
> ated, because the major trend of contemporary theologi-
> cal thought is marked by a blindness of those ways of
> thinking which Harnack practiced not only in his his-
> toriography but also in his judgments of the validity of
> the Christian faith. We therefore direct our attention to
> his insistence that Christianity must be understood as an
> historical movement and that it must be interpreted by
> the historical method.[4]

The main thrust of Pauck's statement resides in the injunction
to understand Christianity as a "historical movement" by way
of the "historical method." But what does it mean to understand the Christian faith as a "historical faith" by way of the
"historical method"? The problematic word is the word "historical," and Pauck, in pointing to the liberal understanding of

[3] Wilhelm Pauck, "The Significance of Adolf von Harnack's Interpretation of Church History," *Union Seminary Quarterly Review* (Jan-
uary 1954), pp. 13–54.
[4] Ibid.

Christianity, has pointed to the problem of history in its relation to the Christian faith as the central theological issue.

The centrality of this issue has been confirmed in the most
recent theological developments. Professor John B. Cobb, Jr.,
writing in the second volume of the series *New Frontiers in
Theology*,[5] points this out. In summarizing the basic issues in
the dialogue between German and American theologians, he
concludes that the critical issue of the current theological discussions is the problem of the relation of faith and history or
culture. Contemporary theology faces a dilemma in its confrontation with the old liberal problem of the relation of faith
and history. The liberal theological solution to the problem
has been rejected. The emasculation of the Christian faith
through a theology of ethical subjectivism is not an acceptable theological solution. On the other hand, the voice of dogmatic confessional objectivism, raised in protest against theological subjectivism, sounds less and less like the voice of a
new prophetic Christianity, and more and more like a voice
crying in bewilderment in the modern world.

In their own way, contemporary theologians have come to
take Pauck's injunction seriously. For it is possible to view the
recent hermeneutical approach to theology as one way of interpreting Christianity as a historical phenomenon by way of
historical method. But as a result of this new interpretative
effort the problem of faith and history or culture has again
been raised to a cardinal position. Contemporary theologians,
as Cobb points out, agree that "in the total occurrence in which
faith occurs culture [history] is ingredient, but they differ in
their views of the ingredience of culture in faith itself." [6] They
differ on how seriously the historical character of faith must
be taken. The crucial question is whether faith and history are
externally or internally related. Cobb divides the partners in
the current theological dialogue into two types. Continental
theologians such as Gerhard Ebeling and Ernst Fuchs are
treated as holding to an "existentialist" view of faith, and

[5] James M. Robinson and John B. Cobb, Jr., eds., *The New Hermeneutic*, (New York: Harper & Row, 1964), p. 220.
[6] Ibid., p. 223.

American theologians, such as Amos N. Wilder and John Dil-
lenberger, are seen as proponents of a "formalist" view of
faith. For the theologians of the existentialist type, culture is
externally related to faith, while for the theologians of a formalist type, culture is internally related to faith. In nuce this
means that for the former, faith is substantively exempt from
change; while for the latter, faith is formally beyond change.
Thus for one group of theologians faith itself escapes history,
while for the other group it does not.

Existentialist theologians, in Ebeling's words, see the formalists as treating faith as "an empty sack whose nature it is
to serve as a container for specific objects,"[7] while the formalist theologians suspect that their colleagues do not take the
historical character of faith seriously. To put it differently, existentialist theologians fear that the formalists are surrender-
ing the Christian faith to historical cultural relativism, and in
turn the formalist theologians claim that the existential view
of faith places the Christian faith outside the common reality
of God's creation and thereby surrenders it to historical-cultural irrelevancy. The dilemma is profoundly simple: Does
historical relativity, when applied to the Christian faith, make
that faith irrelevant, or does historical relativity, when not applied to the Christian faith, make that faith irrelevant? The
merits of either of the two positions are not under consideration; let us simply note that both existentialist and formalist
theologians are facing the problem of historical relativity and
its significance for the Christian faith as a central theological
problem. An adequate treatment of this problem is as yet part
of the unfinished old business of contemporary theology. The
problem is old because historical relativity or historicism was a
central problem of liberal theological thought; it is unfinished
because, while rejecting the liberal solution of the problem,
contemporary theology has not developed a satisfactory answer of its own. The liberal scholars such as Harnack and
Troeltsch wrestled with this problem, which was not of their
own making, and they have bequeathed it to us. Thus when

[7] Gerhard Ebeling, *The Nature of Faith* (Philadelphia: Muhlenberg
Press, 1961) p. 19.

Bultmann and Pauck call for a reassessment of the liberal heritage, they call for an encounter with the problem of historicism and its meaning for the understanding of the Christian faith.

Briefly, what is the problem raised in the doctrine of historical relativity? Put abstractly, historical relativity as a doctrine asserts that the spatio-temporal point of view of an observer enters into his knowledge of reality, so that no universal knowledge is possible. As a consequence no belief or faith can claim universal validity. Put in historical descriptive terms, historical relativity is concomitant with the modern scientific recognition that relativity is a pervasive phenomenon of physical reality itself. In subjective anthropological terms, the pervasive presence of relativity as ingredient in physical and historical phenomena has given rise to the deeply felt experience among all men that being itself, and not just knowledge of being, is evaporated in the stream of becoming. With the disintegration of physical substances into pulsating quanta of space-time configurations which are approachable only by way of statistical averages and are expressive of probabilities and not certainties, there has come as a corollary a radical historical-cultural relativism. Permanency itself is in question as it never was before. Ernst Troeltsch summed up the situation very succinctly when he once told a group of theologians, "Gentlemen, everything wobbles." Men today, as never before, are tempted to say with Aristophanes, "Whirl is king; Zeus is dethroned"; and they feel lost in a whirlpool of a-rational, if not irrational, forces which penetrate the very integrity of their selves. They feel pushed and manipulated by a reality which is beyond control and cognition. Man's labor seems like the labor of Sisyphus, and with John Updike we can see the rabbit run though there is no place to go.

II

In the context of man's experience of what Mircea Eliade has called the "terror of history," the problem of historical relativity and its relation to the Christian faith takes on existential sharpness. If with Troeltsch and H. Richard Niebuhr, we find ourselves "unable to avoid the acceptance of historical relativism," we are faced with the question of whether the validity or certainty of the Christian faith is dissolved by historical relativity and whether the only alternative left to us is either scepticism and agnosticism or a miraculous leap of faith based on a *sacrificium intellectus*? Or, we must ask, is it possible to affirm with Luther, "Spiritus sanctus non est scepticus," and at the same time with Troeltsch, historical relativity? It is the glory of the worshipping Christian community to make, confessionally, direct affirmations of faith; but it is the duty and task of theology to address itself to problems conceptually. Neither of the two stances is a substitute for the other. The issue before contemporary theology is whether the problem posed by historical relativity can be overcome in adequate conceptual terms?

H. R. Niebuhr thought that a theology of "historical relativism" was possible, and he rejected scepticism and subjectivism. Troeltsch too envisioned the overcoming of historical relativism by historical relativity when he challenged "bold and believing" men "to overcome history with history." Let us examine the possibility of a theology of historical relativity by asking what it is in the Christian faith which makes the doctrine of historical relativity a stumbling block and *scandalon*. Upon what does the validity of the Christian faith rest that the recognition of the historically conditioned character of philosophical ideas, religious dogmas, and moral imperatives should put it in question? Could it be that the problems which historicism causes for the Christian faith are not due to historical relativity as such but due to a particular set of metaphysical assumptions embraced in a particular, even if ancient, conception of the Christian faith?

When we study the theological conceptualizations instrumental in the Christian community of faith, we find that a good many theologians of past and present have operated, explicitly or implicitly, with the notion of an absolute as the necessary and essential foundation for the Christian faith. In other words, the validity of the Christian faith was made to rest on an idea of God's perfection in absoluteness. Even H. R. Nie-

buhr, theologian of historical relativity though he confessed
to be, sees the Christian faith in the context of the metaphysical problem of the relation of an absolute and the relative in
history. Professor Helmut Thielicke, in a series of lectures entitled "Revelation and History, the Theology between Historicism and Existentialism," speaks of "the absolute in history,"
implying that this problem formulation emerges directly
from "the fundamental truth of the Christian faith, as summed
up in the prologue of St. John's Gospel, that the word was
made flesh, that is, that [the absolute] God has entered into
history." In the language of another generation, Professor E.
Schaeder in *Pro and Contra History (Für und wider die Ge-
schichte)* sees man's religious predisposition in his striving
after the absolute. And behind the existentialist theologians'
"thinking explication of the one and indivisible faith according to the different structures that necessarily belong to it," as
Karl Barth's successor Heinrich Ott puts it, seems to lurk the
silent "one indivisible ground" of absoluteness as the sus-
taining basis for the Christian faith. Now maybe an idea of
absoluteness is the cornerstone of the Christian faith, and if
it is, then historical relativity is indeed a stumbling block for
the Christian theologian. But then again the notion of absoluteness may not be as central to the historical faith of Christianity as has been assumed.

At the risk of oversimplifying, it is possible for us to construct two ideal types of this "absolute" and the attempts to
relate it to history. On the one hand the absolute may be conceived as ontologically transcendent, that is, as basically and
essentially separated from the world of becoming, as qualifying time but not being qualified by time. On the other hand,
it may be conceived as immanent in the world of becoming,
in which case the world itself is the eternal unfolding of the
absolute. In the first case, the relationship between God and
the world is purely external, lacking immanence save that of
a miraculous ingression; in the second case it is a purely internal relation, lacking any transcendence save that of the
whole over the part.

In the first type the problem is to find an adequate modus of relation; in the second type it is to find an adequate modus of differentiation. When we study Christian thought we find that Christian theology, though not abandoning the notion of God conceived in the perfection of absoluteness, has never been satisfied with the *caput mortuum* of the metaphysical absolute, and as a matter of fact, has always struggled with it. This struggle must be interpreted, not as the attempt to abandon absoluteness as the central notion, but as the effort to speak theologically in spite of it. Thus we find the doctrine of the Trinity modifying the lifeless sterility of the philosophical absolute, drawing on the doctrine of incarnation as the main resource in this effort. Yet given the notion of God as absoluteness, the doctrine of incarnation, which is the center of Christian theology, becomes also the problem center for Christian theology. To say that the eternal God, conceived as the perfection of absoluteness, revealed himself in one specimen of history is indeed a thought which is the downfall of reason. Put this way, the problem is that Christian theology, though beginning with Christology, cannot theologize on the possibility of Christology. As Professor Joachim Iwand once expressed it, "Man has no power to judge (*Urteilskraft*) whether God can enter into time"; the "is" in the sentence "this *is* my beloved son" is exempt from questioning. From this perspective the relationship of God and world becomes the central issue, inspiring new and ever new restatements. The ideal for this type is to maintain both God's perfection of absoluteness and his incarnation.

The second, more rationalistic type, is not faced with the question of how God can become flesh, but with the problem of how one can say that some flesh is not God; for in the Hegelian language of David Friedrich Strauss, "The idea does not like to pour out her total fullness in one single specimen of history, to let her absoluteness be made manifest in one point of history."

Concretely, both these types appear in various forms and combinations, mixing their features and problem solutions, but sharing implicitly or explicitly the assumption that God, conceived in the perfection of absoluteness, is an unquestionable axiom of the Christian faith. Given the difficulties associated with this supposedly unquestionable axiom, one is led to ask why it has been retained as a fundamental assumption of the Christian faith. One answer seems to lie in the concern for the validity, the objectivity, and certainty of the Christian faith. Only self-identical timeless truth expressed through the notion of the divine absolute seems to be able to give value to the transitory character of the temporal process. The exclusion of change from the absolute guarantees reliability. The temporal historical process has value only insofar as the divine absolute gives value to it or expresses itself in it. Permanency, universality, and necessity are the foundation of certainty. God as the absolute in that sense is the guarantor of value.

III

To inject the metaphysical doctrine of the absolute into the theological formulations of the Christian faith seems not to be necessitated by that faith itself. And to formulate the question of the relationship of the Christian faith to history in terms of the problem of an absolute in history compounds more problems than it solves, and has required ever more radical solutions since the formulation of the doctrine of historical relativity. Is it possible to reformulate the relation of the Christian faith to history from a perspective which does not demand a *sacrificium intellectus*, without falling into a complete rationalism? Recent theological attempts are efforts in that direction, and the following is meant as a contribution to the search for a more fully adequate solution to the central conceptual problem facing theology today.

This attempt at reconstruction is motivated by the desire for reasonableness and by the conviction that problems must not be formulated in an either/or fashion. The "either" must modify the "or" and vice versa. Thus God must be viewed, not only from the perspective of the absolute, but also from the perspective of the relative.

When Troeltsch said that he wanted to "overcome history with history" I interpreted that as meaning that relativity can overcome relativism. Now we must recognize that historical relativity does mean that an "essence" of the Christian faith, which is relevant, irrespective of its location in the space-time continuum, cannot be obtained. And it teaches that a *sub specie aeternitatis* view is not only not possible, but would be barren and empty by itself even if attained. Now the search for descriptive metaphysical generalizations is a continuing effort in which one works toward the formulation of those general abstract conditions which could be said to be the prerequisite of all actualizations. This is a legitimate and necessary task of the metaphysician. But we cannot identify the Christian faith or Christian revelation with the concern for abstract metaphysical truth. The Christian faith is concerned with the particularity of actual events, and as such it must exhibit the characteristics of all concretions — relativity and change. The variety of theoretical abstractions by which the Christian community has explored its living faith reflects always the concrete historical situation. In this sense, it is correct to say with Troeltsch that "Christianity is itself a theoretical abstraction. It represents no historical uniformity, but displays a different character in every age." [8] But we do not have to conclude with Troeltsch that this is due either to man's unfortunate condition or to the character of temporality which requires that the absolute oneness of the divine life can only be perceived in refraction. This position does not advance to the insight of the particularity of the object of faith as the basis for the validity of the particularity of faith itself. The unsatisfactory character of this position becomes clear in H. R. Niebuhr's language when he speaks, for instance, of Christian theology as a particular language expressing "ideas about universals." My objection is not directed against the notion of the universal as such, for we may accept as valid the proposition that all particulars require universals. My objection is directed against the priority of importance which is attributed to universals. In other words, I object to the idea that the theological concern is with God as the source and exemplification of abstraction rather

[8] Ernst Troeltsch, *Christian Thought: Its History and Application*, (New York: Living Age Books, 1957), p. 43.

than with God in his concreteness. The primary theological concern must be with God's specific and concrete participation in the process of concretion and not with those abstract universal conditions which must obtain for all structures of actualization. The doctrine of historical relativity restricts us to particularities. If God by virtue of his very nature is excluded from participating constitutively in the relativity of actuality, he is made unavailable. If, on the other hand, God is constitutively partaking of particularity, then particularity receives a finality of meaning and significance. The difficulties posed by historical relativity for the theological explication of the Christian faith can be theologically overcome only if the doctrine of historical relativity is metaphysically generalized to include relativity as an essential qualification of God. The possibilities of such a generalization require serious theological attention. Do we dare let particularity be saved by a divine relativity? But then can we afford not to overcome history with history or relativism with relativity? What is needed is not only a confessional affirmation of God's particularity but also a conceptual exploration of its possibility.

The history of the Christian community is the history of concrete responses to the concrete activity of God. The validity of the Christian faith is a specific validity grounded in God's presence as a specific presence. The fact that historical relativity removes the possibility of a transformation of the Christian faith into an abstraction, valid without reference to space-time, need not disturb us, for God saves the particular in his particularity.

This then is the paradox, the *scandalon* of faith: the foundation of our hope and salvation is not to be found in an unconditioned absolute, but in the particularity of God, the God in Jesus Christ. To our attempts to escape from particularity, God has replied with the NO of the unavailability of truth other than particular truth. To our pride, which attaches importance only to the universal, God has spoken the NO of his own particularity. The God in Christ does indeed reverse the human standard of value, but the paradox of the Christian faith is not that the absolute came into the relativity of time. The Christian paradox is not an unthinkable thought; rather, it is a thinkable thought but a thought which crushes our sense of importance. God in his particularity can love, forgive, and judge as no absolute can. God's claim over us issues from his concreteness, and the basis of our certainty is his particularity. It is a certainty which we have, not in spite of the historical nature of our faith, but because of it.

11

Can Empirical Theology Learn Something from Phenomenology?
BERNARD E. MELAND

That radical empiricists and phenomenologists have things in common is a judgment that has been commonly known for many years. Current literature reviving and reassessing the works of Edmund Husserl is generous in its acknowledgment of the stimulus of William James during the period of Husserl's early efforts to formulate his method of inquiry.[1] It was even said in those years, with Husserl's assent, that phenomenology is a kind of radical empiricism,[2] aiming toward formulating a philosophical method that focused upon *lived experience* as a way of probing acts of perception and reflection. Both James and Husserl sought to go beyond British empiricism and modern idealism in this effort. James was more critical of both Kant and Hegel than Husserl had been and was inclined to heed British empiricists on certain issues,

[1] Cf. the "Introductory Essay" by James W. Edie, ed., in *What Is Phenomenology?* by Pierre Thevenaz (Chicago: Quadrangle Books, 1962), pp. 34–36; Marvin Farber, *The Aims of Phenomenonology* (New York: Harper & Row, 1966), pp. 7, 100–101; Aron Gurwitsch, *Theori du champ de la conscience* (Paris: De Brouwer, 1957), pp. 246ff; Herbert Spiegelberg, *The Phenomenological Movement* (The Hague: Nijhoff, 1960), 1:111–17; John Wild, *Existence and the World of Freedom* (Englewood Cliffs, N.J.: Prentice-Hall, 1963), pp. 28–34, 62–66, 76–83. An impressive account of James's "existentialist turn of mind" and the extent to which he anticipated much that has since developed as existentialist literature stemming from Sören Kierkegaard's influence and Nietzsche's is given by Geoffrey Clive in *The Romantic Enlightenment* (New York: Meridian Books, 1960), chap. 3. Here James' kinship with the phenomenological mode of thought is likewise reflected.

[2] Thevenaz, *What is Phenomenology?* pp. 52, 168.

though he rejected certain of their presuppositions. Husserl, on the other hand, while critical of Hegelian rationalism, found resources in Hegel's thought which served his own efforts in logic; but he had no kind word for British empiricists, other than to acknowledge the pertinence of Hume's skeptical query. This difference in their stance with regard to these two fronts of European philosophy gives hint of a basic difference in the way James and Husserl viewed the philosophical tasks. And this initial difference in their concern with transcendental notions as developed in Kantian and Hegelian thought has persisted as a barrier between the two movements. James was an out-and-out empiricist who resisted with all his might what he deemed the "presumptions" of absolute idealists. Husserl, on the other hand, shared the idealist's concern for a priori certainty in thought, even though he recoiled from the way Kant and Hegel had established it.

Husserl, as is commonly known, found initial reinforcement of his concern to formulate a new way of doing philosophy in James' *Psychology*, particularly in James' development of the *stream of thought*.[3] James' way of singling out the act of thinking as "thought-going-on" seemed to Husserl to pose thought as a phenomenon, stripped of its psychological and historical coloration or accouterments. It provided a direct way of getting to the fact of pure consciousness.

It would be helpful in understanding these initial affinities between phenomenology and radical empiricism if we had some word from William James concerning Husserl's work; but unfortunately, James appears to have been relatively unaware of Husserl's work, or, if aware, indifferent toward it. The obvious explanation of this lack of response on James' part is that Husserl had not published any of his major phenomenological writings during James' lifetime. His *Philosophie der Arithmetik* (1891) and *Logische Untersuchungen* (1900–1901) were investigations in mathematical logic which were not apt to attract James' attention at that particular period. James was aware of *Logische Untersuchungen* but appar-

[3] Farber, *Aims of Phenomenology*, p. 7.

ently took no special notice of it. It is reported, however, that James was informed about Husserl's efforts from time to time through James' correspondence with the German psychologist, Carl Stumpf.

There is more to be found in Husserl's later writings that accords with the direction of radical empirical inquiry than in these earlier works. In his later writings, Husserl's tendency to speak within the Hegelian idiom appears less and less, and his concern with designating the phenomenal field of lived experience (*lebenswelt*) assumes dominance. This fact in itself would seem to bring the phenomenologist and the radical empiricist within range of one another's plea of inquiry, with a common focus on concreteness. However, "concreteness" never seems to mean quite the same thing to the phenomenologist that it means to empiricists.

It is, I think, a rather remarkable historical fact that two movements of thought within the modern period, having even this much in common, could carry on their respective efforts of innovation and reform within philosophy for more than a quarter century, in fact for nearly a half century, without becoming more attentive to one another's concern. One explanation, I believe, is that radical empiricism, for at least the first two decades of this century, was wholly absorbed into pragmatism, and thus, as metaphysical inquiry at least, was driven underground as pragmatism assumed a more prominent role in modern philosophy.[4] What was projected and

---

[4] Many of James' interpreters may object to my distinguishing so sharply between James' radical empiricism and his pragmatism, or to my dissociating the one from the other. I have contended for many years that failure to see them as different levels of interest and inquiry in James results in doing an injustice to the deeper vein of his philosophical and religious concerns. James' evident respect for what he called "the perceptual flux," as conveying much in experience *as lived* that could not readily be conceptualized, led him to acknowledge its primacy as the empirical datum, and to recoil from overzealous efforts to cast its meaning in conceptual terms, or to presume to envisage it imaginatively or abstractly through rational explications. This sense of the "More" in *experience that is lived*, in contrast to the restrictive portions of it that are *conceived*, is what lends a unique degree of outreach and sensitivity to James' thought as compared with that

emphasized in pragmatism was clearly a detour from what had initially interested phenomenologists in radical empiricism. And conversely, except in the form that pragmatism had originally developed in the thought of Charles Peirce, and was later to develop in George Herbert Mead, its focus of interest was not apt to propel it toward phenomenology. In a word, John Dewey appears to have been the lodestar of American empiricism, drawing it out of the orbit in which it had had affinities with phenomenology, into another orbit that had less obvious relation to the phenomenological field of inquiry.

The change in the relationship between the two movements in recent years, evidencing a renewal of rapport, if not a convergence between them, stems from developments in both empiricism and phenomenology. Empiricism has re-

---

of other empiricists and pragmatists. Now James was not content to dissipate this sense of the *More* in mysticism. Although he was sympathetic toward the mystic, he was insistent that we should make some effort to conceptualize experience within appropriate limits by way of relating ourselves creatively and humanly to it; which, in effect, was to put our human stamp upon it. Pragmatism, as a functional mode of conceptualization, seemed to him to be a feasible and appropriate way of addressing this flux of experience conceptually, in so far as one sought to serve immediate ends consonant with action. On more ultimate issues, one senses obvious misgivings in James concerning the adequacy of any conceptual procedure. One sees in his insistence upon pluralism a way of holding such issues open, rather than an explicit way of closing in on them in a definitive formulation. James did not live to complete or carry out these notions, which, presumably might have developed into a metaphysics of radical empiricisms in which adequate controls of conceptual inquiry were more precisely specified and exemplified. Those of his writings gathered into posthumous publications in *Essays in Radical Empiricism* (1912) and *Some Problems of Philosophy* (1911) were obviously experimental pieces, venturing toward such a vision within the sensibilities of the empiricist. It is in these writings that one comes upon hunches, gropings, and tentative formulations moving out from what some of his interpreters today would call his phenomenological stance, first detected in his *The Principles of Psychology* and *Varieties of Religious Experience*; and venturing beyond not only what pragmatism was to become, but beyond his own pragmatic efforts as well. I find Geoffrey Clive's discussion of the differences between James and Dewey, in his *Romantic Enlightenment*, somewhat supportive of the view I have held on this issue through the years.

286

newed inquiry in the more radical empirical sense of exploring the full meaning of experience as concrete event. And phenomenology, veering away from earlier concentration upon logical studies, has been addressing itself specifically to the perceptual field as it illumines the concerns of lived experience.

For some time, now, students of Whitehead have been tantalized by possibilities of seeing similarities between Heidegger's ontology and the Whiteheadian philosophy of organism.[5] The more these apparent affinities have been pursued, however, the less fruitful their comparisons have appeared. A more likely comparison between the empirical thought of organismic and process thinkers and that of phenomenologists has developed with the publication and translation of works by French phenomenologists, notably the writings of Merleau-Ponty. Here a post-Hegelian mode of phenomenology is being consciously pursued. But what becomes more significant, as one examines Merleau-Ponty's writings, is that the imagery of thought is forthrightly in accord with that of the new era of the sciences as represented by the new physics and modern biology, not to speak of modern psychology. In their own way, the French phenomenologists have taken relativity physics and organismic notions seriously in discussing the notions of space and time, or in explicating the nature of the self, or in expounding "lived experience." The self and the world have become for them configurations that permit of no dualism. The subject-object dichotomy, so important to epistemologies of the Humean-Kantian era, and persisting in neo-Kantian philosophies and theologies even of recent periods, has been abandoned. Concern with the transcendental ego, or with ego as such, has been clearly muted, if not dissipated altogether. Subjectivity, while still of prime importance as a dimension of experience, is never viewed just as a closed track of internal reflection or

[5] This attention to Heidegger in relation to Whitehead has occurred mostly on an informal basis in the way of seminars and special study projects. Among process theologians, Schubert Ogden has been most explicit in acknowledging this concern. Cf. his *The Reality of God* (New York: Harper & Row, 1966), chap. 5.

reverie, but as the immediate access to what opens out into the world as lived experience. In this context of relational thinking, the prominent notion of *intentionality* has undergone transformation. Merleau-Ponty has expressed it this way:

> We have just recognized that analysis has no justification for positing any stuff or knowledge as an ideally separable "moment" and that this stuff, when brought into being by an act of reflection, already relates to the world. Reflection does not follow in the reverse direction a path already traced by the constitutive act, and the natural reference of the stuff to the world leads us to a new conception of intentionality, since the classical conception (By this we understand either that of a Kantian like P. Lachieze-Rey [L'Idealisme kantien], or that of Husserl in the second period of his philosophy) which treats the experience of the world as a pure act of constituting consciousness, manages to do so only in so far as it defines consciousness as absolute non-being, and correspondingly consigns its contents to a "hyletic layer" which belongs to opaque being. We must now approach this new intentionality in a more direct way by examining the symmetrical notion of a form of perception, and in particular the notion of space.[6]

As Merleau-Ponty elaborates upon this new notion of intentionality, it becomes, not simply a singular agency of motivation or volition impelling the conscious act, but a dynamic structure of experience, integrating the individual life of the person with the full cultural orbit of meaning and valuation. Like the genetic code, operating at the level of physical inheritance, this funded social inheritance becomes a given, expressing itself concretely in each individual existence as a past selectively merging with immediacies to emerge as a present moment of living in intentional acts. In this formulation of intentionality, Merleau-Ponty, I venture to suggest, re-states within the phenomenological idiom the cardinal notion of

[6] *The Phenomenology of Perception* (London: Routledge & Kegan Paul, 1962), p. 243.

prehension and causal efficacy as it has developed in the philosophy of Whitehead. Stated in the way Merleau-Ponty presents it, the social import of these notions is made more vivid than the metaphysical statement in process thought conveys it, and thus is given greater force in explicating the nature of the self and its history.

It is important to see, I think, that while these two modes of thought converge in the way they think of man as a subjective existence, intimately and organically related to the objective world, they speak about it differently. What they say in these different ways of speaking corresponds in a remarkable way, and thus they supplement one another. Process thought is basically cosmological in its orientation. Its forms of thought about man and events were shaped by the concerns of organismic thinking, as they developed in biology at the turn of the century and became forged as a weapon against mechanism in an explicit philosophy of organism. These forms of thought were given a new dimension in theories of emergent evolution and in the concept of field theory as it developed in the new physics. The fashioning of these new fundamental notions into a metaphysical vision of experience by Whitehead's *Process and Reality* brought radical empiricism to a stage of conceptualization which William James and Henri Bergson had not dared to envisage. And even Whitehead, mindful of the audacity of the undertaking to which he had committed himself, inserted a warning against taking his empirical Summa as a literal depiction of cosmic existence, saying, "Philosophy is a voyage towards the larger generalities," [7] an analogical vision for purposes of entertaining a broader view of events. James had agreed that conceptualization is inescapable if we are to emerge from our individual tracks of perception; yet he held every such venture under question as being an inevitable overreaching of our human capacities to conceptualize what is given in the "perceptual flux."

There are grounds for suspecting that process thinkers, in-

[7] *Process and Reality: An Essay in Cosmology* (New York: Macmillan Co., 1929), p. 14.

sofar as they have sought to employ Whitehead's philosophy of organism for ontological or theological purposes, have not been equally concerned to observe this empirical sensibility. Were one to be faithful to the empirical concern of Whitehead and James in pursuing, for example, the theological task, one would begin one's reflections in this mode of thought, not with a categorial scheme as if one were repeating the classical procedure of rationalism employing literal notions of space and time, but by emphatically acknowledging the primacy of perception as being the cardinal doctrine of process thought. Here one would be introduced to the threshold of a vital immediacy, the depth and mystery of which is such that one would be mindful that in attending it, one confronts holy ground. For in this immediacy of lived experience, all that has transpired as historic occurrence in the far reaches of space and time now transpires as concrete occurrence, merging in the distillations of *history as lived* with an emerging present, and carrying the import of both immediate and ultimate demands. The "thickness" and "rich fullness" of this primal datum, the empirical theologian would observe, must forever put one on guard against venturing heedlessly into capturing it as a clear and distinct formulation. Whitehead once wrote, "Seek simplicity and distrust it." This injunction might be paraphrased to read, "Seek clarity and distrust it," implying a restless concern to summon every clarification of meaning and formulation before the bar of reality as the immediacies of lived experience convey it. Such recognition that reality continually exceeds and eludes the formulated notions by which we seek to grasp or articulate its concreteness would bring empiricism more in line with the sensibilities of modern scientists, who long ago abandoned the notion that models, and the formulas derived from them, could be employed descriptively. One must acknowledge, I think, that empiricists in philosophy and in theology have lagged behind the scientists in their use of conceptual models, and in assessing their limitations and significance for attaining intelligible results.

That Whitehead has provided a metaphysical vision of concrete experience, incorporating the relevant insights of organismic thought and radical empiricism reaching back to the turn of the century, gives the empiricist grounds for feeling that the empirical venture in thought has reached a new stage of maturity, enabling it to attain a degree of generality hitherto not attainable. His systematic formulation thus becomes a formidable resource for all who can avail themselves of his technical structure of thought. But to use this magnificent resource as a closure upon thought, compelling all other insight to be brought within its purview or rejected as being irrelevant to rational experience, is to profane this vision and to forfeit the creative stimulus of its imaginative venture.

It is one thing to be faithful in expounding the intellectual vision Whitehead has achieved. This exposition requires scholarly precision in clarifying the conceptual scheme he has provided. It is quite another thing to avail oneself of the quickening force of this metaphysical creation for illumining theological judgments long held by a community of faith, a faith which has been formative of the cultural experience of Western history. Here one does not shackle the witness of faith with a philosophical framework, as if the norm of historical experience suddenly shifted to this new Summa of thought. As a theologian sensitive both to claims of the historical witness of faith and to the empirical sensibilities of thought, one will acknowledge as a first canon of inquiry the priority of this lived experience and will employ the judgments and conceptual forms of thought provided by this new generalized vision in the tentative and explorative way that any scientist, attuned to the limitations of his discipline, employs his models and formulas. This implies both a discerning and a disciplined way of encountering the realities of experience, and a proportional use of conceptual tools to further one's reflections upon them.

Strange as it may seem, one finds in the writings of present-day phenomenologists such as Merleau-Ponty the very corrective which process thinking sorely needs in order to bring it back to a more empirical orientation in its procedures. For the preoccupation here is the perceptual field. And while phenomenologists have their own way of becoming detoured from concern with this vital immediacy, the tenacity with which they hold to perception as the living center of all that occurs in existence brings them back again and again to this phenomenal field. It is to the occurrences within this vital immediacy, wherein the realities of faith transpire, that the process theologian is to be attentive in interpreting Christian faith within the contemporary idiom.

As I have worked at this task of interpreting Christian faith within the contemporary idiom, I have been more and more impressed by the need of finding a way to exercise the reflective act in a disciplined manner, in probing or even pondering the witness of faith. This act is different from analytical inquiry. It is holistic and appreciative, aiming at opening one's conscious awareness to the full impact of the concrete occurrence. It is very much like allowing one's visual powers to accommodate themselves to the enveloping darkness until, in their more receptive response to the shrouded shapes and forms concealed by the darkness, one begins to see into the darkness and to detect in it the subtleties of relationships and tendencies which had eluded one, but which now yield a visual field. Empiricists working in the field of religion have, I am persuaded, been unduly intimidated by the psychical thrust of this lived experience as they have confronted it in what has been termed "religious experience." In fact, when they have encountered it in this form, suddenly all of the technical resources that have gone into shaping the organismic response to events seem to have deserted them and they have dealt with religious experience as if it presented itself only as an individualized, subjective event that had only the value of an isolated testimony. William James was no exception to this procedure, though it must be acknowledged in his defense that the full import of his own rational thinking had not yet developed into an organismic view. James, while he was skeptical of mystical experience, was not indifferent to it. And he had the patience to ponder the individual reports of experience, one after the other. In the end, while he admitted he had no mystical experience of his own to offer, he had, as he wrote to his friend Edward D. Starbuck, "just enough of the germ of mysticism in me to recognize the region from which their voice comes when I hear it." [8] But among later religious empiricists, even this degree of tentative responsiveness vanishes; hence the report of faith as "immediate" or "lived experience" is rendered suspect until it can be subjected to the rigorous methods of scientific testing, and conceptually reformulated as a rationally defensible observation.[9] In this procedure there is a short-circuiting of what has been given as a witness of faith. What emerges as a "scientifically tested" distillation of belief is clearly something that could have been formulated rationally without benefit of any appeal to experience, or any dependence upon it.

In this shift from the appeal to religious experience as "lived experience" within a specific context, that is, manifesting itself within a community of faith, to a scientifically tested or rationally defensible notion, presumably distilled from experience, a metamorphosis in the grounds of religious affirmation occurs. This, I think, was as true of the modernists of the early Chicago school as it has been of later process theologians. In the shift of perspective, theological words such as love, revelation, or forgiveness, having been given an ontological or instrumental meaning, are then taken to be meaningful simply as words, simply as linguistic realities. The experienceable realities of faith as events somehow become obscured or lost from the theological discourse as theological inquiry assumes more and more the status of semantic and logical explication.

Now back of this preference for dealing with faith at the level of semantics and logic in modernistic and process theology there is to be found a characteristically Protestant turn of mind of recent origin, stemming from disillusionment with all experiential forms of religious faith, especially as such faith had developed among separatist groups of the seven-

[8] Ralph Barton Perry, *The Thought and Character of William James* (Boston: Little, Brown & Co., 1935) 2:346.

[9] Professor Wieman's statement of this point of view in his *Religious Experience and Scientific Method* (New York: Macmillan Co., 1926), is helpful because it is so explicit, and he argues the case at considerable length throughout the book.

teenth and eighteenth centuries, and notably among Pietists. Much of what has gone on among liberal Protestant philosophers and theologians since the nineteenth century by way of bringing "intellectual respectability" or security to religious affirmations can be related historically to this disillusionment with pietistic or evangelical faith, or to subsequent expressions of religious experience perpetuating such piety, albeit in a more critical form. Thus it may be said that modernist and process thinkers carry forward the defensive concern of the seventeenth-century rationalists who sought to stem the tide of inner appeals in matters of faith, lest it become wholly subjective and irrational. This concern is well founded. The debauchery of faith and sentimentality within post-Reformation Christianity that followed from such appeals to inner experience was no illusion in the time of the Enlightenment. And it is no illusion now. The argument of this essay should not be taken to be a defense of that against which rationalists, modernists, and process theologians have contended. The real objective here is to ask whether, in defending religious thought against such maudlin excesses, rationalists, modernists, and process thinkers have not forfeited the very empirical base upon which religious faith, in sickness or in health, ultimately rests.

One comes back to the fundamental thesis advanced by Schleiermacher in *The Speeches* and in the introduction to *The Christian Faith,* namely, that there is no rational or moral alternative to the experiential base of religion given in the elemental stance of the human being. Schleiermacher found this primal, experiential base to be *the feeling of absolute dependence* which, as it was stated in *The Speeches,* points directly to the nexus of human existence wherein man's own humanly contrived efforts shade off from what is given and persistent as an inescapable and indispensable good not our own; or a condition of existence not of one's own making, or of any man's making. To speak of the primal base of faith in this way is to take it out of the subjective dimension of experience. It is, in fact, to cast experience itself in terms other than that of sheer subjectivity, and to see it as the most basic and commonly shared fact of all human experience, whether acknowledged or not.

Now it can be argued that all organismic thinking, insofar as it has addressed itself to the religious datum, has been continuous with Schleiermacher's primal notion of the feeling of absolute dependence, pointing to the elemental nexus of existence. Even the *sensus numinous*, both as it was put forth by Schleiermacher and as it was restated by Rudolf Otto in *The Idea of the Holy* and in his *Religious Essays*, can be seen as a mode of dimensional thinking about man which, in Schleiermacher's case, anticipated the emergent imagery of organismic thought; and in Otto's case partook of it, however remotely, though with modifications offered by his mentor Jacob Fries' notion of *ahnung*.

The fact that the feeling or sense of the numinous in confronting this primal nexus led to an insistence that all our speaking about the realities of faith must be symbolic, that is, language that does not presume to designate literal processes, though one means to hold the fact of such processes in view and within one's sensibilities of thought has in effect insulated religious discourse from all other disciplined discourses. The wisdom of this procedure may ultimately justify itself; but the effect of the procedure has been to render it unavailable to an impressive group of empirical thinkers who have been sorely in need of its stimulus and vision.

However this aspect of the issue is to be resolved, it remains clear that process theology, insofar as it pursues the empirical and organismic side of its mode of thought, instead of capitulating to conceptualism with its logical and semantic demands, can reformulate this primal nexus in its own terms as an inescapable elemental fact of *lived experience*, expressive both in terms of human subjectivity and in terms of creaturely objectivity. Ultimately, as we shall see in a moment, when *lived experience* is understood configuratively, as radical empiricists and phenomenologists alike have presented it, the subjective pole and the objective pole come to the same thing as the inner and outer perspective of the one reality.

I see this reformulation of the primal nexus within process

theology as being, not only a recovery of its empirical stance, but a reorientation of its thought and procedure toward the historic notion of religious experience. Such a reorientation would take the form of revising and, in some instances, abandoning the historically defensive procedures dating from the Enlightenment by which an uncritical appeal to religious experience was countered by an unproportionate appeal to reason.

A live alternative to a singular dependence upon the appeal to reason as a corrective of an uncritical appeal to religious experience is a more disciplined mode of awareness; or, more specifically, a concern to find ways to attain such a disciplined mode of awareness in attending to reports of religious experience and the witness of faith, among both elemental and critically informed human beings. I have tried to speak to this problem in various attempts to present the claims of the appreciative consciousness; [10] but in none of these discussions have I been able to satisfy myself that I have offered a definitive procedure for attaining such disciplined awareness. The reason for my dissatisfaction here, I have come to see, lies in my inadequate grasp, and I would add, the empiricist's grasp, of what is implied in what the radical empiricist has termed "this vital immediacy" that confronts each individual as lived experience. In James and Bergson it was a generalized notion of pure experience or duration as presented within individual tracks of perception. To gather these many instances of immediacy into a manageable term, James employed the notion of "the perceptual flux." As such it conveyed the fullness of concrete ingredients, and it rendered the internal access to meaning as *knowledge by acquaintance* infinitely richer than the *knowledge about* acquired through conceptualization. Yet its very fullness and richness of occurrence presented it as ambiguous reality awaiting definition and a sharpening of conceptual meaning. Little wonder, then,

[10] Cf. "The Appreciative Consciousness" in *Higher Education and the Human Spirit* (Chicago: Univ. of Chicago Press, 1953), chap. 5. (Paperback Ed., Chicago: Seminary Cooperative Bookstore, 1965). See also, *Faith and Culture* (New York: Oxford Univ. Press, 1953), chap. 7.

that empiricists were led to interpret the dictum, "the primacy of perception," to imply priority only in the sense of an elemental antecedent, requiring critical conceptualization to wrest from this ambiguity what was significant and meaningful.

In my own probing of this problem, I came upon a way of insisting on what James called a "More" of existence that eluded our conceptualization. My phrase for it was, "Immediacy and ultimacy traffic together." As a counterpart of this insistence upon the More of experience, exceeding conceptualization, I argued that our conceptualizations provided us with but a margin of intelligibility. To these rather formal designs of immediate experience, I introduced the notion of *the structure of experience*, which carried more concrete meaning, implying the structural distillations of past events as they persisted within the cultural orbit of meaning of a people, given shape in any given period of history, to the individual's field of existence.

All of these notions represent labored efforts on my part to articulate this primal flux of immediacy in ways that would present it as something more compelling than an ambiguous, preconscious flux, awaiting conceptualization. The fullness of lived experience as a present datum of history, as history fronting its present moment of actuality and much more, was given here. These notions, I believe, point the way toward employing an organismic imagery in arriving at an empirical understanding of religious experience and the witness of faith. They at least set these occurrences within the ongoing stream of events that transpires within a cultural orbit; they are thereby delimited within a definite historical field, yet made inclusive of the whole range of relevant relations within that orbit of experience. But there still is lacking in my procedure both a methodical way of focusing these occurrences for religious inquiry, and a method of inquiry suitable to the task of probing their theological import. It is here that I am led to ask whether the recent efforts in phenomenology do not have something to contribute to the empirical effort.

One reason why one might expect this to be so is that phenomenology has historically adhered to exploring and pondering the perceptual field; hence phenomenologists stand to offer to process metaphysics, and to empirical theology being pursued within its perspectives, a greater degree of concrete observation and reflection, based on its preoccupation with the perceptual field. This is brought out in the very way that Merleau-Ponty presents his organismic notion of intentionality.

> Through this broadened notion of intentionality phenomenology can become a phenomenology of origins. Whether we are concerned with a thing perceived, a historical event or a doctrine, to "understand" is to take in the total intention. . . . It is a matter, in the case of each civilization, of finding . . . a formula which sums up in an unique manner of behavior towards others, towards Nature, time and death; a certain way of patterning the world which the historian should be capable of seizing upon and making his own. These are the dimensions of history. In this context there is not a human word, not a gesture, even one which is the outcome of habit or absent-mindedness, which has not some meaning.[11]

Implicit in this phenomenological view of intentionality is the notion that all individual events and persons are structured occurrences. What we perceive in this vital immediacy is not a chaos of unformed impressions awaiting form through conceptualization. We live out of a world that is given, out of structures of meaning, already bodied forth, yet susceptible of reconception and reformulation, even re-creation. But the freedom to partake of a new historical situation is in a way defined and given by the historical fabric of occurrences which now define one's intentionality in this historical moment of time. This freedom, too, is to be conceived, not as a chaos of possible choices, but as openness to possible occasions fulfilling and following from "the lines of intentionality," which trace out in advance at least the style of what is to come.[12]

[11] Merleau-Ponty, *Phenomenology of Perception*, p. 18.
[12] Ibid., p. 416.

It should be said at this point, by way of balancing perspectives, that phenomenologists, by focusing so exclusively upon the phenomenal field in the way they have done, have tended to restrict the context of their inquiry to the human scene. As a consequence, as I have noted, phenomenologists have been able to vivify the world of conscious experience as a social and cultural history in a way that supplements the world of radical empiricists. On the other hand, radical empirical efforts enhance and enlarge the significance of what phenomenologists have made available. This can be noted especially with regard to terms that both of them have in common in their exposition of perception and lived experience. For radical empiricists, these terms have had a wider, more comprehensive field of meaning; for as their perspective has developed, through process philosophy, they have given increasing attention to concerns of cosmology which eventually flowered into a full-blown metaphysics in Whitehead's *Process and Reality*. By virtue of having become a more completely generalized vision, process metaphysics can throw light on what the phenomenologist has been about. In relating the phenomenology of perception as Merleau-Ponty has pursued it, for example, to process metaphysics, one sees more a convergence between his notion of intentionality and Whitehead's causal efficacy. There is, in fact, a fruitful interplay between these notions, for when Whitehead's doctrine of prehension is brought to bear upon his phenomenological notion, Merleau-Ponty's advance upon Husserl in conceiving of intentionality as an organismic event is distinctly illumined. In viewing each individual event as prehending every other concrete event with varying degrees of relevance, one is able to understand how, in reflecting upon subjective interests, as Merleau-Ponty has observed, one is suddenly thrust back into the world. The phenomenological judgment attained through reflexive analysis is thus given metaphysical explication.

I am concerned here, however, not just with what follows from Merleau-Ponty's conception of intentionality, but with the mode of awareness and reflection that is involved in arriving at this notion. To say that it is a brooding kind of inquiry may not express it explicitly enough. It is, however, a kind of confrontation that acknowledges at the outset the complexity of the datum with which one is dealing. Insofar as it employs analytical procedures, these are used to cut away from what persists as a given structure of experience, explicit biographical or historical detail that transposes the discussion to a psychological or sociological level. In this phenomenological inquiry, a deeper operational structure is being sought than these behaviorial sciences can disclose.

Perhaps the way the phenomenologist expresses this bracketing of detail irrelevant to his inquiry makes its meaning misleading. Empirically speaking, there can be no structure of events without the events themselves. Yet the minutia of discussion centering on these historical details can have the effect of obscuring this deeper level of "operative intentionality." Thus, what one means to do is to probe beneath these multiple events to the pattern of history being disclosed in this sequence of occurrences. This mode of probing becomes a way of seeing into events, or of envisaging a broad canvas of events in such a way as to disclose "lines of intentionality that trace out . . . the style of what is becoming." [13]

Both James and Bergson tended to view this kind of knowing as internally oriented. In the way that Merleau-Ponty comes upon such knowledge, however, it is clear that he sees it as a reading of a structure of events that comes to light as one holds events in view and reflectively dwells upon what is before one.[14] I am inclined to think that Merleau-Ponty is correct here; that reflection is not necessarily intuitive or internal, but objective in a way different from observation as commonly practiced in the sciences, and in philosophies emulating scientific method. What one is viewing here is not simply

[13] Ibid., p. 416.

[14] This judgment recalls Whitehead's corrective of Bergson in commenting upon the latter's concern with internal relations in developing his notion of intuition as a new way of doing metaphysics. Whitehead saw these internal relations as having an external structure which could be attended to rationally and lifted to a generalized vision of experience. In a way, Merleau-Ponty's procedure combines or correlates that of Bergson and Whitehead; yet it issues in an awareness of the structure of occurrences similar to that to which Whitehead pointed.

one's own subjective responses, but a vision of relationships the mind's eye has tentatively formed out of recollections that can be checked and verified. Reflexive analysis in this sense is precisely an act of observation addressed to past external events, now revived through contemplation.

But what is engaged in here carries a wider sweep of envisagement than is possible where one is attending to specific objects or processes in direct observation. For in reflection, objects as such are not in focus; rather, what is in focus are relationships and transactions, weaving events into a configuration of occurrences. In this act of reflection there is not simply a direct act of observation, but, as it were, a waiting and an expectancy that what is so envisaged will disclose its fuller pattern of meaning. One should not dismiss this expectancy too readily as being simply a veiled teleology. There may be remnants of this mode of thinking implied in it or lying back of it, but no more so than in any other contemporary efforts to take full account of the organismic reality in nature and experience. The expectancy implied in intentionality is more in the nature of a holistic working in the spirit of *Gestalt* psychology or emergent theory, than of historic forms of teleological thinking. It is a means of taking hold of the creative intention in relations that are living and dynamic, in a way that will focus upon the total event, in which the qualifying, and one might say qualitative, structuring of past history is given weight along with attention to the event of innovation. Emergent theory saw this phenomenon as a spontaneous leap beyond existing structures. The phenomenologist appears to be pressing for more continuity in the organic pattern of relationships, enough at least so that one may anticipate the creative intention, even though one may not anticipate the creative result.

Much of what is implied here is what I have meant to convey in my use of the term *appreciative awareness*; but it is clear that something more than appreciation and awareness is involved. Along with this openness to a wide range of data, dynamically set in a configuration of events, there is active discernment and a relating of events, out of which a pattern of meaning emerges. Awareness and an appreciative response sufficiently arresting to bring one to a sense of the *More* in events under observation serves to restrain, if not to rout, the tendency to let ideas or categories already formulated impose their image upon the realities being experienced. Yet something more than restraint is needed here. There is need for employing this awareness in a disciplined and directed way that can issue in some controlled, yet imaginative discernment of what is being encountered in the immediacies of experience. I am simply raising the question: Does not the procedure among modern phenomenologists, such as in Merleau-Ponty's writings, offer some help here?

The contribution that phenomenology can make to empirical theology, illumining the notion of religious experience as a communal or cultural resource, may have one serious limitation. While ostensibly it is intended to clarify and vivify the structural character of the past as a formative resource of the present, moving toward a future, the direction of its analysis and inquiry tends to be less articulate about the creative élan in this social context which radical empiricism has been so concerned to make vivid. It would be a mistake to ascribe to phenomenology that kind of emphasis upon the past shaping the present that would lead one to assume that its form of analysis implies making the past normative. Nevertheless, by its very preoccupation with the inherited structures of meaning, as developed in the notion of intentionality, it can lend itself to such an emphasis. The force of radical empiricism lies in its attentiveness to the creative moments of history and to the thrust of the Creative Passage with a certain sense of abandon and trust, as it carries life forward toward new occasions and opportunities. This orientation of openness toward the future is too important to be dissipated or dispelled. It is what gives to the modern ethos its vitality and promise. Yet one must be aware, too, that in overvaluing it, or in being wholly sanguine in one's expectations concerning it, as earlier evolutionary philosophies clearly did, one closes one's eyes to the creative dissonance that is of a piece with the traumatic event of past structures' assuming a vital immediacy. Process then becomes a rather vacuous and automatic occurrence in which novelty is celebrated for its own sake. Too much weight and dependence is then placed upon the resources of modernity itself to the point where all sense of limitation and proportion implied in qualitative attainment is lost. What has made Whitehead's philosophy a timely and salutary corrective of pragmatism and evolutionism generally has been his greater sensitivity to the role of past valuations in the creation of novelty and the emerging present. This he has stated abstractly in his organic version of the doctrine of causal efficacy. There is need for pursuing this organic doctrine further, for giving clearer exposition of the formative role of past valuations as a structure of experience that will be consonant with the urgent stress upon creativity itself. Phenomenologists and empiricists can help one another in this effort. And it becomes increasingly clear that they need one another's stimulus and corrective to keep each other's concern fully operative and proportionate.

Regardless of varying emphases or tendencies within these two modes of thought, the primal locus of concern of each, whether as a "phenomenal field" or a "perceptual field," is the *vital immediacy* that designates the present moment of lived experience. Were one to take this vital immediacy with the seriousness of being in the presence of the holy, one would be on the way to seeing what is implied in finding the sacred in the secular. Much of the disillusionment in matters of faith and the exaggerated gestures of negation that erupt when one senses the discrepancy between the language of faith and the language of secular man stem from the fact that, in most instances, faith has been but a matter of language. The Word has actually meant *the words* formulated within a certain idiom of speech. The loss of an idiom has then seemed to mean the collapse of everything in existence to which these words applied.

Now as any discerning historian of religions knows, the *words* as a witness of faith have followed upon occurrences within a vital immediacy. Perpetuating the encounter with that immediacy has been exceedingly difficult to manage as a cultic or cultural practice; thus it has been left to saints or seers, if such there be. But this only accentuates the dualism between faith structured out of the witness of words, and faith as lived experience within the immediacies of existence.

The vogue of secularity in religion, with its proclamation of the death of God and its clarion call that we have entered upon a post-Christian era, has this singular virtue in the present situation. With the daring of a saint incognito, the secularist in religion is ready to abandon all the protective covering of religious words and ecclesiastical protocol, and to see afresh what happens in this state of being "stripped unto our strength and scars."

Insofar as modern ventures in a secular faith partake of the spirit of Bonhoeffer, I see them moving in this direction. As such they are in accord with the iconoclastic mode of historic saints and prophets bent on recovering or attaining what is immediately given as a redemptive good, as a corrective of what had been inadequately, or even corruptly, mediated through the refinements of cultic forms and formulas. But recourse to secularity gives no assurance that a new sense of the sacred in existence will be apprehended. In the mood of William Hamilton, "One may wait and see." And I gather that this is somewhat the mood of Tom Altizer as well; though with his formula of *the coincidence of opposites*, he appears actually to count on negation as an act of provoking or evoking a new creation of the sacred in the midst of an existence shorn of transcendent appeals.

The appeal of radical empiricism, and I would assume of phenomenology as well, is nothing so romantic or mythological; though it is not unappreciative of what is thereby intended. The radical empiricist, stimulated by the sensitive probing of the phenomenologists, is impelled to say that the truth of the faith is *now*, in the midst of this lived experience. Whatever happens to judge or to redeem existence is immediately present to these times of breathing and acting. We avail ourselves of this good not our own or reject it, though not utterly for we are not wholly in command of what transpires in this bodily existence, important as individual response and decision are in each instance of our existing moment.

Both radical empiricist and phenomenologist, relatively indifferent to the conceptual lore that has mediated the witness of faith within Western culture, attend to the secular present as multiple occasions of the perceptual flux in which the deeps of historic moments are mediated along with the innovating occurrences that mark these occasions as a present immediacy. There is no need to brand this immediacy as secular, any more than there is need to designate the depth of its judgment and grace as sacred. In a way the two are implied without being noted. Only, inasmuch as the realities of faith are not so singularly equated with the linguistic symbols that have formed the cultic or doctrinal legacy of faith, they tend to hold the secular and sacred together as being dimensions of the one immediate moment of lived experience.

The efforts of the radical empiricist and of the phenomenologist are not to counter this secular venture in faith where it is adequately envisaged; but to further it, and hopefully to fulfill it as a way of carrying the act of faith beyond linguistic preoccupations to an experience of grace and judgment within this vital immediacy.

12

Intercommunion and the Cultural Reality
JOSEPH A. SITTLER

Intercommunion[1] among members of radically different Christian traditions has passed from an issue to be discussed to a practiced fact to be confronted. And neither the pejorative phrases used by those who would condemn it nor the ecstatic phrases of those who practice it are a sufficient substitute for theological reflection upon the meaning of its occurrence or responsible guides for those who are called upon to make decisions in the area of church order.

In a recent essay, Father Thomas Ambrogi has descriptively analyzed the status of a very broad discussion of this issue, and has affirmed:

> It is in the light of a whole rich development that one must view (the issue). . . . The recapturing of a sense for sign, the reappraisal of theories of real physical change, the emphasis upon the ecclesial and the personalist character of sacramental presence — all of this is intimately related with the contemporary attempts to express the truth of transubstantiation in personalist phenomenological categories which are radically other than those of a scholastic philosophy of nature.[2]

[1] This essay is a rewritten address delivered in the autumn of 1968 to a Roman Catholic liturgical conference. It has been thought appropriate to this volume not only because its appeal for a phenomenology of participation brings its argument close to the empirical insistences that characterize the companion essays, but also because it is theologizing within the church, out of the church and through the church — which is the only kind of theology the writer has ever believed interesting, useful, or indeed possible.

[2] *Una Sancta* 24 (1967): 35.

Assuming, then, an acquaintance with the very general and various discussion about the nature of the Eucharist, the main themes of which are summarized in the paragraph quoted, I propose to get on with the constructive task by the following steps:

1. An effort to specify a theological perspective from within which the issue of intercommunion can, and in my opinion must, be regarded,

2. An attempt at specification of the interior content of the present insistent pressure for authorized intercommunion,

3. Several tactical proposals appropriate to the new time and situation.

I. The Perspective

The general discussion of intercommunion has been carried on within the perspectives afforded by the traditional placements of the issue. And while, to be sure, there are in Scripture, in tradition, in the several classical lines of doctrinal clarification certain fixed testimonies that must be forever honored, a constructive resolution of the issue cannot be achieved by ever so flexible and irenic interpretations that remain thus bounded. For there have occurred and are occurring, with increasing depth and velocity, massive changes within the very fundamental way men of faith today reflect upon the life of the church catholic. Is there a single massive change which is common to all? Is it possible to specify what is going on in the substructure of theological and practical life, and to do that with such generality that each of us, for whom Augustine, or Thomas, or Luther, or Calvin, or Schleiermacher may have been the most influential theologian, will recognize the change when it is stated as true for and within his own experience?

Such a statement, having of necessity a high generality, can in my opinion be made. Let me propose it in a three-phase argument.

1. Doctrine is the "exteriorized interiority" of what is lived and experienced by the entire people of God in their participation in the event of Jesus Christ. It is not sufficient to be

content with the exteriorized resultant of that participation, the formulation of ideal structures. It is, to be sure, quite true that such formulations have a relative autonomy; and true, too, that there is a place for strict logical reason and for development by reflection upon crucial confessional statements. But if theology is to survive at all with any meaning and force for the life of the church, it cannot become a "theology of theology."

2. The general characteristic of contemporary theology (which I have claimed is declarative of a massive shift) is precisely the degree and the gravity with which the theologian (in this true to the life of faith in our time) makes his proposals about doctrine in concert with and in a language informed and enriched by life within the interiority of faith's object, and as passionate subject. That dialogue is the alembic of theology.

A paragraph from Karl Rahner makes this point in the very theological practice of it.

> The lover knows of his love: this knowledge of himself forms an essential element in the very love itself. The knowledge is infinitely richer, simpler and denser than any body of propositions about the love could be. Yet this knowledge never lacks a certain measure of reflective articulateness: the lover confesses his love at least to himself, "states" at least to himself something about his love. And so it is not a matter of indifference to the love itself whether or not the lover continues to reflect upon it; this self-reflection is not the subsequent description of a reality which remains in no way altered by the description. In this progressive self-achievement, in which the love comprehends itself more and more, in which it goes on to state something "about" itself and comprehends its nature more clearly, the love itself becomes ordered. . . . The progress of love is a living growth out of the original (the originally conscious) love *and* out of just what that love has itself become through a reflexive experience of itself. It lives at every moment from its original source

and from that reflexive experience which has immediately preceded any given moment. Original, non-propositional, unreflective yet conscious possession of a reality on the one hand, and reflective (propositional) articulated consciousness of this original consciousness on the other.[3]

Just as that paragraph is representative of the exteriorizing of interiority in the hands of a magisterial figure in the Roman Catholic community, so the paragraph to follow from the work of Professor Bernard Meland is representative of a company of non-Roman theologians who undertake the same enterprise with reference not only to the solitary individual and his love, but to the historical and cultural life of the entire human community.

> The structure of experience, or feeling-content, is the most elemental level of meaning in any culture — it — gives form to our repeated valuations. . . . The history of events presumes to tell the story of this growth of psychical structure. But compared with the actual process of an evolving structure of experience, recorded history is a relatively superficial account.
>
> The structure of experience is not just accumulative. That is, it is not just a blind appropriation of heterogeneous valuations; rather it simulates an organic unity at every stage of history. The struggles and crises of concrete events, the dedications and betrayals, the discoveries, creations, and intellectual triumphs become the formative stuff out of which rises the persisting structure of experience. Great insight at any one point becomes creative in its influence beyond calculation. Stretches of insensitivity, with its consequent brutality and evil, likewise affect the accumulative valuations, not only in an additive sense but in a transformative one. . . . The present movement of time is laden with qualitative meaning. . . . Generations come into an organic inheritance that is greater in depth and range than the perceptions

[3] *Theological Investigations* (Baltimore: Helicon Press, 1961), 1:64–65.

of any living person. . . . Nevertheless, all living persons carry within their conscious existence and in their perceptual nature something of the hidden drives and aspirations which arise out of this accumulated structure of experience.[4]

What both these men are declaring, Rahner by psychological reflection and Meland by a description of the astounding interactions in cultural reality, is nothing less than a demand for a contrapuntal enrichment in theological method. Both are saying that the proposals of Christian theology are forged by the incessant, absolutely penetrative reciprocal action of subject and object. And both, each in a subtle way, urge us to understand that aspects of the object are definitive of the subject, and vitalities proper to the subject bring into focus the reality of the object. This interaction is indeed so profound, so energetic, and so formative of human thought as such that no epistemology that ignores it can any longer be of use to theology.

3. The third angle from which I think it necessary to support and clarify the first step — definition of a new perspective on intercommunion — can be elaborated as follows: man's relation to the world-as-history, and man's relation to the world-as-nature (and these two relations in vigorous and revolutionary effects upon each other!) have undergone such huge and quite novel shifts that no aspects of thought and feeling and action are unshaken. By a radical oversimplification of the account of what has happened and is happening, one must say that in relation to nature the contemporary man is literally in a new operational role. Within the emergence and development of cultures man has studied, modified, invented, made tools, rearranged the world of nature. But before our time he stood over against nature primarily as a *receptor*, in some sense a spiritually and biologically detached (although destructable), centered reflective entity.

The contemporary man is no longer principally a receptor

[4] *Faith and Culture* (New York: Oxford Univ. Press, 1953), pp. 98–99.

in relation to nature. He is the prober, the knower, the manipulator, the recondite or banal operator. Science has no "world view"; but technology has a world ambition and a world program. By the sheer momentum of its capability technology translates the can-be-done into the procedure and the act. So huge is this momentum that man's partial knowledge of the structure of the world-as-nature makes ever more clear that application of this knowledge enables him for the first time in history literally to do with that world what he wills to do.

The issue of the world-as-history is deeply formed by knowledge of and operations upon the world-as-nature. The very fate of the world-as-nature has been drawn into the decisional center of the world-as-history. For history becomes for the contemporary man the theater in which decisions of power force a displacement of older modes of decisional life: decisions of value, of intention, of direction, of end. Indeed it may be claimed that "secularism" will remain a wrongly stated problem if its emergence and forms are not analyzed from within the data of man's new power relation to the world-as-nature.

This description of the new perspective from within which we must view the issue of intercommunion is certainly not adequate, but the components I have elaborated are certainly central. And their bearing upon the issue is obvious, for if the modality of the understanding mind is being profoundly complexified by a theology of reciprocity having the nature of an exteriorizing interiority, and if the requirements for meaning, relevancy, and world- and self-hope are given by man's fresh and astonishing transactions with the world-as-nature, and the effects of that upon his envisionment of his reality as decisional person within the world-as-history, then we have the context within which to make our second step.

II. The Content of the Pressure for Intercommunion

Analysis must begin with the capital fact of our time, namely, that traditional structures of public order have been shattered by the emergence of clamant human facts which these structures are incapable of handling and before which the slow pace of change and the solid resistance of vested interests and habits of mind are destructive of hope. Not only do these structures stumble before need; continuing acquiescence within them has produced a homogenization of mind and a decay of spirit which the selective affluence in society cannot abate. When, therefore, persons decisively formed within this generation look to Catholic tradition and to the churches which honor that tradition they confront two facts.

The first fact is a quite general and even unexpected fastening upon that figure who looms behind and constitutes the Christian reality. Neither the critical sciences of biblical criticism, nor the theological resultant of demythologization, nor the question raised for Christian knowledge of God by the historizing of epistemology, nor the seduction whereby the Christian community has become identified with economic ideologies and with the "embourgeoisment" of society, nor ossification into nonintelligibility of once lively forms of worship, preaching, charity — none of these events has served to dim the haunting allure of that receding historical figure or reduce the force of the judgment and grace that he embodies. By a sure instinct which is as formative in Protestant theology as it became renascent in some documents of the recent Vatican Council, this instinct knows that the core vitality, the ever-engendering center of the church is her life with Christ. And the Eucharist, by its opulent trans-verbal, sign, symbol, and Word symbiosis is the literal embodiment of the church's identity.

If, then, the first fact despite much confusion is the centered christological fixation I have just stated, the second is an equally clear *ethicizing* of the meaning of the Christ so clearly affirmed. And because the clear ethical meaning of the presence of Christ in and through his community for the threatened world is, in my judgment, the clearly fundamental substance of the moment's desire for inter-communion, I expand this point by proposing a kind of typology whereby to specify the nature of the motivations, remembrances, expectations, and hopes which animate it.

313

There are very many whose desire for intercommunion is a natural product of a powerfully renewed vision of the unity of Christ's church. Their vision is ecclesial in the deepest sense. There are, to be sure, some whose notion of unity is closer to the model of corporation mergers than it is to the recovery of an organic oneness constituted by a redemptive act of God and given sacramental visibility in the Eucharist. But these are by no means representative, and current theological energies are rather completely transforming earlier manifestations of this notion of unity.

The larger number in this category are convinced that the unity of the church is not an achievement but a gift. The possibilities of immanent forces are not despised; but their vision of Christ, community, unity is a product of a power, a presence, a hope they know to be not accountable in terms of the resources of immanence. And there seems to be an impressive correlation between the biblical, theological, social, political sophistication of these persons and the vigor of their longing for intercommunion as a sign of that *act* — together in the name and presence of him "in whom all things cohere."

There is a correlation, too, between this desire for coinherence in the Lord of church and world and the cultural fact that models of coherence, as these have historically been proposed by the several branches of human inquiry, are simply not any longer present, or if present not persuasive. Philosophical endeavors are turned to analysis of the relativity and limitation of all types of meaning; art does not presume to mean but only to exist; science has come to the point at which all *general* statements are in principle abhorred. Formation of something which, in the absence of patternedness is called "life-style," is a contemporary substitute for calculated formation according to verifiable and prestigious principles. When Robert Oppenheimer said that "style is the deference that action pays to uncertainty,"[5] he put his finger precisely upon what is both the pathos and the promise of this generation.

A second type includes those who have expressed all that I

[5] *The Limits of Language*, ed. Walker Gibson (New York: Hill & Wang, 1962), p. 51.

have spoken of under the rubric ecclesial, but who are distinguished from the foregoing by the direction and scope of their concern. They, too, know the finite and limited character of all that pertains to man's historical existence; but communion for them is an act that, while centered in the community of faith, has its full reference of meaning and sphere of action in the worldly, the material, the social. It is an act of world-and-life affirmation combined with a violent, and often sardonic, clarity about the meaninglessness that pervades, the recalcitrancies that resist, the stupidities, evils, prides, structures of affluent contentment that stand massively over against a world-idea and a world-re-formation that might make sense amidst the terrors of human need and the fresh dimensions of the human dream.

Within this type are those who know the most about the fateful powers that lie within what I called a moment ago "man's transactions with the world-as-nature." And because all that is characteristically modern has taught them that, from genetic and galactic science on the one side, to man-as-man-among-fellow-men on the other, their life-affirmation of presence and promise as known in Eucharist calls for material-ethical realization, and it is cosmic in scope. The dimensions of celebration which have come to a fresh accenting in the eucharistic liturgies, recovered, rediscovered, or created in our time, are dimensions of reality and dependency that swing in the arc of modern man's at-homeness in a vast system.

The demand for intercommunion, all this is to say, is a function of the life and world context within which communion as such is today celebrated. The "inter" presents itself as a necessary obedience to that reality. For neither doctrinal formulations (as these have developed out of Christian theology's residence for hundreds of years with ways of understanding nature, history, self, and the interlacing network of influences and dependencies) nor ecclesiological limitations and impediments (as these were intelligible when the people of God understood the life and thought of faith as primarily cultic existence within a *corpus Christianum*) — neither of these traditional ways of thinking is appropriate or helpful in the new situation.

What I am suggesting here in historical terms can be illuminated by observation. When one regards closely the changing mood, language, gesture, style of those celebrations of the Eucharist which are most profoundly penetrated by contemporary theological reflection and most obedient to the actualities of present common life and thought and feeling, he senses an added intention in the act. This intention is by no means a repudiation or a heedless forgetting of the accumulated graces and affirmations of the Holy Communion, but the thrust is different because the context has broadened. Cultic incurvature has been displaced by sharp awareness of social estrangements and longings for reconciliation. To the heard and embodied Word of forgiveness and new life has been added a powerful sense of prophetic judgment and challenge to change. To faith's refreshed life in the God-relationship has been added an excruciating sense of the hurt, or distorted, or graceless cords of relation to the fellow man, to the graces that inhere and await us in the fecund earth, the givenness of clear water and pure air.

Not long ago I participated in a service of intercommunion in which elements from Orthodox liturgies, the Roman rite, the Book of Common Prayer, and "certain of our own poets" were madly mixed. And while I remain troubled by the conviction that orthodox teaching was strained, liturgical proportionality was sprung, and traditional gravity was strangely conjoined with vivacious enthusiasm, I am troubled also by the indubitable authenticity of the Presence that was being adored, and by the genuine participation in that Presence as it fed faith and demanded a life-in-the-world-around continuous with and testimonial to the life celebrated *within* the sacrament. And when the celebration concluded with the old Genevan hymn tune to the text of Clifford Bax (1886), I was moved, in St. Paul's words, to "take heart and give thanks."

Earth might be fair, and all men glad and wise.
Age after age their tragic empires rise.

316

Built while they dream, and in that dreaming weep;
Would man but wake from out his haunted sleep,
Earth might be fair, and all men glad and wise.

There is, to be sure, a madness in that vision, and in the frightening scope of it. But there is a holy madness, too, in the eucharistic prayer of Catholic Christendom.

III

In what I have said in an effort to describe two types of motivation toward intercommunion I have, I fear, already invaded the third type. But in the perhaps rationalized conviction that categories that do not leak are defective, I move on to the third type.

In the beginning of this paper I instanced a paragraph from Karl Rahner to illustrate the statement that astounding contrapuntal interactions in cultural reality demand a deepening in theological method. The concrete meaning of that for our time is simply that faith and life have been forced absolutely together. Intelligibility will be achieved by theological proposals to the degree that they illuminate the depths, clarify the interior relations of things. The ethical is not the whole of Christian faith; but what that whole might be cannot even be proposed to this moment if some clear continuity is not established between fullness of faith and fulfillment of life within the tasks and processes of the creation. Discussion of the sacrament of the Lord's Supper comes completely under this demand. Eucharist is not ethics; but if there be no clear relation between sacramental Presence and the operational world of things and potentials and persons, the entire matter will be dismissed, not on the ground of untruth, but on the equally effective ground of disinterest. It follows, too, that just as issues of what might be Christian and ethical for contemporary life in solitude, in family, and in society, cannot be separated from christly fact, so the way our generation encounters christly fact both demands an accent upon the ethical in our Christ-encounter and participation, and imposes upon the presence of Christ in the sacrament of the Supper a

317

peculiar burden, and demands of all traditions a depth and breadth and materiality in their understanding of it which has the possibility of being more catholic than the community of faith has ever known. Because that is a large supposition I must say a bit more about the phrase, "the way our generation encounters christly fact."

The straight, historical way of encounter with Jesus Christ is irrecoverably lost in virtue of the solidly established critical reconstruction of the testimonial, witnessing, faith-to-faith, already interpretative character of the reporting and transmitting documents. The vast complexification of the meaning and role of tradition as this is ever more deeply understood by the Christian community has disclosed the necessary but modified force of formalized doctrine, and has exposed the historical exigencies that shaped both church structure and ethos. But, and for some, surprisingly, just as the demythologization of the New Testament has proved constructive and deepening for theology and for the understanding of faith, so the hermeneutical demand upon thought penetrating into every nook and recess of Christian understanding thrusts forward into absolute cruciality the ancient promise, "Et ecce ego vobiscum sum omnibus diebus usque ad consummatum saecule."

The role that the term and the notion of *Presence* plays in the lives of those who have come to maturity since World War II is a fact that must be attended to if we wish to penetrate to the intentionality that is common to the variously motivated groups that press for intercommunion. A remark made by a student in my seminar last quarter may provide a clue to the force of this term in its present use. The lad said, "The only way of knowing which has any solidity is a way to know about things we are not ultimately interested in knowing about!"

When the relations between the real and the intelligible are shattered, and during the interim when new forms of relation are a-building, the sheer bluntness of what is there and available for joy becomes a center, not only for the mind's reflection, but also for hope's look and vision's horizon. The new re-

lation between the sexes, for instance, is not understandable
save in these terms.

In our time, then, there have come together at the point
of pressure for intercommunion these two realities: the sheer
pathos, power, allure, prophetic passion of that immolated
"outsider" Christ — and an "outsider" human situation for
which the adequacy of all previous forms of life and thought
and environment-ordering and public law and order are
plainly inadequate. And that is why the figure of Christ (who,
given by the Spirit in ever so obscure history, "will never not
have been") is the dominant Christian fact. This fact is so
many dimensional and so deep, so rich in symbolic potential,
so capable of exercising liturgical force in a language-disen-
chanted time, so freighted with promise of fulfillment and so
engendering of expectancy, so transparent to the redemptive
not-self, so serenely *itself* over against the homogenized, dubious, or wan identity of modern man, that his *Presence*, a
term that resists precise analysis, is nevertheless the com-
manding fact.

If, now, there be anything of truth in all that I have said,
is it possible to suggest how the church might obediently and
sensitively order its practical ways of dealing with the situation? I think there is, but only if we displace from controlling position certain principles and priorities which have, in
other times, determined our decisions. In this concluding
paragraph I can only suggest questions that must be asked as
we probe for a new way. But these questions that arise out
of the care for the gospel of God are given unquenchable
force by the fact of the effective grace bestowed by Presence
in orders of sacramental celebration which have been variously called "incomplete, deficient, inauthentic, unauthorized,
illegitimate."

1. The grace of the sacrament is not confined within the
theological explications that formulate its nature, or within
the ecclesiastical guidelines that regulate its practice.

2. The several churches have sometimes spoken of their obligation to "protect" their understanding of the Eucharist. It
must now be asked if the term does not suggest a mode of

protection which is both inappropriate to the sacrament, and a barrier to the mind that seeks for its gracious and generous meaning. The only proper "protection" of the true substance of the sacrament must be served by right proclamation, grave and time-relevant teaching, pastoral care, and judgment sensitively exercised within the particular circumstances that constitute men's needs and drives when in gravity of spirit and in longing for unity with and in Christ they seek sacramental communion with him. Theological protection, that is to say, is kerygmatic! It is promise of grace and judgment. An understanding of protection that relies upon the juridical suggests that the vitality of the Presence is helpless before occasions that would distort, or banalize, or seek to dispose it in ways strange to its holy giftedness. The gifts of God, including the impulse to theological reflection itself, have a way of themselves taking corrective and liberating reprisals upon abuses!

3. It may well be that the alternatives which have come to characterize discussions of intercommunion (doctrinal consensus as the precondition for intercommunion or intercommunion as celebration and means of unity) may be too shallow a reading of both sacrament and situation.

The ancient statement, "I believe in order that I may understand," suggests another way of stating both problem and practice. A clear and urgent desire may be the placenta for the maturation of the reality and unity it seeks. The depth of the meaning of participation and the graces of it may not be actualizable apart from the fact of it. The possible can become actual in the less than ideal circumstance of the quest.

13

Theology as Critique of Expostulation
JOSEPH HAROUTUNIAN

1. *The Question of a Personal God*

The tension, not to say the conflict, between the theologian and the "layman," between "the science of God" and popular piety, continues in the church, to the detriment of both. The people speak of "a personal God," "Father God," "the Lord God." They speak of a God who knows and cares for his people, who responds to prayer, who loves and judges, who in short is a person. The theologian speaks of Being and the Ground of Being, of Ultimate Cause and Ultimate Reality, of Substance, Spirit, Creativity, and the like. He will not say that God is a person. He speaks of the people's language about God as metaphorical, symbolic, figurative. He argues about how it might be analogical. The people complain that the theologian's "God beyond God" is a poor substitute for the God of the Bible and their God, the living and responding God. They do not understand the logic of communion with "Being Itself" or with superpersonal reality, and they turn away from the theologian as from a subtle and suspicious-sounding fellow.

On the other hand, piety itself demands that the theologian do justice to the Latin saying, *Deus non est in genera* (God does not belong to a genus or to a class of beings). Even a little reflection must lead one to say that God, "the Creator of heaven and earth," is not a person as a man is a person; not even a superlative person. The wisdom and the power of God, his worth and authority, his very communion with men, have been so felt and understood by the pious as to forbid an unqualified idea of him as a person. When a man thinks at all

321

about God who "was in Christ," about the Gospel and the Creed, and about the church and the world, he must recognize that God is not a person as *he* is a person; he must recognize, in other words, that God is God and not man.

The tension, not to say contradiction, between God as Creator, Providence, Redeemer, and God as a person, engaged in "give and take" with his people, has always been with us; and there may be no satisfactory way out of it. Even while the believer speaks of the love and the justice of God, he needs to recognize that God works in him in strange ways. Even while he speaks of God as one who speaks and acts, he may not ignore the fact that he does not hear God with his ears and see him act with his eyes. Such observations belong to piety; and when they are ignored, piety becomes not only superstitious, but also degenerate. Such observations have been made throughout the history of the church, and have been integral to Christian thinking. Insofar as the theologians since the beginnings of the church have taught the pious not to speak of God as though he were another man, they have served the church and served it well. A critical attitude toward human language about God is a *conditio sine qua non* for piety itself.

On the other hand, it has been a permanent temptation in theology to regard the language of criticism as the correct language about God. What has offended and continues to offend the believer is the theologian's attitude that "Being Itself" or Primary Cause or Creativity is what is meant by God, so that such expressions, which appear incompatible with the logic of communion, are literal symbols for God, whereas Father, Maker, Provider, Redeemer are metaphorical. It has been hard for the theologian, engaged in the criticism of pious language, not to propose his own as a substitute for the language of the church, not to think and to say that if the pious had critical minds they would speak as he does. There is always the temptation to say, "The real God is not the God of the language of piety," or, "God is beyond the God of piety. When this is said, it is further said that the language of piety is emotive rather than cognitive, or that piety is a matter of the heart rather than of the head. And the people are offended by all this. They either turn away from theology or turn away from their God.

Piety has not been without its theological defenders against "rationalism," and these have taken recourse either to authority or to experience, or to some combination of the two. There has been appeal to "biblical faith" and to the tradition of doctrine in the church. Appeal also has been made to "religious experience," especially an experience of communion with God. Unfortunately, faith as assent to authority can hardly give a rational account of itself, and does not clearly belong in theological activity. On the other hand, "experience" cannot be accepted by the theologian without criticism of its language. Experience and truth are not the same thing, and there is the question of how they go together. In any case, the theologian must be at his business of rational criticism, and such criticism necessarily has to deal with the tension within piety between faith in a personal God and the notion of "God beyond God."

The truth appears to be that "the philosophical theologian" is driven to think of God as "suprapersonal" and thus to alienate the layman. On the other hand, "the kerygmatic theologian" is driven to be endlessly ambiguous in his language about God, and thus to produce both over-belief and skepticism in the church. The total effect of this theological feud in the church is that the pious prefer to worship and to live without taking theology too seriously, and even without the benefit of intelligence. While the theologians dispute one with another, the church carries on with a minimum of theology or reason.

2. An Interpretation of the Issue

The churches believe in a personal God, and their attitude is that there is no alternative to a personal God except no God at all. In the official piety of the church, or as the churches are publicly supposed to believe, God is a person who loves and cares, speaks and hears, thinks and acts. Sunday in and Sunday out, men in pulpits preach "the word of God"; they offer prayers to God; they speak of things God wills and does and of things that are for and against his will and purpose. They speak of communion with God, obedience to God, and love of God. They speak to the effect that good and evil have to do with the grace and the judgment of God, and they commend the lives and the destinies of people to the care of God. Who then does not know that the God of the churches is a person, and that if he is not a person, he is not the God of his people at all? All this may not be consistently and clearly stated, and it may not be believed without doubt by many who "go to church." But there can be hardly a question that it represents "the faith of the church," which the theologian is supposed to subject to critical examination; not so as to discredit it, but so as to prevent the breaking of the bond between faith and intelligence in the church.

Perhaps the first task of the theologian as a critical thinker is to understand the hold that faith in "a personal God" has on the people. The first thing not to forget is that such belief may be an expression of humanity itself. Human beings talk, think, will, feel, and act. They talk to each other; they will with and against each other; they act for good or evil among themselves. Hearing one another and responding one to another, and thus living together in a common world, are actions without which they would severally wither and die. They believe each other and disbelieve each other. They expostulate with each other and try to persuade each other. They become angry one with another and forgive one another. The one hopes to be loved by the other, and the other waits for signs of love from his neighbor. In such ways, people act as human beings, giving and taking, speaking and responding, turning toward and turning away from each other. Thus they are persons, and as persons they are present one to another and live in the indefinite "plenitude of being."

Thus is it that they are with their God. How else are they to be and still be in the mode of their humanity? They are not, unless somehow reduced, otherwise with their God than they are among themselves. The theologian therefore should not be surprised, and perhaps too readily offended, by "the anthropomorphic element in religion," by the traffic between gods and men in "primitive religion," by the arguments of an Abraham or a Moses with the Lord; by all the praying and protesting, the bargaining with God and the yielding to him; even by the criticism of God, done with more or less diffidence and irony—all of which characterize man's natural piety. What has man been doing in his religion but acting as the human being, the being-with, that he is, or simply being human? If talking and listening are being human, together with eating and sleeping, then, if man did not talk to his God and expect to be heard, he would be acting as less than human. He would not be acting as a human being and in his religion he would not be human. Religion is an expression of co-humanity. Therefore, the Other, or God, appears in religion as Co-Person or Person.

Church people who believe in a personal God and who feel, if not think, that God who is not a person is no God, are quite true to their humanity, in a more or less reflective way. People who live by responding to people have a "God who speaks." They may not believe there is a God, and they may be satisfied with their transactions with their fellowmen. They may, for one reason or another, be atheists. But if they do have a God, they have one who is "personal." Since they are not "man beyond man" but fellow men, they can have no traffic with "God beyond God."

The point is that what is at issue with regard to the existence of "a personal God" is the very practice of humanity or human life itself. This may be the reason for the resistance in the church to theologizing which obscures the personness of God, whether empiricistic, or existentialist-ontological, or ontological-rationalistic. Maybe it is in this way that we should understand the suspicion of theology which is very much a part of the mind of the church.

Thus we are left with a dilemma. Critical intelligence among us is at odds with the piety of the Christian people. Follow the former, the God of these people is obscured. Follow piety, and critical intelligence is offended. Theology and the church have drifted apart, and both are in difficulty.

3. Religious Empiricism and the Pretensions of Theology

The basic source of the conflict between piety and theology is that piety is an expostulation with God about reality, whereas theology is commonly a discourse which aims at a coherent or rational view of reality as under the providence of God. The pious mind tells stories which express its feelings about the vicissitudes of life, its fulfillments and frustrations, and its endless and uncanny surprises. It takes attitudes of gratitude and disgust, awe and rebellion, with despair and hope. There is no telling when human beings will be slapped in the face and reduced to impotence in their seeking for life and peace. The inclemencies of the physical world and the inhumanities of their fellow men in their common life come at them mixed together, and there is no way of being safe under their doings. There is no acceptable order to the way men act and things happen, and no *logos* or *ratio* which enables people to place everything where it belongs and to be secure with it. An indomitable unreason pervades life and induces a spirit of expostulation and controversy as well as a spirit of resignation, and man is saved from going to pieces by an irony which lies close to the surface of the stories he tells face to face with reality. The religious man is man as he lives under the threat of chaos, and he cannot make sense of his world. Hence his response to reality is a mixture of reverence and rebellion, of faith and make-believe, of integrity and dissimulation; a response to a permanently perplexing non-cosmos, to a reality without rational and moral unity.

It is not hard to see why the religious man who cannot make sense of his world is suspicious of those who claim to have discovered the *logos* of the world and who present him with a world view in which everything is ultimately in order. The price for this accomplishment is usually a more or less polite degrading of myths, of the stories people have told to express their visions of disorder and surprise in the world. Stories about the gods, their idiosyncrasies, their arbitrary doings, their frequently puzzling conduct among themselves and towards men, are explained away as human inventions showing a failure of reason. The rationalists (and traditionally if not necessarily, philosopher-theologians have been rationalists) are committed to arguing that there are no loose ends, no surprises, no irrational goings-on in their Reality. They set up metaphysics to show that the "really real" Reality, supramundane and eternal Being, *Fons et Origo,* is the Good and Reason itself. It has been the business of theologians to show the rational and moral coherence of the world, to see it as making sense, as the real of *logos* and *alētheia.* In doing this, their business, they have had to argue that the restiveness of man with the vicissitudes of his world is hardly worthy of reason, and that there is a cure for it in a transcendence which demands that a man find Reality, not in the things that happen to him, but in the Being beyond both men and things. The philosopher-theologian has called upon the religious man to overcome his emotion-laden attitude towards the ups and downs of his life; to cultivate a certain "indifference" and "contempt for the world"; to set his mind to the contemplation of eternal verities; to overcome his bewilderments, not so much by talking back to them as well as to his Gods, as by engaging in a "dead-pan" way of talking about transcendent Being and noumenal Reality. In short, philosophical theology has been the enterprise of seeing the Many as One, of discovering the Reason of the world, of unveiling the serenity of Being in the realm of beings. As such, it is incompatible with "natural piety" which as a tragi-comic response to the world draws its very power from a reality in which the chaotic is irrepressible and unreason permanent.

It is true that the religious man, or man as such, has derived much comfort out of theologizing which presents him with transcendent Reality as his refuge from the world of fate and fortune. It is a happy thing to know that behind or above or under the events which go against the human grain, there is a spiritual and intelligible Being which is the solution of "the problem of existence." It is gratifying to know that there is a "Realm beyond" which is not unmanageable and uncanny as is the realm here, or a Truth and Good which are free from or equal to the threat of Chaos. The better reasoned the proc-

327

ess by which the theologian arrives at such happy conclusions, the more satisfying they are to the religious man. Insofar as theology softens the blows of experience which animate piety, it is the ally of religion and will presumably be with us indefinitely.

And yet the tension between man and theology remains. The truth is that there is a built-in resistance to theology in the pious mind. Religious people hope against hope that the theologian will make sense for them out of the surprises which are woven into their experience. But when the theologian comes forward with a "system" which shall explain reality, they become suspicious and wonder if they are not being hoodwinked. Their good sense tells them that this deep and dialectical fellow has somehow hoodwinked himself and is now hoodwinking them. They suspect him of having lost touch with them, of giving answers which are no answers, of, when all is said and done, leaving them where they were before.

The tension between man and theology goes deeper. In a way, theology tends to be a violation of humanity, because it embarrasses the human being in this controversy in the world which he shares with his fellows. When it is shown, with impressive dialectical skill, that it is wrong or silly to argue with Reality, to doubt the *Logos* of Being, or to question the goodness of God or the gods; that it is somehow emotive and anthropomorphic to have a quarrel with Reality, or to be humorous as well as serious about it; that after all man's good and evil may be incongruous with the nature of things, etc.; in short, when man is shown to be both stupid and wrong to respond to the world as a human being, then piety itself is violated and so is humanity with it. Theological criticism of religion, which one way or another disqualifies myth or the stories people tell about their God or gods as primitive or irrational, strikes at the very heart of religion and with it humanity as such. It forbids talking with Gods, murmuring against them, more or less openly treating them with irony, and trying to persuade them to be reasonable. In the name of Reason, of a rational world view, it impoverishes man by disqualifying the "affections" and presents man with a Reality which does not know man and his ways. What theology gives by way of rationality, it takes away by reducing humanity, and in this respect it turns out to be the enemy of religion and a contradiction of it, in mind and in spirit. In short, religion thrives on myth. Theologians go "beyond" myth. The religious man cannot follow them without self-destruction. But, destroy himself he will not.

4. Faith as Expostulation with Reality

Theological disqualification of religion as a full-blooded response to reality is due to a misunderstanding of the believer's posture in the presence of his God or Gods. The theologian who finds the all too human language of the religious man uncritical and superstitious (however polite the theologian may be in calling it metaphorical, or figurative!) misconstrues the phenomenon of faith. Faith itself contains an element of criticism which evades its would-be critic. It is superficial and unperceptive to construe faith as a simple trust in God, or as a vision of reality without shadow or darkness. Faith as we find it in religion, high or low, primitive or advanced, is an endless struggle with and questioning of reality on the part of human beings who are subject to its vicissitudes and must suffer its blows and be, they know not when, overwhelmed by them. The believer's trust in his God cannot be separated from his permanent restiveness in this world. It is not to be contrasted with reason but seen as a distrust which is eminently reasonable. The religious man may present a calm façade with his believing and obeying, his "accepting the universe" and calling his God his Friend. But anybody should know that there is a Job under the skin of every other Johnny, and a Gethsemane inside every other garden. There is no faith without suffering and no prayer without expostulation, and there is no end to the dialectic of rebellion and acceptance; and in this dialectic, stories must be told in which tears and laughter are indispensable ingredients. The theologian who takes myths as quasi-academic theories of Reality, which he may demythologize or translate into a literal language, is so far removed from the mind of "primitive man" that his critique is as destructive as it is ill conceived. Myths are born of expostulation, and they persist through expostulation. Any theology which forbids expostulation or demythologizes religion disqualifies itself as theology or as a criticism of religion the business of which is to improve and not to disprove, to cultivate humanity and not to dry it up at the roots.

The theologian assumes that the expostulating man is like himself, a man after the literal truth, a man who tells his stories as accounts of Reality. But this assumption will not do. The religious man talks back to his God because the world does not make sense to him, because the way things are or the literal truth offends his sense of the good and his own dignity. He may be primitive, but he is not a fool that he should confuse his myths, the products of his expostulations, with the reality which unruffles him and makes him to cry out with the pain of frustration. How intelligent is it to ask him if his myths are true? He does not tell them because they "correspond to the facts" but because as stories they are his responses to reality, with all their pathos and irony as well as their "truth to life." His myths are as much criticisms of reality as they are expressions of reality as it impinges upon him. They are controversies with God about reality. For this reason, they are irrepressibly "anthropomorphic," even while they are solidly realistic.

If religious faith involves a criticism of reality, it is disastrous for theology, which is a criticism of religion, to impose upon religion a norm of truth which is incongruous with the kind of criticism which is inherent to religion. Theological criticism must be a logical treatment of religious criticism and not a repudiation of it. It must be an examination of religion for bringing out the logic of its response to reality and not for disqualifying it as irrational. It must resist the temptation to translate the language of myth into some other language, scientific or philosophical; to give a rational account of religion which exposes man's controversy with reality as itself irrational. Any theology which fails to respect, as a rational human enterprise, man's controversy with his God, in which "God-talk" logically belongs, fails as theology and loses the respect of human beings for whom life without expostulation is being without blood.

5. A Function of Theology: Faith and Reason

Positively, the function of theology is to criticize faith so as to help it as faith or as the expostulation with reality that it is. The first business of theology is not to attack the anthropomorphism of expostulation, but to resist the temptation of man to dehumanize himself by turning his controversy with God into logic-less griping on the one hand and into indifference on the other. If man is going to argue with God, and argue he must, he needs to be intelligent about it. His stories in which he argues with God should reflect the realities of his life and represent the mind's encounter with them. He should listen as well as talk, be open as well as passionate, "disinterested" as well as concerned, mix vehemence with a sense of proportion. But this kind of response takes discipline and intelligence, and even a conversion and a sanctification. It takes grace, which occurs in the midst of his expostulation, and which is a matter for gratitude on his part. It takes grace, not to dispose of him as in the wrong, but to teach him courage and humility, without which his faith is neither rational nor human. Theology indeed is a rational activity, but the end of theology is to keep human beings human.

One must understand the apparently congenital resistance of the religious man to "reason." One must recognize that in spite of the perennial efforts of theologians to make faith and reason to lie down quietly together in the religious mind, there continues to be a problem here. No matter where one puts faith in relation to reason — above, below, against, next to — there is trouble, and the believers remain suspicious of reason. Theologians themselves appear to be talking ambiguously, and the believer is tempted to turn his back on thinking altogether. Now, the theologian's first duty as a critic is to try to understand this perennial tension between the man of faith and the thinking man. Of course, the believer is often afraid that the theologian is going to take away from him some basic belief, one doctrine or another which he believes is his "faith."

But the believer's fear of theology goes further. He suspects that theology as a rational activity disqualifies the very exercise of humanity in his argument with God. Even when the theologian speaks of God as Person or "personal Spirit," it appears that it is somehow in bad taste to talk to this God and with a more or less straight face to complain to him about reality. Reason has a way of speaking of Reality which shames the believer into shutting his mouth, and man with his mouth shut is hardly a man. Reason as a human activity ought to open a man's mouth, as it does in religion and myth, and not shut it as it has done in "metaphysics." This is the quarrel of faith with reason and the source of the perennial estrangement between them.

In a sense, kerygmatic theology, with its doctrine of reconciliation, is more hospitable to expostulation than philosophical theology. Insofar as expostulation is integral to the dynamics of faith, and faith is essential to kerygmatic theology, such theology is from faith and to faith. However, "revealed theology" has its own way of discouraging and disqualifying expostulation. When such theology, in line with the proclamation of the Gospel or the Word of God, insists, supposedly according to biblical witness and "Christian experience," that God who has revealed himself in Jesus Christ is a gracious Father and Friend, it becomes assertive and intolerant of expostulation. It strengthens the hands of religious institutions which seek to cultivate a spirit of "faith" as the opposite of expostulation. The religious man is exhorted and encouraged to be meekly pious and to accept reality by silencing both reason and conscience. He is invited to exercise "faith" for seeing evil as good and wrong as right, and to be dumb before the "secret counsel" of God. Now there is much talk of God's judgment upon sinful man and his kindness toward the undeserving creature. It appears, once for all, altogether wrong to expostulate with God; and right to acquiesce to reality. Now all is rational and moral confusion, and the very nerve of humanity and justice is cut off.

Fortunately, theologians who keep insisting upon faith as trust in God, not as a questioning of God, are usually too intelligent to be consistent in their piety. In response to an irrepressible good sense in the believing community, they keep arguing about "the problem of evil" and end up admitting that they too do not know the solution of it. Thus one does not have to look too far below the surface of their arguments to realize that their theology may conceal expostulation but cannot suppress it. In faith formed by the cross of Christ, expostulation remains as the nourishing ground of both doctrine and life, and theology itself remains an open-ended "science" because of it. This being the case, it is only right that theology, whether philosophical or kerygmatic, should set aside the pretense of giving the expostulating believer a rational account of reality and apply itself to the proper task of keeping faith intelligent and edifying. It can do this only as it respects the preoccupation of the expostulating believer with reality and with God; that is, as it is, and remains, empirical.

In the Bible, after which Christians pattern their conduct before God, people want to know what God says and what he is up to. There commonly is some unpleasantness about something that causes pain and hurt feelings. There is inhumanity and suffering of the body and the spirit. People are hungry and cold. The strong beat down the weak, the rich oppress the poor. There are enemies within and without, and there is no telling when death and destruction will come. There is no sense to the way good and evil follow each other, and no justice to the way they are distributed. The evil man prospers, the good man is indigent. The unrighteous is secure; the righteous man cannot breathe easily. Liars, thieves, murderers become great men; men of truth and compassion are reduced and become nobodies. Reality does not make sense. What is a man to do? "Accept" it? But he cannot accept it because to accept it is to deny reason and life itself. He is a fellow man, and he may not accept it for himself or for his neighbor. He cannot accept it and stay alive. He must expostulate about it. But with whom? With "reality"? A man does not expostulate with reality. He might and does expostulate with his fellow man. But his fellow man is his fellow sufferer, and he is not the Lord of reality. He must expostulate with the Lord of reality, that is, with the Lord God. He must speak out to the Lord, and he must listen to what the Lord says. If he can speak his mind, so can the Lord: the Lord also can speak out. He also can expostulate. He has his own thoughts and his own ways, and He will not be put in the wrong. If a man has a complaint against the Lord, does not the Lord have a complaint against him and against the people to whom he belongs? Yes, but how does the Lord justify reality? He cannot justify it. On the other hand, how does man justify himself? He cannot justify himself. There is no end to this controversy, and a man cannot win. So, he repents, but the thing is not settled. He is silenced, but he cries out again. God is vindicated, but he makes promises. He does make peace, but the struggle goes on. There is the promise of peace, and peace itself, but not without a cry. Thus man acts as a human being, and his God as a person. He is a human being, a fellow man; God is a person, a "covenant Partner." Thus, the God of the Bible is personal.

Man's controversy with reality means conflict and commotion, insecurity and anxiety. There is, therefore, the temptation to put an end to it. One way or another, man seeks to transcend the reality which is the occasion of expostulation. This he does through mystic experience, through "faith" in comforting doctrine, through speculation about a higher Reality, through "worldliness," through "accepting the universe." The poor man wants to rest and have peace, and will turn to anything that will put an end to his humanity.

Now, the function of theology is to guard his humanity; that is, to keep the expostulation going. It will not make out that the controversy is wrong, or irrational, or silly. It will not settle matters by dogmatizing to the effect that man is in the wrong or that God is in the wrong. It will not engage in dialectics aimed to "prove" that God is the Friend and not the Enemy. It will not argue that the wise man will not argue with God, or that God is beyond argument. It certainly will not argue that since there may not be a God, the expostulating man is silly. In short, it will engage in making a critique of expostulation and not in discrediting it.

Theology has its very reason for being in man's expostulations with God, and the theologian as such is bound to use his reason from and by and for such expostulation. "The science of God" is a rational discourse on God in the midst of a controversy of God with man who is in controversy with Him. The theologian is a "believer" in the sense that he acknowledges the argument between God and man as being itself rational. He is a man who shares the man's restiveness with reality as justified by the "empirical facts" of life in this world, and as expressive of his own reason and humanity. He is a "realist" in a vulgar sense and does his thinking in response to the vicissitudes of experience which occasion the "ultimate concern" (to use Tillich's phrase) of the religious mind. He is a believer, not against reason, or beyond reason, but as a rational man who knows good from evil and life from death. But he is a believer also in recognizing with the expostulating humanity that man's argument is with God and not with "the facts." He is rational as a believer in understanding that the logic of the argument entails "God-talk" or that without God, expostulation is nonsense, the same being the case without man. Indeed, reason does not function here as with empirical facts. It is not engaged in sorting and classifying, or in experiment and deduction. But it does function. It functions in expostulation; in acknowledging God who is a party to expostulation and speaks his own word to man about reality. It is the business of theology as science to show forth the reason in the word of God and in the word of man.

The expostulating man acknowledges that there is a word of God as well as his own word. He does not expostulate with a dumb God who lets him act as though truth and right were altogether on his side. In the stories men have told about gods and God, the latter have argued their own case against man, judging him and accusing him of unreason and wickedness. The expostulating man is not an innocent victim of God's enmity. His case against God is qualified and even threatened by God's case against him, so that his expostulation is informed and made petulant by a sense of guilt which mixes his argument with permanent unreason. Even while man judges he is judged; and he speaks as he hears and hears when he speaks. Expostulation is a dialogue, and without the word of God, it would be a farce.

Theology is a critical examination of the word of God and the word of man, to the end of exposing the reason in their interchange, and combatting the unreason which all too readily turns it either into complacency (which is a corruption of faith) or into griping (which is unfaith) on man's part. Unreason corrupts both the word of man and the word of God as man hears it, and theology is faith's resistance to unreason. Unfortunately, theologians, in their zeal to discourage griping, have contributed greatly to the complacency of "faith." Interpreting faith as belief in the truth of doctrine, as trust, commitment, obedience, and the like, they have thrown their authority on the side of "accepting the universe," which, except as an aspect of expostulation, is a violation of humanity. Faith which functions as submission is in truth a failure of reason in religion, and as such irrational; and traditional theology has cooperated with religious institutions, in the name of faith, in promoting and establishing it in the human community.

Theology as envisaged here would function quite differently. According to our interpretation of faith, interpretations of doctrine which discourage expostulation are misuses of reason in theology. For instance, the doctrine of predestination may not be allowed to browbeat the questioning man, or the doctrine of "free will" to solve his problems. God the Creator is the very Being with whom man has a controversy, and may not be so presented as to shut man up. Man the sinner is the man making a case against God. Sin may not be interpreted to mean that God has a case against man and not man against God. When the Incarnation is interpreted as the expression of God's grace, it may not be forgotten that when the Light shone in the darkness, it was not the end of darkness. Certainly the cross of Christ is a matter for expostulation as well as gratitude, and the Resurrection was followed by the advent of the Holy Spirit who is, as seen in "the warfare of the Christian man," the Spirit of expostulation. There is neither faith

nor hope except by expostulation, and love itself without expostulation with reality is "neurotic." A church of nonexpos-
tulation is more dead than alive, and its life is a foretaste of
death. Eschatology itself is the expostulatory utterance at its
purest and without the Spirit of expostulation is turned into
superstition or mystification. It is the business of theology to
keep the doctrines of the community of expostulation from
turning into superstition, which is the very stifling of its life.

Expostulation, like exercising our humanity, is a risky business. When it is suppressed by either faith or unbelief, it has
the tendency to become endless griping which itself turns
into generalized hostility. When it appears futile to quarrel
with reality, the quarrel is turned against humanity itself. Thus
the life of man with man, especially in a world where Fate
and Fortune appear through human powers and accomplishments, is suffused with expostulation turned into quarreling;
enmity is woven into the ways of man with man, and conduct, however accommodating and even friendly, fails to
give people peace. People who will not or may not expostulate with reality, will quarrel with one another and fill their
common life with perduring and perhaps irremovable conflict.
In this way and sense the issue of religion becomes the ethical issue. It is a function of theology as a practical science to
bring to light the chemistry of the transmutation of controversy with reality into a mutual hostility among fellowmen.
Theology is a critique of conduct growing out of the inseparability of faith from life, that is, of expostulation with reality
from expostulation among men. The understanding of this inseparability, involved in struggles of the Spirit with the flesh,
as an aspect of reconciliation, becomes an intrinsic concern
of theology. Such understanding involves also an interpretation of reconciliation which shall prevent it from becoming
itself a source of hostility; for reconciliation as the end of expostulation, whether with God or with one's fellow men, may
be a delusion and a source of virulence in men's mutual hostility. Reconciliation is the very possibility of expostulation,
and thus of "faith and obedience." It is the business of theol-

ogy as a science of conduct, in respect to ethics also, to guard the "purity of heart."

6. God and Reality.

To the critical mind, people expostulating with God have had a strange way of assuming that He exists and communicates with them. Biblical piety and pieties derived from the Bible, in common with the religions of many peoples, have not raised questions either of God's existence or of his being a party to their expostulations about reality. There have been "fools" who have said that there is no God, and certainly many have lived as though God were dead. But the astonishing thing is that the pious who have been uncompromising in their expostulations and have maintained the dignity of man in the face of reality have been strangers to doubting the existence of God with whom they have been at odds. They have been critical of God's ways to the point of blasphemy, but they have not known the critical attitude which questions the reality of God.

This curious phenomenon of religion requires close examination. The "modern mind" is inclined to attribute it to a lack of criticism, or of philosophical and scientific discipline. It appears that the religious man is given to anthropomorphism, so that he thinks of reality as under a personal Power or powers. This is vaguely speaking true. However, the question remains as to why anthropomorphism has been a commonplace of the human mind. The ready answer of the "modern man" to this question is that anthropomorphism is a natural trait of "the primitive mind," or that man is a natural animist. But such an answer explains nothing. It asserts the facts.

It is offhand curious that the primitive man should be unable to distinguish between a person and a tree, or between a tree and a stone. In any case, people who left us the Bible and other ancient literature did know the difference between man and beast; and, what is more to the point, they did distinguish between their God or gods and the things around them. Thus deities were anthropomorphic, not because men saw things as people, but because, as people, they had their troubles with things. They have had God or gods because they were people and because reality was at odds with them. It was in their intercourse with reality that they had gods or God who were anthropomorphic, God or gods with whom they were engaged in vehement discussion about reality. They were expostulators, and God or gods were the logical parties to their expostulation.

The pious man is a human being, engaged in a controversy about good and evil, and right and wrong, with God or gods. He knows that God exists because he is in controversy with him. A man does not argue about reality as a state of affairs. What is, is. It may be frustrating or destructive. A man may be unhappy about it. He may try hard to improve it. But he does not expostulate with it. Given expostulation, it can happen logically only between persons. The other party in expostulation must be men, or gods, or God.

What if people think they are in dispute with God, while they are in dispute with their neighbors; especially since, without their neighbors, they would not even be people, let alone engage in controversy? But this is contrary to the nature of the controversy in question. Even while people expostulate with their neighbors, they do so in the setting of a reality or realities which are other than their neighbors. They are not so thoughtless as to regard their neighbors as the sole agents of the vicissitudes in their lives. As their fellow men, their neighbors share their own discomfiture in the hands of Fate and Fortune. Reality cannot be identified with the human community. In the human community itself, there are institutions and organizations as well as people. But even these totalities with their structures do not exhaust reality. There is "the world," "nature," reality as a whole which is the setting of human life. In controversy, men respond to this reality; and in so doing, they qualify their mutual expostulations with one that has to do with their common lot and condition in their environment.

Hence it will not do to say that dispute with God is a projection of dispute among men. People expostulate about a reality which is not man's creation, and they expostulate with a God or gods who are neither man nor the world. It is not logical for them to engage in controversy with "nature." It is also not logical for them to blame all their troubles on their fellow creatures. Therefore they turn their attention to God or the gods. As controversialists, their business is with God. If there were no God or gods, there would have been no book of Job, and there would be no controversy. But there is controversy, and it is between God or gods and people.

It may therefore well be that the pious man does not question God's existence because expostulation is his rational activity and expostulation in the absence of God or gods is absurd. Since expostulation, which goes with the knowledge of good and evil, and life and death, is a characteristically human activity, the knowledge of God is the work of reason itself, and it is irrational to raise the question of God's existence. And since the pious man, knowing good from evil, is rational, he does not do it.

If God were approached merely as a Being who has the power to deliver a man from evil, then one might wonder if He is not an object of "wishful thinking," an infantile response to reality. Of course, there has been and is much wishful thinking among men. However, expostulation is something else. It has its roots not in the frustrations of the individual but in the condition of man as a social reality. It is a social phenomenon and involves the expostulations of people among themselves. Good and evil come upon people as they transact one with another, as they respond one to another for good or evil. The ground of expostulation is the coexistence of people, and the context of it is their life as rational beings. As rational beings they expostulate, and in expostulating they are human. But their expostulations one with another are inseparable from another expostulation in which they are posited as fellow men before another party. "Wishful thinking" may enter into their controversy with this party, as indeed it may enter into their mutual controversies. But expostulation is one thing, and wishful thinking is another. In fact these are contrary movements of the mind. Wishful thinking weakens expostulation, and expostulation resists wishful thinking. Job was not engaged in wishful thinking, and his opponents were not engaged in expostulation with God.

In expostulation about reality God alone, as distinguished from men and things, is the other party whose existence cannot be, as Expostulator, in question. God's existence can be questioned only as that of God who is not engaged in expostulation. But then he is hardly God, as the nonexpostulating man is hardly man. Expostulation entails existence, and God as expostulating exists. Indeed, the question of God's existence has arisen, and in our culture it is irrepressible. But apart from expostulation there appears to be no satisfactory way of settling it. One may ask whether one knows another man exists on grounds other than that one is speaking with him. The answer is that one does, in that he sees and may touch him. But with God no such answer is possible, since one does not touch and see God. When people try to "prove" God's existence apart from "faith," there is endless disagreement. Given expostulation, such disagreement is endlessly interesting and salutary, and there shall be no end to it. Not given expostulation, it is an exercise in futility.

When the expostulator is pressed about the existence of his God, he insists that he cannot doubt it. He does not doubt it. But when he is critical, he is full of paradoxes. There appears to be no way of speaking about God which does not demand another way of doing it. God certainly exists, otherwise how would one be expostulating with him? But he does not exist as anything exists, because if he so existed, one would not be expostulating with him. The matter may be stated in terms of reality: Is not God real? Certainly he is, for otherwise one would not speak to him. But he is not a part of reality, since it is about reality that one expostulates with God. Is not God a transcendent Reality? Certainly he is, since if he did not transcend reality, there again would be no expostulating with him. On the other hand, were he transcendent Reality as over against the reality which the expostulation is about, one would no longer expostulate at all. One would contemplate it, and thus oneself transcend reality.

The very question of being with regard to God arises from expostulation. An ontologist like Plato, or Hegel, or Tillich, is an expostulator. He is engaged with ontology because of a conflict in reality, because of the threat of meaninglessness in reality. Ontology is a dialectical process, and it receives its impulse from expostulation. Do away with expostulation, and the dialectic of ontology collapses into a play with words. Expostulation is what has kept ontology going and produced the endless discussions about Being and beings, the One and the many, the noumenal and the phenomenal, the Real and the apparent, the Truth and truths, and so on. There is a question of Being because there is a question of God, and the question of God is asked in expostulation. It is not, therefore, surprising that theologians are concerned with ontology and ask if God is Being or a Being. For the same reason, they endlessly argue among themselves, for the one or the other.

Apparently, "Being" is not a literal symbol for the God of expostulation. Man expostulates with God, but he does not know God as he knows the things around him. He neither sees nor hears God, but he keeps arguing with him. He cannot even identify God with an object of his speculation. He says that God is not an idea, and he says that God is not a thing. He says that God is the ground of idea and thing alike. But it is not hard to see that the ontologist who speaks of God as the ground is the expostulator, and that his "ground" is hardly "Being itself." God is rather the mystery of being in the sense that his being together with his ways which cause expostulation are past finding out. We do not know how to speak of his being, and we do not know if we should speak of it at all, except that we may not cease to expostulate with him. In short, ontology does not provide us with a literal symbol for God. On the other hand, it is necessary for expostulation, because without it expostulation is corrupted and threatens not only truth but also "justice, mercy, and peace." And since ontology is necessary, it needs to be done as well as possible for the sake of expostulation itself.

Expostulation gives rise to speculation with regard to being, but it is concerned with empirical reality. It occurs among men in a common world, with regard to the vicissitudes of life and all the things, good and evil, that happen to human beings. It has to do with food and drink and shelter; with good and ill health, and living and dying; with justice and injustice among men, and war and peace in the human community. It has to do with fulfillment and frustration, with power and weakness, with dignity and lack of it, with hope and despair. The expostulator is a confirmed empiricist with regard to the realities that impinge upon him and an earth-bound creature who (like Job) will not be comforted by either lies or fantasies. To him evil is evil and cruelty is cruelty. Hunger is hunger and death is death. Inhumanity is inhumanity and violation is violation. There is no Truth which turns truths to lies, and no Reality which makes realities unreal. There is no Being which devalues being and no Transcendence which de-realizes the empirical world, the scene of expostulation. To the man of faith, ontology is a temptation as well as a corrective. His business is not with Being but with God the Creator. He may not allow "Transcendence" to confuse or invalidate his controversy with God about reality. He is clearly a transcendentalist as he argues with God (rather God with him), but he is such as an empiricist, arguing with God about things no less real than God.

In short, when one considers the traditional languages and preoccupations of theologians, it appears that they need to come closer to the place of the pious who are engaged in an expostulation with their God about reality. They need to participate in this expostulation and to exercise their critical powers toward bringing out and quickening and maintaining the reason in it. They need to avoid any ontology which discredits expostulation and to persist in ontology which articulates it and tends to make it coherent. Thus theology will be justified as a rational discipline in the human community and will function as an authentic aspect of the human enterprise, which is, in one respect, the realization of humanity itself. Maybe then the expostulating man will recognize the theologian as his fellow man and helper instead of this stranger who talks another language and has a rather dim view of his spirit. Maybe then theology will be acknowledged as a legitimate intellectual discipline in the community at large and come to its own as a humanizing activity in a world where man appears to be fighting for his life.

14

New Modes of Empirical Theology
LANGDON GILKEY

That other, competing theologies are in crisis is comfortably
obvious to every contemporary theologian. An inescapable,
but seldom drawn, conclusion from this fact is that *all* theologies are in crisis, even our own. In this essay I shall initially try
to spell out the nature and causes of this crisis and then propose a theological method which may help in this situation.
Whether my proposal is either new or viable, I am not at all
sure. Clearly it has direct ancestors and near relations; and
clearly, sooner or later it will show the destructive tensions
and inadequacies of all points of view. To me it seems to answer what I feel to be the pressures of the moment, and to
open a way ahead; and that is all one can ask. In another
constellation of cultural and religious forces further down the
line of time, at best it will itself become objectified, anachronistic, and so lacking in usefulness.[1]

The theological crisis, as I see it, has two interconnected
focuses. The first centers on the present demand for an "empirical" approach to theology, a parodoxical demand in so far
as such an approach is both required and difficult in our
time; and the second centers on the question, in relation to
this requirement and this difficulty, of the meaning of the symbol "God." Let me discuss first the contemporary question, and
the problematic, of the word "empirical" in theological discourse.

[1] A much more complete defense of my proposal appears in book
form under the title *Naming the Whirlwind: The Renewal of God-Language* (Indianapolis, Bobbs-Merrill Co., 1969). This essay, in somewhat
different form, is soon to be reprinted in *The Secular: Atheistic or
Theistic*, edited by George F. McLean, O.M.I. (New York: Meredith
Press).

345

That theology must in some sense be *empirical* is, I think, well illustrated by the breakup of neo-orthodox or biblical theology in the recent past. The fact of this demise need not be proved to the readers of this volume; they had predicted it long since. The causes are too manifold to outline here. To me the fundamental one is that a theology whose authority, and therefore whose meaningfulness *and* validity, were derived directly only from the experience of the Word received or acknowledged by faith remained in the end too unrelated to ordinary, secular experience to support that weight. For in a secular culture only what is in coherent relation to ordinary life, life six days a week, bears for us the stamp of meaningfulness and of validity. Ultimately, therefore, those biblical symbols had only "eidetic" meanings; they floated, a coherent system, but suspended high above experience and therefore in the end vulnerable to positivistic and existentialist attack. The question of their meaningfulness, their relation to, and so possible verification or falsification in, ordinary experience remained unresolved. Without that empirical base, neo-orthodox theology lost its compelling power, and moved off from the center of the theological stage. The lesson is that in our modern world some aspect of empiricism in theology is a requirement.

That theology, on the other hand, is only with great difficulty empirical — my second point, vis-à-vis method — is probably a less familiar, and less welcome, theme to the Chicago tradition. My point is not that it is hard in our age to be empirical. The age demands it; in fact this demand might be one way to define "secularity," and consequently the empirical disciplines presently flourish. But it is something else again to be empirical in theology, since most theologies deal inescapably with some understanding of the symbol "God," and that symbol generally refers to something, some factor or reality, that transcends in some significant way the manifold of immediate experience. However much that transcending factor may be conceived as active in or imminent within ordinary passage, it or he is not a direct object of experience, as is a rock or a person, nor a direct implication of the sequences

346

of experience, as is a scientific law. Thus theology is not a part of the special sciences, dealing with "matters of fact," with assertions about creatures or events in space time, as do physical and historical science. Though theological judgments concern, and so may either presuppose or even imply assertions about, such matters of natural or historical fact, theological propositions do not *make* such assertions. Natural science and history make these sorts of assertions, and so alone test and validate them (see, for example, the continual rumble over the differences between the historian's and the theologian's roles vis-à-vis Biblical materials). Or, as Whitehead would have put this point, theology does not deal with "abstracted" elements of experience; nor, as the positivists argue, does it propose hypotheses that are falsifiable or verifiable in the manifold of sensory experience. This is, therefore, generally agreed else God be like Kierkegaard's Great Green Bird, an ordinary, though large and "queer," kind of creature and therefore neither holy nor universal and so of neither religious nor ontological significance. How then *is* theology "empirical"; what can the word mean in our kind of discipline?

Generally the answer has been, certainly in the recent Chicago tradition of empirical theology, that which mediates between the immediacy of direct or lived experience and the object of theological discourse is metaphysical or ontological speculation. This is the imaginative "leap" of speculative generalization, which as Whitehead puts it, begins with experience as it comes, and then transcends the stuff of immediacy, with its objects that come and go (sometimes a tiger is there and sometimes not); and in thus imaginatively transcending immediacy, speculative reason can construct a universal, necessary scheme of categories with which every event, here and now, in the past or in the future, in far-off space, in the lowliest existent, or in the everlasting life of the divine, can be understood. Through speculative philosophy a system of language is thus delineated which can mediate between the immediacy of ordinary daily experience, the various elements of culture, and the religious language of faith about the divine. And thus are both the problems plaguing religious language resolved: (*a*) the problem of validity, by the elaboration of a natural theology, and (*b*) that of meaningfulness, by "translating" biblical or traditional language into the precise and universally intelligible categories of the metaphysical system. So far so good.

There are substantial, though quite possibly not fatal, difficulties inherent in this proposal from the side of theology; but I am not concerned with them here. What does concern me is the difficulty of this method from the side of contemporary philosophy. For while many contemporary theologians may ask "Is this *theology*?" almost all present-day philosophers will apodictically assert, "This is not *empirical*." And they will go on to say, "This is far too rationalistic a proposal to be viable in the modern age." By "rationalistic" they mean what is precisely of the essence of this proposal, and so its strength and attractiveness, namely the affirmation that through philosophical speculation a set of categories descriptive of "actuality" can be discovered and can mediate between immediate experience and the divine. Such confidence that philosophical thought is a special mode of *knowing* what is more "real," more "actual," more pervasive, or more fundamental (the "larger" realities, the "concrete" beyond the abstractions of the special sciences) is precisely what most of modern philosophy does not share. Like the fact that they do not have "faith," their lack of confidence in speculative reason, in philosophy as a mode of super-knowing, as a higher and unifying form of science, may be unfortunate; and we may deplore it or castigate them as relativists, skeptics, and cowards. Nevertheless, the *fact* of this doubt is undeniable, illustrated in modern empirical naturalism, in the bracketing movements in phenomenology, in existentialism's critique of objectifying metaphysical speculation and its rejection of the rationality of the world, and above all in the abdication of linguistic philosophy, in both its positivistic, its analytic, *and* its ordinary language varieties, from this classical role of philosophy. If one is going to argue *philosophically*, and this is the essence of this proposal, one must face this difficulty: namely, the radical questioning whether philosophical *know-*

348

ing is a possibility, and consequently whether an empirical metaphysics and its correlate, an empirical theology, are possible.

That metaphysics and ontology are finally and forever "dead," I do not believe, any more than I believe that "faith" or "God" are dead. But that all are at present equally obscured and so in difficulty, there can be no reasonable doubt. Consequently the task for an empirical theology of this mode, like that of a theology founded on revelation, is to begin with immediate experience and to show therein the *possibility* of metaphysics. It cannot begin with the easy assumption that a metaphysics, merely because it begins with experience, is to be dubbed "empirical" as modern philosophy defines that term, and so remains a possibility in a radically empirical age. Process theology has been right to have reminded revelational theology of the need of defending empirically its fideistic assumptions in a secular age. It has been wrong not to listen to the screeches of philosophers, in the same age and for the same reasons, of the need for defending *its* rationalistic assumptions "empirically." Some of the reasons for this strange deafness in an age when philosophy departments have been almost exclusively staffed with anti-metaphysicians are: (*a*) This form of philosophy has in our day on the whole inhabited theological areas and thus could be unconcerned with what practicing philosophers were actually doing. (*b*) In relation to other theological alternatives (though not in relation to philosophy), this philosophical theology *was* "empirical." In that context, therefore, its strongly rationalistic assumptions were obscured and it could pretend to be as empirical as modern thought required. Only when its advocates strayed amongst the linguists did it appear as anachronistic and even pious as it actually was, presupposing an order of objective coherence which sounded very unmodern and so unsecular, and producing a set of categories whose meaningfulness and whose potential validity were fully as ambiguous and as problematic as were the corresponding categories of biblical theology. This then is the crisis in method: if biblical theology is not empirical enough *in* a secular age, and if speculative metaphysics is not empirical enough *for* a secular age, what *are* we to do to construct an empirical theology?

Let us now look at the second focus of the problem, the focus not so much on method, but on the content or object of theological discourse. It is generally agreed that from the point of view of content, the major theological crisis of our age centers on the problem of God. By this I do not mean merely that we do not know *what* we should think or believe about God — what doctrines, categories, symbols, or language systems we should apply to him. Rather, as I have implied already, the focus of the "problem character" of the symbol God is *whether* modern man can think of him at all, whether *any* doctrine of God, revelational and biblical, or philosophical or ontological, is possible in a secular time. Clearly if this be so, it is in a unique way *the* theological problem to which all others are subsidiary. For logically there are no other theological problems of revelation, Christology, eschatology, anthropology, or ecclesiology if this problem be answered in the negative and if it be impossible for modern man to speak meaningfully of the divine, of God. Let me note that unless we are rabid Arians, there is no way of speaking of Christ if we are unable to speak of God. If the doctrine of the Trinity means anything linguistically, it means that language about the divine nature, dimension, or "event" of the man Jesus is language about *God* — else we speak only, as Hamilton and Van Buren wish to do, of the human Jesus. Correspondingly, language about the Word and Holy Scripture is language about *God* if it is more than speech about an interesting ancient religious document. All *theological* language thus is, in our tradition, inescapably God language.

This is, moreover, a church and not just a theologian's problem, puzzling alone to sophisticated seminarians. The sense of the meaninglessness, irrelevance, and emptiness of theological language permeates our church life and is the ground in Christian communal existence for the appearance of the problem within theological reflection. Finally, we should be clear that the problem is not with *a* particular view of God, as if a new or modern view would resolve the crisis; though a revision of traditional views of God may well also be called for.[2] The problem is a serious one precisely because any view of God, of the sacred, or the divine, is in difficulties in the pres-ent situation; and consequently all relevant alternatives — biblical, neo-Reformation, Thomistic, process, Tillichian, and so on — are faced with the same issues. A mere transition from metaphysical to biblical categories, or the reverse; from a transcendent to an immanent view, or the reverse; from epiphany to eschatological theologies, or the reverse; from Thomistic to Hegelian to process, or the reverse, will not answer a secular challenge which, I believe, finds all these views of the divine almost equally unintelligible and empty. The problem, as has been aptly stated, concerns the death of *God*, not of this or that view of God; or, to put the point in modern linguistic terms, the death of the *word* "God," and thus of any view of God at all.

As this last indicates, I agree with many commentators that the basic cause of the problem, in its focuses of both method and content, is the character of the modern spirit, a spirit or *geist* which provides the most fundamental definition for the word "secular." This secular spirit of contemporaneity is risky to characterize, but if we would unravel our present theological difficulties we must take this risk. I assume that contemporary philosophy, while not the only clue to what contemporary men feel about their world and themselves, is as good an entrée into the modern *geist* as any. My own interpretation of this spirit — which is here stated without adequate defense — is as follows: epistemologically the "secular" is characterized by a concentration on *immediacy* as providing the sole grounds for meaningful and valid speech or thoughts; and hence the limiting concern of recent linguistic and "pure" phenomenological philosophy with the two aspects of immedi-

[2] For example, see the views of Leslie Dewart and of Schubert M. Ogden that the main cause of the present problem of God lies in the character of traditional theism. Leslie Dewart, *The Future of Belief* (New York: Herder and Herder, 1966), chaps. 1, 2, and 6; Schubert M. Ogden, *The Reality of God* (New York: Harper & Row, 1967), esp. pp. 16–20 and 46–52.

acy, namely speech and direct experience or essences. Ontologically, this secular confinement of reflection to immediacy
implies an emphasis on the radical, blind, or arbitrary *contingency* of all that is, and on the *relativity* and the *transience*
of all things as the essential and exhaustive structures of the
real. Consequently, there appears in most modern philosophy a denial of any noncontingent, absolute, or permanent
"ground," "reason," or structure to process. The categories of
self-sufficient being, of logos, and of eternity are alike alien
to contemporary ontology, if any ontology is possible at all in
such an epistemological and ontological situation. Contingent
and relative change is all there is. And it is precisely because
of this implicit ontology of radical contingency, relativism,
and transience, in which no universal, rational structure to
be known by speculative reason is possible, that the radically
empirical epistemology of modern thought results. Thus while
scientific inquiry deals with the immanent structures of sensory experience, philosophy can deal only with an analysis
of language or with an analysis of the essential phenomena
that appear in direct experience. Thought and being, man
and the ultimate structure of things, are radically disjoined.
"God is dead" and man has "come of age" in a world devoid
of sacrality, and so cold and meaningless, a world which is
"useful" only insofar as it can be understood and manipulated
for his own moral and social purposes.

As a result of this mood, typically modern "myths," which
embody our fundamental sense of reality and its relation to
value, and so structure our hope, concern neither God, the
universe as a whole, the cosmic process, or even the progress
of history — as did those of the classical Christian tradition,
of liberal progressivism, and of Marxism. Rather, our modern myths are based on the other major category of secularity:
human *autonomy*. What we tend to believe in is not the divine, the rational, or the progressive structure of existence as
a whole, but solely in our own intellectual and moral powers.
The universe outside is mere "nature" as uncovered by
science, and no help or meaning comes to us from it; but if
we only know enough, are aware enough, and will morally

enough, we believe we can control our world, ourselves, and ultimately our destiny. It is this disappearance of any sense of objective rationality or moral meaning in the cosmos, in history, or in universal process, combined with the epistemological "shrinking" referred to above, that makes a metaphysical or natural-theological solution to the problem of God, which solution must presuppose the power of philosophical reason to know reality's ultimate structure, as elusive and difficult in our time as is a revealed solution.

The secular confinement of reality (and so of meaningful and true statements about reality) to the immediate, to what is contingent, relative, and transient, to the things and people around us, has in turn had a vast influence on contemporary religious life. It has manifested itself there as a sense of the absence or elusiveness of God. Our religious and church life is barren of self-authenticating experiences of the divine, as other ages apparently felt them, whether we speak of hearing the Word, of prayer, of experiences of the Spirit, or of sacramental life. Direct experiences of "encounter" with God are talked about theologically but are rarely actual in our personal life. Thus a theological method which begins with "faith's knowledge of God" or "acknowledgment of the Word of God addressed to me," that is, theologies based on the assumptions of revelation of the Word, and of the reception of these by faith, presuppose precisely what is currently being questioned, namely whether we have in fact heard a divine Word at all, and so whether faith, although probably longed for, is a real possibility or an illusionary hope. If faith is vividly experienced by a person, then certainly the reality of God follows directly for that believer from the experience. But if our possession of faith is itself doubted, if we only hope for faith, then there is in faith alone no basis for such certainty about God, nor any ground in faith alone for meaningful language about him. In such a situation the repetition of a theology which presupposes our prior possession of faith and so our certainty of the reality of God will not help.

The result in church life has been that both our experiences of God and our speaking about him have become shaky. No specifically religious experiences seem easily possible to us, and church language consequently seems unreal and meaningless to many. Several important problems for theological method are here implied. If church language is apt to be meaningless to the people who hear it, a linguistic analysis of that some church language will not provide a meaningful basis for theology. A linguistic analysis must assume at the outset that the language game it analyzes is actually "played," that is, that it already communicates in a community, that it is in fact used — and yet just this cannot be assumed about religious language in our churches. Correspondingly, a phenomenological analysis of specifically *religious* experience or "feeling" presupposes the existence of such experiences or feelings as a basis for theology — and yet these, no more than the meaningful usage of religious discourse, can be assumed at the outset. The secular spirit has been a powerful dissolvent and has eaten away, not only the traditional biblical and confessional authorities, and so methodologies of the faith, but also, uncomfortably, even those more modern methodologies — metaphysical and philosophical, and the ways centered in an analysis of language or of religious experience — with which a new answer to the problem might be devised.

How, then, *do* we begin? Unless we are to presuppose what precisely is doubted (that is, a faith knowledge of God or the possibility of rational speculation in philosophy), we must begin, apparently, with immediacy. Nor can this immediacy be a "religious" one as it was for Schleiermacher or for Otto, for religious feeling or experience is elusive to us, and our words about it are empty. We must, then, start with the immediacy of *secular* experience. But what can we know about God-language *there*? Secular experience is, on the one hand, not "faith" experience and thus cannot be assumed to know either a revelation or a divine Word that could establish biblical God-language. On the other hand, secular immediacy in itself, without rationalistic assumptions themselves philosophically problematic, cannot generate an ontology or a metaphysics that could lead to philosophical God-language.

If, then, we can begin neither with faith nor with philosophical ontology, language about God seems to be precluded from the start. A beginning in secular immediacy can, therefore, only provide us with a prolegomenon to discourse about God. Secular experience, taken "as is" and taken with all its ambiguity and variety, cannot by itself produce "natural theology" and thus out of itself generate any positive theological language.

Although it cannot for this reason "prove God," such a prolegomenon is by no means useless. It can show that religious discourse is *meaningful* because it is related to important and pervasive aspects of ordinary secular experience. We cannot here establish the meaningfulness of religious language by pointing to its "use" — for that is queer and elusive indeed in a secular culture. Rather we can establish it by showing that there are in fact ranges or regions of experience which, because of their particular and unique character, call for religious symbolization. A language game can be said to be "meaningful" if there are areas of experience which it, and it alone, thematizes and brings to clarity. For meaning is basically an interaction of linguistic symbols and shared experiences — which interaction alone makes communication through language possible. If such areas of common experience relevant to religious discourse can be shown to be there in secular life, then religious language is established as a meaningful part of human culture. Correspondingly, a secular self-understanding that blocks out such areas of secular experience, and so such forms of language, is shown to impoverish if not endanger the full life of man. The prolegomenon I propose, then, will seek to establish the meaningfulness of the general language game of religious discourse by unveiling aspects of ordinary experience to which religious symbolization is appropriate and essential, where, so to speak, something "appears" which requires the thematization of religious language. Investigation of the reality or the ontological nature of what it is that appears is not a part of such a prolegomenon; such ontological questions are "bracketed out." Or, put linguistically, the question of the validity of particular statements or claims about the sacred is not investigated. This is an analysis of the secular "situations" to which religious usages of words might apply, and not a testing of the truth of particular religious propositions. This is a prolegomenon to theological discourse, not an example of it. But the prolegomenon is essential to the renewal of theological language; for religious discourse must be related to ordinary secular, day-to-day experience so that its symbols through that relation have given back to them their life and their meaning. The main thesis of my prolegomenon, then, is, to paraphrase Kant,[3] that secular experience without religious symbols is blind, unarticulated and so terrifying; religious symbols, without content of secular experience, are empty and meaningless.

As is evident, one of the presuppositions of this proposal is that there is a split or a disjunction between the secular self-understanding as outlined above and secular experience as it is actually lived. That is, it is assumed that cultures can apprehend and thematize their experience in ways which at certain crucial points do not fit the felt tonalities, the real dimensions, and the actual characteristics of their experience. Such an assumption, I take it, is necessarily implied in any historically relativist view which recognizes the variety of cultural self-understanding amid a basic and universal mode of human being in the world. A second point of the prolegomenon, then, will be to show that at certain definite points secular experience belies the secular self-understanding, that elements or dimensions appear in actual secular experience which the symbolic accounts of that experience — as *merely* contingent, relative, transient, and autonomous — do not in fact successfully thematize. The appeal here is to the characteristics of secular experience itself, not to religious norms; but the *content* of the appeal is the assertion that secular experience manifests a religious dimension, a dimension of ultimacy

[3] I owe this "re-usage" of Kant to my phenomenological colleague Eugene T. Gendlin, whose excellent *Experiencing and the Creation of Meaning* (Glencoe: Free Press, 1962) provided the source for many of the fundamental ideas of this proposal.

and sacrality which only religious symbolization can express and clarify.

Put in terms of religious language, the essence of secularity was that the cosmos was drained of ultimacy and sacrality: the gods have long since fled from field and stream; even the biblical and the philosophical gods are now dead, and only flux is king. Further, I said that for secularity the ground of our hopes and the source of our norms reside only in man's own autonomous capacities. If this be so, a prolegomenon which aims to show the error of this restrictive self-understanding and of its myths of autonomy will seek to establish that in and through *both* our autonomy and the cosmos which is our setting a dimension of ultimacy and of sacrality reveals itself.

Our autonomy is experienced in secular life as essentially ambiguous and often helpless — and therefore not the resource for our norms and our hopes which modern myths believe. Correspondingly, the values and meanings of our existence find their roots, not in our own powers, but in the "given." That which in various ways grounds and establishes our capacities, and so that which we can neither create nor control, is the basis of whatever value our autonomy itself can muster — something on which we absolutely depend. Thus a secular self-understanding that locates meaning solely in autonomy, and finds the "given" devoid of grounds for hope, is at variance with our actual experience of life. Central to the prolegomenon, then, is the effort to show that both within our secular experience of the "given" in life, and in our experience of our own autonomy, a nonsecular dimension appears, namely a dimension of ultimacy and of sacrality with which religious language peculiarly deals, and which can be thematized in no other terms. What is shown is that man is a religious being whose experience of the sacred, both positively as the ground, limit, norm, and resource of his life, and negatively as the infinite and uncontrollable threat to his life, characterizes his humanity and provides the only way of understanding rationally the positive characteristics of man's autonomy and of his creative powers, and the negative uses he makes of those powers. In all human experience, *including* modern, secular experience, such a dimension reveals itself negatively and positively, and alone accounts for the unique structures of human experiences. Consequently the forms of language appropriate to this dimension of experience, religious language, are both meaningful and essential to man's life. What the mode of reality or "nature" of this sacred may be, is here for the moment bracketed out; that the sacred appears, I seek to show and thus to show, in terms of their referents in ordinary experience, the meanings of religious language.

Methodologically, therefore, I am proposing a phenomenological hermeneutic of secular experience to uncover the latent, but very significant, religious dimension there, the dimension with which all religious language is concerned, and so, with which Christian theological discourse is also concerned. My thesis is that a dimension of ultimacy does in fact appear at the center of each significant facet of man's being in the world, and that it is this dimension which grounds man's powers, possibilities, and joys, and also which man experiences as a threat to his being and his value. It appears, therefore, not directly but indirectly, as the *basis* of our dealings with the world, ourselves, and our history, as the *limit* and even the *threat* to these dealings, and as the *resource* for our confidence and hope. Our deepest joys and anxieties alike, our most significant norms and our most important hopes, likewise find their roots, and so their comprehensible symbolic thematization, in this region of ultimacy. To show the religious character of man, as being in the world, in relation to a horizon or dimension of ultimacy, is the fundamental purpose of the prolegomenon I propose. Here is the ground in ordinary secular experience for the language we call "God-language," and it is these experiences of ultimacy within ordinary experience to which the symbolic forms of Christian discourse refer and which, in part, Christians *mean* when they talk about God and his activities.

If this dimension of ultimacy or sacrality does not appear

directly in secular experience — as it certainly does not — then where and how do we look for it there? I suggest that it appears in dim awareness or in apprehension — "prehended," as Meland says, if not explicitly noted in consciousness — in four areas of our ordinary experience: (1) when we experience the *grounds* or the bases of our being or our powers: (2) when we experience the *limits* of our powers, and thus an unconditioned threat to them; (3) when we experience the *ambiguity* of our destiny and of our freedom, and both the possibility and the threats in that apprehension; and (4) when we experience a *resource* or a basis for our hopes and our confidence. In each of these cases an experience of ultimacy, of unconditionedness, and of sacrality is present, and any discourse about these regions of experience has the character of religiously symbolic discourse. That is, it is multivalent or symbolic in a special sense, speaking of the finite, but the finite only in so far as it is in relation to an ultimacy or a sacrality which appears within and to it.

This experience of ultimacy and sacrality — as ground, limit, and in ambiguity and hope — appears, moreover, in relation to every significant aspect of man's being. For man is man on all his levels in relation to this dimension, and must be so understood if he is to be comprehended — as his life must be so lived if it is to manifest its fullest possibilities. Thus ultimacy appears with regard to man's being, to his knowing, his meaning, his valuing, his decision-making, his experience of isolation, guilt, and stain, to their resolution in self-acceptance and reconciliation, and finally to his temporality or death. In each of these "areas," so to speak, the unconditioned appears as the ground, limit, threat, and resource to all man is and does. In essence, therefore, what my prolegomenon seeks to do is to take each category of the secular spirit: contingency, relativity, temporality and autonomy, and to show how these fundamental "ontological" categories of our being, as viewed by modern man, imply for our modern *existence*, if not for our modern thoughts, a religious dimension. Each of these categories in the self-understanding of modern man has led to a secular view of the world as merely contingent, relative, transient, and autonomous. Each of them, when *lived and experienced* by modern man, as by his predecessors, leads inescapably to an apprehension of an ultimate threat, an ultimate ground and an ultimate hope which provide the real horizon within which even modern man lives. For he too is threatened by the deepest anxieties, the possibilities of despair and of meaninglessness, by his own demonic reactions, and by the fear of isolation and of death which other ages have felt, and which can be understood only in terms of the category of ultimacy and unconditionedness. Correspondingly, modern man too lives by "myths"; he models his life on sacral images; and he directs himself and his history by religious hopes beyond the evidence — all of which likewise presuppose this dimension. Thus does the phenomenological evidence centered on the fundamental categories of the secular spirit refute its own self-understanding and drive to the recognition of a religious dimension in human existence. And by implication, if this religious dimension is there, religious language is necessary and meaningful if man is to be fully man.

Through this prolegomenon, therefore, the region of religious discourse and the essential character of that discourse are established, and the possibility of its meaningfulness in a secular age is assured. The region is the experience of ultimacy and sacrality as it appears in each facet of human life. The character of religious language is correspondingly defined as fundamentally symbolic or polysemic in form, referring to the infinite and the sacred that appears within the finite and the profane, grounding it, limiting it, threatening it, and providing to it ultimate structure, meaning, and hope. Thus does religious discourse form the basis of every creative activity, as well as of every demonic propensity of man. It is language always implying man's total self-involvement, since it refers to that which grounds both his being and his value, and so that which can threaten all he is and does. It is also language productive of ethical norms and models for his life, since all his important relations to the world and to others are determined at this level. And finally it is language related to his questions of identity and of hope, and thus the language in which his "faiths" are always couched. Hence, as always, religious language is: (*a*) referent to the ultimate or the sacred, (*b*) involving existential or ultimate issues, and (*c*) productive of models and standards by which a community lives its life. It is also true that such symbolic forms and such myths as deal with this area of experience and discourse are communally borne and transmitted over historical time, and that each man relates himself to answers at this level in terms of accepting and subsisting within some community which bears symbolic forms which give, for him, relevant and valid answers to life's ultimate issues.

If this analysis of secular experience, uncovering its religious dimension and so its usage of religious language — if only in surreptitious forms in a secular culture — is successful, I have, then, established the meaningfulness of this realm of discourse and also established the referent in ordinary experience for the particular symbolic forms of any given religious tradition. It is our ordinary secular experiences of contingency that the symbol of creation is talking *about*; our search for meaning that providence is *about*, and so on. These theological symbols have potential meaning (that is, reference to actual experience) because they do refer to real aspects of ordinary experience, and in locating *those* referents, I have, potentially at least, delineated part of the meanings of theological symbols. However, as I have noted, such a prolegomenon is not yet theology; it can make no more positive assertion than that a sacred dimension appears in phenomenal experience. What that ultimacy and sacrality is or is like involves more than an analysis of general experience, in which all imaginable possibilities of characterization of the sacred — as Being or as Void, as meaning or the negation of meaning, as love or condemnation — are possible. Thus just as linguistic analysis cannot test particular assertions with regard to their validity, and phenomenology brackets questions of reality or ontological structure, so my prolegomenon provides the grounds for theological or religious language, but is not itself an example of it.

How then is *God* talked about in our age? Is a secular and yet a *Christian* theology possible? An analysis of our general usage of language, or an analysis of general experience, will not in a secular culture of itself provide, I believe, the bases for positive theological assertions. The linguistic effect of the secularization of our cultural life is precisely that religious language is *not* any longer an essential part of ordinary usage (except when we are upset!), of common-sense language, of political or moral speech, of scientific discourse, and so on. Accordingly, what happens is that religious language, insofar as it remains in all cultural life, is driven "underground" and reappears as the tacit or unacknowledged scientific, political and social mythologies by which we live. And even a careful phenomenological hermeneutic that might uncover a "religious" dimension in experience uncovers too much or too wide a variety of religious possibilities for theological assertions: an experience of an ultimate void, the appearance of demonic absolutes, as well as the creative presence of the sacred. Positive theological assertions cannot be grounded in this sort of generality, but must stem from particularity, from some deep but *particular* apprehension of the nature of things which excludes alternatives and thus makes a *claim* about the nature of what is real and what is of value.

Thus necessarily a "break" appears in the movement from prolegomenon to theology, a "new" departure based on some definite and special stance — or what Paul Ricoeur has called "a wager" — that is taken. Such stances are universal in human experience. They found each cultural *Weltanschauung*, and within that wider matrix, they are the implicit and often unacknowledged ground for each "point of view" in philosophy, and they are the explicit and celebrated basis for each religious community. Human thinking, valuing, man's total existence rest on such presuppositional attitudes with regard to what is real, how the truth is to be known, and what is of value — what Stephen Toulmin calls our answers to "limiting questions."[4] The origin of these particularist attitudes on perspectives is difficult to determine; generally they come from our cultural or communal surroundings. Ultimately they arise when there is received some apprehension of the ultimate nature, structure, and purpose of things which gives illumination, clarity, direction, and healing to a man's existence; and this apprehension, set slowly within communal symbols, is then passed on in a tradition.

Thus even in secular life we can, I believe, speak legitimately of "hierophanies" or "revelation" of the sacred, if we take these words as describing a manifestation of the ultimate sacral structures or horizons of our ordinary common life. Every positive point of view, in secular or religious life, reflects such a particular but fundamental perspective, originating in a existential apprehension and borne communally, be it one mediated through culture as a whole, centering about the scientific, the political, or the social communities of secular life, or be it mediated through a religious tradition. As I have argued, since the dimension of ultimacy and sacrality lies back of all thinking and doing, religious language is necessary to express the foundation of every human point of view. More concretely, an apprehension or revelation of this dimension — revelation because we do not "discover" it or "think to" it, since it founds our powers of discovery and of thought — lies back of each positive point of view, and so in unraveling the philosophies and stances of men we arrive ultimately at a specific religious symbolization based on a particular hierophany of the sacred. Our modes of apprehending the world, of thinking about it, and of valuing within it are, therefore, given to us historically and communally, by the community in which we spiritually exist (be it the scientific community, the democratic community, *das Volk*, or the church) and mediated to us by the (often tacit) symbols and norms of that community's life. Revelation of the sacral ground of life is thus *universal* and *general*, else there would be no life, no meaning, no thought, no valuing, and no hope

[4] Stephen Toulmin, *Reason in Ethics* (New York: Cambridge Univ. Press, 1964), esp. chap. 14.

in human experience; but each example or illustration of this universal apprehension of the sacred is *special* and historical, originating in some particular hierophany of the sacred through definite media and passed on historically by a particular communal tradition by means of its quite particular symbolic structures appropriate to that original apprehension.

Christian theology is reflection upon one of these many stances in life from the point of view of one within that communal stance, and so it represents in terms of reflective thought a commitment to one mode of apprehension of the sacred, one set of symbolic forms, one set of definite norms for truth and for value, and one form of hope. To stand within this communal perspective, which is what is meant by "faith," is to view the sacred, and thus our own life and destiny, in the light of this community's history and in terms of these symbolic structures. And the reason one does this is that *here*, in this community and through these symbolic forms, illumination, clarity, direction, and hope have been experienced; here the ultimate and the sacred ground of our life, our meanings, our truth, our freedom in community, and our destiny has manifested itself to us.

This is not a "queer" or even a nonsecular thing to do. Each human lives in some historical and spiritual community, and looks at things from the point of view of its symbolic structures and norms, because there illumination, direction, and hope has been experienced. There are no universal positions or universal symbolic forms — though most of us like to think ours are. In the next valley even the most objective philosophy seems alien. In this sense traditional symbols, norms, and something like "faith" are prerequisites for any assertions or any testing of validity — be they the tacit acceptance of community, the more explicit acceptance of such a symbolic structure by political and social communities, or the quite open acknowledgment of all of this in traditional religious communities. Formally, therefore, there is no vast difference between theology and other types of thinking, although the particular type of community in which theological reflection occurs and whose ethos theology explicitly represents, and the particular symbols of which it reflects, are of course unique. In any case, in order for *any* positive assertions to be made about what is real, how the truth is to be known or verified, what in life is of value, and what are our grounds for hope, some stance is required, some community inhabited, and some set of symbolic structures and norms affirmed. Speaking about God in a Christian way, then, implies "faith," subsistence in the historic community, and the utilization of the symbols of the Christian apprehension of the sacred.

Theology, however, cannot be merely the repetition, or even the expression, of traditional symbols, as is often the case in biblical or traditional theologies. For as I argued in the second section, religious discourse, of which Christian theological assertions form one variety, has *meaning* only insofar as it thematizes ordinary, secular experience, namely the range of experience where ultimacy and sacrality are apprehended. Thus theological symbols, explicated without reference to ordinary experiences, "mean" only eidetically in terms of their inherent structures or intentional meanings; they do not yet have *religious* meaning for us (though we who study them may realize sympathetically that they have *had* some such meaning for others and even what that meaning was). Consequently they will have no religious usage among *ourselves* and in *our* situation. Such eidetic meanings of religious symbols by and to others are available to us in the careful study of religions; but we must not mistake a understanding of their eidetic meanings for the *religious* meaning for *us* of these symbols in our contemporary situation. That meaning is possible only when these symbols are united to the experiences in our actual contemporary life which they symbolize, when they are conceived and understood as answers to the questions the ordinary life we lead raises; and such a union is the task of theology and of preaching. This means, in turn, that religious, or in this case Christian, symbols are not to be understood as answers to "religious" problems; and consequently they do not find their "meanings" solely or evenly mainly in church, in faith or Word-events, or in the area of religion itself. They are symbols expressing experienced answers to the problems of ordinary and so secular life. Thus the task of systematic theology is to conceive of the symbols of its tradition in terms of the experiences of ultimacy within secular life, or, alternatively, to understand the dimension of ultimacy and sacrality, as it is apprehended in ordinary life, *through* the symbols of the Christian tradition. A Christian is thus one who names Christianly and so apprehends Christianly the sacred, which is experienced universally in and through his contingency, his search for meaning, his knowing, his experiences of valuing, of renewal, and of hope. That is, he names this sacred "God," the father of Jesus Christ, as that symbol has been expressed in what theology calls the "Word" and thence in the wider system of symbols inherent in Christian history. A Christian theologian is one who understands reflectively that symbol ("God"), and its whole correlate system of symbols, by comprehending it solely as an answer to the experiences of ultimacy which ordinary life possesses.

Systematic theology, Christian speaking of God, then, has three elements or stages, all of which are essential. (1) The prolegomenon, a phenomenological hermeneutic of secular experience, achieved by an analysis of the way in which modern man experiences his being in the world as characterized by contingency, relativity, transience, and autonomy, which analysis will manifest the positive and the negative appearance of the ultimate and the sacred within these aspects of our being in the world. For theology this prolegomenon functions in two ways: (*a*) establishing the *meaning* of religious discourse by showing the experiences which religious symbols thematize; and (*b*) by passing on to theology these "potentialities for meaning" through its delineation of those experiences which religious symbols *mean* and in terms of which these symbols are to be comprehended. For example, our experiences of our own contingency provide the experiential situations to which the symbol of creation potentially refers and which it might in its own way "mean."

(2) Second, there is the eidetic analysis (or in another sense

of that oft-used word, a "hermeneutical" analysis [5]) of the community's symbols, both biblical and traditional. Here the objects of analysis are the eidetic or intentional meanings of these communal symbolic forms. Every such form and system of symbolic forms (i.e. every particular "religion") has a definite, unique meaning, and this uniqueness of its meaning gives to each religious tradition the possibility of mediating to communal experience a definite, unique apprehension of the sacred. The sacred is universal, but it is experienced differently in each tradition because of the unique *gestalten* of the community's symbolic structures. The theologian thus analyzes the symbols of his community and its tradition to see the unique meanings which they each possess, alone and as a system of symbols, and so the unique apprehension of the sacred which that community mediates to us.

(3) Finally, systematic theology is the mutual interpenetration ("correlation" was Tillich's term) of experienced questions and symbolic answers, the one being a means for the understanding of the other. This is *not* an understanding of symbol by and through itself, and so of "God" by himself. Meaning is an interaction of symbol and *experience*, and so in religious meaning an interaction of the experience of the sacred with religious symbols which *mediate* and *thematize* that experience. Thus theology is an understanding of the biblical symbols in terms of the secular experiences of ultimacy, and these experiences in terms of the symbols; together they form "Christian" meanings. Correspondingly it is an understanding and speaking of God in terms of his relations *to*, his activity *in*, and his appearance *through* creaturely life. If "creaturely symbols" are, as Eliade and Tillich have insisted, the finite media through and in which the sacred appears, a *symbolic* understanding of God is an understanding of this

[5] This latter is the meaning of this elusive word in the "hermeneutical" theologians, and the way in which Paul Ricoeur uses it in his *Symbolism of Evil* (New York: Harper & Row, 1967), pp. 347–357. For my own use of this word to describe my prolegomenon as a "phenomenological hermeneutic," cf. Herbert Spiegelberg *The Phenomenological Movement*, (The Hague: Nijhoff, 1960), esp. 318–26, and 694–98.

appearance in and to ourselves as finite creatures: as contingent, relative, transient, autonomous, and guilty — an apprehension comprehended in terms of the whole structure of Christian symbolism. And that structure of Christian symbolism is, of course, itself based on the originating "creaturely symbols" of Israel's history and the person of Jesus through which, for this community, the sacred has manifested itself normatively. Through this mutual interaction of contemporary experience and traditional symbols theology is *properly* "demythologized" and rendered "existential," but it is not thereby rendered into mere anthropology. It is *Christian* discourse about the *sacred* as it appears in and to human existence, and therefore it speaks of "God" the "father of Jesus Christ" as he manifests himself in the total range of our ordinary secular contemporary existence.

The criteria or modes of validation of Christian discourse about God follow from this its character as speech within this community, speech based on these symbols, and speech concerning these ultimate or foundational issues in secular human existence. (1) First of all, since this speech originates in an experience of illumination and renewal *in* this community, and mediated *through* these symbols, such speech — expressive of the ethos of this community — is "valid" only if it faithfully reflects the meanings of these symbols as they have functioned in that community's life. A theology is validated first by showing the legitimacy of its use and interpretation of the biblical and traditional symbols. (2) Second, this is speech which "means" only as it celebrates felt joys and expresses felt answers to real problems, issues, and crises. Thus a theology is valid only if it illumines the existential or ultimate questions of ordinary life, and provides useful models and directions for contemporary decisions and creditable grounds for hope. The second validation of a theology is in its relevance to contemporary and to ordinary experience as a symbolic structure making that secular experience intelligible, bearable and hopeful. (3) This speech purports to give symbolic expression to the foundations of human being in the world, and so to all the various elements of human culture. It is validated, therefore, insofar as it is able to elaborate its symbols into intellectual categories expressive of the foundations of inquiry, of art, of social structures, of psychology, of ethics, and so on. As with any total viewpoint in philosophy, a theology can claim to be "true" only if it can provide on its own terms a secure intellectual foundation for all of our creative life in the world. Insofar as theology purports to be dealing with *ultimacy*, this claim of universal applicability is, of course, inescapable. And this requirement inevitably leads theological speech towards ontological elaboration, towards becoming a "Christian philosophy" and so capable of mediating between ultimacy and the proximate, between religious speech about sacrality and cultural speech about science, art, literature, politics, and the supermarket.

Thus the fidelity of its interpretation of traditional symbols, its relevance to contemporary and secular experience, and its width of cultural scope are the three "objective" criteria of theology in terms of which it finds warrants for its arguments. Of course, however, the character of religious discourse itself, namely, that it is speech in response to an involved apprehension of the sacred within the finite, means that the most important "criterion" is existentially subjective and not objective, namely that there be that involvement itself implied in any apprehension of sacrality. For without an existential reception of the hierophany, an apprehension of the sacred in and through the symbols, there is no multivalence, no religious use of language, no positive or assertive *religious* speech at all, and so neither a valid use of symbols nor any relevance to ordinary experience. Thus descriptions, historical or sociological, of the visible surface of religious institutions and behavior, and even of existing systems of doctrine, are not yet themselves *religious*. Unless through those descriptions of the finite media, the sacred manifests itself, there is as yet no religious speech. There is only secular speech about "religious things," and so only secular criteria of meaning and of validity, scientific or historical, are applicable and relevant.

Ordinary experience does reveal the presence, and the brooding absence, of ultimacy and sacrality, and thus, I believe, it cannot be understood or dealt with on a purely secular basis, separated from the symbolization that makes this apprehension possible. Theological symbols, whose task it is to thematize this dimension of life in the world, have in the past removed themselves into the cloister or the chapel, existing apart and self-sufficiently confined in their inherent meanings and not their experienced ones; thus have they become empty and finally expendable when life is lived in the world, as it is now by all of us. A secular Christian theology will understand ordinary experience in terms of Christian symbols, and its symbols in terms of ordinary life, the first providing the "matter" of experience of our being in the world, for which the second provides the "form," the symbolic thematization. This is, I am convinced, what religious discourse and so theological language is "for," what the usage of this language is and so where its meanings lie: to articulate, to clarify, and to bring to stronger and so controllable expression the dimension of sacrality prehended or dimly experienced in ordinary life. And correspondingly, it is this alone which can add celebration and serenity to secular existence, which is at present unaware of the sacral glories that ground its being and its meanings, and unable to cope with the ultimate anxieties of which it is not at all symbolically conscious.

Biographical Notes

JERALD C. BRAUER is professor of church history and the dean of the Divinity School of the University of Chicago.

LANGDON GILKEY is professor of theology in the Divinity School of the University of Chicago. He was formerly on the faculty of Vassar College and of the Divinity School of Vanderbilt University.

JOSEPH HAROUTUNIAN, before his death in 1968, was professor of systematic theology in the Divinity School of the University of Chicago. He previously taught in Wellesley College, and for many years was professor of systematic theology in McCormick Theological Seminary.

BERNARD E. MELAND is professor emeritus of theology of the University of Chicago. Before coming to the Divinity School of the University of Chicago he taught in Central College, Fayette, Missouri, and Pomona College, Claremont, California. Following retirement he was visiting professor of theology in the Divinity School for three years, and recently visiting professor of philosophy of religion in Union Theological Seminary, New York.

SCHUBERT OGDEN is University Professor of Theology in the Divinity School of the University of Chicago. He was formerly professor of theology in the Perkins School of Theology in Southern Methodist University.

JOSEPH A. SITTLER is professor of theology in The Divinity School of the University of Chicago. For many years he was on the faculty of the Lutheran School of Theology in Maywood, now located near the campus of the University of Chicago.

FRED BERTHOLD, JR., is professor of religion and chairman of the department of religion in Dartmouth College. He is the author of *The Fear of God* (1959), and an editor of *Basic Sources of the Judaeo-Christian Tradition* (1962).

JOHN B. COBB, JR., is Ingraham Professor of Christian Theology in the School of Theology at Claremont, California. He formerly taught at Young Harris College and at Emory University. He is the author of *Varieties of Protestantism* (1960), *Living Options in Protestant Theology* (1962), *A Christian Natural Theology* (1965), and *The Structure of Christian Existence* (1967). He is co-editor of the series, *New Frontiers in Theology.*

ROGER HAZELTON is Abbot Professor of Christian Theology in Andover-Newton Theological School. He formerly taught at Colorado College, Andover-Newton Theological School, Pomona College, and the Claremont Graduate School, and the Graduate School of Theology in Oberlin College where he was also dean of the School of Theology. He is the author of *The Root and Flower of Prayer* (1943), *The God We Worship* (1946), *Renewing the Mind* (1951), *God's Way with Man* (1956), *New Accents in Contemporary Theology* (1960, *New Testament Heritage* (1962), *Christ and Ourselves* (1965), and *A Theological Approach to Art* (1967).

PHILIP J. HEFNER is associate professor of systematic theology at the Lutheran School of Theology at Chicago. He formerly taught at the Hamma School of Theology and the Lutheran Theological Seminary at Gettysburg, Pa. He is the author of *Faith and the Vitalities of History* (1966), editor of *The Scope of Grace* (1964), and co-editor of *Changing Man: The Threat and the Promise* (1968).

BERNARD M. LOOMER is professor of philosophical theology in the Berkeley Baptist Divinity School and in the Graduate Theological Union at Berkeley, California. For many years he was dean of the Divinity School and professor of philosophy of religion in the University of Chicago.

HUSTON SMITH is professor of philosophy at the Massachusetts Institute of Technology. He formerly taught in Washington University, St. Louis, Missouri. He is the author of *The Religions of Man* (1958), and *Condemned to Meaning* (1965). Samuel Todes, with whom Professor Smith collaborated in preparing his essay, was also on the faculty of the Massachusetts Institute of Technology, and later taught at Northwestern University.

PAUL SPONHEIM is associate professor of systematic theology at Luther Theological Seminary, St. Paul, Minnesota. He formerly taught in the College of the University of Chicago, Lutheran Theological Seminary, Gettysburg, Pennsylvania, and Concordia College, Moorhead, Minnesota. He is the author of *Contemporary Forms of Faith* (1967) *and Kierkegaard on Christ and Christian Coherence* (1968).

GERHARD E. SPIEGLER is provost of Haverford College. Before going to Berkeley, California where he was professor of contemporary theology at Berkeley Baptist Divinity School and the Graduate Theological Union, he had been professor and chairman of the department of religion in Haverford College. He returned to Haverford as professor of religion in 1964 where he was later made provost. He is the author of *The Eternal Covenant* (1967).

DANIEL DAY WILLIAMS is Roosevelt Professor of Systematic Theology in Union Theological Seminary, New York. He was formerly on the faculty of Colorado College, the Chicago Theological Seminary and the Federated Theological Faculty of the University of Chicago. He is the author of *The Andover Liberals* (1941), *God's Grace and Man's Hope* (1949), *What Present-day Theologians Are Thinking* (1952), and a recent work, *The Spirit and the Forms of Love* (1968). He was co-editor of *The Ministry in Historical Perspectives* (1956) and has been a contributor to various books edited by others.

Acknowledgments

Several of the essays which appear in this volume* were presented at the Alumni Conference of the Theological Field of the Divinity School, November 7–9, 1966 in celebration of the seventy-fifth anniversary of the University of Chicago and the one-hundredth anniversary of the Divinity School of the University of Chicago. The paper by Professor Williams was given as a public lecture in Bond Chapel, opening the conference. Various faculty members and alumni participated in the conference as critics and discussants of the papers: Carl Bangs, Fred Berthold, Eric Dean, E. Thomas Lawson, William Reese, Jr., and Gerhard Spiegler.

I wish especially to acknowledge with gratitude the extensive and valuable help of Larry Greenfield and Fred Reisz who served as editorial assistants in preparing the manuscripts of this volume for publication.

Grateful acknowledgment is also made to the following publishers for permission to quote from works published by them, acknowledgment of which appears in a footnote reference: Augsburg Publishing House, Basil Blackwell, Publisher, George Braziller, Inc., Doubleday & Company, Inc., Duquesne University Press, William B. Eerdmans Publishing Co., Harper & Row, Hill & Wang, Inc., Holt, Rinehart and Winston, Inc., *The Journal of Philosophy*, The Macmillan Company, Martinus Nijhoff, The M.I.T. Press, The Open Court Publishing Company, *The Philosophical Review*,

* Papers by Schubert Ogden, Daniel Day Williams, Huston Smith (in collaboration with Samuel Todes), Roger Hazelton, Philip Hefner, John Cobb, Jr., and Bernard M. Loomer.

375

ACKNOWLEDGMENTS

Princeton University Press, Random House, Inc., Routledge & Kegan Paul Ltd., SCM Press, Ltd., *Union Seminary Quarterly Review*, The Westminster Press, Yale University Press. Acknowledgment is also made to Professor Harmon R. Holcomb, for permission to quote from an unpublished paper on "Natural Theology: New Explorations in an Old Tomb."

Index

direct, 352, 353; elements of, 347; evidence, 118; facts, of, 6, 7, 12, 38; flux of, 54; human, 67, 93, 94, 176, 178, 179, 180, 186, 222, 224, 295, 358, 364; immediacy of, 213; immediate, 38, 97, 297, 346, 349; lived, 37, 52–54, 56, 283, 285, 287, 288, 290, 291, 293, 295, 296, 297, 299, 303, 304, 305, 347, 348; mode of, 81; modern, 152; moral, 8; mystic, 292, 334; nature of, 55; object of, 346; ordinary, 110, 346, 347, 355–59, 361, 368, 369; phenomena, 3; pure, 296; reflexive, 309, 310; religious, 8, 10, 11, 12, 34, 145, 177, 178, 292, 293, 296, 297, 302, 323, 354; secular, 354, 356–58, 361, 365, 367, 369; sense, 8, 77, 90, 91, 98, 99, 108, 160, 352; structure of, 177, 178, 288, 297, 300, 303, 310, 311; totality of, 91; of ultimacy, 359, 366; ultimate dimension, 37; understanding of, 77–79, 82, 87; unmediated, 130

Explanandum, 106, 107

Explanans, 106

Explanation, 105; causal, 106, 126

Faith, Christian, 17, 22, 43, 45–47, 62, 66, 74, 76, 77, 88, 95, 101, 115, 116, 122, 159, 199, 228, 271–80, 292, 317; community of, 44, 180, 291, 315

Farber, Marvin, 283 n, 284 n

Fechner, G. T., 41

Ferry, W. H., 217 n

Feuerbach, Ludwig, 52, 224

Flew, Anthony, 108 n, 127, 128

Fodor, J. A., 137 n

Forgiveness, 293, 316

Foster, George B., 14 n, 15, 16, 17

Free will, doctrine of, 336

Frege, 145

French revolution, 23

Freud, Sigmund, 149, 217 n, 224

Fries, Jacob, 295

Fromm, Erich, 197

Fuchs, Ernst, 272

Functional method, 15, 16, 17, 26

Geist, 243, 250, 263, 351

Gendlin, Eugene T., 356 n

Gerhard, John, 251

German: dialectical method, 166; modes of thought, 264; theologians, 272

Germany, 236

Gerrish, Brian, 58, 61

Giacometti, 182, 183

Gibson, Walker, 314 n

Gilkey, Langdon, 57, 58, 345

God, 87, 90, 106, 140, 151, 158, 159, 161, 210, 211, 214, 215, 221, 223, 225, 233, 246, 259, 260, 264, 277, 279, 321–44, 347, 353, 362, 365, 366, 367; absence of, 353; acts of, 114, 164, 169, 190, 191, 226, 280, 314; assertions about, 114; being of, 175, 177, 191, 226; conception of, 20, 27, 70, 166; conceptual nature of, 167; concreteness of, 167, 280, 281; consequent nature of, 33, 50, 81, 86, 167; contingency of, 169; as creator, 74, 75, 130, 131, 165, 191, 207, 213, 256, 321, 322, 336, 343; death of, 16, 49, 52, 57, 141, 165, 166, 199, 221, 227, 228, 229, 238, 260 n, 304, 349, 351, 352; doctrine of, 161, 165, 175, 177, 189, 190, 191, 194, 350; existence of, 71, 74, 116, 119, 338, 339, 340, 341; grace of, 75, 76, 117, 121, 170, 324, 336; image of, 170, 202, 251, 261; immanence, 73, 74, 176, 229, 276; impassibility of, 175; judgment of, 46, 321, 324, 332; knowledge of, 74, 75, 236, 313, 340, 353, 354; language of, 57, 58, 99, 322, 323, 330, 335, 350, 353, 354, 355, 358, 368; nature of, 40, 74, 162–64, 167, 168, 221; omnipotence of, 176, 207, 208; ontological argument for,